The Will to Believe

NEW STUDIES IN U.S. FOREIGN RELATIONS

Mary Ann Heiss, editor

The Will to Believe

Woodrow Wilson, World War I,
and America's Strategy for
Peace and Security

❋ ❋ ❋

Ross A. Kennedy

The Kent State University Press
Kent, Ohio

© 2009 by The Kent State University Press, Kent, Ohio 44242

ALL RIGHTS RESERVED

Library of Congress Catalog Card Number 2008035887

ISBN 978-0-87338-971-6

Manufactured in the United States of America

LIBRARY OF CONGRESS CATALOGING-IN-PUBLICATION DATA

Kennedy, Ross A.

The will to believe : Woodrow Wilson, World War I, and
America's strategy for peace and security / Ross A. Kennedy.

p. cm. — (New studies in U.S. foreign relations)

Includes bibliographical references and index.

ISBN 978-0-87338-971-6 (hbk. : alk. paper) ∞

1. World War, 1914–1918—Diplomatic history. 2. National security—United States. 3.
United States—Foreign relations—1913–1921. 4. Wilson, Woodrow, 1856–1924. I. Title.

D619.K45 2009

940.3'2273—dc22   2008035887

British Library Cataloging-in-Publication data are available.

13 12 11 10 09   5 4 3 2 1

To my dad,

James Stirling Kennedy,

And my wife,

Larissa

Contents

Acknowledgments

There are many individuals and institutions I would like to thank for their support as I worked on this book. First, this project would not have been possible without the education and aid I received from one of the great centers of higher education in the world, the University of California at Berkeley. Doe Library provided me with the bulk of my research material, and the Berkeley history department generously helped to fund my work with several scholarships. My teachers at Berkeley also made a lasting impression on my intellectual development. Leon F. Litwack's incomparable American survey course first inspired me to study history as an undergraduate. In different ways, Charles G. Sellers and James H. Kettner taught me how to think about the role of ideas in American politics. Professor Kettner's graduate seminar on colonial America stimulated the basic question in my mind that ultimately led to this book: Whatever happened to America's fear of standing armies? I am also grateful to Lawrence W. Levine for his insightful reading of my doctoral dissertation and for sharing his views of William Jennings Bryan. My deepest appreciation goes to my dissertation advisor and friend, Paula S. Fass. She taught me how to write and how to analyze historical arguments in a critical, logical way. Even though our fields of study were different, she enthusiastically encouraged my work and, with her probing questioning of my arguments and careful editing of my writing, vastly improved it.

In addition to Professor Fass, I have been fortunate in having three other important mentors in my career. I first met Martin Sherwin while a student at the Fletcher School of Law and Diplomacy. He has remained a friend and advisor ever since, always happy to exchange ideas and help out in guiding me through life as a diplomatic historian. William Rope was the American director of the Hopkins-Nanjing Center for Chinese-American Studies when I taught there in 1995–96. A gifted diplomat and administrator, he was the most patient and fair boss one could hope for, and he never fails to inspire me with his intellectual curiosity, keen intelligence, and profound dedication to public service. Jerald Combs was department chair when I taught at San Francisco State University. At a time when jobs were hard to find, he kept me in the game while offering a treasure trove of sensible advice about academia. I will always be thankful for his wise counsel.

The quality of the book has been improved by advice from several scholars who were kind enough to read summaries or chapters of the manuscript. I am especially indebted to Lloyd E. Ambrosius, John Whiteclay Chambers II, and Roger Baldwin for their thoughtful suggestions and incisive criticisms. My colleagues at Illinois State University—Roger Biles, Anthony Crubaugh, Alan Lessoff, and Richard Soderlund—also offered invaluable comments on this project at various stages, from the book proposal to the final manuscript. Most of all, I am grateful to Professor Mary Ann Heiss, my series editor at Kent State University Press. Professor Heiss edited an early draft of the manuscript with extraordinary care, pushed me to clarify my interpretive points, and guided the work through the peer review process with exemplary professionalism. One of the very best parts of writing this book was working with her.

I would also like to thank Joanna Hildebrand Craig at Kent State University Press for her encouragement and support in meeting all of the key deadlines connected with the work; Mary D. Young at Kent State University Press for shepherding the manuscript through its last stages; John Kostelnick, who produced the excellent maps that accompany the manuscript; and Lawrence Castriotta, who helped me with archival research on the League of Free Nations Association I otherwise would have missed.

Finally, I am grateful to my family. My daughters Sidney and Eliot patiently competed with this book for my attention, rejuvenated me with Post-It note fights, and even offered to check the page proofs for misspellings. My wife, Larissa, served as both sounding board and editor and never allowed her disdain for Woodrow Wilson's China policies to interfere with her willingness to help in anything I asked her to do. And last, but certainly not least, I thank my dad, James Stirling Kennedy, for everything.

Introduction

December 1918. Woodrow Wilson's train slowly rolled through Hoboken, New Jersey, its tracks lined with cheering crowds who had interrupted their morning work to wish their president farewell. Wilson was on his way to the USS *George Washington,* an army transport ship, which would take him to France, where he would begin a round of triumphant parades and speeches before attending to his main task, the writing of the peace treaty that would end the Great War and shape world politics for years to come.

Upon arriving at the ship's berth, Wilson ate breakfast in his train, then walked up the gangplank and went to an office that had been prepared for him. He was not in a good mood. He had a cold and was "surprised" by what he saw in the morning papers. Theodore Roosevelt, his old rival, had denounced Wilson's peace program, the Fourteen Points, as "thoroughly mischievous" and "so vague and ambiguous that it is nonsense to do anything with them until they have been defined and made definite." Roosevelt also stressed that Britain's navy and the Allied armies had done the most to defeat Germany. America's role in the peacemaking was therefore "to stand by our allies," not seek to dominate them.

Joined by three reporters in his office, Wilson rejected Roosevelt's statement. "He virtually says that England won the war and should have everything she wants," complained the president. "I don't believe our boys who fought over there will be inclined to feel just that way about it. We won the war at Chateau Thierry," insisted Wilson. He then objected to Roosevelt's naval views, asserting that "militarism is equally dangerous when applied to sea forces as to land forces." The idea that the United States and Britain should "act as the sea patrol of the world is only a new kind of militaristic propaganda," argued Wilson. "No power, no two powers, should be supreme. The whole world must be in on all measures designed to end wars for all time."

Wilson's emphasis on the equality of nations and the collective enforcement of peace abruptly diminished, however, when he was asked how the United States should deal with a refusal by Britain to reduce naval arms. In that case, Wilson declared, "the United States should show her how to build a navy." The president related how America had the ability to match Britain "or any other power" in naval construction. "We now have greater navy yards, thousands more shipbuilders than we ever had before," Wilson boasted, "and an abundance of raw materials such as would make it possible for us to have the greatest navy in the world." On that note, the interview concluded.

A short time later, Wilson's ship eased out of its berth and left New York Harbor, escorted by tugboats, launches, airplanes, and, at one point, a huge navy dirigible. It was a clear, cold day, and a bright sun shone upon President Wilson and his party. "In fact," recorded Dr. Cary Grayson, Wilson's personal physician, "no person could have wished for a more auspicious commencement of an eventful trip."[1]

The contradictory ideas expressed on that cold December morning—the endorsement of both a collective effort "to end wars for all time" and a unilateral arms buildup to coerce other states into naval disarmament—provide a glimpse into the complexity of American national security debates during World War I. Much more so than Americans after World War II, Wilson and his contemporaries engaged in a wide-ranging analysis of how to achieve American national security in the modern world. No consensus existed on fundamental issues such as the nature of the international system, the impact of security policies upon domestic freedom, the value of alliances and multinational organizations, and the relationship between democratic political systems and peace. All of these issues remain active today, as both Democrats and Republicans try to define the meaning of "Wilsonianism" for a post–September 11 world and to lay claim to its legacy.[2]

This book focuses on how three competing coalitions of American leaders dealt with these and other national security issues from 1914 to 1920, when the existing international system violently collapsed and a new world order had yet to be built. "Pacifists" were made up of four powerful political groups: agrarian Progressives led by three-time Democratic presidential nominee William Jennings Bryan; leftist Progressives and moderate Socialists such as Jane Addams, Lillian Wald, Paul Kellogg, and Crystal and Max Eastman; Republican Progressive insurgents including, most prominently, Sen. Robert La Follette; and mugwumpish liberals such as the manager of the *Nation* and the New York *Evening Post,* Oswald Garrison Villard. Through their speeches and media outlets, and through the Left's two chief peace organizations, the American Union against Militarism (AUAM) and the Woman's Peace Party (WPP), the pacifists reached a massive—and receptive—audience, especially among farmers and the urban working class. Woodrow Wilson and a diverse set of opinion makers outside the administration led a second group, "liberal internationalists." These included the editors of the *New Republic;* Samuel Gompers, the head of America's largest labor union, the American Federation of Labor (AFL); and members of the League to Enforce Peace (LEP), an organization of largely conservative businessmen, academics, and lawyers led by former president William Howard Taft. Theodore Roosevelt, Henry Cabot Lodge, and Elihu Root best represented the views of "Atlanticists." Their chief lobbying organization was the business-dominated National Security League (NSL), formed in December 1914 by S. Stanwood Menken, a lawyer from New York.[3]

Most of the leaders of these groups—and in particular of the pacifists and liberal internationalists—believed that the existing international system of "power politics" was inherently unstable and would never produce peace for any lengthy period of time. Perceiving the alliances, arms races, and coercive diplomacy of this system as essentially European phenomena, they also believed that active, long-term participation in great power politics by the United States would militarize American society and destroy America's democracy and domestic liberties. They pointed to the outbreak of the world war as evidence for these assertions, and, indeed, events during America's participation in the war reinforced these ideas still more. These political and military fears underlay both isolationism and varying efforts to build collective security. Chiefly designed by Woodrow Wilson, the program to create a new system of collective security dominated policy debates. It did so because it promised to preserve America's safety in the modern world without the need for large-scale armaments that could lead to militarism at home. The president and his supporters had great difficulty distinguishing a collective security order from the balance-of-power system it was supposed to replace, however. Ultimately, because Wilson's effort to end power politics depended on containing the power of Germany, such a distinction could not be made in practice—an outcome suggesting that his whole project of reforming world politics was deeply flawed.

This study departs from the existing scholarship on Wilsonianism in several ways. Rather than examine only Wilson or only his critics, as most other historians do, I analyze the entire national security debate from 1914 to 1920, including all major perspectives from across the political spectrum. This comprehensive approach best illuminates the basic assumptions about national security affairs that pervaded American political culture in the early twentieth century. Unlike other scholars, I see the fear of arms races and militarism as a key component of that culture and as heavily influencing which national security policies rose and which fell in popularity. Although ideas about the moral and political superiority of the United States gave American leaders confidence that their policies would work, such notions of American exceptionalism, in my view, did not provide the key stimulus behind the drive by liberal internationalists to transform the international system. Finally, even some of the best literature on Wilson and his contemporaries understates the degree to which strategic desires to contain Germany's power animated the president and both complemented and contradicted his efforts to reform international politics. By overemphasizing the role of missionary idealism and trade concerns in Wilsonian diplomacy, scholars have ended up paying too little attention to the paradox at the heart of Wilson's national security strategy—that of practicing power

politics to end power politics. This book explores that dilemma in depth, revealing an American national security policy during World War I at once strategically
prudent and tragically self-defeating.[4]

The chapters that follow are organized both thematically and chronologically.
The first three analyze, respectively, how American leaders from 1914 to 1917
viewed the concept of militarism and the character of the existing international
system, how they assessed the implications of the war for American national security, and how they envisioned the goal of international reform. The remaining
chapters trace President Wilson's pursuit of a new world order through neutrality,
war, and peacemaking, as well as examine how policy advocates outside the administration reacted to his diplomacy. The book then concludes with a brief look
at how Wilson's approach to American national security cast a long shadow over
American policymakers for the rest of the twentieth century and beyond.

1

Militarism and Power Politics, 1914–17

The outbreak of war in late July 1914 immediately provoked an intense debate in the United States about militarism, the nature of power politics, and the status of American national security. Pacifists, liberal internationalists, and Atlanticists all feared that under certain conditions militarism at home could undermine America's free way of life, but they disagreed about the specifics of those conditions and the likelihood that they would occur. The three groups also all believed that the system of power politics was unstable, but they differed in their analysis of the degree to which this was a problem as well as why it existed in the first place. Finally, as discussed in Chapter 2, they sharply diverged in their assessment of how the war's outcome might affect America's security. As the debate over these questions unfolded between August 1914 and January 1917, it became clear that, despite their differences, pacifists and liberal internationalists had more in common with each other than with the Atlanticists. United in their intense fear of militarism and power politics, pacifists and liberal internationalists managed to marginalize the Atlanticists—the only group in American politics with a relatively positive view of the balance-of-power system.

More than anyone else, pacifists raised dire warnings that any significant increases in America's military establishment above the levels that existed in 1914 might trigger an unraveling of liberty and freedom at home. Created after the Spanish-American War, the existing force structure—a standing army of professional volunteers numbering about 100,000 men, a navy ranked third in the world in warship tonnage, and a reserve force of about 112,000 active National Guardsmen—was safe from the standpoint of preserving America's domestic way of life. Any large-scale defense expansion, pacifists argued, any "big army and navy programs with their accompanying propaganda," would be nothing less than "a menace to democracy."[1]

Pacifists outlined in some detail the logic that lay behind this position. Drawing on fears about professional standing armies dating back to the Revolution, they asserted that military service, especially if made compulsory through a program of universal military training (UMT), would undermine the citizenry's democratic spirit. "Free minds, and souls undrilled to obedience," lectured Crystal Eastman of the American Union against Militarism (AUAM), "are vital to the life of democracy." The whole point of "military drill," however, was "to develop unquestioning obedience, so that the soldier will move forward in the face of danger and even certain death." At the same time, trainees confronted an organization that was "aristocratic" in nature, with a "fixed line between officers and men." "Cringing before men who abuse their power," taught to "stop thinking" and respond blindly to the will of others, it was no wonder to the editors of the Nation that a man exposed to military training became "an automaton."[2]

Pacifists also stressed that military officers harbored antidemocratic attitudes that led them into aggressively antidemocratic behavior. Officers were used to giving orders and, "clothed with power to gratify caprice," dominating others with arbitrary commands. Consequently, they showed little patience for civilian authority. Such officers, complained Oswald Garrison Villard of the Nation, arrogantly asserted that they alone had the wisdom to decide military and foreign policy, actively lobbied Congress to increase the armed forces, and pressed for new national defense councils to determine public policy in "secret session."[3]

The policies that military officers advocated added to their power. Any "expert" in any field, observed Villard, tended to get so absorbed in his specialty that he was likely to "subordinate everything to the development of that specialty." Military experts acted no differently. "Their entire training leads them . . . to fear the oncoming of the enemy and they habitually think of every possible combination that may be brought against them." They were therefore obsessed with organizing the country for war—an outlook that would "inevitably make for the subordination of everything civilian to the military." Jane Addams believed that she saw the outcome of military thinking already taking shape in war-torn Europe, observing, in mid-1915, that a "military party" had become ascendant in each of the belligerent states. Censorship of the press had become rampant, and, she worried, "the military power is breaking down all of the safeguards of civil life and of civil government." Fearing that excessive preparedness could spark a similar process in the United States, Addams became an early and central leader of the AUAM.[4]

If the "military-naval oligarchy" embodied dangerously antidemocratic ideals and policy aspirations, so too did its chief allies, the "capitalists, imperialists, and war traders" who profited from defense spending and aggression overseas. Nearly all of the major pacifist spokesmen charged that propreparedness movements were "stimulated by interests whose purpose was not entirely the undiluted welfare of the majority." To the pacifists, preparedness programs furthered the interests of those who "look down with undisguised contempt upon the masses" and who undermined the forces of democratic progressivism.[5]

Reactionaries benefited from preparedness programs in several ways. Most obviously, corporate munitions makers reaped huge profits from preparedness, as did bankers who helped to finance arms purchases made by the American government and by belligerents overseas. Their efforts to push defense increases through Congress by whipping the country into "a panic" distracted attention from economic and political injustices at home, and by identifying themselves with patriotism and security, reactionary preparedness advocates made passage of legislation aimed at curbing their power difficult.[6]

Perhaps most disturbingly, expansion of the military served the interests of America's "upper and leisure classes" by providing them with the means to pursue "class . . . aggression" at home and abroad. The "real basis for . . . preparationist propaganda," alleged a Progressive single-tax journal, the *Public,* was "to provide an army to over-awe labor unions" and to "repress" them. James Maurer, a Pennsylvania labor leader active in the AUAM, pointed out that stepped-up military forces could be used "to dragoon the working people of the country" into corporate America's "battles for trade" overseas. Imperialist adventures could only further stimulate demands for military forces—and thus further strengthen the hand of the reactionary plutocracy that advocated preparedness and imperialism in the first place.[7]

Pacifists were not alone in associating military preparedness with a threat to American democracy and liberty. Liberal internationalists agreed with much of their diagnosis. Like the pacifists, President Wilson associated militarism with the size and composition of America's armed forces. In his annual message to Congress in December 1914, the president argued that the ability instantly "to put a nation in the field, a nation of men trained to arms" meant an abandonment of "America's present political principles and institutions." A volunteer army supported by the National Guard was an appropriate force for the United States, and Americans should certainly consider ways to encourage men to join it. But anything "more than this," Wilson warned, "carries with it a reversal of the whole history and character of our polity."[8]

About one year after this speech, Wilson shifted course and proposed significant increases in America's defense forces. He called for increasing the army by about 40 percent, to 140,000 men, building a navy that by the early 1920s would rival Great Britain's, and creating a new 400,000-man force of army-trained federal reserves, the so-called Continental army. The motives behind this policy will be discussed in subsequent chapters. Here, though, it is important to note that Wilson's decision to expand America's military establishment in no way indicated that his fear of militarism had suddenly disappeared. Instead, it revealed his belief that America could tolerate a larger military establishment than the pacifists thought wise; his basic concerns about militarism, however, still remained fixed.[9]

Even as he advocated greater preparedness for the United States, Wilson did not support a program of UMT, the central plank of most propreparedness platforms.

In part, the president steered clear of UMT because he knew it had little support in Congress. But he also genuinely believed that compulsory training risked generating militarism at home. His program, he emphasized in late 1915, stepped up the voluntary enlistment of "citizen soldiers," most of whom would only serve three years before retiring to their civilian pursuits. "What we all wish to accomplish is that the forces of the nation should indeed be part of the nation and not a separate professional force," he explained. America "does not want to be ruled by the spirit of any class," and certainly not by "the spirit of a military class"; "militarism," Wilson stressed, "is the end of progress. There cannot be any progress when the professionalism of the soldier dominates in a national polity."[10]

In addition to refusing to endorse UMT, Wilson resisted calls by propreparedness forces to increase the regular army up to 250,000 men. The House of Representatives would not support such an increase, but, in any event, Wilson considered it "much too large." "We are not asking for armies," Wilson informed a crowd in St. Louis, "we are asking for a trained citizenry which will act in the spirit of citizenship and not in the spirit of military establishments." That was why he limited his increase of the regular army to 40,000 men: it was the figure Wilson considered "adequate to the uses of peace" and faithful to the fact that he was "just as much opposed to militarism as any man living."[11]

Wilson echoed pacifist anxieties about the reactionary potential of preparedness as well. To be sure, he did not explicitly address the idea that expanding the military establishment would sabotage Progressive reform, nor did he endorse the charge that munitions manufacturers manipulated defense programs for their own selfish power and profit. At one point, in fact, Wilson said that such a charge was "preposterous." But the president did not totally dismiss the pacifists' worries about the anti-Progressive character of preparedness either. Wilson avoided UMT, for example, in part because he believed voluntary training would spur the sense of civic virtue that most reformers associated with Progressivism; it would make Americans "a little less careless of the general interest of the nation, a little less thoughtful of their own peculiar and selfish interests." In addition, although he downplayed the notion that munitions manufacturers influenced preparedness planning, Wilson also assured Americans that he was not a "dupe" of the arms business. "I know the points of danger," he confided to an audience in Des Moines, and he therefore urged Congress to expand government ownership of armaments plants. In sum, while Wilson associated militarism more with the military itself than with reactionary corporate interests, he clearly harbored some fears on this score too.[12]

Wilson further signaled his desire to link preparedness with Progressivism by suggesting that voluntary military training could be accompanied by "a great system of industrial and vocational education." Under such a program, explained Wilson, "men will think first of their families and their daily work, of their service in the economic fields of the country, of their efficiency as artisans, and only last of all of their serviceability to the nation as soldiers and men at arms." In this way, preparedness could work in the interests of the many instead of the few.[13]

Finally, the president went out of his way to defend his naval program in the language of antimilitarism. Again, this made good political sense, but Wilson had said the same thing before he had formulated and started campaigning for his preparedness plan. The navy's ships "have no suggestion of bluster about them," he asserted, and "are commanded by men thoughtful of the duty of citizens as well as the duty of officers." Americans had always supported a powerful navy "because they seem to think that, if you can keep your fighting men at sea, they are not in danger of disturbing your peace of mind or the character of the national life." In so defending his naval buildup, Wilson again revealed that while he judged the risks involved with military expansion differently than the pacifists, he nevertheless still shared their belief that, under certain circumstances, militarism could threaten America's domestic freedoms.[14]

The editors of the Progressive journal, the *New Republic,* the most articulate proponents of liberal internationalism in the press, essentially agreed with Wilson's perspective on preparedness. They especially stressed the idea that professional military forces possessed a political outlook at odds with democracy. An America that had "a small standing professional army which was really no more than a national police force," wrote chief editor Herbert Croly, had "no reason to fear the corruption of its democratic institutions and ideals by a military caste or spirit." But increasing that army to a size where it could instantly defeat any invader would be a different story. That kind of force, warned Croly, would "have a profound reaction on American domestic life, because as a consequence of its increased size and authority it will be constantly making imperative demands upon the civil authorities which they will be reluctant to grant and which will raise the issue between civil and military control over American policy."[15]

Like the pacifists, the *New Republic* also associated preparedness advocates with anti-Progressive elements in American life. Editor Walter Weyl in particular made this point. He argued that the "dominant classes" in Europe had long agitated for preparedness and had manipulated the "constant fear of war" to "allay domestic discontent and to oppose democratic progress." While he thought that American preparedness campaigns cut across more diverse groups, Weyl still believed, at least "to a certain extent," that conservative forces in America hoped to use military expansion to achieve "political quiescence and domination." Just as the pacifists did, Weyl perceived "a reactionary shape" in the preparedness movement.[16]

"If preparation for war meant only what it means to many of the defense societies and military agitators," agreed Croly and Walter Lippmann, then America could not pursue preparedness "without being false to national ideals as well as its traditions." Their concern about the character of the preparedness movement did not lead the *New Republic*'s editors to reject all types of military expansion, however. In line with President Wilson, they did not believe that military training per se would undermine a person's democratic character and "turn citizens into mere military automatons." On the contrary, the editors asserted, voluntary training could be a "stirring and illuminating episode" for an enlistee, teaching him "moral discipline," not in a "servile" way but "as part of a system, to which as a civilian he had given his consent."[17]

Compulsory training fell into a different category. If UMT was necessary to combat America's "prevailing tendencies towards faction and disintegration," and the editors thought it might well be, then it had to be combined with sweeping advances in Progressive reform. Specifically, the *New Republic* could only go along with UMT if it was accompanied "by the nationalizing of essential public services, like the railroads," by government ownership of vital natural resources, and by a "strengthening of the trades unions and their frank recognition as an independent member of the official industrial organization." Without an attempt "to make the American commonwealth better worth defending," warned the editors, an upgraded military featuring UMT "might be as demoralizing as an armament intended plainly for undemocratic aggression."[18]

The League to Enforce Peace (LEP), the most conservative component of the liberal internationalist coalition, represented a variety of views concerning militarism. Some members, such as the *Independent*'s editor, Hamilton Holt, shared Wilson's conviction that a "large standing army" was "the greatest foe of liberty" and supported the president's defense program as the best way to achieve preparedness "in consonance with American spirit and American traditions." Other members, such as conservatives Edward Filene and William Wadhams, ignored the charges often made by Progressives that professional military forces possessed an antidemocratic outlook. But they did worry that excessive preparedness might lead to huge tax increases and "serious class strife" harmful to America's political stability. Still others, such as William Howard Taft, Theodore Marburg, and A. Lawrence Lowell, considered Wilson's defense program weak; indeed, Taft supported UMT.[19]

In adopting this position, Taft and other conservatives in the LEP tilted toward the Atlanticist perspective on the relationship between the military and American democracy. At first glance, the Atlanticist approach to military matters starkly contrasted with that of the pacifists and Progressive liberal internationalists. Roosevelt and his supporters demanded that preparedness go well beyond Wilson's plan. At a minimum, they wanted a standing army of 250,000 men supported by UMT and a faster naval buildup than the one proposed by the president. Atlanticists also tended to dismiss the proposition that munitions makers stimulated preparedness for profit; whenever speakers mentioned this charge at the 1916 convention of the National Security League (NSL), the audience always burst into laughter. Finally, Atlanticists had no hesitation in urging that Congress rely upon the advice of military officers in making defense policy; they evidently were not concerned that this would undercut the principle of civilian control of the military.[20]

Nevertheless, Atlanticists betrayed that they too believed that America was vulnerable to militarism. Repeatedly, they expressed deep reservations about relying solely upon professional forces for defense. "I do not believe in a large standing army," announced Roosevelt in late 1914. "Most emphatically, I do not believe in militarism." Roosevelt did not elaborate much on the reasoning behind this position, but he did suggest, as did pacifists and liberal internationalists, that it was dangerous to the Republic to withdraw "our population from civil pursuits, such as occurs among the great military states of the European Continent."[21]

Their fear of professional standing forces helps explain the Atlanticist endorsement of UMT. A system of compulsory training for all able-bodied young men, they argued, was the proper method of preparedness for a democracy. "If you put the son of the workingman and the son of the millionaire side by side in the ranks," explained Luke Wright, a former secretary of war and a member of the NSL, "it does not build up a military aristocracy, but it builds up a democratic body of men who love their country and its institutions." The UMT method of "democratic preparedness" would train a man "to realize that he is a partner in this giant democracy," added Roosevelt, "and has duties to the other partners." Echoing the claims of liberal internationalists about the moral and educational benefits of voluntary military training, Roosevelt also insisted that enlistees, and in particular immigrants, would "acquire habits of order, of cleanliness, of self-control" and learn how to provide for the growing families Roosevelt thought provided a cornerstone of national power. Universal military training thus amounted to a way of improving democracy while providing for preparedness without a large standing army and without isolating the armed forces from civilian life. In Roosevelt's words, it would allow for a military defense as effective as Germany's "without loss of our own democratic spirit."[22]

UMT, moreover, was a cheaper way to defend America than reliance upon professional forces. This benefit attracted Atlanticists to UMT because they worried about Americans' "wasting our substance in continual readiness for war." Even Henry Cabot Lodge, who did not discuss the threat of militarism as much as the other Atlanticists, alluded to this problem, observing in 1915 that "the grave objections to overwhelming and exhausting armaments are economic." From this perspective, large-scale professional forces threatened America's economic stability, a threat that UMT could counter by providing a way "to secure an economical and inexpensive army."[23]

The different shades of antimilitarism among American leaders were matched by varied analyses of great power politics. Pacifists emphasized that the international system that produced the war was inherently unstable. In the existing system, they explained, nations strove above all else to maintain a "balance of power" between each other. In theory, international law, "the conscience of mankind," as the *Nation* called it, restrained nations from pursuing power politics with unlimited force. But in practice nations paid little attention to international law as they struggled to maintain a balance of power. The Europeans and Japanese focused instead on negotiating "secret and open alliances," concentrating foreign and defense policymaking in the hands of executive authority, and building massive military establishments. By maintaining a balance of power, the world's leading states hoped to deter aggression; they believed, as Bryan put it, that "fear is the only basis upon which peace can last."[24]

This hope was a delusion, argued the pacifists, as the outbreak of the Great War obviously demonstrated. First, power politics exacerbated emotions of anger, suspicion, and hate that made the peaceful settlement of disputes difficult. Bryan elaborated on this problem at length. Power politics, he perceived, "presupposes the existence of an enemy who must be hated until he can be overcome." Hatred, however, "begets hatred" and pervaded the whole system. Twisted by their rage and fear, nations in the balance-of-power system succumbed to "the spirit that expresses itself in threats and revels in the ultimatum." Genuine negotiations became virtually impossible, as was clearly shown, Bryan thought, in the crisis that led to the war. "Firmness, supported by force," had ended in disaster for all concerned.[25]

Pacifists also saw a logical flaw in the proposition that a balance of power could preserve peace. Suffused with "an atmosphere of fear" and built on the "doctrine that force must rule our affairs," power politics encouraged arms competitions and preemptive surprise attacks. In the logic of the existing system, argued Samuel Danziger of the *Public*, "adequate defense" meant creating "an armament more powerful than any possible combination of foes could bring against us." But that would only be a start, "for our potential foes might suspect that we were planning to attack them, just as we suspect them of planning to attack us. They would attempt to outstrip us in building armaments." To stop such a "race" in arms, one side either would have to quit, which made little sense given the assumption that only a balance of power could maintain peace, or "would have to find some pretext to attack the other when conditions for victory would seem most favorable." The behavior of the Europeans showed all too clearly which alternative was likely to be chosen; "preparations for war," concluded Danziger, "only lead to war."[26]

If they easily agreed on the nature of power politics, pacifists somewhat varied in their analyses of its sources. The dominant position attributed the balance-of-power system to the ability of undemocratic, reactionary, militaristic groups to influence—indeed, to control—the foreign and defense policymaking of the major powers. Frederic Howe, a prominent social reformer and the commissioner of immigration at Ellis Island, provided the most in-depth treatment of this thesis in his 1916 book *Why War?* The foreign policies of the European great powers, Howe believed, were run by an alliance of three reactionary groups: the "old aristocracy of the land," who dominated the diplomatic and officer corps; the "new aristocracy of finance," who sought investments and concessions overseas; and the "munitions makers," who made "colossal" profits from armament sales. "These classes," Howe claimed, "own or control great portions of the press. They mould public opinion. They control political advancement. They are society. These forces are the state." Operating "in the dark behind closed doors," they promoted and practiced the power politics—"the preparations for war, the irritations and the jealousies, the suspicions and the controversies"—that caused modern war in general and the Great War in particular.[27]

The reactionaries embraced power politics for various reasons. The old aristocracy saw itself as "a caste apart," considered war its special "calling," and thought "almost exclusively in terms of its profession." "It is a mind which views democracy with contempt," argued Howe, "which thinks of the state as something separate and apart from the people, and for the preservation of which the peasant and the workman are but fodder for guns." The new aristocracy of the financial classes promoted power politics as a means to protect their imperialistic investments overseas. They pressed the policy that "the flag follows the investor," thus transforming the state, with its "narrow militaristic psychology," into the "insurance and collection agency for the investing classes." Their ultimate goal was "to secure a complete and exclusive monopoly" in their overseas concessions or territory "from which all other financiers and countries can be excluded," a goal that inevitably led to international conflict when it was pursued, as Howe thought it was, by each of the great powers. Finally, munitions makers fomented power politics because they made money out of it. To Howe, they, more than anyone except the "great financiers," were responsible "for the agitation for armament and 'preparedness' and for the increase in war expenditures which has taken place during the last twenty years."[28]

In contrast to the old and new privileged classes, ordinary people gained nothing from power politics and war. Instead, they suffered "in lower wages, in higher costs of living, in burdensome taxes." Laboring classes suffered the most; they bore the cost of war and preparedness, according to Howe. "Labor really gives its all," he lamented. "It gives life; it gives health; it gives home, family, and the few comforts which labor enjoys. And labor enjoys none of the profits." At the same time, war and war scares gave reactionaries an opportunity to reverse social legislation, cut money for "social needs," and whip up emotions of hate and vengeance that "shattered the foundation of the democratic mind and entangled the highways of democratic advance." Ultimately, Howe suggested, reactionary influences promoted power politics more for political than economic reasons: to maintain their power at home.[29]

Over the course of 1914–17, leading pacifists embraced all or most of Howe's argument about the origin of power politics. Although the leaders of the Woman's

Peace Party (WPP) emphasized that male aggression and ambitions were a primary cause of power politics, they alluded to Howe's analysis in their platform, condemning "the economic causes of war" and calling for "democratic control of foreign policies." *Survey,* a leading social welfare journal, printed one of Howe's many articles, as did *La Follette's Magazine,* and La Follette himself praised *Why War?* as a "very able work." Even Villard, probably the least progressive of the leading pacifists, blamed arms races and the war on munitions manufacturers, military officers, and "small ruling cliques, who, apart from the masses of the people, . . . cling to the old shibboleths and still lust for conquests."[30]

In sum, pacifists believed that power politics and militarism were twins born of the same reactionary parents. Military officers, plutocratic imperialists, decadent aristocrats, and greedy munitions makers conspired together to provoke war scares, propagandize for preparedness, and defend exclusive spheres of interest around the globe. They either operated in secret, with little democratic oversight, or, when necessary, by manipulating the normally peaceful masses through fear and appeals to patriotism into supporting their schemes. Their intrigues both enhanced their power at home at the expense of democratic progress and militarized international diplomacy, thus making war almost inevitable. And war, of course, could only further perpetuate their power and wealth, both domestically and in international relations. Which came first—domestic militarism or power politics—was not clear. The way pacifists described it, the two were cause and consequence of each other, feeding on each other to put the world on a road toward dictatorship and destruction.

Pacifists, however, sometimes suggested that other forces might lie behind power politics too. Bryan at one point noted that fear of invasion rather than internal militarism "led the European nations to convert themselves into armed camps." In August 1916, the editors of the *Nation* asserted that "no nation can make itself so strong as to avoid all risk of attack," and they connected this danger to a condition of "anarchy among nations." They also frequently hoped for "a better world where national security is written into international law, rather than propped on bayonets." Similarly, Edward Devine of the *Survey* wanted the United States to help put some sort of "law in place of anarchy in international relations," a goal endorsed in general terms by the WPP, the AUAM, and La Follette as well. These comments implied that the structure of the international system, and not simply reactionary political groups, had something to do with the development of power politics. More specifically, they implied that anarchy—the lack of a ruling authority over states—and uncertainty—the fact that states could never take their security for granted—provided the environment that gave rise to balance-of-power behavior.[31]

But pacifists did not pursue this line of analysis. They recognized that the anarchical structure of the system was a factor in alliance building, arms racing, and war, but they focused their analysis of the cause of power politics on the presence of antidemocratic forces operating within the various great powers. Thus David Starr Jordan of the AUAM began one of his analyses of the war by asserting that "the great conflict of our century is that between law and anarchy." Yet he went on to blame armies for "the spirit of international hate" and "privileged classes" in the officer corps for keeping alive "the idea of the righteousness and necessity of war." Anarchy as a cause of power politics faded from view, just as it did in the writings and platforms of other pacifists.[32]

Liberal internationalists shared much of the pacifist assessment of the international system. They certainly agreed with the pacifists on its basic characteristics. President Wilson summed up the prevailing outlook on the system in his famous "peace without victory" address to the Senate on 22 January 1917. In the existing order, nations sought to achieve "equipoises of power," and in so doing, they pursued an array of policies that enmeshed them in "a net of intrigue and selfish rivalry." They handed "peoples about from sovereignty to sovereignty as if they were property," closed off the free flow of international trade, based international rights on the "individual strength" of nations, built "great preponderating armaments," formed "entangling alliances" that drew them into "competitions of power," and constantly "planned for war and made ready for pitiless contest and rivalry." Pacifists could not have described the system of power politics any better.[33]

Liberal internationalists also agreed with the pacifists that the system was profoundly unstable. International law provided some measure of security for nations, but not much. It had failed to prevent the war, which broke out precisely because the world lacked any real mechanism for upholding international order. "Have you ever heard what started the present war?" Wilson asked an audience in Cincinnati. "So far as I can gather, nothing in particular started it, but everything in general." The intrigues of power politics, combined with the "powder magazine" of large-scale armaments, generated "a mutual suspicion, an interchange of conjectures about what this government and that government was going to do"— a mix of emotions Wilson suggested was bound to end in conflict. The maintenance of "great preponderating armaments" in itself left nations with "no sense of safety and equality," added the president, thus making peaceful relations difficult to maintain. If power politics persisted after the war, warned Wilson in October 1916, "sooner or later, you will have just such another war."[34]

Arms races and the prospect of preemptive attacks especially troubled liberal internationalists; Wilson, in fact, called the issue of armaments "the most immediately and intensely practical question connected with the future fortunes of mankind." To the president, "preparing a great machine whose only use is for war and giving it no use to which to apply itself" was a formula for disaster. The "men who are in charge of edged tools and bidden to prepare them for exact and scientific use grow very impatient if they are not permitted to use them," he feared. Thomas Raeburn White, a member of the LEP's Executive Committee, perceived

the same danger in arms competitions. Nations engaged in a "struggle for supremacy in armaments," he argued, were "only waiting a favorable opportunity
to strike the first blow." Convinced that attacks could come "without warning,"
nations involved in the balance of power kept themselves "on edge," maintaining
forces in an "instant readiness to repel attack."[35]

Liberal internationalists had a more complex view of the origins of power politics than did the pacifists, however. In part, they agreed with the pacifist thesis
that antidemocratic groups within states promoted the existing system for their
own narrow purposes. Wilson believed that autocratic structures of government
brought on wars: "They are never brought on by peoples." "Democracy," he added,
was "the best preventive of such jealousies and surprises and secret intrigues as
produce wars among nations where small groups control, rather than the great
body of public opinion." As revealed in his analysis of militarism, Wilson thought
that professional military leaders, in particular, had aggressive, self-aggrandizing
tendencies. At home, this led the military to view civilians and civil institutions as
objects of, or obstacles to, military efficiency. In facing the outside world, it led to
a paranoid, warlike foreign policy. "The purpose of militarism," as the president
maintained to the 1916 graduating class of West Point, "is to use armies for aggression." Autocratic, military-dominated groups, he agreed with one correspondent,
"may easily be led into ordering mobilization and entering upon war out of mere
apprehension of danger from their neighbors." Wilson also suggested more than
once that he agreed with Howe's argument that "privileged interests" promoting
imperialism were a factor in the "countless irritations, conflicts and diplomatic
contests" of power politics. Finally, the president, as discussed earlier, was wary
of the influence of munitions makers in government. He therefore not only called
for greater public ownership of American munitions plants but also thought that
other nations should do the same thing with their own munitions industry. In
fact, Wilson initially included government control of the manufacture and sale of
munitions in his proposal for a pan-American peace pact.[36]

Other liberal internationalists indicted reactionary forces within nations for
power politics as well. Franklin Giddings of the LEP thought that "the monstrous
egotism and the medieval-mindedness of the absolute monarchs" and the "manufacturers of artillery and powder" helped to bring on the war. Theodore Marburg,
another leading figure in the LEP, suggested that "autocratic government" had
something to do with the cause of war, while Weyl, more broadly, identified power
politics with the political ambitions of "financial-military" elements in society.
Imperialism and power politics, argued Weyl, were due in part to the "dominant
classes'" using "the constant fear of war" as a means to "allay domestic discontent
and to oppose democratic progress." Lippmann described similar groups lurking
behind imperialism and arms races, as did Samuel Gompers. The *New Republic*
even applauded Howe at one point, claiming his "main thesis that competition

for investment opportunities is at bottom responsible for most of the aggression and international strife that have occurred since 1880, will be disputed by hardly anyone who has made a expansionistic study of recent history."[37]

In line with this argument, liberal internationalists blamed autocratic states for tensions and conflict in the international system. At times, they singled out autocratic Russia for condemnation. But Germany was the target of most of their criticism. To all of the leading liberal internationalists, Germany appeared to respond to the international system's anarchical character with an especially aggressive, irrational form of power politics. At the same time, its domestic militarism was more pronounced than that of any other state. Soon after the war broke out, Wilson condemned Germany's attack on Belgium and complained that "German philosophy was essentially selfish and lacking in spirituality." On 14 December 1914, Wilson suggested that although Germany was "not alone responsible for the war," it did bear more responsibility than others, and he implied that the militarized, autocratic character of its government helped explain its aggression. He continued to express this view in 1915 and 1916, to the point of explicitly denouncing "Germany's responsibility for this world-wide calamity" to his chief advisor on foreign policy, Col. Edward M. House.[38]

Other liberal internationalists also scorned Germany. The *New Republic* considered Germany's autocratic leadership "the aggressive party" in the war, who planned and prepared for it "not to resist but to conquer." The German regime, declared Croly, embodied "autocratic militaristic aggression," and it seemed bent on a "headstrong career of . . . militarist nationalism." Its attack upon Belgium, argued the editors, was an "assault on international morality," its submarine warfare a "revolting" and "barbarous" challenge to international law. Similarly, Holt thought that the German kaiser wanted to be "the dominant power in Europe" and that the Germans and the Austrians had "no just occasion for the war on which they have embarked." Marburg's language was even stronger. Belgium, he exclaimed in a letter to Wilson, "is being trampled to death simply because it lay in the path of a war-mad government." Germany was "dominated by a heartless military class" with an "utter disregard of the international code . . . and of the moral law." Taft agreed with these views, as did Gompers.[39]

While they saw autocracy, military officers, and corporate reactionaries as important generators of power politics, however, liberal internationalists put even more emphasis on other factors. First, they identified the anarchical structure of the international system as a central cause of balance-of-power behavior. Wilson perceived that the governments contesting the war "believe the very life and political integrity of the nations they represent to be involved." They felt they had to fight the war to its conclusion "in order to make themselves secure in the future against its renewal and against the rivalries and ambitions which brought it about." They fought, in other words, for their national survival and their future security.[40]

Other leading liberal internationalists agreed with Wilson's analysis. Lippmann, as noted, thought that "special interests" in nations helped to provoke imperialism and power politics, but he ascribed the system and its instability fundamentally to the deep anxieties nations had about their place in the world's hierarchy of power. Weyl shared the views of his colleague. Narrow imperialistic motives emerging from the influence of reactionary groups in government certainly influenced the behavior of states, but more basically, Weyl argued, nations sought resources and territory to preserve their "physical well-being and economic ambition." They struggled to find and to monopolize resources for survival, which brought them into explosive conflict with each other around the globe. "A nation in danger of annihilation cannot indulge in the luxury of sentiment," Weyl observed. "Each nation is compelled to enter into offensive and defensive alliances, and these alliances, perpetually suspecting each other, are compelled to prepare for instant war." The lack of democracy contributed to but did not cause this dynamic—the "prevailing circumstances" of anarchy did.[41]

For the LEP, likewise, the root of power politics lay not in the domestic sphere but in an "international realm . . . in which each nation is equally sovereign." In this system, asserted Holt, "the only way for a nation to secure its rights is by the use of force," a fact that led to arms races, coercive diplomacy, and war. Lowell, one of the key leaders of the LEP, likened the existing system to a lawless frontier, where nations frantically tried to protect themselves with ad hoc vigilante committees. Filene also made this analogy and asserted that the alliances that emerged in the system were inherently unstable given clashing "national interests" and the lack of "some method other than war to deal with the differences that are bound to arise." Indeed, argued Marburg, "the central idea" of the LEP "is that wars are the result of the condition of international anarchy out of which the world has never yet risen." In the eyes of these commentators, the structure of the system explained the balance of power much more than the internal politics of the various states.[42]

Liberal internationalists also perceived that the lawlessness of the existing order allowed people free rein to self-destructive emotions. Wilson pointed to the consequences of the Franco-Prussian War of 1870–71 as an example. France, "hopelessly beaten," desired revenge; Germany, victorious, "began to dream greater dreams of conquest and power." Both sides proceeded to arm heavily for another round of fighting. Given the lawless structure of the system, there was nothing to restrain their fears and ambitions and no incentive not to arm to acquire the means to get what they wanted, be it vengeance or more territory.[43]

These self-defeating insecurities and ambitions were not confined to antidemocratic elites or autocratic governments. Wilson implied that they infected whole peoples. In his private memorandum on the war, the president did not distinguish between peoples and their governments. He instead referred to the emotions and behavior of "nations." He also wrote, in describing the psychological consequences of victory, that "the victorious nation, as the man, gets 'cocky' again, places another chip on its shoulder and becomes unendurable as a neighbor." Here the president clearly seemed to universalize the emotional dynamic under discussion; it applied not just to leaders or to particular groups but to everyone. According to Wilson, even the American people had been guilty in the past of aggressive "selfish passion" in their conduct toward other nations, most notably in their war against Mexico in the 1840s. Human nature, combined with the anarchical character of the system, encouraged grasping, militaristic power politics, not the internal political character of states.[44]

Wilson's conception of political leadership also ran counter to the idea that the balance of power could be traced to the machinations of authoritarian-minded groups at home. Wilson believed in the merits of strong executive decision making, emphasized that few peoples had attained the maturity needed for successful popular government, and doubted the ability of ordinary people to form sound opinions on complex issues. As Wilson's brother-in-law Stockton Axson recalled, the president's "faith in the people has never been a faith in the supreme wisdom of the people, but rather in the capacity of the people to be led right by those whom they elect and constitute their leaders." In line with this philosophy, and with what his leading biographer calls his "egotism, secretiveness, and urge for dominance," Wilson believed "that the President alone must make and control foreign policy, governed only by public opinion and his conception of what was the right thing to do." Indeed, Wilson told Colonel House in November 1914 that "when newspaper men asked questions involving his foreign policy, he felt entirely justified in lying to them." This elitist outlook on politics was perfectly consistent with Wilson's belief that the democratic masses were only marginally more likely than autocrats or plutocrats to tolerate the insecurity and resist the lust for power inherent in an anarchical world.[45]

Similarly, the *New Republic* and the leaders of the League to Enforce Peace questioned the wisdom of common people on national security matters. "When the war fever is on," observed Marburg, "the people are the last to be trusted." Mass emotions, agreed Lippmann and his colleagues, were volatile and easily shaped by leaders—facts that complicated the argument that selfish elites alone were to blame for the war.[46]

To a significant degree, Atlanticists shared the view of the international system put forward by Wilson and his supporters. They, too, closely connected power politics with international anarchy. "In international matters," Roosevelt asserted, "we are still in the stage that individuals were in certain western communities where . . . I lived thirty years ago, that is, there is no international police and there are certain nations which can be withheld from wrongdoing only by fear of the consequences." With "no real homology between international law and internal or municipal law," states could not trust in treaties to protect them from attack, feared for their security, and therefore had no choice but to be prepared to defend their rights and interests themselves. They had to develop their military strength; "a nation must be strong," preached Roosevelt, "otherwise it can neither preserve the friendship of friendly nations or the respect of possibly hostile nations." Liberal internationalists would not have disagreed with this description of the existing system at all.[47]

Atlanticists also perceived that some of the worst impulses of human nature found expression in the lawless environment of the existing international order. With nations competing "for trade and wealth, for honor and prestige," as they sought to protect themselves in the jungle of the existing system, sometimes "selfishness and greed" and incendiary posturing overcame them. In 1905, for example, during the first Moroccan crisis involving Britain, France, and Germany, Roosevelt thought that "wild talk, . . . inflammatory and provocative talk" about war, especially by the British public, had greatly aggravated tensions. He saw the same dynamic at work during his second term as president, when popular hostility and discrimination directed at Japanese immigrants in California so irritated Japan that Roosevelt worried that war could break out. Pressed into a corner by his own peoples' "fatuous policy of insult and injury" toward another nation, Roosevelt had to combine a variety of military and diplomatic moves to defuse the crisis.[48]

Prior to 1914, Root developed in the most detail the idea that popular self-righteousness stimulated power politics. He noted that wars could arise out of a logic of preemption: the "suspicion by one country that another intends to do it wrong, and upon that suspicion, instinct leads the country that suspects the attack, to attack first." According to Root, this "suspicion" came from "exasperated feeling" produced "of the acts and the words of the people of the countries themselves, not of their governments." Apparently unable to control the base instincts of "man's original savage nature" that Root saw as the ultimate cause of war, the ordinary masses—"the men on the farms and in the shops, the men with the pick and shovel in their hands"—reacted to international disputes with "race and local prejudice, . . . exaggerated national *amour proper*, . . . [and] the . . . assumption, often arrogant, often ignorant, that the extreme claims of one's country are always right are to be rigidly insisted upon as a point of national honor." This warped patriotism produced preemptive attacks and, at least in part, the arms racing and alliance building that preceded them.[49]

While both the anarchical structure of the international system and the primitive aspects of human nature were largely behind power politics, Atlanticists agreed with other American leaders that the internal character of nation-states played a role as well. They in particular saw autocratic governments as fomenters of the insecurity intrinsic to the existing system. In part, autocracies suffered from the same deficiencies as the mass public: they were emotional and impulsive in their approach to foreign policy. Because autocracies centralized power in one person, it followed that if that leader was incompetent, power hungry, or paranoid, the foreign policy pursued by that leader's government would be too. Moreover, unlike democracies, autocratic governments were based on the idea that the leader had a "God-given right to govern the people." An autocracy, stressed Root in late 1915, protected itself and ruled largely by "arbitrary power" rather than by "the rule of law." And law, including international law, was a fundamental constraint upon humanity's "powerful, innate tendencies which survive from the countless centuries of man's struggle for existence against brutes and savage foes"; law was "the only means yet discovered by man to limit those tendencies." Unrestrained in their use of power at home, unfamiliar with the need to reach accommodations with others "based upon justice," autocracies like Germany did not think twice about repudiating "every element of fundamental right upon which the law of nations rests," including "the right of every nation to continued existence."[50]

Despite the dangers of war generated by anarchy, aggressive autocracies, and the belligerent masses, Atlanticists, in sharp contrast to pacifists and liberal internationalists, did not see the existing world order as inherently unstable. Before 1914, in fact, Lodge, Root, and especially Roosevelt developed an elaborate theory of why the international system was becoming increasingly peaceful. The "civilized" nations, as Roosevelt called the United States, Britain, France, Russia, Italy, Austria-Hungary, and Germany, maintained world peace, first of all, through military preparedness. Strong military establishments deterred attack, argued Atlanticists. "So far from being in any way a provocation to war," asserted Roosevelt in 1901, "an adequate and highly trained navy is the best guaranty against war, the cheapest and most effective peace insurance." America's navy secured the Western Hemisphere against attack, just as the navies and armies of the other powers safeguarded their interests too. Arms races imposed an unfortunate economic and budgetary burden upon states, but, in and of themselves, they had little to do with the outbreak of war. In fact, warned Roosevelt in 1905, "at present there could be no greater calamity for the free peoples, the enlightened, independent, and peace-loving peoples, to disarm while yet leaving it open to any barbarism or despotism to remain armed." Thus arms races did not cause war. Weakness did.[51]

Preparedness by the great powers also allowed them to dominate and to "police" undeveloped nations—the "barbarous or semi-barbarous peoples" in Roosevelt's lexicon. Imperialism backed by military power was a force for peace, Atlanticists contended, because it tended to spread "law, order, and righteousness." Undeveloped nations lacked political stability and the capacity to fulfill international financial and political obligations to other states. Such areas of the world benefited from the guiding hand of a stronger, civilized power—and, with the uplift of more and more peoples on the "scale of civilization," the world benefited too.[52]

Prior to 1914, Roosevelt and other Atlanticists had little doubt that civilization was on the march. "The last century has seen a marked diminution of wars between civilized powers," Roosevelt reported to Congress in 1902. "Wars with uncivilized powers are largely mere matters of international police duty, essential for the welfare of the world." Increasingly, he asserted, "the civilized peoples are realizing the wicked folly of war and attaining that condition of just and intelligent regard for the rights of others which will in the end, as we hope and believe, make worldwide peace possible." International conferences of the world's leading powers at The Hague "gave definite expression to this hope and belief and marked a stride toward their attainment." Gradually, Atlanticists thought, an international moral code was developing, expressed in international law, treaties, and arbitration agreements. A "great nation must often act," Roosevelt affirmed in 1906, "and as a matter of fact often does act, toward other nations in a spirit not in the least of mere self-interest, but paying heed chiefly to ethical reasons; and as the centuries go by this disinterestedness in international action, this tendency of the individuals comprizing a nation to require that nation to act with justice toward its neighbors, steadily grows and strengthens." Such gradual moral advancement was a force for peace, as peace, Roosevelt was certain, "is normally the hand-maiden of righteousness."[53]

Preparedness and an increasing sense of morality merged together as forces for peace in Roosevelt's axiom "speak softly and carry a big stick." The aim of all "enlightened nations," he argued in his fourth annual message as president, should be "the attainment of the peace of justice, of the peace which comes when each nation is not merely safe-guarded in its own rights, but scrupulously recognizes and performs its duty toward others." In part, this meant that nations should refrain from and condemn "wanton or useless war, or a war of mere aggression—in short, any war begun or carried on in a conscienceless spirit." But it also meant that a nation should never make threats, promises, or treaties that it would not or could not keep. To do so would be to destroy a nation's credibility, as well as, if treaties were broken, the momentum of international morality the Atlanticists thought was advancing throughout the globe. The fabric of international peace would consequently be threatened. As Lodge discerned, "The nation that disregards its treaty obligations will soon find the world unwilling to enter upon agreements with it and, what is far worse, will also find itself constantly embroiled with other nations in regard to questions of good faith and upright dealing which are more likely than any others to bring on war." The "just man armed," the nation that most contributed to peace, was the nation that shunned hypocrisy, respected the rights of others, and delivered on what it said it would do, with force if necessary.[54]

Balance-of-power politics and the development of an international "golden rule" might not guarantee the stability of the international system, but they appeared to offer the best hope of doing so over the long run. The outbreak of the world war thus came as a shock to Atlanticists. "What occurred in Europe is on a giant scale like the disaster to the *Titanic*," mourned Roosevelt. The war was a "horror," a "hideous event" that left him "inexpressibly saddened." For one thing, the war obviously called into question the idea that international moral development was a force for peace. The "very foundations of international law," the code of ethics the Atlanticists thought helped to diminish the chances of war, had been "rudely shaken," Root admitted, if not destroyed. Lodge, deeply distressed at the destructive spectacle of modern battle, was more blunt. "The veils of what we call civilization have been torn away," he moaned. "Primitive man" had been reborn.[55]

Atlanticists also began to doubt the efficacy of power politics as a means to peace. Both Root and Lodge speculated that arms competitions had led to the war. Roosevelt, for his part, concluded days after the war started that it had been "inevitable." The various belligerents, he thought, "are, each from its own standpoint, right under the existing conditions of civilization and international relations." Ensnared in anarchical world politics, "each nation has cause for the fear it feels," and each felt compelled to protect itself in the July 1914 crisis that led to the war. "Under existing conditions," asserted Roosevelt in late 1914, "each nation was driven by its vital interests to do what it did." Roosevelt even suggested that mutual fears of preemptive attack might have triggered the conflict. "The power sending the ultimatum and making the attack," he wrote in an allusion to Germany's assault upon Belgium, "may do so merely because it is so obvious that the other side is preparing to strike first." The whole logic of competitive power politics, including especially that of arms races, Roosevelt appeared to say, caused the war.[56]

Yet Roosevelt, Root, and Lodge drew back from fully embracing this conclusion. Despite their evident uncertainty about the fundamental stability of balance-of-power politics, they still clung to their prewar argument that military preparedness could virtually guarantee a state's national security. Just as criminals attacked "the helpless" whenever they could, "aggressive and militarist nations attack weak nations where it is possible. Weakness always invites attack." Preparedness might not always deter assaults, Roosevelt conceded, but "unpreparedness for war has invariably invited smashing disaster, and sometimes complete conquest." After all, he pointed out, Belgium and China made little effort to maintain a robust military establishment—they "inspired no fear" in others—and look what had happened to them. Germany occupied Belgium while Japan, like other powers before it, brutally violated China's integrity and neutrality. Britain's failure to keep up in the pre-1914 arms race with Germany had contributed to the outbreak of fighting as well, in Roosevelt's view. "Because you had the Channel," he wrote Rudyard Kipling, "your people have not thought it worth while to arm when Europe was arming." If Britain "had had an army as effective in preparation to your size, as Switzerland has had, there would have been no war, for Germany would not have entered upon the war." Britain might have been armed, but it did not arm enough. Its *failure* to practice power politics—its failure to balance Germany's power prior to 1914—brought on the war, not any defect in the system of power politics itself.[57]

The other key cause of the war lay in Berlin, in the immorality and stupidity of the Reich's leaders. "I am sure," Roosevelt conceded in commenting on the German invasion of Belgium, "that nine tenths of the German people have acted primarily from fear—from an honorable fear . . . that German civilization would be wiped out if they did not strike their foes." But the other 10 percent, "including the bulk of the men high up," were another matter. "The Government of Prussianized Germany for the last forty-three years has behaved in such fashion as inevitably to make almost every nation with which it came in contact its foe," Roosevelt charged, "because it has convinced everybody except Austria that it has no regard for anything except its own interest, and that it will enter instantly on any career of aggression with cynical brutality and bad faith if it thinks its interest requires such action." Belgium had never threatened Germany or any other nation, and its neutrality was guaranteed by all of the major European powers, including the Germans. Yet Germany had "carefully planned for a score of years" to attack Belgium anyway; Germany's leaders took "the ground that in matters of national moment there are no such things as abstract right and wrong." All Germany's "intelligent and despotic upper class" cared about was ruthlessly maximizing their country's power. It was this attitude—the imperial government's amoral aggressiveness—that started the war, not any fundamental flaw in the balance-of-power system.[58]

The Atlanticists' analysis of power politics and of militarism did not gain them many allies in the debates over those topics that began after August 1914. First, pacifists and most liberal internationalists had very similar ideas about the nature of militarism and how it could undermine American democracy. They both perceived that professional military officers possessed attitudes and ambitions fundamentally at odds with America's free way of life. Most of them also associated military preparedness agitation with reactionary elements in American society. In their view, professional military officers and reactionaries sought to manipulate national security fears to enhance their own power. Both groups wanted to militarize American life to suit their own agendas—the military to prepare the country for all-out war against every conceivable opponent, the reactionaries to snuff out democratic reforms and organizations that might threaten their wealth and political dominance. Pacifists and liberal internationalists did disagree over the precise military force structure that might begin to generate militarism. Their differences here were important, as pacifists objected to any sizable defense increase while liberal internationalists argued that American democracy could withstand a significant military buildup, especially if it featured voluntarism. Still, in the context of their shared anxiety about military officers and reactionary preparedness groups, this disagreement did not loom very large.

In contrast, the Atlanticists' stated concerns about massive professional forces undermining democracy appeared disingenuous given their calls for UMT and a standing army of 250,000 or more. Moreover, unlike the other two groups of commentators, Atlanticists dismissed the argument that corporate interests helped to promote preparedness for their own selfish reasons. These positions made it easy to mark Atlanticists as outside the mainstream of thought on the issue of militarism, all of their protests notwithstanding.

Indeed, Atlanticists seemed out of step not just with the existing political center on the question of militarism but also with dominant American opinion on the topic stretching back to the Revolution. From the first days of the Republic, American leaders expressed a grave suspicion of professional military forces, which they associated with European monarchical tyranny. Alexander Hamilton, for example, believed that professional forces were at best a "necessary evil" that citizens had to strive to limit. A large army and the fear of foreign attack that gave rise to it in Europe "enhances the importance of the soldier and proportionably degrades the condition of the citizen," he warned. "The military state becomes elevated over the civil." Throughout the nineteenth century, Americans scorned the regular army as "dangerous to our civil and political institutions, not only on account of its physical force, but also on account of its moral effects, its contaminating influence over our principles, feelings and habits." They therefore kept the army very small relative to the size of those in Europe and relied on a mixture of regulars, militiamen, and temporary volunteers, along with naval forces, to fight America's wars.[59]

Even after the Spanish-American War, which revealed glaring deficiencies in the nation's military establishment and resulted in a commitment to defend a new colonial empire, Americans still remained wary of a professional military. Prodded by the Roosevelt administration, Congress created a general staff but refused to set up a new federal reserve force, as it would put "a part of the citizen soldiery" under control of "the standing army of the country." Although lawmakers raised the army's authorized ceiling from about 28,000 men to about 90,000, they failed to appropriate the funds to maintain it and refused to give the president authority to increase the army on his own without their specific approval. "The importance of an army in any government, and most of all in a republican government," argued one congressman, "is so great that it is a dangerous grant of power, and I believe one that can not be paralleled even in the constitutional monarchies, to bestow upon the Executive such authority in fixing the number of the Army." Despite the military's expansion at the turn of the century, traditional suspicions about its role in domestic politics remained intense—a fact that worked against Atlanticists in the national security debates of 1914–17.[60]

The argument that preparedness agitation reflected and promoted hostility toward Progressivism also hurt the Atlanticists. At a time when rapid industrialization, mass immigration, urbanization, political corruption, and the rise of populism and socialism all led to widespread apprehension about America's ability to adapt its democratic institutions to the demands of modern life, the conservative

character of the preparedness movement deeply alarmed most of the leading advocates of pacifism and liberal internationalism. They worried that military expansion could become, in the hands of reactionaries, a weapon to thwart Progressive
reform—and Progressive reform, to them, offered the best hope of reconciling social stability and democracy with modern capitalism. With America struggling to
adjust its democracy to modernity, militarism, especially as a vehicle of anti-Pro-
gressivism, thus loomed as a larger potential threat than ever before. And Atlanticists, from this perspective, seemed not just indifferent onlookers to militarism but
supporters of it.

Theodore Roosevelt's presence in the front ranks of the Atlanticists did little to
assuage the fears of pacifists and Progressive liberal internationalists. Although he
claimed that he still supported the Progressive Party platform of 1912, Roosevelt,
by 1914, was no longer in the forefront of the fight for Progressive reform. Partly
this reflected his belief that anything he did on domestic issues would be construed as a bid for power and would hurt the cause of reform. But it also was due
to his own sense that the Progressive movement had moved in directions he had
trouble supporting. In late 1914, Roosevelt accused Progressives of going "every
which way" and denounced La Follette and other Republican insurgents as part of
"the lunatic fringe." A year and a half later, Roosevelt found reasons to oppose two
of the most important Progressive legislative achievements of 1916, the Adamson Act, mandating an eight-hour day for railroad workers engaged in interstate
transportation, and the Keating-Owen Act, restricting child labor. More basically,
by late 1914, Roosevelt simply no longer had much interest in promoting domestic
reform, as his attention was focused almost entirely on the war and preparedness.
For all of these reasons, Roosevelt's leadership of the Atlanticists did nothing to
blunt the politically damaging charge that preparedness forces aimed to sabotage
the reforms that America needed to preserve its democracy.[61]

In addition to their fundamental agreement on the issue of militarism, pacifists
and liberal internationalists also held similar views about power politics. Despite
their different analyses of why the balance of power existed, pacifists and liberal
internationalists both believed it was a fundamentally unstable and self-defeating
way of conducting international politics. They argued that arms races, alliances,
and imperialism generated warlike emotions and, most crucially, incentives for
preemptive attack that made the peaceful resolution of disputes virtually impossible. They pointed to the outbreak of the war—a war preceded by imperialism,
arms races, and intrigue and precipitated by a crisis in which military calculations
apparently short-circuited diplomacy—as irrefutable proof of their case. Atlanticists, in contrast, did not think balance-of-power behavior necessarily always
ended in war. On the contrary, they argued, so long as a nation kept up its military
defenses and maintained its international credibility, it could almost always deter
attacks upon it, no matter how foolish or aggressive its foes. It was this thesis—the

idea that arms races led to peace, so long as the competitors stayed even with each other and matched their actions to their words—that most alienated pacifists and liberal internationalists from the Atlanticist position on the balance of power.

The outlook of the three groups on the cause of power politics overlapped and diverged in a more complex manner. In the broadest sense, pacifists, liberal internationalists, and Atlanticists all agreed that the more democratic a state, the less likely it was to engage in power politics and outright aggression. But on the specific details of this issue there was marked disagreement and uncertainty. Pacifists attributed power politics almost entirely to the lack of democracy within states; if democratic social, economic, and political reforms went forward, they suggested, power politics would fade away. But even as they asserted this argument, they betrayed some doubts about it. At times they indicated that international anarchy was related to power politics. In addition, by portraying ordinary people as easily whipped up by "war scares" and patriotic appeals into supporting arms races and imperialism, pacifists implied that the spread of democracy might not ensure peace after all. They clearly wanted to believe that a democratic world would be a peaceful one, free from the balance of power, but their own analysis suggested otherwise.

Liberal internationalists and Atlanticists ranked the factors behind power politics in a different way. Like the pacifists, most liberal internationalists tended to see corporate reactionaries and military-dominated autocracies as aggressive practitioners of power politics. Atlanticists said little about corporate interests causing international strife, but they too thought that autocracies were guilty of aggression and of foolish strategic overreach. Both liberal internationalists and Atlanticists also put much of the blame for the war on the imperial regime in Germany, as did some pacifists. Still, neither Wilson's nor Roosevelt's supporters believed that the spread of democracy would guarantee an end to power politics. Ordinary people might be relatively less susceptible to the lust for power that appeared to grip autocratic elites, but they were hardly free from bellicose emotions that could lead to war. Moreover, both liberal internationalists and Atlanticists believed balance-of-power behavior derived, fundamentally, from international anarchy. The lawlessness of the existing system drove states to act as they did, not a lack of democracy within them.

Overall, the Atlanticists' perspective on militarism and power politics put them in an awkward position. Their position on military issues made them unpopular, but, at the same time, they actually reinforced the idea that America, under certain conditions, could be vulnerable to militarism. It was their different estimation of how exactly militarism might be triggered that estranged them from their rivals, not any clear rejection of the proposition itself. In addition, while Atlanticists questioned the notion that democratic public opinion was a force for peace, they simultaneously lent support to this idea by portraying autocracies as aggressive and autocratic Germany as the primary culprit for the war. Finally, despite their repeated insistence that military preparedness preserved peace, their comments about power politics causing the war pointed to a different conclusion. As the debates over militarism and power politics demonstrated, the Atlanticists did represent an alternative perspective on international security affairs—but in crucial ways they buttressed an emerging framework of beliefs deeply hostile to any American national security strategy based on active involvement in the balance of power.

2

National Security, 1914–17

Lurking behind the debate over militarism and power politics that broke out after the start of the war stood a third issue: the question of how the conflict overseas related to American national security. On this crucial question, it appeared that pacifists, rather than Atlanticists, stood alone; unlike Atlanticists and liberal internationalists, pacifists did not believe that the outcome of the war would in any vital way affect the security interests of the United States. When it came to analyzing the implications of how specific different endings to the war might affect the safety of America, however, the apparent unity of Atlanticists and liberal internationalists broke down. The two groups agreed that a German victory in the war would threaten the United States, but they sharply diverged when it came to estimating the implications of a decisive Allied win. This divergence reflected the different positions of Atlanticists and liberal internationalists on militarism and the stability of power politics—and it further marginalized Atlanticists in the national debate over international security affairs.

Pacifists were united in their conviction that however the war turned out, the arms races, alliances, and hair-trigger diplomacy they identified with great power politics would remain European and Japanese problems, having little to do with the United States. To be certain, they were not oblivious to the war's impact on America. They perceived that America's interests were "entwined" with those of other nations and that Europe's conflagration brought "disturbance . . . in every department of human activity." "Already we have been deeply affected by the war," wrote Villard in March 1915. "We have been drawn into it spiritually by our sympathies, economically through our sufferings and through the contributions of our granaries, our arms, and our powder factories; politically because of the appeals to us to act as judge of wrong-doing." Pacifists never described these effects of the war as seriously damaging to the United States, however. America might be inconvenienced by the conflict, and the life of the nation even disrupted to some degree, but none of this amounted to evidence that the war actually endangered America's fundamental economic, political, or social well-being.[1]

Equating national security with America's ability to deter invasion and to defeat any would-be conqueror, the pacifists stressed the significance of geography and potential military strength in their assessments of the nation's safety. "We are protected on either side by thousands of miles of ocean," declared Bryan in mid-1915, and "additional protection" lay "in the fact, known to everyone, that we have the men with whom to form an army of defense if we are ever attacked; and it is known also that we have the money too." America's distance from the other great powers made it almost impossible to invade: "No nation could possibly land 100,000 men here," argued the *Nation*'s editors, "save after weeks and months of preparation."[2]

America's existing military establishment further buttressed the security advantages conferred upon the nation by geography and resources. "Our coast defenses are the strongest in the world," applauded La Follette, "making an overseas expedition against us . . . practically an insuperable undertaking." Testifying before Congress in early 1916, representatives of the AUAM stressed that they saw no need for any expansion of America's armed forces, but they approved of "a reasonable outlay for coast defense by submarine or other weapons, proved by recent experience to be effective for that purpose." The editors of the *Nation* added that they did not oppose a "reasonable enlargement of the navy" either, to reinforce America's existing deterrent. Most pacifists also endorsed a congressional investigation of America's defense needs in light of the war, partly to slow down the momentum for preparedness but also to make the nation's military forces more modern. In short, they believed that modest, up-to-date preparedness appropriate to America's location in the world made the nation virtually invulnerable to direct attack.[3]

Pacifists further argued that the war actually enhanced America's enviable position of security. Repeatedly, they insisted that whatever the outcome of Europe's conflict, "the result will mean such an exhaustion of resources, such a weariness of war, that no member of either side is likely to attack us for years to come." Victory in the war, the pacifists implied, would not replenish the victor's power or add to it in any significant way. The hostility between the Central Powers and the Allies generated by the fighting, moreover, would likely continue after the war, which meant that the Europeans would remain absorbed with security threats from each other rather than with plotting against the United States. As AUAM leaders reasoned, a victorious Germany would not adopt a "'bullying' policy" toward the United States because it would be "surrounded by jealous European foes who would not hesitate to spring again at her if she gave them an excuse." European power politics did not threaten American security at all in this analysis. On the contrary, the more the Europeans struggled against each other, the more secure became the United States.[4]

Pacifists were not very worried about the war's implications for American trade either. While they supported more equal, open terms for international trade and denounced exclusive, imperialistic trade policies as one of the worst features of power politics, they never described an "open door" for American trade as vital to its economic well-being. "The United States is not dependent upon foreign commerce in the sense that Germany and Great Britain are," reported the *Public*. "We are a small world to ourselves that cannot be starved or beaten by isolation." America, agreed Villard, was "practically a self-supporting nation" that had no national security need to protect its commerce overseas. This economic reality would not end anytime soon, regardless of the course of the war.[5]

This is not to argue that pacifists were indifferent to how the war ended. As the next chapter discusses, they wanted it to end in a way "as will prevent this war from being but a prelude to new wars." But here it is crucial to realize that none of the pacifists from 1914 to 1917 perceived that the United States had any essential security stakes involved in this issue. Because the United States "was not in any immediate danger of invasion," Crystal Eastman saw no reason even to discuss "questions of purely national policy." She focused on fighting "the agitation for increased armament" at home and on promoting "an overpowering sense of the sacredness of life, so that war will be unthinkable." Bryan thought it "a waste of time to discuss hypothetical questions or to try to decide whether our nation would be aided or injured by the triumph of this nation or that." The Europeans "are fighting over questions which do not affect our welfare or destiny," declared Bryan in August 1915. Undoubtedly the United States should urge the belligerents "to substitute cooperation for hatred." But regardless of whether or not they followed that advice, America's national security, as the pacifists defined it, was assured.[6]

Liberal internationalists completely disagreed with this outlook. They thought that the war had profound—and disquieting—implications for American security. If Germany won the war, liberal internationalists believed that the United States would face immediate dangers. President Wilson voiced fears about the consequences of a German victory soon after the war broke out. On at least three separate occasions in the first six weeks of the conflict, Wilson confided to friends and to Britain's ambassador to the United States that if Germany succeeded in Europe, "we shall be forced to take such measures of defence here as would be fatal to our form of Government and American ideals." "If the Germans win out," agreed Theodore Marburg, "the use of their methods will have been justified and we will see an enormous spread of the curse of militarism." The prospect of a "triumphant" Germany, "able to annex new territory and to terrorize Europe," frightened Croly, Lippmann, and Weyl of the *New Republic* as well. "A world in which a helpless and inoffensive country like Belgium is violable is not one in which a peace-loving democracy has any chance of surviving." Confronted with a victorious Germany, the United States would have to "arm heavily" and thus run the risk that militarism would destroy its free way of life at home.[7]

America would have to pursue such a course in part because of Germany's evident hostility toward the United States. As early as November 1914, Wilson thought the Germans were trying to construct secret military bases on American soil; by August 1915 he was convinced that "the country is honeycombed with German intrigue and infested with German spies." His ambassador in Berlin, meanwhile, sent Wilson a steady stream of reports about Germany's resentment toward the United States, with the kaiser at one point openly threatening to "attend to America when this war is over." Germany's submarine warfare campaign provided still more evidence of this attitude, as it violated international codes that Wilson and other liberal internationalists associated with American security and world peace.[8]

Aggressive, indifferent to international law, and, if it won the war, sure to have its power enhanced, Germany would probably challenge the Monroe Doctrine. With Germany dominant in Europe, Marburg feared, "America . . . will be open to the dangers of actual attack by men of boundless ambition and inhuman callousness." Walter Hines Page, America's minister to Britain, and embassy legal counsel Chandler P. Anderson saw the same threat. On 15 October 1914, Page advised Wilson that if Germany won the war, "we shall see the Monroe Doctrine shot through," and America "shall have to have a great army and a great navy." Just a few weeks later, when Colonel House remarked that Germany disliked the United States and had ambitions in South America, Wilson "replied that the war was perhaps a Godsend to us, for if it had not come we might have been embroiled in war ourselves." In late 1915, the president also listened as House and Robert Lansing speculated about whether German colonization of a South American country would pose a danger to the United States if Germany were a republic rather than a monarchy. House thought German republicanism would make a difference while Lansing did not; in any case, their choice of Germany as a possible aggressor, and Wilson's lack of any objection to the discussion, is revealing. The conversation was not surprising, though, given that by October 1915, according to historian Arthur Link, Wilson and Lansing knew that "German agents had been busy all summer encouraging strife in Mexico in an obvious effort to involve the United States." Still later, in March 1916, Wilson agreed with House that "the Germans and others" were opposed to the administration's proposed system of mutual security guarantees in the Western Hemisphere, the Pan-American Pact. Here too Germany's ambitions in the region seemed not speculative but real.[9]

Indeed, liberal internationalists embraced greater military preparedness for the United States in part because they worried about the vulnerability of Latin America, an area they deemed vital for their nation's safety. "Nobody seriously supposes . . . that the United States needs to fear an invasion of its own territory," Wilson explained to an audience in New York in January 1916. "What America has to fear, if she has anything to fear, are indirect, roundabout, flank movements upon her regnant position in the western hemisphere." Incursions by other powers into Latin America threatened what Wilson viewed as the most vulnerable point in the security of the United States—not its territorial inviolability but its "national political integrity," its "great ideals which gave birth to this government." Americans treasured "unmolested development and the undisturbed government of our own lives upon our own principles of right and liberty," asserted the president. If hostile powers threatened the hemisphere, he suggested, the ability of the United States to pursue its "self-chosen lines of national development" would be threatened. That was why Americans "made common cause with all partisans of liberty on this side of the sea, and have deemed it as important that our neighbors should be free from all outside domination as that we ourselves should be."[10]

In accord with this analysis, liberal internationalists saw the Entente as a shield for the United States. On 25 November 1914, for example, Wilson "expressed pleasure" to Colonel House at news that Italy and Rumania might join the Allies "and hoped those two countries would not delay too long." A few days later, the president "agreed" with the colonel that "it was not good for the United States to have peace brought about until Germany was sufficiently beaten to cause her to consent to a fundamental change in her military policy." In September 1915, the president went even further, telling House that "he had never been sure that we ought not to take part in the conflict and if it seemed evident that Germany and her militaristic ideas were to win, the obligation upon us was greater than ever." House was surprised at this comment, but it was consistent with Wilson's earlier assertions that a German victory would force America "to give up its present ideals and devote all its energies to defence which would mean the end of its present system of Government."[11]

Wilson also indicated agreement with his advisors' statements about America's common security interests with the Entente. In late 1915, House recorded in his diary that he urged Wilson to tell the Allies "that we considered their cause to be our cause, and that we had no intention of permitting a military autocracy [to] dominate the world." House declared that it was "impossible to maintain cordial relations with Germany" and that "unless we did have a complete and satisfactory understanding with the Allies, we would be wholly without friends when the war was ended and our position would be not only perilous, but might become hurtful from an economic viewpoint." Wilson responded "that we should let the Allies know how our minds are running" but not in writing. About two weeks later, House found Wilson determined to stay out of the war and "not quite as belligerent as he was the last time we were together." House again pressed upon the president "the necessity of our having the Allies on our side for the reason we would have to undertake the task alone when Germany was ready to deal with us." Wilson agreed with this point—"He admits this," noted House—but now he was unwilling explicitly "to let the Allies know we are definitely on their side," for reasons explored in subsequent chapters. The president shared House's sense that the Entente's resistance to the Reich enhanced America's safety, in other words, but did not endorse his advisor's recommended policy for acting on it.[12]

Unlike the case with Germany, Wilson did not worry about the Allies using their power directly to challenge America's vital security interests. "I feel," he wrote British foreign minister Sir Edward Grey a few days after the war started, "that we are bound together by common principle and purpose." Britain, the most powerful member of the Entente, "has already extended her empire as far as she wants to—in fact, she has got more than she wants—and she now wishes to be let alone in order that she may bend all her energies to the task of consolidating the ports [parts] of her empire." A victorious Britain would not challenge the Monroe Doctrine, implied Wilson, so an Entente victory in the war would not "hurt greatly the interests of the United States" and would not pose any immediate danger to America's safety.[13]

Other liberal internationalists agreed. Members of the LEP considered Britain and America to be, at the least, de facto allies with a mutual interest in "putting down the law-breaker"—namely Germany. Similarly, the New Republic argued that the United States "could not regard with indifference even a partially successful attempt to crush Great Britain and break down her control of the sea. British sea power has been on the whole a protection rather than a menace to the United States, and we may need that protection even more in the future than we have in the past." The Monroe Doctrine, which the editors saw as a policy to keep the Americas free from "European suspicions, antipathies and international aggression," had always "depended upon British good-will, and no matter what form it assumes in the future, it cannot escape such dependence." America shared a border with British Canada, moreover, as well as "a common language and legal tradition" with Britain, Canada, and Australia. For all of these reasons, the New Republic did not think that the United States could afford to allow the Allies to lose the war.[14]

Fortunately for America's physical safety and its ability to avoid militarism, liberal internationalists expected the Allies to prevail over Germany. Once the Entente stopped Germany's advance on Paris in September 1914, the war became, in Wilson's words, "a great endurance test" likely to favor the Allies because of their superiority in men and resources. At best, all the Germans could hope to do was to stave off inevitable defeat for an indeterminable length of time.[15]

Clearly the Allies evinced a grim determination to defeat their enemies completely. In defiance of accepted international law, they attempted to cut off trade not only with German ports but also with neutral ones near Germany. In public and private statements they also declared their intention to rout Germany's army to the point that the Reich's autocratic system of government collapsed. As British prime minister Herbert Asquith put this aim in late 1914 and again in 1916, Britain would not make peace "until the military domination of Prussia is wholly and finally destroyed." The British would fight to get "a knock out," David Lloyd George emphasized in a press interview in late 1916; they would make war "until the Prussian military despotism is broken beyond repair."[16]

The determination of the Allies to defeat Germany decisively—as opposed to their evident ability to prevent the Reich from winning the war—alarmed most liberal internationalists. In part, it concerned them because it would require "arming and encouraging Russian aggressive ambitions that in the long run would be more dangerous," in the *New Republic*'s view, than allowing Germany to retain some of its power. House and Wilson worried early on in the war that an Allied victory might produce "the domination of Russia on the Continent of Europe." Given that liberal internationalists believed that Russia's government was nearly as militaristic as Germany's, such an outcome might threaten America in a manner not unlike what might happen if the Reich won the war.[17]

Japan's presence in the Allied coalition also appeared to concern some liberal internationalists. Long-simmering tensions between Japan and the United States over America's immigration policies and Japan's ambitions in East Asia accounted for this anxiety, and relations became further strained when Japan forced Germany out of Shantung, China, and made demands threatening Chinese sovereignty in 1915. The Japanese demands on China made Wilson "very uneasy," a feeling that no doubt increased when he received news that Russia and Japan had formed an alliance with each other. French ambassador Jean Jules Jusserand, House told Wilson, also thought Germany might "drift into that alliance" after the war and direct it against the United States. Similarly, Walter Lippmann grouped Japan with Germany and Russia as the "serious troublemakers in the world"; it would be a "nightmare," he thought, if the three ever combined in a coalition against "the western world."[18]

Notwithstanding their anxieties about Japan and Russia, liberal internationalists did not dwell on the possible dangers those two powers might pose to the United States in the aftermath of a decisive Allied victory. They rarely discussed Japan, implying that it was at the outer periphery of their security concerns. As for Russia, Wilson never elaborated on his perception of the threat it posed, but he appeared to change his mind about it by late 1914. In an off-the-record interview with the *New York Times* on 14 December, the president revealed little anxiety about Russian aims in the war. "Russia's ambitions are legitimate," he remarked, "and when she gets the outlets she needs her development will go on and the world will be benefited." A few weeks later, Chandler Anderson informed Wilson that Russia wanted "Constantinople and the Dardenelles" and that Britain would probably go along with these objectives. The president expressed no alarm at this prospect, saying "in regard to Constantinople that he had anticipated that it would either be neutralized or would be taken by Russia." Following this exchange, Wilson did not mention Russia much in his analyses of the war; even after

House warned him of the possibility of a Russian-Japanese alliance against the United States, Wilson did not voice any fear that victory for Russia over Germany in itself would somehow threaten America.[19]

The president and other liberal internationalists harbored fears about a decisive Allied victory for reasons other than those dealing with Russia and Japan. Although the Allies were vague about their exact war aims against the Central Powers, their language about destroying Prussian militarism could be interpreted to mean that they wanted to impose debilitating territorial and economic demands upon the Reich. As Wilson put it, if the Allies inflicted a total military defeat upon Germany, they might be tempted to impose an "unjust peace . . . sure to invite further calamities." The president equated such a peace with terms designed to weaken Germany through "the annexation of her colonies, the allot[t]ing out of the territory of her allies, and an indemnity" to pay for rehabilitating the nations Germany had invaded and for some of the "military expenses" of the Entente. Unjust terms meant those aiming at "the division of spoils" rather than the reconciliation of the belligerents. They meant terms, in Marburg's words, that would "dismember Germany" or "keep her in permanent subordination to the will of the Allies."[20]

Liberal internationalists assumed that even a rump Germany would be a formidable nation, however. If the Entente achieved an overwhelming military triumph and then dictated the sort of settlement outlined earlier, they believed that sooner or later Germany would somehow recover and retaliate, just as France had sought to do after its defeat at the hands of the Germans in 1871. "Such an outrage to [Germany's] pride would never be forgotten," the president predicted; "it would rankle in her breast as did the rape of Alsace-Lorraine to the French." Peace would never last in such a poisoned environment. Eventually, alliance intrigues and arms competitions would resume in earnest, leading inevitably to another catastrophic war.[21]

Liberal internationalists were convinced that the perpetuation of unstable power politics in Europe would threaten American national security. It would do so because, as Edward Filene of the LEP put it, the war "has shaken down about our ears the House of Isolation." If the conflict overseas showed anything, declared Wilson in late 1916, it showed that "there is no more anywhere a division between one arrangement of politics and another." The war "profoundly" affected the United States, in his view. Almost immediately, it had sparked a preparedness movement in America that Wilson considered "nervous and excited" and that included proposals for UMT and sharp increases in the army that he thought might lead to militarism. The war also provoked a major financial panic, damaged and then boomed American trade, and led to pressures from ethnic groups to enact policies, such as an arms embargo, that Wilson believed the belligerents would see "as an unneutral act." In fact, both sides of combatants complained bitterly about the administration's posture toward the war, and both sides blatantly violated U.S. neutral rights as they sought to cut off each other's access to American supplies. Repeatedly, Wilson found himself compelled to choose between sacrificing those rights and, as he saw it, undermining "the honor of the United States," or upholding them at the risk of war. By January 1916, after a series of crises with Britain and Germany, Wilson lamented that "now we are completely surrounded by this tremendous disturbance," and he worried it could "touch us to the quick at any moment."[22]

America would not be able to isolate itself from the dangerous currents of power politics in the future either. Wilson's own preparedness program testified to this fact, as its major component, the naval buildup, would not be completed until the early 1920s. In May 1916, the president was quite specific about what the future might bring, suggesting to the AUAM that all nations, including the United States, would have to arm "indefinitely" in a world ruled by the balance of power. Hamilton Holt of the LEP agreed, arguing that if power politics persisted after the war, "we shall have to arm to the teeth and enter the deadliest race of military madness the world has ever known."[23]

Such a policy would not make America safe. By engaging in an endless arms competition with foreign powers, the New Republic warned, "we should merely be organizing insecurity at a tremendous cost, adopting militarism for the sake of protecting ourselves against it." If another general war broke out, it promised to be even more calamitous than the current "vast, gruesome contest of systematized destruction." Trends in weapons technology appeared to confirm one's worst fears about what another war would look like. Already, Page reported to Wilson in July 1915, many in Britain believed that massive air strikes against cities held out the best hope of ending the war quickly. Wilson found this scheme "incredible," but he conceded it looked "as if Europe had finally determined to commit suicide." A few months later, Wilson read a letter from Edward Grey asserting that "the use of poisonous gas by Germany and the indiscriminate use of Zeppelins make it evident that, after the war, there will be no security in future against the use in war of the most horrible methods that science can devise. The whole world will be busy devising means of extermination and of protection against such." Given how quickly and easily the war rendered America's neutral position "all but intolerable," and given the disturbing developments in the scale and character of modern warfare, it is no wonder that Wilson concluded that "this is the last war of the kind, or of any kind that involves the world, that the United States can keep out of."[24]

For liberal internationalists, then, a decisive Allied victory in the war would ward off the dangers to America posed by a German win, but only at the risk of creating other security problems for America in the not-too-distant future. In time, the power politics generated by a peace dictated by the triumphant Entente would produce arms races and an even more terrible world war. Frightened Americans would react with demands for preparedness, raising the danger of militarism at home. Again the belligerents would vie to control each other's ability to get American supplies, resulting in violations of U.S. neutral rights and war-threatening crises between them and the United States. In such circumstances, militarism or war or both could easily engulf America. This nightmarish scenario was more remote than the dangers posed by a victorious Germany, but it existed as a real possibility in the minds of Wilson and other liberal internationalists—and it made a decisive Allied victory appear almost as menacing to U.S. security as a German win.

In discussing the threats that a world caught in the grip of power politics would pose to the United States, liberal internationalists paid relatively little attention to America's interest in an open door for trade. Leaders of the LEP only occasionally analyzed how postwar tariff walls could hurt America while neither Wilson nor the *New Republic* considered overseas markets vital to American security. Weyl, the *New Republic*'s economic expert, provided the most extensive treatment of this issue in his book *American World Policies,* published in 1917. Detailing America's increasing levels of foreign investment and trade since 1898, Weyl observed that Americans were "beginning to overflow our boundaries." He had little anxiety about this development, however. Manufactured products were at the heart of the world's trade competition, according to Weyl, and America's "fundamental welfare does not absolutely depend upon this exportation." In fact, he noted, "our export of manufactures still forms but a trifling part (perhaps one thirtieth) of our total product." Weyl also suggested that the domestic pressures to export that did exist could easily be alleviated through Progressive reforms to stimulate consumer demand at home. In keeping with his view that they helped to cause arms races and wars, Weyl certainly opposed discriminatory trade barriers. But he, like his colleagues at the *New Republic,* did not consider such barriers in and of themselves to be any serious danger to America's way of life.[25]

Similarly, Wilson, both before and after taking office as president, asserted that "our industries have expanded to such a point that they will burst their jackets if they can not find a free outlet to the markets of the world." Wilson also vigorously pursued policies designed to increase America's exports, including efforts to create a government-supported merchant marine, lower the tariff, promote overseas banking, and allow American companies to cooperate in their export businesses. Not surprisingly, some historians have taken all of this as proof that Wilson perceived a vital American interest in trade: "The expansive needs of American capitalism," according to one scholar, led the president to see the trade barriers that made up part of power politics as the key threat to the United States.[26]

But this interpretation overstates and misinterprets the evidence. First, as David Kennedy argues, Wilson may have promoted American exports because he saw the "parochialism of American businessmen" as potentially undermining the political support he needed to reform international politics. Certainly, Wilson frequently indicated that he did not see exports as economically crucial to the United States. For example, he did not blame the 1913–14 recession on a lack of markets abroad for American goods. Instead, he argued that ten years of Progressive criticism of business had made businessmen "feverish and apprehensive" and thus, he suggested, hesitant to expand and invest. He also pointed out that although "the business depression is world-wide . . . the depression is less felt in the United States than anywhere else," implying that the condition of overseas markets had little impact on U.S. prosperity. This conclusion was consistent with the president's perception, stated in 1916, that exports did not constitute a significant share of America's economy. "If you take the figures of our commerce, domestic and foreign included," the president lectured at a Cincinnati luncheon, "you will find that the foreign commerce, even upon the most modest reckoning of our domestic commerce, does not equal 4 per cent of the total." "Now," Wilson asked, "is 4 per cent creating the 96 per cent?" He did not think so, attributing American prosperity instead to his Progressive reform legislation.[27]

Significantly, Wilson did not mention America's supposedly vital need for export markets on other occasions when it would have made sense for him to do so. In late 1914 and early 1915, when the nation was still in an economic slump, the administration engaged in an all-out campaign in Congress to secure passage of a bill to create a government-owned and -operated merchant marine. In defending the ship purchase bill, Wilson did speak of "the great need for immediate action in this matter," noting increased shipping rates and arguing that the bill would "tend to remove that great impediment to the shipment of our goods." But he did not invoke the specter of a depression if the bill did not pass. He stressed, rather, that Latin Americans badly needed U.S. goods at a time when the war in Europe had interrupted their usual lines of trade. The United States had a "duty and opportunity" to meet this need and seize new markets. In addition, Wilson saw the bill as "a fight between the people on one side and special interests on the other"—it was a battle against reactionary Republicans who supported private shipping interests out to maximize profits. If the bill failed, "we shall have to have a new struggle for liberty in this country," Wilson confided to a friend, "and God knows what will come of it." The political ramifications of a defeat worried the president much more than the economic damage that might result, again revealing that he did not consider an open door for trade to be a vital economic interest for the United States.[28]

Atlanticists likewise occasionally expressed concern that America's well-being depended on its access to foreign markets, and they sometimes voiced fears about an "industrial war" between the United States and Europe after the war ended. But again, like other commentators, they made this argument relatively rarely. While he was president, in fact, Theodore Roosevelt noted that he tried "once or twice" to open new channels of trade "by diplomatic activity" but found, to his surprise, "little public feeling . . . for any such effort." He displayed no anxiety about the public's apathy on the subject, however, and a few years later, in 1910, he told President Taft that America's open door trade policy concerning Manchuria was not worth a war with Japan, as America's interests in the region were "unimportant." As historian Howard K. Beale argues, Roosevelt and Lodge saw America's involvement in international economics not as important in and of itself, that is, as a crucial means to preserve the nation's economic health, but as only one element among many in America's overall "power and prestige."[29]

The security analyses of the Atlanticists therefore focused on other issues. Most frequently, they stressed that America, as Lodge described it, lay "open to the world, rich, tempting, and easy prey to the armed." Under presidents Taft and Wilson, they charged, the United States had allowed its military preparedness to slip to a dangerously weak level. "Every nation should have sufficient military and naval defense to maintain its own peace and security," Lodge told the 1916 NSL convention. "This Nation has not such defense." So long as their recommended defense program remained unenacted, argued Atlanticists, the United States lacked "a sword for defense" adequate to guard the Monroe Doctrine and its own territory from attack. At a minimum, this security perimeter included "Alaska, Hawaii, the Panama Canal and all its approaches, including all the points of South American soil north of the Equator, and . . . our own coasts and the islands of the West Indies." Yet, far from being able to fend off any assaults upon this extensive zone of interests, the United States could not even protect itself against an invasion of its continental heartland.[30]

Atlanticists identified Germany as the nation most likely to pursue aggression against the United States. Roosevelt discussed this idea at length, especially in his private correspondence. As explained earlier, Roosevelt believed that Germany was led by a ruthless, aggressive regime bent on increasing Germany's power at almost any cost. Before, during, and after his presidency, Roosevelt thought that Germany disliked the United States and had ambitions in the Western Hemisphere. Once the war started, Roosevelt had no doubt that if the Reich won it, "within a year or two she would insist upon taking the dominant position in South and Central America and upon treating the United States precisely as she treated Japan when she joined with Russia and France against Japan twenty years ago and took Kiaochow as her share." An arms race between a victorious Germany and the United States would surely then develop, Roosevelt believed, and ultimately end in war.[31]

Other Atlanticists shared Roosevelt's assessment of the potential threat that a triumphant Germany would pose to the United States. "If Germany conquers France, England, or Russia," warned Lodge in September 1914, "she will dominate Europe and will subsequently seek to extend that domination if she can to the rest of the world." The "issue" in the war was "simple" to the senator. "It is whether democratic government, as it exists in England, France and the United States, can survive Prussian militarism." Root, like Roosevelt, was sure that Germany would challenge the Monroe Doctrine—leaving an isolated, frightened America no choice but to heavily arm itself. Speakers at the NSL convention in 1916 expressed similar fears; one predicted that a German victory in the war would mean "the conquest of Canada and the planting of the German Empire, with perhaps a million veteran soldiers, upon our northern frontier." Germany's defeat of the Allies, another speculated, would secure for it "freedom of action in the southern half of the Western Hemisphere," an opportunity it would "inevitably" seize. Whether a victorious Germany directed its aggression north or south of the United States, Atlanticists were in any case certain that it would seek to expand its power in the New World—an outcome they implied would mean war between Germany and the United States.[32]

Germany also threatened the United States because its illegal behavior in Belgium and on the high seas undermined international law. As noted in Chapter 1, Atlanticists believed, as did the liberal internationalists, that the world's various treaties, conventions, and legal norms marginally improved the safety of all nations, at least to a minimal degree over what would otherwise be the case. Germany's violations of international law thus diminished American security. Root explained this idea most forcefully in a major foreign policy speech he delivered in February 1916. Germany invaded Belgium, he argued, "in repudiation of the faith of treaties and the law of nations and of morality and of humanity." The law that Germany violated "was our law and the law of every other civilized country." The United States had helped develop it, had spent money and energy promoting it, and had bound itself to it. "That law was the protection of our peace and security," declared Root. "It was our safeguard against the necessity of maintaining great armaments and wasting our substance in continual readiness for war." In trampling upon that law, Germany therefore not only wronged Belgium but also threatened America's safety.[33]

In their apprehension of Germany, then, Atlanticists differed very little from the advocates of collective security. The two groups diverged in their view of how a decisive Allied win might affect America, however. Although Roosevelt early on urged the Allies not to cripple and dismember Germany, because he believed that the West needed the Reich to balance Russia's power, neither he nor other Atlanticists ever showed any doubts about the desirability of an Allied victory in the war. "I think the Allies will win," Roosevelt confided to Spring Rice in February 1915. "I know they ought to win." Trusting that the British goal of destroying Prussian militarism did not signal an intention to dismember the Reich, Roosevelt never criticized Allied war aims. He wanted and expected the Allies, including Russia, to overwhelm the Central Powers—and he, along with Lodge and Root, saw such an outcome as both a triumph of right over wrong and the only way to start to build a more peaceful, secure world.[34]

To be sure, Atlanticists did not expect the postwar international system to be completely free of conflict, even if the Allies defeated Germany. Balance-of-power politics would persist, which meant that the United States had to maintain military preparedness adequate to defend its security perimeter against "aggressive military powers" from any quarter. "Alliances are very shifty and uncertain," Roosevelt noted in late 1914 in a *New York Times* article, and while Britain was a friend, the United States could not expect any help from it in the event of a war with some other nation. Ultimately, indeed, every nation had to be ready to take care of itself. It was "not wise for any people, certainly for any people as rich as we are," agreed former secretary of war Luke E. Wright, "to depend for our security upon the good will of any foreign power." This point took on added weight for many Atlanticists, because the war would make all the European powers desperate to recover their losses. The pacifist thesis that an exhausted Europe would "never attack" the United States was wrong, Lodge stressed. On the contrary, he shouted to applause at the 1916 NSL convention, "there is no nation on earth so dangerous as a nation fully armed and bankrupt at home." Eager to repair themselves, Root predicted, the Europeans would look to make incursion into "the new world" and to challenge the Monroe Doctrine. Regardless of the outcome of the war, America had to be ready for them.[35]

Atlanticists, then, no less than pacifists and liberal internationalists, directly connected their view of power politics and militarism to their assessment of the war's implications for American national security. Convinced that the balance of power was inherently unstable and that American democracy could never withstand participation in its arms races, coercive diplomacy, and warfare, pacifists recoiled from the idea that the war exposed the United States to serious threats from overseas. Conceding that a threat existed, or would emerge in the war's aftermath, meant admitting that America's relative isolation from the balance of power was over, which could only open the door to defense increases certain to produce militarism at home. Pacifists therefore sought to minimize the dangers that the war might pose to the United States. They did this by narrowly defining "national security" to mean safety from physical invasion of America's territory. Deploying this concept of national security allowed them to focus on the advantages afforded the United States by geography and by the nation's great potential military resources—advantages that made it appear "impossible . . . for Germany or any other country to ever bombard or land a soldier on our coast."[36]

The pacifist position on national security suffered from a serious problem, however. In a variety of ways, their own reaction to the war contradicted their contention that America, for all practical purposes, was somehow immune from outside threats. First, their endorsement of modest upgrades to the nation's existing defense establishment revealed a certain degree of apprehension about the war's possible impact on American security, despite their claim that "we are in less danger from a foreign foe than ever before in the history of our country." Their argument that America would be safe even if Germany won the war, moreover, assumed that the Germans would be exhausted by their victory and that the defeated Allies would not be reduced to mere satellites of the Reich. After all, the pacifists stressed that Europe's rivalries and conflicts were crucial to inhibiting Europe's great powers from challenging U.S. interests in the Western Hemisphere. If those rivalries faded because one power achieved hegemony over the continent, the pacifists implied that the United States might be endangered—especially if the hegemonic nation was imperial Germany, a state many pacifists identified as unusually aggressive and militaristic.[37]

The pacifists' response to the preparedness movement, and to President Wilson's defense program, also belied their faith that America's impregnability ensured its national security. The war, they recognized, provided preparedness enthusiasts with an atmosphere conducive to enacting sharp defense increases: "The present conflagration," as the *Nation* put it in late 1914, "is to be made the excuse for a wild raid on Congress for more soldiers, more sailors, and more ships." Wilson made it clear that the war had much to do with his preparedness scheme, as he noted repeatedly in defending it that "the world is on fire, and there is tinder everywhere." In fact, he told representatives of the AUAM in May 1916 that America had to step up its defenses in part because "all the world is seeing red," and "no standard we have ever had obtains any longer."[38]

The world war, in other words, allowed the preparedness movement to move from the fringes to the center of American politics. For the pacifists, it followed that militarism was already engulfing America and undermining its democracy. Even Wilson's moderate defense program struck Bryan as "revolutionary," as "an abandonment of the historic policy of his party and the traditions of his country." The president, moaned Bryan, was "joy-riding with the jingoes and . . . grieving those to whom democracy is a religion." Villard thought Wilson's preparedness policy might have "far-reaching consequences" for America. "For you are sowing the seeds of militarism," he wrote the president, "raising up a military and naval caste, and the future alone can tell what the future growth will be and what the eventual blossoms." The various proposals to increase armaments that lay before Congress, the AUAM warned Wilson in May 1916, were "the indication of an invading militarism—undemocratic, unsound, un-American, and threatening to the fundamental institutions of the land." Amos Pinchot and Lillian Wald saw particularly striking signs of "the enemy in our midst" in New York laws calling for compulsory military training for boys aged sixteen to nineteen. For Wald, these measures showed how foolish it was to think that America could never succumb to militarism. "It seems to me," she bitterly told Wilson, "that the evidence we have that it can and may succumb is overwhelming."[39]

This conclusion—confirmed in the spring of 1916 when Congress intensified the nation's "militarist infection" by enacting most of Wilson's preparedness program— raised doubts about the soundness of the pacifists' equation of national security with America's safety from invasion. Despite the pacifist insistence that America was and would continue to be safe from direct attack, clearly large numbers of

Americans were frightened by the war. Of course, pacifists saw this fear as "hysteri-cal" and blamed it on the paranoid, power-hungry machinations of the military of-ficers, munitions makers, and upper classes who made up the preparedness move-ment. But that explanation did not alter the fact that the war had allowed the forces of militarist reaction to capture the president and the Congress and, as the AUAM lamented, pump "enough downright militarism into the cherished body politic to poison us for the next ten years." Evidently, then, the United States *was* deeply af-fected by the course of power politics overseas, even though it had not been in-vaded. Far from being the "small world to ourselves" depicted in their rhetoric, the pacifists' own analysis of the domestic political fallout from the war indicated that the well-being of American democracy was directly connected to the balance of power. They refused to confront this uncomfortable reality, preferring instead sim-ply to denounce the preparedness movement's "sinister and even sordid" motives and to hope that somehow the "sanity" of the American people would reassert itself and resist the calls for greater defense.[40]

If the pacifists turned away from the idea that America's democratic integrity was intertwined with the balance of power, liberal internationalists did not. Most of them feared militarism as much as the pacifists and were equally alarmed by the panicked enthusiasm for preparedness that appeared to grip significant seg-ments of the American public. They saw the agitation for preparedness as more than a troubling episode that sooner or later would hopefully fade away, however. To liberal internationalists, the preparedness movement was prime evidence that America's relative detachment from the balance of power was over, and, disturb-ingly, it provided a glimpse of the militaristic path Americans would likely take if power politics persisted after the war.

This perception, along with their conviction that power politics was inherently unstable, profoundly shaped how liberal internationalists analyzed the meaning of the war for American national security. To them, Germany's power, ambition, and hostility toward America all suggested that the United States would face a grave threat from abroad if that country won the war—a threat that would pro-voke defense measures menacing to the nation's domestic freedoms. Conversely, the more likely outcome of a complete Allied victory on the battlefield would open the door to a dictated settlement aimed solely at eviscerating Germany's power. Consistent with their analysis of the instability of power politics, liberal internationalists expected such a peace to enrage and embitter Germany and to lead the Germans to strive to overturn the settlement at the first opportunity. Sooner or later, another round of arms racing would commence, and the fears and preemption incentives sure to accompany it would produce a second world war even more destructive than the first. The United States would be faced with a choice between arming itself in isolation, out of a generalized fear of war or as a hedge against a German victory, or joining in the Allied effort to uphold, with armaments and perhaps war, a peace settlement that never should have been made in the first place. Given their belief in America's vulnerability to militarism, liberal internationalists perceived this as no choice at all—either alternative risked ruining democracy at home.

The crosscurrents of opinion concerning the war and American national security did not work in favor of the Atlanticists. The tendency of liberal internationalists to focus on the dangers to America deriving from an Allied attempt to crush Germany narrowed the gap between them and the pacifists on security matters. Like liberal internationalists, pacifists distrusted all of the belligerents and feared that a victory by either side would perpetuate an inherently unstable system of power politics. If either the Allies or the Central Powers won "so complete a victory as to be able to dictate terms," predicted Bryan, "it will probably mean preparation for another war." Similarly, the platform of the WPP warned against a peace settlement that arbitrarily stripped away the territory or economic rights of any country and denounced the idea of trying to build a peaceful postwar world upon the shaky foundation of a "balance of power." Thus, even if they did not agree with the fears for the safety of America voiced by liberal internationalists, pacifists did share their thesis that decisive victories on the battlefield were not a pathway to peace.[41]

Furthermore, pacifists agreed with prevailing opinion that the Entente would eventually win the war. No one sympathized with "any aggressive military ambitions of the central powers," observed Edward Devine in the *Survey* in late 1916. One need not worry about them, however. "That those aims have already been thwarted, notwithstanding the present position of the actual fighting lines, seems certain." This meant that the main danger to future world peace would derive from an Allied-dictated, vengeful peace, not a German one. On this score, too, pacifists and liberal internationalists could agree.[42]

Atlanticists, meanwhile, failed to concentrate their threat assessment on the dangers a victorious Germany would pose to the United States. Had they done so, they would have underscored national security fears they had in common with liberal internationalists and brought to the surface a key point of difference between the latter group and the pacifists. Instead, Atlanticists spent much of their time discussing vague scenarios of unnamed powers assaulting the Western Hemisphere after the war ended, to recoup losses suffered in the fighting in Europe. This discourse only further bolstered the view, central to the outlook of both liberal internationalists and pacifists, that the existing balance-of-power system was inherently unstable and that a decisive Allied victory would simply add to that instability.[43]

The Atlanticists contributed to their own marginalization in security debates in an additional way. In insisting that America needed to arm heavily to meet any possible threat to the Western Hemisphere, Atlanticists strengthened the position of liberal internationalists against the pacifists. To a large degree, as previously discussed, the latter two groups shared common beliefs about power politics and militarism. What separated the two was their differing assessment of the viability of relatively disarmed isolation as a national security policy. Pacifists saw no reason for that policy to change. Liberal internationalists, in contrast, argued that the policy could no longer provide America with a comfortable level of safety in the modern world. The war, and the response of the American people to the war, confirmed this new reality. Consequently, they asserted, the United States confronted a future of armed isolation, with a high danger of militarism and war, unless international politics somehow fundamentally changed. The more Atlanticists pressed for a steep military buildup to guard America's defense perimeter, the less convincingly pacifists could contest this argument. The preparedness campaign of the Atlanticists, in short, was the best debating point that liberal internationalists had.

3

The Vision of Collective Security, 1914–17

By late August 1914, shortly after the war began, President Wilson was already thinking about how to end power politics by reforming the international system. If only the Europeans had moved toward disarmament and some sort of procedure of frequent international consultations in 1913 or 1914, he suggested to Colonel House, the war might never have started. During the next several weeks, as Wilson focused on how the war's outcome could perpetuate power politics and threaten America's ability to avoid a future of militarism and war, he became convinced that he would have to lead the world toward a new international order. As preparedness agitation arose in Congress and it too began to assess the implications of the war for American security, the editors of the *New Republic* and the leaders of what would become the League to Enforce Peace reached the same conclusion. Somehow America had to end the war in a way that would eclipse power politics "and see peace assume an aspect of permanence." Given the way liberal internationalists analyzed national and international security affairs, only such an outcome to the war would ensure America a future free from the arms races and fears that could militarize its way of life.[1]

As liberal internationalists developed their program between late 1914 and early 1917, pacifists and Atlanticists had difficulty formulating a compelling alternative to it. Pacifists feared that President Wilson's vision of a world order based on collective security might perpetuate the balance of power rather than end it. But they also supported Wilson's conception of the peace settlement as the most likely to lay the groundwork for changing the existing international system. Atlanticists objected to the president's proposed peace terms and questioned the assumptions of collective security theory. But they put forward their own version of international reform too, apparently validating the wisdom of making that goal a strategic priority for America. Thus, despite the serious criticisms that pacifists and Atlanticists raised about the program of Wilson and his supporters, it increasingly dominated America's national security debates as the war wore on.

. . .

This outcome was all the more remarkable given that liberal internationalists themselves failed to articulate a coherent explanation as to how their program would end
power politics. They even appeared unclear and uncertain about the basic premise
of collective security. Usually they claimed that a reformed world order was possible
because, as Wilson asserted, "the world is no longer divided into little circles of interest. . . . The world is linked together in a common life and interest such as humanity never saw before." The unprecedented interdependency of the modern world
meant that political conflicts were difficult to contain. "The politics of the world
used to be local," Wilson explained in an October 1916 address. "But the world has
been drawn together now, so that there is no more anywhere a division between
one arrangement of politics and another." William Howard Taft more bluntly made
the same point: "To-day war in any part of the world may rapidly manifest itself in
another part." Because the world's nations were interdependent, war anywhere affected everyone, or at least had the potential to do so. All nations therefore had a vital stake in deterring or suppressing conflict anywhere it occurred: "If lawbreaking
is permitted at one point," the New Republic warned, "the anarchy infects everyone."
For their own safety, everyone had to uphold order everywhere.[2]

But even as they asserted this theory of collective security, Wilson and his supporters betrayed lack of faith in it. Although they most often described a league
to enforce peace as universal in scope, guarding the world from "every disturbance
of its peace that has its origin in aggression," sometimes they suggested that they
had a more narrowly focused organization in mind. In his first major public speech
calling for the creation of a peace league, for example, Wilson argued that it could
have stopped "this war" from breaking out in 1914, implying that its aim should
be to prevent future great power conflict. Similarly, the leaders of the LEP almost
always spoke of a league as an organization "between great nations," devoted only
to the task of preventing a war between them. The editors of the New Republic occasionally described their vision of a peace league in a like manner. Limiting the
scope of a peace league's authority to conflict between the great powers certainly
made sense given that a great power war would likely affect the whole world. But
it also contradicted the premise of collective security that *any* war, anywhere, was
a threat to everyone.[3]

The murkiness of the theory and proposed scope of collective security was
underscored by another issue. All liberal internationalists agreed that an enforced
cooling-off period during international disputes would be a vital component of
any "concert of power" to preserve peace. "Nobody," Wilson pronounced, could
be allowed to disturb "the peace of the world without submitting his case first
to the opinion of mankind." The time involved in conducting an international
review of a crisis would allow passions to diminish and "misunderstandings" to
be "cleared up," making conciliation more likely between the parties involved. An

enforced investigation procedure under the auspices of a collective security league would also probably reveal how world opinion divided on the issue, raising the possibility that one party might find itself too isolated to attempt a war to achieve its ends. As Wilson explained in May 1916, the current war arrived "suddenly and out of secret counsels, without warning to the world, without discussion, without any of the deliberate movements of counsel with which it would seem natural to approach so stupendous a contest. It is probable that, if it had been foreseen just what would happen, just what alliances would be formed, just what forces arrayed against one another, those who brought the great contest would have been glad to substitute conference for force." In this way, the spotlight of world opinion could help to deter war, by illuminating the collective will of the many to oppose the wrongdoing of the few.[4]

Liberal internationalists were divided over whether the enforcement of a cooling-off period would be enough to preserve peace, however. Wilson and the *New Republic* strongly asserted that more would be necessary. The latter wanted the judgments of the league enforced, equated American participation in a league with a commitment to uphold the peace of Europe, and thought a league should manage the development of colonial areas and assume some sort of legislative power over its member states. Wilson, in his 27 May 1916 address to the League to Enforce Peace, asserted that he expected a league to provide its members with "a virtual guarantee of territorial integrity and political independence." On 22 January 1917 he also stated that a "League for Peace" would have the task of "guaranteeing and preserving" the "treaties and agreements" ending the war. For the president and the *New Republic,* ending power politics required a collective security system with a broad mandate—a mandate well beyond enforcing arbitration and conciliation procedures.[5]

The leaders of the League to Enforce Peace were wary of creating a collective security regime with such sweeping authority. In part, they preferred limiting the league to arbitration and conciliation matters because they saw codifying international law—a major focus of the prewar peace movement—as an important part of building collective security. But they also objected to a league with extensive responsibilities, implying they had doubts that a collective interest in world peace actually existed. A political-territorial guarantee, they argued, amounted to an a priori enforced judgment concerning political and territorial issues between nations, a posture with grave risks in the eyes of the LEP. It would force the peace league to uphold whatever status quo existed at the time of its formation, something the great powers might be unlikely to do if their own specific vital interests were at stake in some future conflict. States would be willing to submit their case in a political or territorial dispute to a hearing, suggested the LEP, but only if they knew in advance that they could reject whatever judgment came out of it and still go to war to protect their interests.[6]

The status of the Monroe Doctrine under a peace league also raised tricky problems for liberal internationalists. Under a league's cooling-off provisions, the United States would presumably have to submit any dispute concerning European encroachment in the Western Hemisphere to a conciliation hearing. Apparently perceiving that many Americans might object to allowing foreign governments to have any say in an issue involving the Monroe Doctrine, Wilson, when he first began formulating his ideas about international reform in late 1914, envisioned one set of security guarantees for the Western Hemisphere and one for Europe. After deciding a year later to support U.S. involvement in a global peace league, Wilson said as little about the Monroe Doctrine and collective security as possible. When he did, he simply asserted that under collective security, "the nations should with one accord adopt the doctrine of President Monroe as the doctrine of the world." One of the LEP's vice presidents, however, William D. Foulke, thought that the United States would react to any threat to the Monroe Doctrine immediately, without submitting the issue to any conciliation process. "We would have to act instantly or not at all," he argued, "and if we acted instantly the entire military power of the League of Peace would be invoked against us." Marburg and Taft replied by noting the help a league could give to the United States in upholding the doctrine, a point emphasized by the New Republic as well. But this argument evaded the more basic question Foulke raised: Would the United States in practice really follow the league's procedures when it came to an issue vital to its interests? Foulke did not think so; he thought that if the United States joined a peace league, it would have to exempt the Monroe Doctrine from the league's authority.[7]

In contrast to the issues surrounding the premises and scope of collective security, Wilson, the LEP, and the New Republic had an easier time agreeing on the mechanism necessary to uphold a league's authority, whatever the extent of that authority turned out to be. Whether it sought to enforce a conciliation procedure or guarantee territorial boundaries, any league would have to wield "a threat of overwhelming force" to coerce nations into following its commands. It would have to have so much "force" at its disposal "that no nation, no probable combination of nations could face or withstand it." Establishing "law and order" in the world—ending anarchy and power politics—required "overwhelmingly preponderant" power to intimidate potential aggressors. "As the evil-doer must be restrained by force in our local communities," reasoned Thomas White of the LEP, "so the evil-doer must be restrained by force in the community of nations."[8]

This level of power could not be attained without the participation of the United States. "No covenant of cooperative peace that does not include the peoples of the New World," declared Wilson, "can suffice to keep the future safe against war." As the Europeans struggled against each other, their economic power declined relative to that of America's, Wilson perceived. "Our resources are untouched," the president bragged in April 1915. "We are more and more becoming, by the force of circumstances, the mediating nation of the world in respect to its finance." By the end of 1916, U.S. naval strength was increasing too, something that could only add to the power America could use to uphold collective security. Had a peace league including the United States existed in 1914, the war probably would not have occurred, Wilson told the LEP on 27 May 1916. "If we ourselves had been afforded some opportunity to apprise the belligerents of the attitude which it would have been our duty to take, of the policies and practices against which we would feel bound to use all our moral and economic strength, and in certain circumstances even our physical strength also, our own contribution to the counsel which might have averted the struggle would have been considered worth weighing and regarding." Most likely, any would-be aggressor, if confronted with a collective force for peace that included the United States, would opt to talk rather than fight.[9]

The *New Republic* and the League to Enforce Peace agreed with Wilson's perception of the importance of America's power to the project of reforming world politics. The Europeans would find themselves economically weakened by the war, noted Taft. "The primacy of the United States among the nations of the world will thus become clearer than it ever was," he predicted. "And this, taken with its real neutrality, must give it a great influence in a council of nations which can and ought to be exerted for the world's benefit." The *New Republic*'s editors, along with Lowell and Taft, also applauded the weight that America's military power could bring to a peace league. Military preparedness, Taft argued in early 1917, put the United States "in a position to contribute our share to any force that we may be called upon to furnish in a joint exercise of power by the world to suppress war." Coupled with the British navy, added the *New Republic*'s editors, America's navy could give a league "unassailable maritime supremacy" and thus, they implied, enough power to deter aggression.[10]

America's moral authority, no less than its economic and military power, would enhance the ability of a collective security organization to uphold peace as well. President Wilson best articulated this argument, which was also voiced by the *New Republic* and the LEP. Wilson deeply believed that the United States had a unique character among nations and a duty "to do mankind service." America's exceptionalism, he argued, lay in the success of its political system of democratic federalism; its embracing of equality of opportunity for its citizens; its diverse population, "drawn from all the nations of the world"; and, finally, its lack of territorial ambition and its detachment from the immediate "causes and questions" involved in the world war. These peculiarities cast the United States in a special role in history: "The mission of America in the world is essentially a mission of peace and good will." To be sure, Wilson acknowledged that U.S. policies in the nineteenth century toward Mexico and Native Americans featured "unpitying force" and differed little from the "aggressions" of other strong states against the weak. But the nation's westward expansion had led Americans to sympathize

"with freedom everywhere" as well, Wilson claimed. Regardless of their assertive-
ness in conquering a continent, Americans, in Wilson's eyes, were "the champions
of humanity and of the rights of men." America had "the distinction of carrying
certain lights for the world that the world has never so distinctly seen before, certain guiding lights of liberty and principle and justice." It was, thought Wilson, an
"ideal destiny" for a nation chosen by "the Providence of God" to be like no other
"in the whole annals of mankind."[11]

To reform the international system, the United States and other nations also
needed to embrace the concept of self-determination and, in Wilson's words, the
right of peoples to enjoy "free access to the open paths of the world's commerce."
As the president explained on 22 January 1917, in a major address to the Senate,
self-determination involved "the principle that governments derive their just powers from the consent of the governed, and that no right anywhere exists to hand
peoples about from sovereignty to sovereignty as if they were property." If this
ideal was ignored in the peace settlement that ended the war, Wilson feared that
"the ferment of spirit of whole populations" would be aroused, threatening the
project of building a world based on collective security. Similarly, "freedom of the
seas," free access to the oceans, and, as Wilson suggested in other speeches, the
"open door" or nondiscrimination in trade would all foster "trust" and "intimacy"
between nations and diminish the jealousies that contributed to war.[12]

Exactly how and where to apply these principles was unclear, however. The
LEP, in fact, largely ignored trade issues in its discussions of world reform and was
openly skeptical of the wisdom of self-determination. "The consent of the population to transfer of territory is a dangerous principle," Theodore Marburg argued,
"because it logically involves the right of secession." Such a right "would be fatal
to strong and just government" and "would ultimately lead to the erection of a
great number of small States." The anarchy and conflict inherent in the existing
international system would be exacerbated, Marburg predicted; the proliferation
of small states "would be against the current of history, which has brought wider
and wider areas of peace through union and the spread of dominion." Perhaps
because of Marburg's objections to it, the principle of self-determination was left
out of the LEP's program for world reform. "The question of whether a colony or
a portion of a nation should be entitled to its independence," Thomas Raeburn
White emphasized in a speech explaining the LEP platform in 1916, "is not a matter for judicial settlement, nor would it come within the comprehension of this
scheme, or of any international institution."[13]

Wilson may have sensed problems with the idea of self-determination too, as
he avoided spelling out how it would apply in Europe. He did indicate he agreed
with the LEP that it would not be employed to change the colonial empires held
by the belligerents outside of the continent, however. While it is true, as Arthur

Link argues, that Wilson "utterly detested the exploitative imperialist system that had reached its zenith by 1913," the president nevertheless did not think all peoples were ready for statehood. A native Virginian, Wilson believed in a "hierarchy of race," in the words of historian Lloyd Ambrosius, with "white Americans of European ancestry" on top. Just as he never questioned the South's system of racial segregation and disenfranchisement of African Americans, Wilson never called for an end to Europe's colonial empires, even as he criticized their exploitative character. In 1900, he also defended American annexation of the Philippines on the grounds that the Filipinos were unfit for self-government and, in 1916, backed off a bill definitely promising independence to the islands after it encountered opposition in Congress. Nonwhite peoples—and, as Ambrosius points out, peoples in south Central Europe that Wilson considered politically immature—needed a long period of uplift and guidance from the "advanced" powers before they might evolve into sovereign nations. Wilson's interventionist policies in Latin America reflected this outlook, as did his failure to oppose colonialism in his 22 January address to the Senate. His endorsement of self-determination and equality between states applied to peoples he considered economically and politically developed, such as the Poles and Belgians—people whose claim to sovereignty was either compromised or controlled by German expansion during the war.[14]

In supporting the president's blueprint for world reform, the *New Republic* also implicitly endorsed the principle of self-determination. But, like the president, the editors restricted its application for the foreseeable future to only the "more advanced economic nations." In their analyses of how to reform international politics, the editors never called for an end to Europe's colonial empires. Indeed, they considered "Africa, large parts of Asia, and the middle Americas" to consist of "weaker peoples and of disorderly states," ill prepared to function as fully independent sovereignties. The denial of self-determination to such "politically archaic" people was not in itself a threat to peace, according to Croly, Walter Lippmann, and Walter Weyl. Colonialism instead caused difficulties when it involved monopolistic economic concessions that bred jealousies and nationalistic competition among the great powers. A collective security regime could end this problem by mandating an open door for trade and investment in such "backward" areas and, ideally, by actually taking over their administration. Such a policy, the editors argued, would remove a key source of conflict in international affairs, while also building the sense of "world citizenship" and common purpose vital for the credibility of collective threats to enforce peace.[15]

If liberal internationalists varied in their view of the roles self-determination and an open door for trade should play in international reform, they were somewhat more united in their assessment of the need to democratize foreign policymaking around the world. On the one hand, their faith that a cooling-off period would defuse international disputes rested in part on the idea that the masses usually recoiled from war. On the other hand, as Chapter 1 discussed, liberal internationalists also had doubts about the peaceful character of ordinary people, however. Consequently, when they described how a peace league would work, they said relatively little about specific measures to enhance democratic control of foreign policy, although Wilson and the *New Republic* did support government control of the manufacture and sale of war munitions. Overall, except for the special case of Germany, liberal internationalists focused more on changing the anarchical structure of the international system than on promoting peace through democratic reforms within states.[16]

Once some sort of mechanism for collective security was in place, its advocates fully expected plans for arms limitation to go forward. For one thing, America's presence in a collective security organization would allay fears of how it might use its new military and economic strength, fears that could lead other states to balance America's power with armaments and alliances. A peace league's enforced conciliation procedure would also take away the advantage of surprise attack and so would tend "to lessen the need of preparation for immediate war." Hence, arms reduction, in Taft's words, was "a corollary to our League's proposals."[17]

Neither arms limitation nor any other aspect of collective security could become a reality, however, until the war ended—and how the war ended, liberal internationalists perceived, would heavily affect whether or not a peace league got off the ground at all. Yet despite the importance of this issue for their goal of international reform, Wilson, the *New Republic,* and the League to Enforce Peace had difficulty defining the peace terms most conducive to collective security. They all agreed that, at a minimum, the peace settlement should be based on the status quo antebellum, which meant that peace would be based on the Central Powers' evacuating territory in western and eastern Europe that they had occupied at an enormous cost in lives and treasure since 1914. The extent of the additional terms that liberal internationalists favored was unclear, however. Wilson and the *New Republic* wanted the Germans to commit themselves to disarmament talks and the principle of collective security, but the LEP was silent on those issues. Perhaps encouraged by the Entente's embracement of arms limitation and the general idea of a peace league, the president privately mused that France should have Alsace-Lorraine and Russia take Constantinople. Publicly, on 22 January 1917, he called for the creation of an independent Poland and implied the territorial settlement should be based on the principle of "government by the consent of the governed." The *New Republic,* meanwhile, usually opposed any Allied territorial ambitions beyond a return to the prewar status quo. Yet the editors applauded Wilson's speech of 22 January, which appeared to call for changing the 1914 map of Europe. Finally, the leaders of the LEP sympathized with Allied war aims implying significant territorial gains for France, Italy, and Russia. For a new world order to be built, Germany had to relinquish all of the gains it had made in the war—but what else it would have to give up was ambiguous.[18]

Rolling back Germany's power was crucial for ending power politics for several reasons. Most basically, reversing Germany's gains in the war and getting it to commit to arms limitation would end the threat to American security posed by a German victory. As explained in Chapter 2, Wilson and other liberal internationalists believed a victorious Germany might challenge U.S. dominance in the Western Hemisphere, a possibility that could cause America to militarize its society in preparation for meeting the attack. According to Wilson's own analysis of international affairs, the defeated Allies, meanwhile, would likely be absorbed in plotting and arming to wreak revenge upon the Germans, just as France had done after its defeat in 1871. In such an atmosphere of intense insecurity, power politics could hardly be moderated, let alone banished. Instead it, and the domestic militarism that accompanied it, would flourish.[19]

The retraction of Germany's power would have the opposite effect. It would leave the Allies and the United States feeling more secure. "The ideal of the typical military nation has been Germany," Wilson observed in May 1916. "She must, within years, be so armed and powerful that she could take care of her interests as against all the rest of the world." Limiting the Reich's power would help to allay American and British fear of having to live with an overbearing state that both considered a threat. It would also create, in the *New Republic*'s words, "a chastened Germany . . . with whom liberal Europe could begin to negotiate." After all, by agreeing to terms based at least on the status quo antebellum, the Germans would be demonstrating a readiness to embrace the ideals of a new international system rooted in collective security. They would be repudiating power politics in the most concrete way possible—by giving up the gains they had made in the war. With international security thus enhanced, the task of constructing a new world order could much more easily go forward.[20]

In theory, the peace program sketched out by liberal internationalists contributed to Germany's security as well. If the president's vague statement of 22 January 1917 served as the basis for a peace settlement—a statement that staked out a position on terms somewhere between the status quo antebellum and those asserted by the Allies—the Germans, in Wilsonian parlance, would not be "crushed." The Reich would have to pull its army back within its borders, and it might, at worst, lose Alsace-Lorraine and perhaps some territory in the east to Poland. But it would be doing all of this voluntarily; its army would remain intact pending a mutual agreement on arms limitation; it would probably still exert dominance over the Balkans, or what the *New Republic* called "Middle Europe"; and it could still claim a right to its overseas empire. It would, most importantly, gain entry into a collective security regime that offered safety without arms races for all of its members. The Allies, at the same time, would be restrained from pursuing their more extreme economic and territorial aims, which would rob Germany of its legitimate security and thus prime the world for another round of arms competitions and war.[21]

The security calculations underlying Wilson's peace program were closely related to another issue: the democratization of the Reich. Given their view that military autocracies in general and Germany in particular were aggressive, war-prone states, all liberal internationalists doubted that the Reich would be a suitable member of a peace league. "Germany as motivated today," Marburg alerted A. Lawrence Lowell in October 1916, "would not be a desirable partner in a league of peace because it could not be trusted"; the "professions" of the kaiser's autocratic regime, he declared, were "valueless." Echoing this analysis, Secretary of State Robert Lansing wrote a receptive Wilson that because only democracies could be trusted to keep their word, only democracies should be allowed into a league. Otherwise the league would be "constantly menaced by factions resulting from inharmonious conceptions of duty and right and from radically different motives by the governments bound to carry out its objects." Such a league would not work to uphold peace—it would be "inherently defective," argued Lansing. Wilson agreed. "This is so interesting a paper," he replied to Lansing, "and it is so *true*." Collective threats to punish aggressors would most probably be effective if the members of the collective had confidence and faith in each other's character and intentions, a condition unlikely to be obtained if autocracies were part of the group.[22]

Liberal internationalists therefore hoped that the war would produce democratic reforms inside the Reich. Most of the leaders of the LEP believed that only the complete overthrow of Germany's armies would accomplish this goal; this was one reason, indeed, why they tended to sympathize with Allied war aims more than the *New Republic* or Wilson did. "Germany must be beaten to her knees," Marburg insisted in September 1914, " . . . to free the German masses themselves from the grip of bureaucracy and ruthless military class and to arrest militarism itself." Negotiations with Germany were pointless, maintained Marburg. "There is no reasoning with mad dogs and now only force will answer," he declared. So long as Germany possessed foreign territory, moreover, it would hold "trump cards" in peace talks. No talks could occur and no league could be created, then, until Germany's armies and the military class that led them were destroyed and "a new Germany" created. For Marburg, this was "a fundamental consideration, dominating every other."[23]

Marburg's insistence on making the democratization of the Reich a precondition for international reform went too far for Wilson, the *New Republic,* and even most of his colleagues at the LEP. They thought that the democratic masses could fall prey to warlike fears and ambitions, it will be recalled, and, as revealed in their peace terms, they wanted *any* German government, regardless of its political makeup, to give up its gains in the war. Moreover, a peace league without Germany would not be a true collective security organization at all, Harry Garfield pointed out to Marburg—it would be "nothing better than an alliance." Such a league would simply mask power politics, not change it; to bind up the fate of international reform with the democratization of Germany might therefore easily doom the whole project.[24]

The more prudent course was to support peace terms requiring Germany to retreat to its borders while quietly hoping—but not openly demanding—that this outcome would trigger the democratization of the German government. This was certainly Wilson's position, as he told Lansing that it would be "unwise" to insist that only democracies be allowed in a peace league and publicly declared that a league should be a "universal association of the nations." Although Taft and other LEP officials no doubt sympathized with Marburg's desire for a decisive Allied military victory in the war, presumably because they thought it would increase chances of a German democratic revolution, the LEP formally endorsed "a League of all the great nations," with no stated conditions laid upon German member-ship. With the league in place, perhaps democracy would then flourish, the *New Republic* explained. "A little stability will encourage a little more democracy," in Lippmann's words, "and democracy in its turn by reducing aggression will add to stability." Whatever happened inside the Reich, though, once its wartime gains in power had been reversed and it was committed to the principles of international reform, the creation of a world free from power politics could go forward.[25]

In addition to their security and political implications, the settlement terms preferred by liberal internationalists also laid down, in Wilson's view, the "essential basis" of a lasting peace—"the psychological basis." In giving up their quest for a "crushing" victory, the Allied peoples and governments, no less than the defeated-but-not-crushed Germans, would emerge from the war remembering, most of all, "the uselessness of the utter sacrifices made." Already, Wilson reflected in a private memorandum on the war in late 1916, the "modern processes of battle" had cre-ated a yearning for peace. "The mechanical game of slaughter of today has not the same fascination as the zest of intimate combat of former days," he observed; "and trench warfare and poisonous gases are elements which detract alike from the excitement and the tolerance of modern conflict." Ending such suffering "with the objects of each group of belligerents still unaccomplished" would surely discredit war itself, Wilson reasoned, and eliminate it "as a means of attaining national am-bition." Purged of their desires for conquest and selfish gain, deterred by the fear of suffering from ever engaging in war again, the peoples of Europe would be free to build a "new peace structure on the solidest foundation it has ever possessed."[26]

There was another psychological element to the collective security peace pro-gram as well. Although they differed in the degree to which they wanted to change the 1914 distribution of power to Germany's detriment, liberal internationalists all wanted to avoid what Marburg called "vindictive" peace terms aimed at allowing the Allies to dismember or dominate the Reich. Dictated, unequal peace condi-tions, Wilson in particular emphasized, "would be accepted in humiliation, under duress, at an intolerable sacrifice, and would leave a sting, a resentment, a bitter memory upon which terms of peace would rest, not permanently, but only as upon quicksand." If the war was "decided by slow attrition and ultimate exhaustion," moreover, "resentments must be kindled that can never cool and despairs engendered from which there can be no recovery." A harsh peace, on the heels of a brutal war, would make reconciliation between the belligerents impossible. All "hopes of peace and of the willing concert of free peoples will be rendered vain and idle." Only by ending the war with "a peace without victory"—a peace that limited but did not destroy Germany's power—could this outcome be avoided.[27]

Pacifists found much to support in this argument, but they did not agree with it entirely. Most importantly, unlike Wilson, the *New Republic,* and the League to Enforce Peace, pacifists did not link American national security to the goal of radically changing the international system. As Chapter 2 discussed, in their view, the war did not signal an end to America's relative isolation from balance-of-power politics. Blessed by its remote geographic location, great potential military power, and the unending rivalries of the other great powers, America had nothing to fear from either group of belligerents, regardless of what happened in the conflict raging overseas. The pacifists' analysis of militarism, moreover, indicated that if the United States did become involved in the war, for whatever reason, its democratic way of life at home would be in grave danger. The chief security interest for the United States with regard to Europe's struggle, then, was simply to stay out of it: "This war," as Bryan put it, "is not our war."[28]

Yet pacifists, no less than liberal internationalists, saw the war as an opportunity to transform the international system. While they did not link this goal to the preservation of American national security, they did see attaining it as a moral imperative. The "universal sense of humanity," they claimed, was outraged as never before by the specter of global conflict and the suffering it caused. Echoing the proponents of collective security, pacifists thought that this common sentiment made it possible for a league of nations to strike at arms races, alliances, and war by binding its members to conciliation procedures and disarmament.[29]

In contrast to Wilson, the LEP, and the *New Republic,* however, most pacifists were reluctant to invest any kind of peace league with the authority to coerce nations into following its rules, especially if that coercion involved military force. Such an organization, Stoughton Cooley of the *Public* worried, "would partake too much of the nature of the 'balance of power' that has filled Europe with jealousy and suspicion." William Jennings Bryan agreed, declaring that he opposed debasing his own cooling-off conciliation treaties, negotiated when he was secretary of state, with a "gattling-gun attachment." The *Nation* leaned toward this position as well, as the editors respected the power of "moral forces" to advance peace and felt that the LEP would have a stronger claim to public support if it put less stress on using force to back up its program. Although Paul Kellogg, David Starr Jordan, and Edward Devine all endorsed using both "moral force" and "physical force" to maintain a peaceful world, the other social activists clustered in and around the WPP and the AUAM did not. Significantly, the WPP at first called for an "international police force" to safeguard peace but then, in January 1916, proposed that "economic pressure and non-intercourse" be employed instead. Given its goal of "arousing the nations to respect the sacredness of human life," this shift made perfect sense.[30]

Pacifists especially questioned the wisdom of linking preparedness to international reform. "'Fighting the devil with fire' has long been a popular amusement," observed Bryan, "but the effort has never been successful." The logic of "advocating an armament that will lead to disarmament" escaped the *Public* as well; whatever interest other powers had in arms limitation would dissipate the moment they saw "the wealthiest nation in the world entering upon a great military program." When Wilson explained his position to AUAM leaders in May 1916, arguing that America had to contribute "her element of force" to make a league effective, Lillian Wald was not convinced. "Would that not, Mr. President, logically lead to a limitless expansion of our contribution?" she asked. Wondered another participant in the meeting, how did Wilson's plans to enforce peace "differ from the ideal which has prevailed in Europe all along in the matter of the piling up of arms?" The president's assurances that his policy was "radically different" failed to sway his audience; the AUAM continued, throughout the rest of 1916, to predict that Wilson's defense program would "seriously menace our relations with every other great world power" and provoke a disastrous postwar arms race.[31]

More explicitly than other pacifists, Bryan also thought that U.S. participation in a coercive peace league would lead to needless conflict with other nations and undermine American democracy. It would "involve us in the quarrels of Europe— quarrels which have their origin in centuries of antagonism, in race hatreds and in commercial rivalries." It meant the "surrender" of the Monroe Doctrine and thus potential clashes with the Europeans in the Western Hemisphere. And it would leave Congress with little choice but to follow the league's decisions and "furnish our quota of men and money for the enforcement of decrees which may not represent the wishes of our people." In Bryan's analysis, collective security was not a way to end power politics and militarism, but a path leading the United States directly into both.[32]

Clearly uncomfortable with the schemes for coercion lying at the heart of the collective security vision for world reform, pacifists preferred to link the goal of a lasting peace to the spread of democracy around the globe. Nearly all pacifist leaders and organizations called for governments to own their nations' munitions plants; "democratic control of foreign policies," which meant, for most of them, no secret treaties, "legislative ratification of future treaties," and some version of a

popular referendum on war declarations; and greater political and social democracy in all states. "Democracy not only in Europe but in America is the first step toward peace," declared Frederic Howe, "and no permanent peace is possible so long
as the privileged classes rule." Bryan also promoted his cooling-off principle as a
vital element in any peace plan, arguing that a yearlong investigation into international disputes would allow peoples' natural reason to assert itself and demand
peace. By mid-1916, the WPP and the AUAM began trumpeting another version
of this idea: the use of informal citizens' commissions to facilitate the resolution
of international disputes without violence. Actually implemented by the AUAM at
Crystal Eastman's suggestion during a crisis between America and Mexico in June,
the joint commission proposal seemed like a perfect way to organize democratic
opinion for peace without the need for any formal league of nations.[33]

Howe and most other pacifists put almost equal weight on the importance of
anti-imperialism to the cause of international reform. While most of them fell
short of calling for an end to the world's colonial empires, leading pacifists did
insist that a lasting peace depended in part on reforming imperialism's monopolistic and predatory characteristics. To ensure that colonialism was no longer, in
Kellogg's words, "a scourge to backward races and a spur toward war among their
exploiters," pacifists called for neutralizing the world's seas, straits, and canals;
lowering trade barriers and equalizing access to colonial markets; and stripping
foreign investors of the protection they enjoyed from their home governments.
Even if these measures would not destroy imperialism immediately, they would,
thought the pacifists, defuse and humanize its operation while undercutting the
influence of antidemocratic groups inside the colonizing states.[34]

If pacifists and liberal internationalists significantly diverged in their assessment
of the proper elements of a new international order, they agreed much more on
how to end the war in a way conducive to international reform. Pacifists enthusiastically cheered Wilson's "peace without victory" address to the Senate on 22 January
1917, and they embraced some of the reasoning behind its proposed peace terms.
To be certain, they did not share the president's fears of how a victorious Germany
might use its power against the United States; they saw no reason to worry about
American security even if Germany kept its conquests and defeated the Entente.
But they did endorse the idea that a smashing victory by either side of belligerents
would make for trouble in the future. If such an outcome occurred, contended
Bryan, "the peace that would follow would be built upon fear, and history proves
that permanent peace can not be built upon such a foundation." A war ending with
a decisive victory by one side, added other pacifists, would mean a war of "plun-
der, revenge, and conquest" sure to embitter the losers and sow the seeds of future
conflict. International reform would be furthered, instead, by ending the war on
the basis of a return to something like the status quo antebellum, a "draw" which

left "such a feeling of disgust that it will be comparatively easy to bring about the desires of our League to Enforce Peace."[35]

Pacifists also hoped, like Wilson, that a peace without victory would produce democratic reform in Germany. This desire was consistent with their more basic assertion that democratic advances in all nations were necessary to purge the world of militarism, arms races, and war. Pacifists perceived that democratic reforms might not happen immediately, however, and, if a peace league was established, that it would be "dangerous" to exclude Germany from it, regardless of whether or not it had democratized. Leaving Germany out of an international peace organization, predicted the *Nation,* would simply divide the world into "two great leagues menacing one another by their armaments." Hopefully, implied the pacifists, the psychological impact of a peace without victory would be enough to propel both democratic and international reform; if the former lagged behind the latter, even in Germany, international reform should still go forward.[36]

The debate over the meaning of a peace without victory and of a reformed international system was not limited to pacifists and liberal internationalists. Atlanticists joined in as well, offering a contradictory vision of a new world order. In several ways, they, like the pacifists, made penetrating criticisms of the ideas about international reform advanced by Wilson, the *New Republic,* and the League to Enforce Peace. Theodore Roosevelt especially took aim at the LEP's requirement that nations submit their disputes to arbitration or conciliation before going to war. As he read this provision, it meant that if a nation suffered an attack upon its vital interests or honor, it had to wait to defend itself until the cooling-off period had ended. If it failed to wait, if it made war instantly upon the attacker instead, "then the League to Enforce Peace would itself go to war, not against the wrongdoer . . . , but against the nation which declined to submit even for a moment to [the] crime!" Even Bryan's cooling-off treaties had not included such a "silly" and "base" provision, Roosevelt noted. In practice, he argued, no nation would delay in responding to an assault upon its vital interests. That being the case, liberal internationalists were evidently urging America to make promises it would not keep. Such a course, to Roosevelt, was both "thoroughly immoral" and destructive to the diplomatic credibility America needed to preserve its security.[37]

Atlanticists made a more basic indictment of the collective security proposals of Wilson and the LEP in early 1917. The most detailed and direct attack came from Lodge, in a major speech delivered to the Senate on 1 February 1917. The league under discussion by Wilson and his supporters, Lodge argued, implied an international police organization with the power to order armed forces around the globe "to maintain the peace of the world." Lodge doubted that nations would comply with such orders, because doing so might not be in their interest. Certainly he doubted that the United States would comply. "Washington declared that we had a set of interests separate from those of Europe and that European political questions did not concern us," Lodge reminded his fellow senators, and, he added, "I have the greatest possible reverence for the precepts of Washington." If a league sought to uphold Wilson's principle of "freedom of the seas" and the right of nations to have access to the ocean, moreover, Americans would find themselves involved "in some very difficult questions wholly outside our proper sphere of influence." The United States had its own specific national interests to protect, argued Lodge—it did not have an overarching stake in world peace. To pretend that it did would lead to promises the United States would not and should not keep.[38]

Despite their harsh assessment of key elements of the collective security peace program, Atlanticists nevertheless appeared to endorse aspects of it as well. In late 1914 and early 1915, Roosevelt even outlined a detailed plan for a "world league for the peace of righteousness." Under his proposal, "the efficient civilized nations," which he listed as "Germany, France, England, Italy, Russia, the United States, Japan, Brazil, the Argentine, Chile, Uruguay, Switzerland, Holland, Sweden, Norway, Denmark, and Belgium," would solemnly agree "as to their respective rights which shall not be questioned." These rights would include such matters as a state's "territorial integrity, honor and vital interest," however a state chose to define them. Once a "status quo at some given period" was agreed upon, the rights of each "contracting" power would be "mutually guaranteed." Any signatory violating another's rights would face the military power of its victim, who would have the right to fight back against the aggressor without waiting for a cooling-off investigation to take place, plus the combined military strength of the other contracting powers, who would be required to hasten to the victim's aid. Minor disputes outside of the contracting nations' rights would be referred to a league-appointed arbitral court for judgment, with the decrees enforced by the military power of the league. A short list of secondary powers would also be allowed into the organization, but if they attacked each other the first line of contracting powers could choose not to get involved. In essence, then, Roosevelt's plan focused on deterring the great powers from encroaching upon each other's self-proclaimed vital spheres of interest. If conflict occurred within one of those spheres, even if it occurred between two independent states, Roosevelt's peace league would not take any action.[39]

Roosevelt's defense of this scheme invoked much of the same reasoning that liberal internationalists used to promote their own versions of a league. Like Wilson, Roosevelt sharply contrasted his "World League" with traditional alliances. Based on "self-interest," the latter "must continually shift," while, in the former, "the test would be conduct and not merely selfish interest, and so there would be no shifting of policy." Roosevelt also argued that his peace plan could lead to "a limitation of armaments that would be real and effective" and to "the admission of the peoples everywhere to a fuller share in the control of foreign policy."

Most importantly, Roosevelt's peace plan, like Wilson's, assumed that America and the world's other leading nations had an equally vital stake in preventing a great power war from breaking out.[40]

Of the three key Atlanticist leaders, Elihu Root, who had been a prominent supporter of expanding international legal institutions prior to the war, probably had the deepest interest in collective security ideas. The growth of international transportation, communication, and commerce "are creating an international community of knowledge and interest, of thought and feeling," he declared in mid-1914. "Gradually, everything that happens in the world is coming to be of interest everywhere in the world." The war, of course, involving "almost the whole military power of the world," underscored this new reality. In December 1915, Root therefore urged that private and public efforts be stepped up to strengthen international law "by the process of codification," so that it covered far more aspects of international relations than was currently the case. He also proposed that breaches in international law no longer be treated "as if they concerned nobody except the particular nation upon which the injury was inflicted and the nation inflicting it." To make the law of nations more "binding" and respected, "violations of the law of such a character as to threaten the peace and order of the community of nations must be deemed to be a violation of the right of every civilized nation to have the law maintained and a legal injury to every nation." Every nation had "the right to exist, . . . the right to independence," as far as Root was concerned. "The repudiation of these principles . . . anywhere within the confines of civilization," he insisted, "is dangerous to the peace and safety of the whole community of nations."[41]

From 1915 to 1916, Henry Cabot Lodge also endorsed the general concept of a league to enforce peace. He praised a collection of Roosevelt's articles on the war, which included Roosevelt's sketch of a peace league backed by armed power. "Nothing can be truer," he told Roosevelt, "than your main theme of the folly, if not the wickedness of making treaties which have no force and no intent of enforcement behind them." Appalled by the war and its "unchained physical force multiplied beyond computation by all the inventions and discoveries of an unresting science," Lodge, in June 1915, announced that peace could only be maintained by the united force of the world's great nations. He reiterated this point in a speech to the League to Enforce Peace in May 1916, speaking from the same platform as Wilson. Voluntary arbitration, he declared, had reached its limit. "I think the next step is that which this League proposes and that is to put force behind international peace." Lodge stopped short of actually endorsing the LEP's program, but his support for the idea of collective security was clear: some way had to be found to put "the united forces of the nations . . . behind the cause of peace and law."[42]

As Chapter 6 discusses in more detail, both Roosevelt and Lodge muted their support for a league as the proposal became increasingly bound up with Wilson's diplomatic and military policies. Yet even when Lodge raised serious questions about collective security theory in his speech of 1 February 1917, he compromised his attack in an important way. Given Wilson's assertion that peace had to be founded on the "equality of nations" and "equality of rights," Lodge assumed a league that would operate according to the rule of the majority, which meant that smaller nations could conceivably "precipitate the greater nations into war." The incredibility of this scenario—of small nations ordering the great powers into battle—preoccupied Lodge in his speech, and he related it closely to his point that, in practice, nations would act only to preserve specific national interests rather than a theoretical collective interest in world peace. Yet neither Wilson nor the LEP had said anything about the details of a league's voting procedure. In denouncing the prospect of small powers' ordering the United States into war, Lodge was attacking a collective security organization no one had proposed. His more compelling point—that nations might not have an equally overriding stake in global peace—was thus somewhat obscured in his argument.[43]

If Atlanticists more than faintly echoed the calls of liberal internationalists for structural reform of the international system, they lent even greater support to the idea that democratizing Germany was central to building a lasting peace. To be certain, they displayed some of the same doubts as Wilson's supporters about the validity of this notion. The growth of democracy in Europe as a result of the war, mused Roosevelt in late 1914, "would render it probably a little more unlikely that there would be a repetition of such disastrous warfare." But the spread of democracy would not prevent the "possibility" of more armed conflict. Early on in the war, when he was still advocating a peace league, Roosevelt also included Germany in his list of "contracting powers" without any reservation or condition.[44]

More strongly and consistently, however, Atlanticists implied that they wanted and expected Germany's autocracy to be destroyed by the war. A peace that left in place "militarism and autocracy," Roosevelt declared in late 1914, would be a "worthless truce." Lodge suggested soon after the war started that he shared Britain's definition of it as a "battle of freedom and democracy against militarism and autocracy," and he never questioned the wisdom of Britain's stated intention to crush the latter. Neither did Roosevelt or Root. Anything less than a total victory by the Entente, any "premature and disastrous end to the war," Roosevelt emphasized, "would mean that it would all have to be fought over again in a few years, and perhaps under far more disadvantageous conditions." Regardless of what happened concerning a peace league, Atlanticists saw the defeat of the Reich, its democratization, and the imposition of Allied peace terms upon it all as central to minimizing the chances of another world war.[45]

Overall, the debate over peace terms and international reform tended to marginalize Atlanticists, just as the discourse over militarism, power politics, and American national security did. It did so despite serious shortcomings in the national security strategy put forward by President Wilson, the *New Republic*, and the League to Enforce Peace. Liberal internationalists argued that ending international anarchy and power politics would best ensure America's future safety. They insisted that this was a feasible goal because the war revealed the existence of an interdependent world—a world in which war and the destructive effects of battle could so easily spread from one part of the globe to another so that all nations had a vital stake in world peace. But at the same time, they refused to commit themselves clearly to a policy of having a league suppress any war, anywhere; they were divided over whether or not a peace league should uphold the territorial integrity and political independence of all nations; and at least some of them doubted that the United States would submit a threat to the Monroe Doctrine to any league-mandated conciliation process. Liberal internationalists themselves, in short, appeared to harbor grave doubts about the actual extent of the interdependency between nations—yet it was the central premise of collective security theory.

The president and his supporters also failed to define the peace terms necessary to create a doorway to international reform. They all insisted that Germany could not be allowed to gain anything from the war, as that would threaten American and Allied security and cause those nations to focus on competing for power against the triumphant Germans, an outcome ruinous for a peace league. They also agreed that a settlement too biased in favor of the Allies would similarly frighten, embitter, and alienate Germany, causing it to plot to renew the war so as to gain revenge on its foes and recapture its own security at the expense of others. Liberal internationalists could not decide, however, when peace terms designed to frustrate Germany's ambitions degenerated into a "complete crushing" of the Reich. Wilson usually favored some changes in the status quo antebellum, but he also warned against taking territory from Germany and its allies. The *New Republic* opposed any changes in the status quo antebellum, but the editors also applauded Wilson's 22 January 1917 address to the Senate, which explicitly demanded an independent Poland. The leaders of the League to Enforce Peace supported Britain's call for significant Allied gains at the expense of the Central Powers but also urged the British not to be "vindictive" toward their enemies. Somewhere, a line existed between the legitimate containment of Germany's power and illegitimate power politics sure to destroy any chance to reform the international system—but where it was no one could say.[46]

Similar vagueness surrounded the peace terms most likely to trigger democratic reform in Germany, a hoped-for but not necessary component of the liberal internationalist program for a lasting peace. "What terms of peace have you in mind that would suffice to teach Germany that aggression does not pay," George Santayana asked the *New Republic*, "while not inflicting any wound, such as the loss of properly German territory, which would rankle and call for revenge?" Croly and his fellow editors thought they had an answer to this question, but it was a strained one. Terms going beyond the status quo antebellum weakened Germany too much, they argued, and "would tend to keep alive in the German people those real and reasonable apprehensions of peril from Russia upon which the ruling class in Germany rely for their hold upon the nation." At the same time, the editors wanted Germany's wartime gains reversed and observed that this setback would leave the German people "in a morass of debt, frustration, and anguish." The Germans would not feel insecure and vengeful toward the Entente as a result of this outcome, claimed the editors, but would instead blame their own autocratic government, overthrow it, and embrace the peace terms responsible for their own suffering. Why this would be the case was left obscure; the journal's assertion seemed to be based on a leap of faith more than anything else.[47]

The inability of liberal internationalists to articulate the peace terms necessary for international reform reflected a profound contradiction at the heart of their program, namely that it aimed both to end power politics and to contain the power of the belligerents, especially Germany's. These two objectives ran directly counter to one another. Logically, if a universal interest in peace existed, based on the notion that modern warfare had become so destructive that it threatened all nations, then the distribution of power in the world at the end of the war was irrelevant to international reform. In collective security theory, the enemy was "war," not any specific state. Yet Wilson and his supporters demanded that international reform begin with the retraction of Germany's power and with the assurance, more vaguely, that the Allies would restrain their own ambitions against the Central Powers. In effect, liberal internationalists rejected the security aims of other states as irrational, counterproductive objectives bound up with the discredited system of power politics while, at the same time, they pursued strategic aims of their own. The more they focused on their strategic goals, the more they obviously contradicted their own theory of international reform, and the more they risked alienating the Europeans—and in particular Germany—from the whole project of ending power politics. Unwilling to take that risk because they assumed a perpetuation of the existing international system would be a disaster for America and the world, they struggled to find peace terms that would somehow both arrange a balance of power in America's favor and be consistent with ending power politics—an impossible task.

Liberal internationalists sincerely believed that the paradoxical project of using power politics to end power politics could work, regardless of its logical inconsistency. Their faith in American exceptionalism especially gave them confidence that the contradictions in their program could be resolved. If America was truly different from other powers, if it uniquely embodied universal values of liberty, democracy, and justice, then it was more plausible that other nations would go along with the peace terms America declared were necessary to build collective security—even if those terms meant sacrificing their own strategic aims. Whatever difficulties a peace league faced in ironing out its scope and procedures, moreover, would surely be overcome with the leadership of the United States. The principles to underpin a new world order, after all, were American principles. If problems developed in interpreting them, the United States could solve them, and the world's other powers would presumably defer to its leadership.[48]

Although pacifists and Atlanticists made cogent criticisms of the vision of international reform put forward by Wilson and his supporters, they failed to offer a clear-cut alternative national security strategy of their own. Atlanticists, as discussed earlier, sensed that all nations probably did not have an equally vital stake in world peace, or even peace between the great powers. When the time actually arrived for a nation to intervene in disputes not immediately relevant to its own national interest, it likely would not do so. If it did—if it acted as if it had a stake in upholding peace everywhere—it would find itself wasting its power in armed conflicts with which it really had no concern. Yet simultaneously, Atlanticists offered their own plans for a peace league, praised the expansion of arbitration and international law, and suggested that those measures could pave the way for disarmament. Similarly, they cautioned that the spread of democracy in Europe would have only a marginal impact on prospects for peace but also applauded the Entente's claim that overturning Germany's autocracy would diminish chances of another war. If the collective security program was fundamentally contradictory, the Atlanticist approach to preserving America's future safety was inconsistent, to say the least.

Lodge's best biographer, William C. Widenor, attributes the Atlanticists' awkward posture on collective security to their concern with domestic politics. Lodge and Roosevelt initially supported the league idea, Widenor argues, chiefly because they saw it as a way to entice a predominantly indifferent public into supporting preparedness and an Allied victory in the war. When they realized that Americans associated a collective security league with Wilson's brand of preparedness rather than their own, and with mediation of the war, they dropped the idea and denounced it.[49]

This interpretation makes good sense, but it does not by itself adequately explain why Atlanticists failed to present a more coherent alternative to the collective security program. They failed to do so because, in significant ways, Atlanticists shared the perspective of Wilson and his supporters on national security affairs. As noted earlier, Atlanticists took the threat of militarism to America seriously, and in the decades before the war, they had heralded the slow development of international law and morality as a force for peace. Once the fighting started in 1914, they openly expressed doubts about the efficacy of power politics as a way to avoid war. They therefore became more interested than ever in international peacekeeping institutions and, more specifically, in the concept of collective security. Even Lodge confessed that when he first began to consider a league to enforce peace in 1915, "it presented great attractions to me." It appealed to Atlanticists because it offered a way to reassert the need for civilized norms to moderate power politics, a goal that had acquired unprecedented urgency with the outbreak of the war. It attracted them too because it relied on threats of force to deter aggression, something in accord with the Atlanticist conviction that moral exhortations by themselves were worthless for maintaining peace. Like liberal internationalists, Atlanticists also believed that the democratization of Germany would contribute to a lasting peace because it would eliminate a regime that had proved itself an amoral aggressor. They did not, then, support aspects of the liberal internationalist program merely as a political tactic to attain other objectives. They saw some possibility for protecting America in the collective security strategy as well. Consequently, they ended up suggesting that a decisive victory for the Allies could be the basis for some kind of international reform—a stance not unlike that of the League to Enforce Peace.[50]

Similarly, although pacifists perceived that a coercive peace league could lead to endless preparedness, war, and a decline in Congress's war powers, they supported much of President Wilson's peace program anyway. Echoing collective security theory, most pacifists stressed that the war affected all of humanity and that future wars therefore needed to be prevented. Even if, as they also argued, American national security did not depend on international reform, they still believed that the immorality of modern warfare and its widespread economic dislocation were reasons enough for the United States to join with other nations to promote peace. Likewise, pacifists embraced Wilson's proposed peace terms not because of their implications for American security vis-à-vis Germany, but because they promised, as Wilson asserted, to promote self-determination, break down imperialistic trade barriers, and lead to disarmament. Far from questioning the plausibility of defeating Germany while reconciling it to the project for international reform, pacifists enthusiastically endorsed that policy.

Thus, regardless of its dubious assumptions and muddled logic, the approach to reforming the international system put forward by President Wilson and others held a dominant position in American national security debates by the time Wilson summed it up on 22 January 1917. In one way or another, Wilson's goal of ending power politics forever appeared to be shared by all, even though little agreement existed concerning how to achieve it. Indeed, the key issues involved with international reform—the questions of how to contain Germany without embittering its population and how to organize a league of independent nation-states to deter war—were unresolved. President Wilson and his supporters tried to address them, but profound ambiguities and contradictions marred their analysis—problems that showed up too in the policies Wilson pursued to convince the belligerents to end the war and to build a reformed world.

President Woodrow
Wilson, c. 1916. Library
of Congress, Prints and
Photographs Division
[reproduction number LC-
USZ62-107577].

Woodrow Wilson and William Jennings Bryan, 25 January 1913. Library of Congress,
Prints and Photographs Division [reproduction number LC-USZ62–68294].

Right: Crystal Eastman and Amos Pinchot, c. 1914. Library of Congress, Prints and Photographs Division [reproduction number LC-DIG-ggbain-21959].

Far right: Jane Addams, 1914. Library of Congress, Prints and Photographs Division [reproduction number LC-USZ62-10598].

Below left: Hamilton Holt, c. 1915. Library of Congress, Prints and Photographs Division [reproduction number LC-DIG-ggbain-27968].

Below right: William Howard Taft, c. 1915. Library of Congress, Prints and Photographs Division [reproduction number LC-USZ62-11453].

Theodore Roosevelt, c. 1908. Library of Congress, Prints and Photographs Division [reproduction number LC-USZ62–93318].

Elihu Root, c. 1914. Library of Congress, Prints and Photographs Division [reproduction number LC-USZ62–37254].

Henry Cabot Lodge, c. 1916. Library
of Congress, Prints and Photographs
Division [reproduction number LC-
USZ62–36185].

The American Commission to Negotiate Peace, Paris, 18 December 1918: from left to
right, Col. Edward M. House, Robert Lansing, Woodrow Wilson, Henry White, and Gen.
Tasker Howard Bliss. Library of Congress, Prints and Photographs Division [reproduc-
tion number LC-USZ62–80161].

Extent of Central Powers' expansion, 1918.

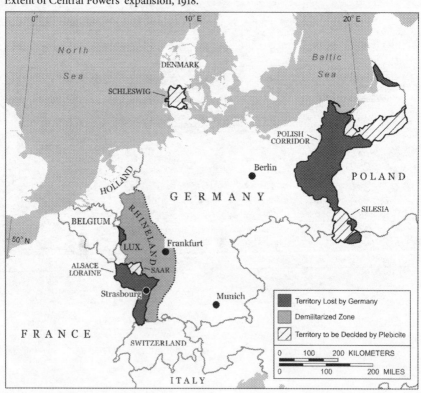

Germany and the Versailles treaty.

Territory held by the Central Powers, end of 1915.

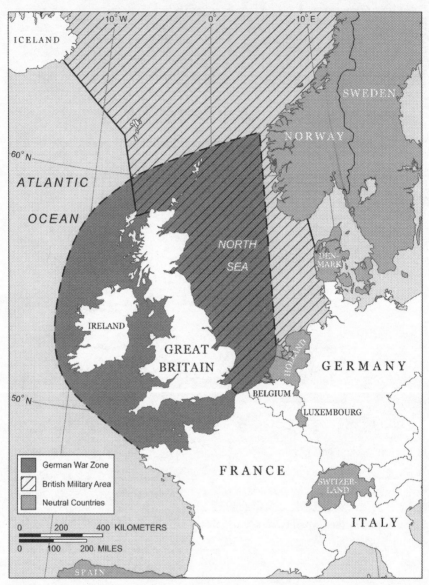

The war in the North Atlantic.

4

Pursuing a Wilsonian Peace, 1914–15

The central policy question facing liberal internationalists between August 1914 and February 1917 was straightforward: How could the United States persuade the European powers to embrace peace terms associated with international reform? President Wilson's approach to this issue is examined in this chapter and the next; the views of other liberal internationalists and of the pacifists and Atlanticists are analyzed in Chapter 6.

By late September 1914, Wilson had arrived at certain basic conclusions about the war that gave him a foundation for a diplomatic strategy toward the belligerents. He had decided that a German victory would threaten America's ability to avoid a future of militarism; that the Allies had blunted Germany's western offensive and so were likely, in the long run, to win the war; that a decisive Allied military victory might lead to a continuation of power politics threatening to America's security; and, finally, that the Allies seemed to be interested in building a new world order based on disarmament. These perceptions suggested to Wilson, in 1914–15, that his best chance of attaining peace terms conducive to international reform was in a policy of limited, informal cooperation with the Allied war effort. In so doing, he could help ensure that Germany did not win the war, a necessary precondition for world reform. Frustrated in their bid for victory, the Germans might also recognize the wisdom of embracing Wilson's peace program, if for no other reason than to avoid a crushing defeat at the hands of the Allies. Even if Germany did not immediately reach this conclusion, a policy of helping the Allies could gain Wilson influence with them—influence he could use to persuade them to abandon their quest for a total victory in the war. At the same time, by not overtly and formally aligning the United States with the Entente, Wilson hoped to retain Germany's trust in him as a mediator dedicated to a fair peace, maintain public backing for his diplomacy, and diminish the chances that the Allies would be able to destroy the Reich.

. . .

The thrust of Wilson's approach to the belligerents began to emerge almost immediately after the war started. On the one hand, he proclaimed America's official neutrality in the conflict, noting his desire "to play a part of impartial mediation and speak the counsels of peace and accommodation, not as a partisan, but as a friend." On the other, he began to implement policies favorable to the Allies. This stance could first be seen during the "ship purchase" controversy of 1914–15. Eager to reduce the nation's dependence on foreign-owned merchants, Wilson, in mid-August 1914, proposed that Congress create a government-owned corporation to buy merchant ships, including ones owned by Germany, that sat idle in American ports and to use them in trade with Latin America "and elsewhere." Britain immediately expressed alarm about this plan, as it could provide the Germans with money and prevent the capture of some of their merchants by the British navy. If the United States insisted on buying the ships, British foreign secretary Sir Edward Grey demanded that they not be used in trade with the Reich or with any neutral ports "near Germany." Even though Robert Lansing noted that such conditions violated U.S. neutral rights, Wilson informally went along with them anyway. He assured Grey that the ships would not be used on any German trade routes. Any ship transfers to the United States, then, could not "be . . . regarded as an effort to relieve the present economic pressure on Germany or to re[-]create anything that Great Britain had a right to destroy." The shipping bill ultimately died in Congress, killed by conservatives opposed to government involvement in the merchant marine business and to any policy that might lead to trouble with Britain. But Wilson's position on the bill was nevertheless significant. It revealed a willingness to defer to the British on issues that they indicated were important to their war effort, even if acquiescing to their demands might deviate from the rules of neutrality.[1]

President Wilson's 1914–15 policies toward Britain's maritime system and mediation of the war revealed the same thing in a far more unambiguous way. At the outset of the conflict, Britain immediately moved to use its naval superiority to cut off Germany's trade with the outside world. Its first formal order in council outlining its system for isolating Germany was issued on 20 August 1914. The British declared their intention to seize all "absolute contraband" (goods such as munitions and war production materiel clearly intended for the armed forces of a belligerent) and "conditional contraband" (commodities that might be used by armed forces, such as clothing) bound for Germany or for neutral ports near Germany, on the assumption that goods going to neutrals might find their way into the Reich. The British made it clear that they themselves, in British prize courts, would seize the contraband if they merely suspected it was bound, directly or indirectly, for Germany.[2]

The most significant aspect of this system was the way it dealt with foodstuffs. Under existing international law, as recognized by Britain, food was conditional contraband and could therefore only be seized if the blockading nation could prove it was destined for the enemy's armed forces—a difficult standard to meet.

An unratified new code of maritime warfare, the 1909 Declaration of London, eased this criterion, allowing food to be intercepted if it could be shown that it was consigned to the enemy government. Unfortunately, from Britain's point of view, however, the declaration also explicitly stated that conditional contraband, such as food, could only be seized if it was bound directly for a belligerent port; it could not be taken if it was going to a neutral port, even if the blockading nation thought that it could prove that it would end up in the hands of the enemy. The declaration, moreover, included a long list of other items, including cotton, that were never to be considered contraband at all. For this reason, when the war broke out, the Wilson administration urged all the belligerents to follow the declaration's rules, because doing so would benefit America's trade.[3]

Determined to prevent Germany from receiving food supplies from any other state, the British decided to assert the rules from both existing law and the Declaration of London that most supported what they wanted to do. Thus Britain announced that the German government had taken over all of the Reich's food supply, that food was therefore conditional contraband, and that shipments of food would be seized even if they were bound for neutral ports near Germany rather than for Germany itself. In effect, the British followed neither existing international law nor the Declaration of London but blurred the two sets of rules together to give themselves legal cover for starving Germany into defeat.[4]

Britain did not fool the State Department's legal experts, however. As the British added more items to their contraband lists and intercepted ships bound for Europe's neutral ports, State Department counselor Robert Lansing; James Brown Scott, chair of the interdepartmental Joint Neutrality Board; and Harvard law professor Eugene Wambaugh grew increasingly disturbed. By mid-September 1914 they were convinced that Britain was grossly violating international law. To Wambaugh, in fact, Britain's policy was "so injurious to neutral commerce and so inconsistent with general International Law as to bring it wholly within the legal rights of a neutral . . . to protect its commerce by war." On 27 September 1914, Lansing sent Wilson a draft protest to Britain, urging the president to approve it. "I cannot but feel," Lansing argued, "that the action of the British Government calls for unqualified refusal of this Government to acquiesce in its legality and that our objections should be clearly and firmly stated." Failure to do so, the draft note asserted, might be regarded "as evidence of unfriendliness" toward Britain's enemies; at the least, it would place America "in a position where its neutrality and impartiality are doubtful or open to question." The British system, Lansing added in his cover letter, seemed like "the obnoxious Orders in Council of the Napoleonic Wars"—orders that had contributed to the War of 1812 between Britain and the United States—and would "cause severe criticism in the press."[5]

Wilson took Lansing's warning seriously. He reread the analysis of the War of 1812 that he wrote in his 1902 textbook, *History of the American People,* and found, he told House, that "the circumstances of the War of 1812 and now run parallel." James Madison, he argued, had been forced into war by "popular feeling" against Britain's maritime system. The same thing could happen now, as Britain again mobilized its sea power to combat a would-be European hegemon.[6]

The State Department's draft protest note against the British system reached Wilson just as his first serious effort to mediate an end to the war reached its conclusion. On 18 September 1914, as the French drove the German Army back from its threatening advance upon Paris, Colonel House told Wilson that Germany's ambassador to the United States, Count Johann Heinrich von Bernstorff, was willing to open informal talks with his counterpart in Washington, Sir Cecil Arthur Spring Rice. Britain, House thought, "would probably be content now with an agreement for general disarmament and an indemnity for Belgium," and Germany, he believed, "would be glad to get such terms." It quickly became clear, though, that Britain had no interest in pursuing any talks with Bernstorff. Germany hoped to destroy Britain, Grey told the administration on 19 September. British leaders did not trust Berlin, believed that any peace now would just be "an uneasy respite during which preparations for renewing the struggle would go on," and were determined to "fight and starve the Germans out if it takes years to do it." If Wilson pressed ahead with mediation, former ambassador James Bryce warned, Britain would not accept it, and prospects for a successful intervention by the president later might be "prejudiced."[7]

To confront Britain now over its maritime system while pressuring it to explore talks with Germany, then, would most likely alienate British leaders. Undoubtedly, the British would see both actions as constituting a pro-German policy, and both would therefore threaten any chance Wilson had to influence the British to end the war on his terms. Consequently, Wilson decided to abandon his tentative mediation efforts in deference to Britain's wishes. Informed, on 28 September, that Bernstorff still wanted "to discuss peace measures" and that he hoped House would go to London to prod the British government into talks, Wilson demurred: "This would not be advisable at the moment," he told House.[8]

With this decision Wilson chose to align his peace moves with the progress of the Allied military campaign against Germany, just as the Allies desired. To be certain, Wilson and House agreed that mediation could occur "if the war became a draw." But what they meant, more precisely, was that mediation would have its best chance of success once Germany's military situation deteriorated. Germany's "purpose had already largely failed," House told Wilson on 28 September. If the Reich was beaten back some more, hopefully the Allies would see that their foe need not be "entirely crushed" in order for them to get a "permanent" peace based on "disarmament." The Germans, for their part, would probably welcome talks even more than they did now, because, again in House's words, "they would know the end was not far off." Rather than risk alienating the British with demands for mediation now, it was wiser, as Spring Rice told House on 8 October, to wait until London gave Wilson a "hint" to act.[9]

On 27 and 28 September, Wilson also decided to curry favor with Britain by sidetracking the State Department's official protest of London's maritime system. Rather than issue the protest, he informally floated proposals to the British designed to allow their maritime system to proceed without aggravating proneutrality and pro-German elements among the American people. One way to do this, the administration argued, was for Britain to accept the Declaration of London, which would appeal to American public opinion, but then to interpret its provisions in a way to justify the existing blockade against Germany. After Grey rejected this scheme, Wilson withdrew the suggestion and directed the American embassy in London to protest British seizures of American exports on a case-by-case basis, under existing international law. He hoped that the British found this course "satisfactory," he confided to Spring Rice in October. Of course, there was no reason why they should not—Wilson had for all practical purposes decided not to confront them with a choice between a crisis with the United States or a loosening of their blockade.[10]

The president continued this policy into November and December 1914. "England is fighting our fight," he commented to his secretary, Joseph Tumulty, "and you may well understand that I shall not, in the present state of the world's affairs, place obstacles in her way." Wilson failed to protest Britain's mining of international waters in the North Sea and allowed Ambassador Walter Hines Page, who Wilson knew had "intense feeling . . . for the English case," to handle the case-by-case protests on the blockade. On 9 November, House also sent Spring Rice a "message from the President" telling him not to worry about American-British relations. "Some serious protests will have to be made as to action supposed to be injurious to American interests," Spring Rice reported to Grey, "but general sentiment inside & outside the administration was sympathetic and was gradually realising the true nature of the struggle and that it affected this country most nearly." Wilson personally told the ambassador a few days later that "ninety per cent of the American people are very strongly in favor of the Allies." German-American agitation in favor of the Reich was having "an extremely exasperating effect upon American public opinion," however, and Wilson complained that it had hurt the administration in recent congressional elections. "For this reason," as Spring Rice quoted Wilson in his cable home, "the United States Government will no doubt have to make rather a strong ex-parte statement as to their action in the matter of contraband." The president's message was clear: whatever protests or statements the administration made about Britain's maritime system were for domestic political purposes only; they were not meant to confront or threaten London about its illegal behavior.[11]

Not surprisingly, the British ignored the half-hearted protests filed by Page in London in early November. They also began seizing neutral ships carrying food to neutral ports near Germany without even bothering to try to show that the goods were destined for the Reich. By early December the blockade was tighter—and more at variance with international law—than ever.[12]

With anger at the British rising in Congress and American exporters complaining to the State Department, the administration finally felt compelled to act in mid-December 1914. State Department solicitor Cone Johnson, Lansing, and Secretary of State Bryan composed a formal protest to be delivered to London and sent it to Wilson for his approval on 17 December. It noted Britain's seizures of American ships; declared that the seizures justified American "resistance"; characterized British policies as "novel," "arbitrary and inconsistent," and destructive of "well recognized principles of international law"; and called the situation "critical." After extensive revisions demanded by Wilson, the protest went off to Page in London on 26 December 1914.[13]

The revisions that the president and his advisors made to the note seriously weakened it, as did other signals sent to Britain around the same time. About two weeks before the revised note was finished, Lansing, alerting Spring Rice that a note might be coming, told the ambassador that Wilson wanted good relations with Britain in order to mediate an end to the war; only pressure from Congress might force the president to denounce the blockade. When Wilson received the first draft of the note on 18 December, he angrily rejected it for poor English and for using language sure to give the British offense. He told House to forewarn Spring Rice that a protest was near and that Britain should release detained American ships. When Grey defended Britain's procedures, Wilson did not complain further. Instead, he thanked Spring Rice for Grey's message, adding, "I hope and believe that all these matters, handled in this frank and reasonable way, will be worked out without serious or lasting embarrassment." Protest or not, the United States was not about to threaten its relations with Britain by seriously challenging the British maritime campaign.[14]

This policy was further underscored by the character of the final version of the note of 26 December. Gone was the reference to possible American "resistance" to the British interdiction of American ships. At times the note barely sounded like a protest against the blockade at all, as it asked for "information" as to how the British implemented their policy and referred to ship detentions that appeared to be illegal "so far as we are informed." It even undercut its strongest section, which stated that British policy was "not justified by the rules of international law," by adding the clause "or required under the principle of self-preservation." This implied that if Britain claimed it had a vital security interest in violating the laws of war, it could do so. Finally, the note concluded not with any threats but with the hope that Britain would, in the future, "conform more closely" to international maritime rules. With language like this, even Spring Rice found the note "very fair, just and courteous."[15]

Wilson watered down the 26 December protest to Britain for the same reasons he had gone along with the British order in council in the first place: while he wished to avoid an open alignment with the British, he also needed to stay on friendly terms with them to gain their support for his mediation, and he wanted them to defeat Germany's ambitions in France. This rationale surfaced quite clearly in a long conversation Wilson had on 9 January 1915 with Chandler Anderson, a State Department official who had just returned from London. Repeating an argument he had outlined for the president on 21 October 1914, Anderson recommended that the administration "acquiesce" in Britain's maritime system because the British would not back off their policy "even at the risk of a quarrel with us." Britain was "fighting for national existence," declared Anderson, and it could not endanger its military position by allowing holes to develop in its blockade. Moreover, by confronting Britain over its maritime system, the United States "would lose not merely its extraordinary opportunity for usefulness as a peacemaker when that time comes, but also the opportunity of working in close friendship and harmony with Great Britain in the reorganization of world influences which will follow this war." According to Anderson, the president "apparently agreed to all of this, and said that . . . he felt that the policy he had laid down was exactly in accordance with the views I had expressed."[16]

Certainly mediation was again on Wilson's mind that December, as he reconfirmed his policy of acquiescing in Britain's blockade. On 15 December, House received a letter from the German undersecretary of state for foreign affairs, Arthur Zimmermann, indicating Germany's willingness to discuss peace if the Allies made some "overtures" in that direction. The next day, after learning of the letter, Wilson directed House to talk to Bernstorff about it and then, perhaps, go to Europe "to initiate peace conversations." The basis for the talks would be an "indemnity for Belgium and a cessation of militarism," that is, disarmament. Wilson and House also began planning a collective security regime for the Western Hemisphere to "serve as a model for the European Nations when peace is at last brought about."[17]

After Bernstorff informally affirmed Germany's possible readiness to negotiate on the basis House suggested ("evacuation and indemnity of Belgium and drastic disarmament which might ensure permanent peace"), the colonel and President Wilson had a series of contacts with the British government about the matter in late December and early January. To their disappointment, Grey, through both Spring Rice and Chandler Anderson, "emphatically" argued that "the time had not yet come for peace overtures or even the discussion of possible terms of peace." As Spring Rice explained to House, he "could not understand why Germany would consent to peace parleys now when they seemingly were so successful, and he did not believe the German military party or the German people as a whole would permit such conversations being brought to satisfactory conclusions." In any case, with Germany "in possession of a large part of Belgium and a portion of France, . . . it would be to her advantage and to the disadvantage of the Allies to begin parleys now." All of this seemed perfectly obvious to British leaders, which meant that Germany's peace overtures were not sincere. The Reich was merely trying to make Britain appear responsible for a continuation of the war and to divide Britain from the United States. Peace talks, then, could not even be contemplated until the military advantage shifted to the Allies; the Allies would only talk from a position of strength.[18]

Despite Britain's evident opposition to peace talks, Wilson decided, on 12 January 1915, to send House to Europe to feel out the belligerents face-to-face. "It was time," as House put it, "to deal directly with the principals." This decision reflected the same evaluation of the state of the war Wilson and House had discussed back in the fall. Because its initial offensive had not forced France to surrender, and because its subsequent attacks in the west had not achieved a breakthrough either, Germany, the Americans believed, was probably going to lose the war. As House told Spring Rice on 23 December, the "proper attitude" for the Allies "to assume was one of absolute confidence in the ultimate defeat of Germany." German leaders, the colonel again confidently declared, "knew that the war was already a failure," and they did not want to risk fighting on, "provided they could get out of it whole now." Their peace overtures might therefore reflect not their desire to take advantage of a position of military superiority but their desperation to get the best terms possible before the Allies decisively defeated the German army. That was why they were apparently willing to talk peace on the basis of evacuating Belgium and France—and it was why Wilson and House saw a chance to end the war in a way conducive to international reform.[19]

On 30 January 1915, House sailed for Europe aboard the Lusitania, fated to be torpedoed later that year. The futility of his peace mission, and the conclusions House drew from its failure, became apparent soon after he reached his destination. In London, the British reiterated the views they had conveyed to the administration before House left Washington. The Allies, in their opinion, had "not achieved sufficient military success to insure acceptance of their demand for permanent peace," and they were "determined not to enter into any peace negotiations unless permanence is insured." Thus they had no interest in House's peace mission.[20]

By 15 February, a few weeks before he went to Berlin, House realized that Germany was also unlikely to be receptive to peace talks. The Reich, he thought, was "now almost wholly controlled by the militarists," and, he emphasized in a letter to Wilson, "as long as the military forces of Germany are successful as now, the militarists will not permit any suggestion of peace." In fact, no one in London believed that Germany was ready for a "permanent settlement and evacuation and indemnity to Belgium." By 18 February this suspicion appeared confirmed, House reported, as he passed on to Wilson letters from America's ambassador in Berlin, James Watson Gerard, and from Zimmermann, saying Germany would pay "no indemnity to Belgium or anyone else." Any remaining doubts concerning Germany's position disappeared in early March, when Zimmermann observed that

House's peace terms took "as a basis a more or less defeated Germany or one nearly at the end of her resources." Because, as Zimmermann put it, "this is not the case," Germany would not evacuate France and Belgium, let alone pay any indemnities to its foes.[21]

For House, Germany's attitude confirmed the wisdom of deferring to British views and staying in "close and sympathetic touch" with Grey, "the one sane, big figure" in London. The colonel summed up his views on 29 March, in a cable to Wilson sent shortly after House visited Berlin. Pressuring the British to accept "freedom of the seas as one of the peace conditions" might induce Germany to give up Belgium, House speculated, but he presented no firm promises from German leaders regarding this proposal. Instead, House emphasized, "the blockade is pinching Germany" and "tends to increase peace sentiment." The sound course was to take up the free seas idea with Grey while doing "nothing to upset our amicable relations with the Allies consistent with our position of neutrality"—a position that effectively meant abandoning any peace efforts until Allied military fortunes improved.[22]

Wilson showed little if any disagreement with House's stance. When the colonel had at first hesitated to visit Berlin because the Allies opposed the trip, Wilson did urge him not to go "too far" in allowing them to dictate his plans. But the president failed actually to order House to go to Germany in defiance of the British; he left it to House to judge how to deal with the situation. More significantly, Wilson responded positively to House's message about free seas in warfare, the impact of the blockade upon Germany, and the need to remain on good terms with the Allies. "Your full cable of Monday received and read with deep satisfaction and approval," Wilson telegraphed House. "I warmly admire the way in which you are conducting your conferences at each stage. You are laying indispensable groundwork and sending me just the information I need." Far from questioning House's faith in the wisdom of coordinating mediation with improvement in the military position of the Allies, Wilson appeared to agree with it.[23]

It is conceivable, of course, that Wilson was happy that talks were taking place at all and that his encouraging words for House should not be interpreted as an endorsement of the colonel's deference toward the British. Wilson never expressed *any* disagreement with House's messages, however. As he reflected about House's peace mission on 27 April 1915, moreover, the president explicitly agreed with the argument that Germany's success in the war undermined prospects for peace. Writing to Secretary of State Bryan, Wilson noted that he was "keeping in as close touch as possible with what the men in authority at Berlin, Paris, and London have in mind" regarding terms for ending the war. He discovered, he wrote, that "there are no terms of peace spoken of (at any rate in Germany) which are not so selfish and impossible that the other side are ready to resist them to their last man and dollar. Reasonableness has not yet been burned into them, and what they are thinking of is, not the peace and prosperity of Europe, but their own aggrandizement, an impossible modern basis . . . for peace." Germany, in short, needed to suffer military reverses before peace talks on Wilson's terms would have any chance of success.[24]

Wilson's policy of de facto cooperation with the Allies had unintended consequences threatening to his peace program, however. Ironically, Wilson's stance toward the war actually annoyed British leaders, who found the administration's policy confusing and weak. On the one hand, Wilson told them that he shared their fear of Germany. "Everything that I love most in the world is at stake," he confided to Ambassador Spring Rice. If Germany won, America would "be forced to take such measures of defence here as would be fatal to our form of Government and American ideals." As evident in Wilson's approach to peace terms and mediation, he also clearly signaled the British his agreement with their minimum war aim of forcing Germany to withdraw from France and Belgium. On the other hand, the administration pursued policies, such as the purchase of idle German merchant ships and the request that Britain endorse the Declaration of London, that could interfere with Britain's effort to strangle Germany's economy—an effort Grey described as absolutely crucial to Britain's chances for success in the war.[25]

The first signs of British exasperation with the administration appeared in mid-October 1914, as they resisted the administration's Declaration of London scheme. "Do you mean that we should accept it [the Declaration]," Grey asked Page, "and then issue a proclamation to get around it?" Page noted the foreign minister's "irritation" at a plan Page himself felt "could not be made to appear wholly frank and friendly." From Grey's point of view, the administration asked Britain to put its credibility at risk, as well as conceivably the effectiveness of the blockade, so that Wilson could more easily deal with political opponents at home critical of his policies toward Britain's maritime system. It seemed like a lot to ask, to say the least, when Britain, in Spring Rice's words, was in a "life and death struggle" with the Germans.[26]

When the administration shifted course to a policy of weakly protesting the existing British order in council, Britain's opinion of it dropped still further. As noted earlier, Wilson and his advisors themselves apologetically explained the protests as necessary to "satisfy Congress," an argument that made Wilson look like a weak political leader. In January 1915, in fact, Grey openly accused Wilson of losing control of "German societies" and "German members of Congress under the open direction of the German Ambassador" who wanted to cut off British war supplies while opening the door for contraband to Germany. After all, argued Grey, Wilson, as of 22 January 1915, had not protested anything Germany had done; only Britain, evidently, was "worthy of reproach."[27]

Privately, as historian John Coogan shows, the British "expressed little but disdain and contempt" for the administration. Prime Minister Herbert Asquith, for example, considered the protest of 26 December nothing more than a "nuisance."

He also thought Wilson feared "powerful money interests" who wanted to press American exports to Europe. The way the British saw him, Wilson was a craven leader who cared more about scoring political points at home than about helping Britain defeat the Germans—hardly the sort of man the British could trust to mediate an end to the war on the terms they demanded.[28]

While Wilson's effort to support Britain looked insufficiently vigorous to the British, it was nevertheless clear enough to alienate both German Americans at home and, more ominously, the German government. In part, Germany's anger stemmed from Wilson's adherence to one part of international law that the president did follow to the letter, namely the right of neutrals to sell munitions to any belligerent able to buy them. Britain's control of the sea allowed it to take advantage of this well-established principle of international law; Germany could not. Even though the Reich admitted that the arms sales were legal, they infuriated German leaders. "The bitterness of their resentment towards us for this [the munitions exports] is almost beyond belief," House reported to Wilson from Berlin in March 1915. "It seems that every German soldier that is now being killed or wounded is being killed or wounded by an American bullet or shell."[29]

When Germany announced, on 4 February 1915, that its submarines would sink, without warning, enemy merchants in a war zone surrounding Britain, however, it did not cite America's arms sales as a justification for its new policy. Instead, the Germans asserted that they had a right to retaliate against the illegality of Britain's "starvation" blockade and against neutral submission to it. "For her violations of international law Great Britain pleads the vital interests which the British empire has at stake," the German government noted, "and the neutral powers seem to satisfy themselves with a theoretical protest." Because neutrals had thus evidently accepted "the vital interests of belligerents as sufficient excuse for every method of warfare," Germany would respond in kind. It would "appeal to these same vital interests to its regret" and allow its submarines to attack enemy merchants in the war zone without first searching them and providing for the safety of those on board, in violation of the international laws covering cruiser warfare and regardless of the dangers this posed to neutral shipping.[30]

Even before the submarine warfare announcement, Wilson knew that his pro-British policies ran the risk of enraging the Germans. His public and private protests to the British over the blockade, although weak, were one way he tried to appear neutral and so mitigate this danger. He also supplemented his formal announcement of American neutrality by discouraging American bankers from making loans to belligerent states. Such loans, Secretary of State Bryan argued in a Wilson-approved statement on 15 August 1914, were "inconsistent with the true spirit of neutrality." The Allies complained that this policy was prejudicial to them, and Wilson soon modified it, allowing "bank credits" to be extended to belligerent governments for the purposes of trade while still banning the sale of bonds issued by belligerent states. Nevertheless, Wilson's early position on loans stood as a potent symbol of his alleged commitment to true neutrality.[31]

Wilson also defended his neutrality policies in elaborate public statements. In lengthy letters to Hugo Münsterburg, a German American leader who had bemoaned Wilson's pro-Allied posture, and to the Senate Foreign Relations Committee, the administration insisted it had not shown "partiality" toward the Allies in the war. Of the two most important issues—arms sales to the Entente and the administration's accommodating posture toward the British maritime system— the first was easy enough to explain: arms sales to belligerents were legal under national and international law. An arms embargo would thus not be a neutral act at all, as it would clearly be aimed at the side with the naval power necessary to import arms, namely the Allies.[32]

The second issue was much harder to address. Charged with being too submissive to Britain's blockade, the administration noted that the United States itself, during the Civil War, had "contended for a liberal list" of contraband and had also interfered with trade going to neutral ports. "The Government," the administration asserted, "therefore can not consistently protest against the application of rules which it has followed in the past, unless they have not been practiced as heretofore." The administration then pointed out that it had, despite America's own track record, sent a note to Britain in December 1914 "strongly" contending for "freedom of trade in articles of conditional contraband not destined to the belligerent's forces." Wilson had done his best to protest the blockade, he seemed to be saying, even though he really did not have good grounds for objecting to the British system at all.[33]

Unsurprisingly, Wilson did not rely much on this strained argument to demonstrate his neutrality in the war. He put more energy into trying to maintain amicable relations with Germany, despite his hostility to the Reich and its conduct of the war. Though privately appalled by Germany's invasion of Belgium, Wilson remained silent about it in public. When a group of Belgian representatives appealed to him at the White House for some comment on the conduct of German troops in Belgium, Wilson refused, saying the "day of accounting" would come after the war was over. Right now, he emphasized, "it would . . . be inconsistent with the neutral position of any nation which like this has no part in the contest, to form or express a final judgment." Wilson would not issue a statement explaining his silence on Belgium either, as he was afraid it would sound too legalistic and technical. Rather than present a "lawyer's point of view" of the issue or state what he really felt, which would inflame Germany, he chose to say nothing at all.[34]

To be sure, in response to Germany's submarine war zone announcement, Wilson sent a sharp note to the Reich. Even though Lansing thought that the German explanation of its policy—an explanation stressing Germany's right to retaliate against Britain's blockade while deploring the failure of neutrals to challenge Britain's behavior—was "a strong presentation of the German case," Wilson disagreed. He rejected Germany's claim that America had acquiesced in illegal acts by Britain, saying the United States government had a "clear conscience" with regard to the blockade. With House in London at that very moment trying to translate good relations with Grey into British support for peace talks, Wilson decided to issue a strong warning to the Germans. If German war vessels "should destroy on the high seas an American vessel or the lives of American citizens, it would be difficult for the Government of the United States to view the act in any other light than as an indefensible violation of neutral rights which it would be very hard indeed to reconcile with the friendly relations now so happily subsisting between the two governments." The administration would hold Germany to a "strict accountability" for such acts and would "take any steps it might be necessary to take to safeguard American lives and property and to secure to American citizens the full enjoyment of their acknowledged rights on the high seas."[35]

The contrast between this statement and the 26 December 1914 note to Britain was striking. In the latter message, Wilson observed that Britain *was* breaking international law on matters "critical . . . to the commercial interests of the United States." But the president made no implied or explicit threats about holding Britain "strictly accountable" for its actions. Nor did he suggest that he might escort American merchants with warships to prevent their illegal interception by the British navy. As we have seen, the president only demanded more information about the British system and called for the British to make it conform "more closely" to international norms. The note to Germany sounded ominous; the one to Great Britain did not.[36]

However much Wilson was anxious to take a hard line with the Germans, especially while House was in London, he did not seek a confrontation with them. At the same time that he sent his "strict accountability" note to Berlin, he also protested against the hoisting of the American flag by British merchants as a *ruse de guerre* to avoid German attacks. This practice, he argued, made American shipping more likely to be struck by German U-boats. By sending a complaint to London, Wilson hoped to stop the flag deceptions and thus diminish the chances of an American–German crisis over the submarine war.[37]

More significantly, Wilson tried to broker a deal between Germany and Britain to defuse the dangers posed by Germany's submarine campaign altogether. The Germans, Bryan told Wilson on 15 February 1915, might be willing to withdraw their war zone declaration in return for an end to Britain's efforts to shut off Germany's food imports. Germany further promised "to give assurances that the imported food will not be taken by the Government and is even willing that American organizations shall distribute that food." Bryan, fearful that a "disaster" could occur in the German war zone ruinous to German–American relations, urged Wilson to propose the deal. The president immediately approved; three days later he signed off too on a similar, more detailed proposal. Eager for an agreement, Wilson also told House to press the deal in London, saying it would generate "favorable opinion" toward Britain in the United States.[38]

The proposed arrangement quickly collapsed, however. Germany wanted the agreement to cover more than just food; it demanded free transit for raw materials such as copper—a demand unacceptable to Britain. By 10 March 1915, the British signaled, through Page, that even a deal limited to food imports was out of the question, as Britain thought it a poor trade given the ineffectiveness of Germany's submarines. The British were also convinced that the German government had "so commandeered the food supply as to make all food subject to army use if need be." The proposed food-sub deal therefore probably never had much of a chance of being accepted. But in pushing it, Wilson had taken a concrete step to prove his impartiality to the Germans.[39]

The president further tried to demonstrate his trustworthiness as a neutral mediator by trumpeting American exceptionalism. The war, he announced in his neutrality proclamation, offered a chance for America to show herself as "a nation fit beyond others to exhibit the fine poise of undisturbed judgment, the dignity of self-control, the efficiency of dispassionate action; a nation that neither sits in judgment upon others nor is disturbed in her own counsels and which keeps herself fit and free to do what is necessary and disinterested and truly serviceable for the peace of the world." Americans, Wilson declared in October 1914, were the "custodians of the spirit of righteousness, of the spirit of equal-handed justice, of the spirit of hope which believes in the perfectibility of the law with the perfectibility of human life itself." Unlike other nations, America harbored no territorial ambitions, was not in any immediate physical danger from other states, and was not "jealous of rivalry in the fields of commerce or of any other peaceful achievement." "We are, indeed," Wilson enthused, "a true friend to all the nations of the world, because we threaten none, covet the possessions of none, desire the overthrow of none." All of these qualities gave Americans their "greatness" and made them "the champions of peace and concord."[40]

Wilson illuminated America's distinctive character by refusing, in late 1914, to support a buildup of the nation's military forces. Commencing a program of military expansion while the war raged overseas would not only lead to the development of militarism at home, to "a reversal of the . . . character of our polity," Wilson warned in December 1914. It would also signal the belligerents "that we had lost our self-possession, that we had been thrown off our balance by a war with which we have nothing to do, whose causes can not touch us, whose very existence affords us opportunities of friendship and disinterested service which should make us ashamed of any thought of hostility or fearful preparation for trouble." Holding off on preparedness measures would show that America lived up to its own self-image and embodied the spirit of "amity" necessary to lead the belligerents to peace.[41]

Certain of America's exceptionalism, Wilson believed other nations perceived it too—that Germany and Britain saw America the same way he did. Armed with this belief, Wilson no doubt had greater confidence that his diplomacy would succeed than otherwise would have been the case. His strained defense of his policy toward the British maritime system, his silence on Germany's invasion of Belgium, and his attempt to broker the food-sub deal between Germany and Britain did not really amount to very convincing evidence of his evenhandedness toward the belligerents. The overwhelming facts remained that, in late 1914 and early 1915, Wilson essentially supported Britain's illegal maritime warfare against Germany and embraced peace terms obviously premised on Germany's deciding that it had lost the war. Why, then, should the Reich view the United States as anything other than a de facto ally of its enemies, intent on containing its power? Only by believing in American exceptionalism and by doing his utmost to promote it could Wilson answer that question in a way consistent with his goal of mediating an end to the war.

Unfortunately for the president, it soon became apparent that the belligerents did not see American policy the same way he did. The British, from early 1915 to early 1917, continued to be disappointed in what they saw as America's lack of support for their war effort. The Germans, even more angry, considered Wilson's policies to be all too clearly biased in favor of the Entente. Determined to retaliate against Britain's blockade and to shut down Britain's supply line from America, they persisted in their submarine campaign, provoking a series of crises with the United States. America's exceptionalism, it seemed, was not enough to induce the belligerents to turn to Wilson to mediate an end to the war. The president would have to find other ways of persuading them to do so.

5

Pursuing a Wilsonian Peace, 1915–17

From 1914 to early 1915, President Wilson pursued his goal of international reform through a policy of "ostensible neutrality" toward the war—a policy designed to appear neutral while in fact the United States cooperated with Britain's war effort. Ideally, the policy would increase U.S. influence with the Allies while containing Germany but not alienating it, thus positioning Wilson as a mediator between the combatants. At the same time, the policy would appeal to public sentiment in favor of neutrality, thus shoring up Wilson's political standing at home. As this strategy unfolded, however, tensions developed between the United States and both sides of belligerents, and important segments of public opinion, including especially German Americans, criticized the administration for a lack of neutrality toward the war. These problems intensified after early 1915, as Britain tightened up its blockade, Germany implemented its submarine campaign, and rival policy advocates at home, as Chapter 6 discusses in more detail, increasingly charged that Wilson's course was detrimental to American security. To address these developments, Wilson introduced two new components into his diplomatic strategy: first, he promised the belligerents that if they settled the war on his terms, the United States would join a postwar collective security organization to uphold the peace, and, second, he proposed a new program of American military preparedness. These actions were intended to enhance America's credibility as a partner in world reform, to deter attacks on U.S. rights, and, implicitly, to warn the Europeans of what kind of military policy they could expect from the United States should international reform fail to occur. On a rhetorical level, the president also redoubled his attempts to link his diplomacy with American exceptionalism, both because he believed in its tenets and because it could increase support for his diplomacy at home and abroad. Finally, in late 1916, Wilson threatened to end his policy of de facto cooperation with the Allies if they did not agree to move toward ending the war on his terms.

. . .

Despite these new elements in his diplomacy, its cornerstone remained good relations with the British, even as the president became increasingly willing to coerce them over the mediation issue. This was especially evident in Wilson's response to Britain's announcement, on 1 March 1915, that it would intensify its blockade against Germany in retaliation for the Reich's submarine warfare. Henceforth, the British declared, they would intercept any ship they thought traded in any way with Germany, either directly or through neutral ports. In essence, they were now going to engage in unrestricted economic warfare against the Reich.[1]

Although Wilson agreed with State Department experts and his secretary of war that the British system constituted "a proposed course of action previously unknown to international law," he responded placidly to it. After a full month of deliberation, the president sent a protest to London warning the British not to interfere with America's legitimate trade with neutral ports. If they did so, they should "be prepared to make full reparation for every act" violating America's neutral rights. They also should expect America "to enter a protest or demand in each case" in which its rights were violated. Nowhere in the message did the administration threaten the British with reprisals of any kind; nowhere did Wilson state that America would hold Britain to a "strict accountability" for its actions; nowhere did Wilson indicate that "friendly relations" between America and Britain were at risk because of Britain's stated new policy. The note, in sum, bore little resemblance to the one sent to Germany concerning the submarine warfare declaration—it was hardly a warning, or even a protest, at all.[2]

Wilson did not threaten the British over the blockade primarily because he did not want to endanger his standing with them as a potential mediator. At the very same time Wilson decided how to respond to the new order in council, he was in the midst of digesting the results of House's peace mission to Europe. House's trip confirmed Wilson's inclination to mediate on the basis of Britain's minimum terms, not Germany's, as well as his belief that his chances for mediation depended on British goodwill and the Entente's ability to frustrate Germany's aims in the war. Taking a hard line with Britain over the blockade would only alienate British leaders, as Page pointed out to Wilson on 3 March and again a week later. It was useless to press the British on the blockade, Wilson told Bryan later that month. "We are face to face with *something they are going to do,*" he emphasized, "and they are going to do it no matter what representations we make." He also noted Page's assurance that the British would "be careful not to offend us in act" and that American trade was showing "no sign of slackening" even though it had dwindled to almost nothing with Germany. There seemed, from the president's point of view, no benefit—and potentially political and economic setbacks—to challenging or retaliating against Britain's blockade.[3]

Wilson recognized a need to state America's view of its rights, however, and to tell Britain that it would be held "to a strict responsibility" for interfering with them. To do anything less, he agreed with Lansing, "would invite strong criticism" at home, "furnish the opponents of the Administration with a plausible argument as to the weakness of our foreign policy," and undercut future legal claims American traders could make against the British. "Argument in the circumstances," Wilson felt, "is a waste of time," but a "statement" as to America's neutral rights, "in friendly language," was another matter.[4]

The challenge, Lansing told the president, was to write a "strong declaration of rights" while avoiding language that would "force this Government to employ drastic measures to compel their recognition." The United States needed "to file a *caveat,* to permit their violation under protest deferring settlement until peace has been restored." Wilson saw his first draft note, which was even milder than the final version, as meeting this test, as it contained "nothing necessarily inconsistent" with Lansing's suggestions. The president nevertheless used some stronger language concerning American rights in his revised protest, which Lansing applauded, as it would facilitate getting claims out of Britain after the war ended. Lacking any sort of confrontational tone, the note, sent on 30 March 1915, promised to meet the administration's legal and domestic political needs while allowing Britain's blockade—and amicable American–British relations—to go forward.[5]

Wilson's concern with maintaining a supportive relationship with Britain animated his response to Germany's submarine warfare as well. Although Wilson also tried to avoid war over the U-boat campaign, his desire to retain diplomatic credibility with Britain in the name of mediation and international reform nonetheless drove him to take a hard line with the Reich in 1915 and 1916.

The president's anxiety about how the submarine war could affect his standing with Britain emerged with the first great crisis over the U-boats, the sinking of the British passenger liner *Lusitania* on 7 May 1915. Almost 1,200 people died in the attack, including 124 American citizens. "Our action in this crisis will determine the part we will play when peace is made," House quickly cabled Wilson from London, "and how far we may influence the settlement for the lasting good of humanity. We are being weighed in the balance, and our position amongst the nations is being assessed by mankind." According to Page, opinion in London echoed House's. The British, he related to Wilson on 10 May, believed that "if the United States submits to German disregard of her citizens' lives and of her property and of her neutral rights on the sea, the United States will have no voice or influence in settling the war nor in what follows for a long time to come."[6]

These messages deeply impressed the president. "It is a very serious thing to have such things thought," Wilson commented to Bryan after reading Page's cable, "because everything that affects the opinion of the world regarding us affects our influence for good." The president's "strict accountability" note, moreover, limited Wilson's room for maneuver. "We defined our position at the outset and cannot alter it," he believed. Failure to respond to Germany's flagrant violation of international law would be devastating to America's diplomatic credibility overseas; he had no choice, Wilson thought, but to take a stand.[7]

On 11–12 May, Wilson composed a virtual ultimatum to Germany. The "lives of non-combatants," he declared, " . . . cannot lawfully or rightfully be put in jeopardy by the capture or destruction of an unarmed merchantman"; belligerents, according to international law, had to "visit and search" unarmed merchants and provide for the safety of those on board before attacking them. Submarines, Wilson argued, could not follow these rules and were therefore, he implied, illegal. The United States expected Germany to disavow the behavior of its U-boats, make reparation for the injuries they caused, and "prevent the recurrence" of any such acts in the future. When German leaders, on 28 May, charged that the *Lusitania* had been transformed by the British into an armed merchant carrying munitions, Wilson dismissed their argument as "irrelevant" to the issue of attacking the liner without warning and reiterated the demands of his original note.[8]

In adopting this course, the president rejected more conciliatory options for how to deal with the crisis. Germany, Bryan argued, would view Wilson's note, in conjunction with America's inaction on Britain's food blockade, as "partiality" toward the British, "an impression which will be deepened in proportion to the loudness of the praise which the allies bestow upon this government's statement of its position." To preserve America's standing as a potential mediator and "to insure us against war with Germany," Bryan wanted the president to issue a simultaneous protest against the blockade, agree to an investigation of all submarine issues between America and the Reich, "warn American citizens against going into the danger zone on foreign ships," and refuse port clearance "to belligerent ships carrying American passengers and . . . to American passenger ships carrying ammunition." Lansing, although much more hawkish toward Germany than Bryan, also recommended a protest note to Britain as well as to Germany, "as it will evince our impartial purpose to protect American rights on the high seas, whoever is the aggressor."[9]

Wilson, however, believed that a strong note to Britain would be a mistake. "We cannot afford even to seem to be trying to make it easier for Germany to accede to our demands by turning in similar fashion to England concerning matters which we have already told Germany are none of her business," he told Bryan on 20 May. "It would be so evident a case of uneasiness and hedging that I think it would weaken our whole position fatally." And, he added to the cabinet on 1 June, "when we had before us a grave issue with the Germans, it would be folly to force an issue of such character with England." As for Bryan's other suggestions, Wilson rejected them as feeble and hesitant. A warning to American travelers to the war zone "seems to me both weak and futile," he asserted to Bryan. "To show this sort of weak yielding to threat and danger would only make matters worse." Nor was there any time to regulate American travel overseas or any way to call for an investigation of the submarine campaign "without hopelessly weakening our pro-test." With his international prestige on the line, and in particular his credibility with Britain, now was not the time to show weakness.[10]

To be certain, Wilson modified the demands he made of Germany in his third *Lusitania* note of 21 July 1915, for reasons that will be discussed later. Specifically, he observed that submarines apparently could follow accepted rules of maritime warfare if they tried; so long as they did so, Wilson did not object to Germany us-ing its U-boats against its enemies. Nevertheless, Wilson still demanded that the German government disavow the actions of the U-boat involved in the *Lusitania* sinking and offer reparation for the deaths of American citizens. He concluded the note with a stern warning: any repetition of Germany's violations of neutral rights "must be regarded by the Government of the United States, when they affect American citizens, as deliberately unfriendly."[11]

As Germany's submarine attacks against shipping continued over the course of August 1915 to March 1916, Wilson found it difficult to retreat from even his scaled-back *Lusitania* demands without severely damaging his credibility at home and abroad. The American people, he perceived, wanted him "to keep us out of this war" and, equally passionately, "to keep the honor of the nation unstained." When a U-boat sank another British liner, the *Arabic,* on 19 August 1915, this dilemma immediately became apparent. "Everybody," Lansing told Wilson on 20 August, "takes the position that the declarations in our notes are so strong that we must act, that otherwise it will be said that our words have been mere 'bluff,' and that it would place the United States in a humiliating position to temporize." Wilson agreed. If the U-boat had fired on the *Arabic* without warning, Wilson told Edith Bolling Galt, his soon-to-be second wife, "this would appear to be what we told Germany we should regard as 'a deliberately unfriendly act,' knowing the signifi-cance of the words we used." Germany, Wilson charged, was "insolently ignoring the protest and the warning of our three notes." Failure to act, the president agreed with House, "would disappoint our own people and would cause something of derision abroad," a contempt that would leave America "no influence when peace is made or afterwards."[12]

Wilson therefore threatened Germany with a break in relations unless it dis-avowed the *Arabic* attack and stopped assaulting passenger ships without warning and without "safeguarding the lives of non-combatants." He did this recognizing that severing diplomatic relations could lead to war, although he hoped war could be avoided. To be certain, the threat was somewhat muted, as it was delivered through leaks to American newspapers and signaled in private talks between Lansing and Germany's ambassador in Washington. But the threat nevertheless was delivered, with Wilson's full awareness that it might not be heeded. "We are walking on quicksand," he gloomed to a friend at the height of the crisis. Ameri-ca's "self-respect," however, demanded nothing less.[13]

Eventually, in October 1915, Germany met Wilson's demands regarding the *Arabic*. The president continued to have sharp exchanges with the Central Powers over submarine warfare in late 1915 and early 1916, however, and, in March 1916, another crisis broke out when a German U-boat sank yet another passenger ship, the British liner *Sussex*. At first, Wilson was reluctant to accept that his approach to the submarine campaign had led him to a breaking point with the Reich. Alarmed at the president's reluctance to act, House impressed upon Wilson "that he would soon lose the confidence of the American people, and also of the Allies, and would fail to have any influence at the peace conference. I tried to make him see that we would lose the respect of the world unless he lived up to the demands he has made of Germany regarding her undersea warfare." Evidently affected by House's argument, Wilson ordered the colonel to see Ambassador Bernstorff "and say to him that we were at the breaking point and that we would surely go into the war unless some decisive change was made in their submarine policy." If Wilson had any doubts about this decision, they probably disappeared when he received a letter from Page. The British, the ambassador reported, increasingly saw the United States as "of no use" as a peacemaker because "we do not even keep our own pledge, made of our own volition." Having promised Senator Stone that he would not break relations without first notifying Congress and, one can speculate, eager to reassure the British about his backbone, Wilson then opted to reinforce his ultimatum in the most public forum possible, in a speech to a joint session of Congress, rather than leave it in Bernstorff's hands.[14]

Wilson's confrontational posture toward Germany's submarine campaign reflected more than just his desire to retain diplomatic credibility with Britain. By insisting that Germany follow the rules of maritime warfare, Wilson could also lessen the effectiveness of the submarines against British trade. This factor was a tangible consideration in Wilson's policymaking, especially from June through August 1915, when Wilson received a series of negative reports about the Allied war effort. The Germans were building more and bigger submarines, James Gerard reported from Berlin, while, House and other advisors stressed, the Allies' hopes for winning what had become a war of attrition rested on their ability to import supplies. "I think it is going to be *a great endurance test*," Wilson emphasized in mid-August, "and that the Allies are on the whole more likely—being open to the rest of the world, to survive that test than the Teutonic monarchies are." This calculation—that the Allies could only gradually wear down Germany if they were "open" to the world—no doubt reinforced Wilson in his determination to restrict the Reich's submarine campaign.[15]

The president's perception of the Allies' need for American war supplies contributed to another decision he made as he confronted Germany over the *Arabic*: ending the administration's opposition to the floating of belligerent loans in the United States. Partly, he took this step to ensure the well-being of America's economy. As we have seen, though, Wilson more often than not downplayed the importance of trade to American prosperity; the economic benefit of selling goods to the Allies was probably not the most important factor weighing on the president's mind in lifting the loan ban. He was likely more concerned with buttressing his relations with British leaders, who had complained about their inability to get loans in America back in January 1915 and who, House told Wilson in early August, were irritated at the administration for not doing enough to defeat Germany. Fully aware that the Allies needed American supplies to batter Germany's army, Wilson could, through his approval of a new policy on loans, improve his standing with them in the best way possible—by directly helping their war effort. Finally, as Wilson told Treasury Secretary William G. McAdoo, "the *Arabic* affair puts a new and all comprehensive phase of the situation before us and action on that will dispose of everything, in all probability." It was the resolution of the new submarine crisis that would determine German–American relations, not the status of loans to the Allies, so there was no reason why the latter should not go forward.[16]

Throughout the submarine episodes of 1915–16, Wilson continued to acquiesce in Britain's blockade against Germany. Despite violations of international law that Lansing considered "beyond belief," mounting public anger over them, and his own recognition that "diplomatic consistency" required a formal objection to them, Wilson delayed sending another public protest to London until 21 October 1915—almost seven months after the blockade note of 30 March. The October note declared the methods of the blockade "ineffective, illegal, and indefensible" but, as usual, contained no threats of American retaliation. Whatever force it had was also weakened by its timing: it went to London at virtually the same time that House, with the president's full approval, told Grey of Wilson's interest in another mediation bid, provided it met with "the approval of the Allies." After British leaders received the note, Wilson let them sit on it while he pursued his mediation negotiations with them. In March 1916, he even told Spring Rice that he would be "glad" if London "delayed for a time" a reply to his protest. Wilson's actions gave the British little reason to take his protest seriously.[17]

Wilson was far more interested in coordinating mediation with the British than in confronting them over the blockade. Agreeing with Lansing in August 1915 that the Allies would reject and resent any peace bid by America while Germany held the upper hand on the battlefield, Wilson made no sustained mediation effort until October. He then acted on the basis of a pro-Allied scheme developed by House. Germany, the colonel warned Wilson, "looked as if she had a better chance than ever of winning, and if she did win, our turn would come next, and we were not only unprepared but there would be no one to help us stand the first shock." The president needed to "do something now—something that would either end the war in a way to abolish militarism or that would bring us in with the Allies to help them do it." House proposed that he ask the Allies, unofficially, to alert him when "it would be agreeable to them to have us demand that hostilities cease" and peace talks begin "upon the broad basis of both military and naval disarmament." The Allies would accept the demand; if the Central Powers refused it, the United States would enter the war against them.[18]

Wilson was at first "startled" by this plan. But he went along with it, with minimal modification. In mid-October he approved a letter to Grey outlining House's proposal; the only change he made was to qualify what America would do if the Central Powers refused the offer of mediation. In that event, the letter stated, "it would *probably* be necessary for [America] to join the Allies and force the issue." In December, after House reported some encouragement from Bernstorff regarding another mediation attempt, Wilson sent the colonel to Europe for talks with the belligerents. The chief result of the trip was the so-called House-Grey memorandum, a paper negotiated by House and the British that repeated the colonel's intervention plan. Further underscoring its pro-Allied character, the memorandum included a list of peace terms "not unfavourable to the Allies" that America would support if peace talks occurred. Wilson endorsed the paper on 6 March 1916. Again, the only alteration he made to its text was to water down a pledge to enter the war against Germany if the Germans did not agree to pro-Allied peace terms; Wilson insisted upon stating that America would "probably" become a belligerent on the Allied side in that event. Other than that, Wilson embraced the memorandum "in toto," in House's words, expressed his "admiration and gratitude" for what House had done, and personally typed up the cable to Grey confirming his endorsement of the document.[19]

If Wilson's policy of pro-British "neutrality" continued along the same lines in 1915–16 that it had earlier in the war, some important new elements did nevertheless enter into his diplomacy. One key development involved the president's evolving conception of America's exact role in creating a new world order free from power politics. In late 1914 and early 1915, Wilson saw American mediation of the war on the basis of a German withdrawal in the west, disarmament, and the establishment of a *European* security system as the best path to international reform. The administration, in fact, had offered to help broker an arms limitation agreement between Britain and Germany before the war had started, in the spring of 1914, with the proviso that America would "have no alliances of any character." On 30 August 1914, Wilson and House agreed that a European security system could also be strengthened by a mechanism "for the principals to get together frequently and discuss matters with frankness and freedom as Great Britain and the United States were doing." This idea animated Wilson in December 1914 as well, when he and House drew up a collective security plan for the Western Hemisphere that "would serve as a model for the European Nations when peace is at last brought about." At this stage of the war, Wilson perceived a security stake for America in international reform, but, consistent with traditional isolationism, he wanted to limit America's role in attaining a new world to that of a broker and exemplar rather than that of an active participant.[20]

By November 1915, however, Wilson had changed his mind. As early as late 1914, British leaders indicated that they were more likely to agree to a mediated end to the conflict on Wilson's terms if the administration pledged to uphold the resulting peace settlement. As 1915 wore on, they ever more insistently linked Wilsonian peace terms to an American commitment to uphold the peace. The whole point of arms limitation, Grey noted in September in a letter to House, was "to get security for the future against aggressive war." But this sense of security would have to precede disarmament; only in the context of a league to enforce peace could the "diminishing of militarism and navalism" take place. "How much are the United States prepared to do in this direction?" demanded Grey. When Wilson and House answered the foreign minister's query with the letter outlining House's mediation-intervention plan, Grey pointedly asked if the proposal involved peace talks on the basis of both disarmament and a collective security league involving America. House urged Wilson to make a positive reply. "We should do this not only for the sake of civilization, but for our own welfare, for who may say when we may be involved in such a holocaust as is now devastating Europe." Wilson immediately concurred: "Message approved," he told House. To entice the British into ending the war on the terms he wanted, he realized, he had to promise that America would use its power to uphold the security of a new world system.[21]

Tempting the British into mediation with the promise of American help for their security was one new component of Wilson's approach to the war in 1915–16. He also began to indicate that continued rejection of his peace terms might alienate the United States—with dangerous results for the Europeans. The president's preparedness program, certainly, demonstrated a willingness to step up American armaments to unprecedented peacetime levels if an international arms limitation agreement was not concluded. Most significantly, if completed, the program would leave the United States with a navy "second to none" before 1925, a development that could only complicate British defense planning. While German–American relations and domestic politics were central to Wilson's decision for preparedness, the very existence of the policy nevertheless gave Wilson a tool he could use to coerce the Europeans into embracing his vision of international reform.[22]

The president began to use this leverage shortly after formally announcing his preparedness plan on 4 November 1915. In early January, he allowed House to tell British leaders that America might pursue "an isolated life" if it decided that conditions were not favorable for joining a new international organization. "If this were decided upon, I told them," House reported, "we would increase our army and navy and remain within our own hemisphere." In defending his preparedness program in a series of public speeches in late January and early February, Wilson hoped that the war would produce "some sort of joint guarantee of peace on the part of the great nations of the world." But, he pointedly added, "it has not done that yet." Until it did—until the Europeans agreed to mediation on his terms—the "only thing" that kept America "out of danger" was the nation's ability to protect its rights by force, if necessary. Arming in isolation, he implied, was America's answer to an unreformed world. In case the British missed this message, the House-Grey memorandum approved by Wilson on 6 March 1916 also alluded to it. If the Allies "delayed accepting" Wilson's offer of mediation, "and if, later on, the course of the war was so unfavourable to them that the intervention of the United States would not be effective, the United States would probably disinterest themselves in Europe and look to their own protection in their own way."[23]

Both new tactics in Wilson's approach to the British—dangling the carrot of American participation in collective security and brandishing the stick of American competition in arms races—were in play in spring 1916. During and just after the *Sussex* crisis with Germany, Wilson urged British leaders to act on the House-Grey memorandum and call on America to intervene diplomatically in the war. The longer they waited, the more likely that sooner or later the submarine issue would force America into the conflict, with disastrous results for international reform. "It would probably lead to the complete crushing of Germany," predicted a Wilson-approved letter to Grey on 11 May, and to an Allied scramble for "spoils" at the expense of building a future peace league. Picking up on Germany's hints that it would "welcome mediation" from the United States, Wilson told Grey that "the wearing down process, as far as Germany is concerned, has gone far enough to make her sensible to the power we can wield." American public opinion was growing impatient with the war too, and Americans increasingly viewed the Allies as "more determined upon the punishment of Germany than upon exacting terms that neutral opinion would consider just." They also wanted the administration to assert America's "undeniable rights against the Allies with the same insistence we have used towards the Central Powers." Now was the time to move toward peace: "Delay is dangerous," warned Wilson, "and may defeat our ends."[24]

When Grey yet again rebuffed the president, saying the Allies would view mediation as "premature," Wilson and House backed down, suggesting that they would put off a peace effort until after the Entente's summer offensive on the western front. But the president's statements in May nevertheless indicated that the United States was nearing a "crossroads." One path he outlined in a major speech to the League to Enforce Peace on 27 May 1916: the path of a peace based on Wilson's terms, made secure by the partnership of the United States "in any feasible association of nations formed in order to realize these objects." The other road, suggested in letters to Grey, in well-publicized remarks to the AUAM, and in Wilson's preparedness program, pointed in a very different direction. It led, in the short run,

toward an assertion of U.S. rights against the blockade and, in the longer term, to a
navy rivaling Britain's and, perhaps, to a more "aggressive" American nationalism
in trade. Nothing would aid the "world movement to maintain peace" more, House
advised a receptive Wilson, than the inauguration of "a big naval programme" by
the United States. "We have the money and if we have the will, the world will realize that we are to be reckoned with," maintained the colonel. "I greatly value your
suggestion about the navy programme," Wilson replied, although, with the administration's naval bill working its way through Congress, he need not have bothered
to assure House on this point. The legislation—and Wilson's all-out support for it
in the spring and summer of 1916—spoke for itself.[25]

Wilson's commitment to a policy of ostensible neutrality, biased heavily in favor
of the Allies despite the hints of coercion that entered into his diplomacy in the
first half of 1916, was matched by his determination not to alienate Germany. He
tackled this task in 1915–16 in much the same manner as he had earlier in the war.
Just as he remained silent regarding Germany's invasion of Belgium, he restrained
himself in responding to revelations of German subversion in the United States in
later 1915. While he leaked documents incriminating the German embassy to the
press, demanded the recall of Austrian ambassador Dumba, and expelled some
lower-ranking German diplomats from America, Wilson did not order the dis-
missal of Bernstorff. He feared that it would imply a "diplomatic breach" between
America and Germany, and he knew German leaders were growing bitter over the
whole episode. The president probably wanted to do more about German subversion, but he also wanted to preserve relations with the Reich—so he handled the
matter with caution.[26]

Similarly, Wilson strove to avoid war with Germany over the submarine conflict in the Atlantic. The president's view of America's domestic politics in part
accounted for this decision. The American people wanted him to preserve the nation's "honor" in the crisis with the Reich, he thought in early 1916, but they wanted
their president "to keep us out of this war" too. In accord with his concerns about
America's vulnerability to militarism, Wilson also perceived that involvement in
the conflict overseas could empower reactionary groups at home. "Every reform
we have won will be lost if we go into this war," Wilson predicted to Secretary of
the Navy Josephus Daniels in late 1914. From a domestic standpoint, the president
saw nothing to gain by intervening in the "terrible mess" going on in Europe, and
much to lose.[27]

Intervention would also ruin Wilson's chances for mediating a peace settlement
on his terms. It would internally divide the American people, weaken America's
growing material power, and cost Americans their "position as the trustees of
the moral judgment of the world." Once a belligerent, Wilson feared, the United
States would "lose all chance of moderating the results of the war by her counsel

as an outsider." The war would be "prolonged" by American entry because "there would be no one to lead the way out" and because the Allies would be emboldened in their policy of trying to crush Germany. In Wilson's estimation, intervening "actively" in the conflict would also undermine America's leverage with the Allies. The United States would be formally committed to helping the Allies to achieve victory, and it would be difficult, if not impossible, to abandon them, regardless of the aims they pursued against the Reich. Aware of this reality, the Allies would feel free to ignore Wilson's recommended peace terms and perhaps ignore his project for international reform altogether.[28]

These calculations dictated a temperate policy toward Germany's submarine campaign. Despite his threat to hold Germany to a "strict accountability" for the acts of its U-boats, Wilson did nothing in response to three incidents that occurred prior to the sinking of the *Lusitania* on 7 May 1915. These episodes involved the sinking of the British liner *Falaba*, which killed an American citizen, Leon C. Thrasher (28 March 1915); a German airplane's bombing of an American ship, the *Cushing* (29 April 1915); and a German torpedo's striking another American ship, the *Gulflight*, killing three crew members (1 May 1915). It took Wilson three weeks even to write a draft protest to Germany over the *Falaba* attack, and, when both Bryan and Lansing warned that Germany would see the note "as unfriendly, and as further evidence of our partiality for the Allies," Wilson backed off and did not send it. "Perhaps," he wondered to Bryan, "it is not necessary to make formal representations in the matter at all." Wilson had little reaction to the *Cushing* or *Gulflight* incidents either and apparently intended at most to send some sort of "representation" to Germany about them while postponing any final settlements until after the war. Before he could act, the attack upon the *Lusitania* occurred.[29]

As we have seen, Wilson felt compelled to respond vigorously to the sinking of the *Lusitania* and to subsequent U-boat incidents because he thought it vital for his relationship with Britain. Nevertheless, he consistently tried to resolve the crises with Germany without going to war. "There is such a thing as a man being too proud to fight," Wilson declared in public three days after the *Lusitania* attack. In line with that sentiment, the president scaled back his appeal, made in the first *Lusitania* note, that Germany abandon its submarine campaign against merchant ships, demanding only that the Reich follow the accepted rules of cruiser warfare with its U-boats. He settled for a qualified German acknowledgment of illegal behavior in the sinking of the *Lusitania* as well. Similarly, when an Austrian submarine sank an Italian liner, the *Ancona*, in November 1915, Wilson at first took a hard line with the Austro-Hungarian government but then retreated. By late December he decided to calm down the crisis by moving toward arbitration or prolonged discussion of the incident. Standing up to the Central Powers over the U-boat campaign was crucial to Wilson's policy of ostensible neutrality, but pressing them all the way to the point where war was highly likely was not.[30]

Even in the two most serious submarine crises in 1915–16, the attacks on the *Arabic* and the *Sussex,* Wilson tried to minimize the likelihood that war would occur. As Arthur Link points out, the president refused to issue a formal, public ultimatum to the Germans over disavowing their U-boat's assault on the *Arabic.* Nor did he try to get them to pledge not to attack all merchant ships without warning. In the *Sussex* incident, Wilson felt he had no choice but to issue a public ultimatum threatening to break relations with Germany unless it abandoned its "present methods of warfare against passenger and freight carrying vessels." This formulation of the ultimatum was weaker than the one Lansing recommended, however: the secretary wanted the president to break relations immediately and keep them broken until Germany actually changed its submarine campaign. Like-wise, House and Mrs. Wilson declared Wilson's draft ultimatum note "weak" and wanted tougher language in it. While they managed to get the president to make some minor changes to it, he resisted more extensive revisions, arguing that they "would mean a declaration of war, and he could not declare war without the con-sent of Congress." He did not want a war in any event, and keeping the *Sussex* ultimatum in the form he wanted made it easier to avoid one.[31]

Wilson also attempted to defuse the submarine issue altogether. Aware that Ger-many justified the submarine campaign as retaliation for the British blockade, Wil-son repeatedly pressed British leaders in private to reduce their interference with America's neutral trade. He tried to get them to respond by telling them that if they did not, Congress might place an embargo on overseas arms shipments. At the height of the *Lusitania* crisis, the president attempted to address the blockade from a different angle. He again embraced the idea, first floated back in February 1915, of Germany's ceasing its illegal submarine attacks on merchant ships in exchange for Britain's stopping its seizure of food and other noncontraband shipments destined for neutral ports. Again, however, the deal foundered on Germany's insistence that the British allow raw materials through the blockade that could be used in muni-tions manufacturing. Still, Wilson had tried, seeing in the trade a way to remove friction from America's relations with both Britain and Germany in one stroke.[32]

A more elaborate move to work out an accommodation with Germany on the submarine campaign occurred in early 1916, when the administration proposed that Germany follow international law in its U-boat war in exchange for the Al-lies' disarming their merchant ships. With Lansing advising that this "modus vi-vendi" could "prevent the horrors" that characterized submarine warfare, Wilson approved pitching the deal to the belligerents on 10 January 1916. Even after the British immediately rejected the idea on the ground that it violated existing inter-national law and favored the Germans, Wilson continued to press it, as he allowed it to leak to the press on 28 January. The president backed off the proposal only after receiving direct evidence that it threatened to do serious damage to British–American relations. Grey, on 5 February, personally cabled the administration to denounce the proposal, stressing that it would "ensure" the "effectiveness" of the U-boats to the "great disadvantage" of the Allies. House, in the midst of negotiations with the British over how and when Wilson should intervene diplomatically in the war, also strongly urged Wilson to hold the modus vivendi "in abeyance." On 15 February the administration in effect withdrew the proposal, and Wilson, in a major battle with Congress, went on to reassert the right of Americans to travel on defensively armed merchant ships. Again, though, the attempt to push the modus vivendi was revealing, even if it failed: desperate to do something to resolve the submarine crisis that so threatened his goals, Wilson, however briefly, had flirted with a scheme that strained his prized relationship with Britain.[33]

The president's decision to step up America's military preparedness was aimed in part at pacifying relations with Germany too. As we have seen, his preparedness policy quickly became connected with his understanding of how a postwar collective security organization would have the power necessary to deter aggression. It also almost immediately became a component of his diplomacy toward Britain, as he began pointing to the proposed military buildup as a preview of what the United States might do if Britain obstructed his efforts to reform international politics. Both of these motives for pursuing preparedness appeared after the president had already decided to embark on a new military policy, however; the initiating impulses for the new course lay elsewhere.[34]

One source lay in domestic politics. As Chapter 1 discussed, Wilson embraced preparedness in part to stimulate the sense of civic virtue that he and other Progressives associated with democracy. In addition, the Lusitania incident sharply increased the public debate over preparedness, and Atlanticist leaders such as Theodore Roosevelt and Henry Cabot Lodge discerned some movement among the American people toward their proposals for large-scale defense increases. Although antipreparedness forces almost certainly still held a majority among the public and in Congress, Wilson picked up on the shift in favor of a defense increase, seeing in it a "demand for reasonable preparedness" that was "clear enough" to him. With an election year looming, the president could hardly avoid seizing control of an issue that had the potential to damage him politically.[35]

Wilson's political calculations probably reinforced a decision he was inclined to make in any case, because of the submarine crisis with Germany. No less than the public, Wilson was alarmed by the Lusitania attack. Right up until early May 1915, the president had opposed any military expansion. Then, on 21 May, two weeks after the Lusitania was sunk, he issued a public statement urging a buildup of the navy. The attack itself, not the political shifts occurring in the months afterward, triggered the president's determination to change his defense policy.[36]

In one sense, Wilson's decision for preparedness reflected some uneasiness with America's readiness to fight should the submarine confrontation with Germany abruptly end in war. If an "armed uprising of German sympathizers" occurred in

America in the event of a break with the Reich, the president feared that he lacked sufficient forces to deal with it. America's "tiny army is so scattered (a few hundred here, a few hundred there)," he complained to Edith Galt in August 1915, "that at the first—not knowing *where* to be ready—we would be unable to do anything effective." In late 1915 and early 1916, moreover, he publicly expressed concern about America's ability to defend the Monroe Doctrine against foreign aggression. This sense of weakness must have unnerved Wilson as tensions with Germany mounted, contributing to his decision to expand the military.[37]

No preparedness program could alleviate America's deficiencies overnight, however, as Wilson certainly knew. His defense policy was therefore designed not so much to prepare for war as to demonstrate U.S. resolve to the Reich and to remind German leaders of America's great military potential. Such a signal, Wilson hoped, would help to manage the submarine crisis by deterring Germany from persisting in its illegal actions. The Reich, Chandler Anderson advised Wilson on 13 July 1915, was using its U-boats to bully America into either embargoing munitions exports or forcing Britain to abandon its blockade. "The German Government evidently is proceeding on the assumption that the United States does not want to go to war," calculated Anderson, implying that as long as German leaders held this assumption, they would continue their submarine campaign. "With these considerations in mind," he argued, "the conclusion is inevitable that nothing short of fear of war with the United States will induce Germany to yield to the demands of the United States." Wilson agreed; five days after he received Anderson's memorandum and a similar analysis from House, he formally ordered the War and Navy departments to draw up defense recommendations. "I love peace," Wilson explained as he promoted his preparedness program a few months later. "But I know that peace costs something, and that the only way in which you can maintain peace is by thoroughly enjoying the respect of everybody with whom you deal."[38]

Of course, to mediate an end to the war on the terms he desired, Wilson needed to do more than defuse the submarine crisis or deter German actions that could lead to war. He also needed to gain Germany's trust. To this end, the president made some limited attempts to engage the Germans in talks about how mediation could occur, although these contacts never approached the intimacy or frequency of the administration's contacts with the British. During the *Lusitania* crisis, for example, Wilson privately told Bernstorff that if Germany met U.S. demands regarding the U-boat situation, the administration would "press for the ending of the English hunger blockade policy." Once that issue was settled, Wilson promised the ambassador, "a beginning would be made for a peace move in grand style, which he [Wilson] would like to get under way as the head of the neutrals." The terms for peace could include "a neutralization of the seas," something Wilson knew the Germans, with their inferior navy, cared about a great deal. House, with Wilson's approval, also revealed to Bernstorff the gist of his late 1915 diplomatic intervention plan. Concealing the fact that the plan hinged upon approval by the Allies, the colonel portrayed Wilson as interested in pushing for peace on the basis of eliminating "militarism" and "navalism." House's second wartime trip to Europe in early 1916, when he negotiated the House-Grey memorandum, included a visit to Berlin, where the colonel felt out Chancellor Theobald von Bethmann Hollweg about peace terms over dinner and beer. Nothing came of the talks but, in holding them at all, the administration had made a gesture toward evenhandedness in its mediation probes.[39]

More consistently, Wilson tried to underscore America's character as a mediator in the same way he had earlier in the war: by proclaiming that "America was born into the world to do mankind service" and that its "peculiar and particular mission in the world" was to act in "the service of justice and righteousness and peace." With German–American tensions escalating because of the submarine campaign and his acquiescence in the British blockade, the president had more reason than ever to herald American exceptionalism to the world. His policies obviously aligned America's power with the Allies against Germany, something the Germans did not fail to notice, as they continued to complain, vehemently, about the administration's failure to insist on its rights against Britain. Somehow Wilson had to convince them that he was not engaged in balancing America's power against theirs, because if they believed that he was, they would never trust him as a mediator.[40]

He did this by portraying his stance toward Germany not as a product of power calculations but as a consequence of America's "sense of duty as a representative of the rights of neutrals the world over." It was true, he conceded in February 1916, that the Central Powers were "practically shut off" from the outside world by Britain's blockade. But that was something "over which we have no control." Americans, he claimed, were "genuinely neutral" concerning the war. They were, in fact, reluctant to confront Germany over its submarine attacks, Wilson noted as he delivered his ultimatum after the *Sussex* incident to the Reich. "But we cannot forget that we are in some sort and by the force of circumstances the responsible spokesmen of the rights of humanity, and that we cannot remain silent while those rights seem in the process of being swept utterly away in the maelstrom of this terrible war." The United States owed it to itself, to other nations, "and to a just conception of the rights of mankind to take this stand now with the utmost solemnity and firmness." A desire to help Britain contain Germany's power had nothing to do with U.S. policy toward the Reich, in other words; true to their exceptional character "as the trustees of the moral judgment of the world," Americans acted only "to hold high the standards which should govern the relationship of nations to each other."[41]

Similarly, the president did all he could to distance himself from a discussion of specific peace terms with the belligerents. These always included a German withdrawal from France and Belgium. Rather than focus on that aim, which was so clearly biased in favor of the Allies, Wilson tried to get talks going in 1915–16 on

the basis of "(a) military and naval disarmament and (b) a league of nations to secure each nation against aggression and maintain the absolute freedom of the seas."
Americans, he instructed House before the colonel left for Europe, "have nothing
to do with local settlements,—territorial questions, indemnities, and the like,—but
are concerned only with in the future peace of the world and the guarantees to be
given for that." That this was demonstrably untrue, as evidenced in the calls for the
restoration of Belgium, the terms in the House-Grey memorandum, and the principles in Wilson's 22 January 1917 address to the Senate, was beside the point. Wilson
wanted to obscure his concern for containing Germany's power, not draw attention
to it. Framing his proposed peace terms in a manner most consistent with America's
missionary exceptionalism was the best way to accomplish this end.[42]

The president recast preparedness in the light of American exceptionalism and
a peace league too. Concerned that it might provoke Germany and that pacifists
thought it undermined prospects for neutral mediation and for ending power politics, Wilson stressed that his preparedness program was not aimed at any particular
power. The "dangers" America faced were instead "infinite and constant" as the belligerents, in their struggle against each other, assaulted the nation's neutral rights.
The United States had to deter such attacks and, if necessary, defend itself against
them, and not merely to protect American lives. It had to act to preserve its "honor"
and "ideals," because those ideals were "intended to regenerate mankind." Because
of its exceptional character, the United States, in arming to defend itself, was actually
"standing for the rights of mankind, when the life of mankind is being disturbed by
an unprecedented war." Moreover, Wilson argued, the United States had to be ready
to "keep law alive while the rest of the world burns" in order to increase the chances
that the war would result in "some sort of joint guarantee of peace on the part of the
great nations of the world." By asserting "in times of war the standards of times of
peace," the United States could make a lasting peace more likely for all nations. Its
armaments, then, had nothing to do with traditional power politics at all.[43]

Wilson's efforts to mediate an end to the war began to culminate in late 1916, in a
formal peace note he sent to the belligerents. Several factors lay behind this move.
First, British–American relations deteriorated over the second half of 1916 as London displayed a near-total lack of concern with American complaints about the
blockade and refused to call on Wilson to intervene diplomatically in the war. At
the same time, the president learned from House that liberal public opinion in
Britain had been stirred by Wilson's endorsement of U.S. participation in a peace
league and might now support a peace bid by Washington. Finally, even as the
German government decided to restrict its U-boat operations in the spring of
1916 rather than face war with the United States, it indicated that its decision was
conditional on Wilson's confronting the British over the blockade. In October,
German leaders essentially told the administration that if some move to ease the

blockade did not happen soon, they would have to resume their unrestricted submarine warfare campaign. Convinced "that unless we do this now, we must inevitably drift into war with Germany upon the submarine issue," the newly reelected president resolved, in mid-November 1916, "to write a note to the belligerents demanding that the war cease."[44]

Wilson was careful, though, to avoid alienating the British with this initiative. He still saw his goal of international reform as bound up with them and their ability to prevent a German victory in the war. Consequently, although he secured legislative authority from Congress to ban British merchant ships from American ports, he did not actually use this power to coerce the British into embracing his peace bid. He did exert other economic leverage over the Allies by discouraging American banks from investing in short-term Allied treasury notes. But he almost certainly knew that Britain's financial situation would not really reach a dire condition until March 1917, which meant that the president could always change course before he inflicted any real damage on Britain's war effort. Far from demanding a peace conference, moreover, the final version of Wilson's peace note simply called for a statement of terms from each side and expressed hope for an end to the war soon.[45]

Even before all the belligerents replied to his message, Wilson decided to prod them further toward talks by publicly detailing his own view of how to end the war. Delivered before the Senate on 22 January 1917, his speech marked the climax of the diplomacy he had pursued since late 1915. His proposed peace terms could easily be interpreted as a call for the Central Powers to withdraw from the Allied territory they occupied and, perhaps, to give up additional territory as well, revealing yet again the president's conviction that international reform depended on reversing Germany's advances in the war and his hope that the Allies would join him in working for peace. In his next breath, he emphatically denied that his proposed terms had anything to do with the power politics of the existing international system: "Mankind," he declared, "is looking now for freedom of life, not for equipoises of power." America's principles of peace reflected not its common security interests with the Allies but its unique mission to "show mankind the way to liberty." Germany, then, should trust Wilson, see that he was "speaking for liberals and friends of humanity in every nation," and embrace his peace program. Finally, Wilson emphasized, "there is only one sort of peace that the peoples of America could join in guaranteeing." If the peace arranged by the belligerents failed to "engage the confidence and satisfy the principles" of Americans and their leaders, the United States would not underwrite it by joining a league of nations. The United States would protect its safety in its own way in a world still trapped in power politics, Wilson implied, which presumably meant that it would continue to build up its own military forces. The belligerents faced a stark choice: meet Wilson's demands and build a future "safe against war" or "struggle for a new balance of power" and alienate the strongest nation on earth.[46]

Wilson's magisterial "peace without victory" address of 22 January 1917 did not impress the British. From mid-1915 to late 1916, the drawn-out character of the president's submarine diplomacy and his failure to demand Bernstorff's recall, despite the ambassador's apparent involvement in subversion inside the United States, dismayed British leaders. To them, Page observed, Wilson's course was "proof of weakness" and showed, along with the president's protests over the blockade, an inability to understand the "moral meaning of their struggle against a destructive military autocracy." The administration's silence on Belgium, America's "tradition . . . against any sort of intervention in outside affairs," its desire to keep the Monroe Doctrine, and its lack of military preparedness all indicated to Spring Rice, moreover, that Wilson's pledge to join a peace league was merely "a pious wish." Grey concurred. Reports "that public opinion in the United States is determined at all costs to keep out of war," the foreign minister informed House, "makes people ask whether even with a League of Nations the United States could be depended upon to uphold treaties and agreements by force." Others were blunter. "The man is surely the quintessence of a prig," steamed historian G. O. Trevelyan to Lord Bryce days after Wilson's address to the Senate. "What a notion that the nations of Europe, after this terrible effort, will join him in putting down international encroachments by arms, at some future time, if he is afraid to denounce such encroachments even in words now."[47]

As for the Germans, their declared interest in peace in late 1916 and early 1917 was less of a genuine effort to get talks going than a stratagem to pave the way for the resumption of unrestricted submarine warfare. They had no desire to use Wilson as a mediator in any event. "When the President wants to put an end to the war," the kaiser groused upon receiving Wilson's peace note, "he needs only to threaten the English blockade pirates with a munitions embargo and a blocking of the market for loans, and take reprisals against robbing of the mails and the black list. Then the war will be ended without notes, conferences, etc. I won't go to any conference! Certainly not under his chairmanship!" Paul von Hindenburg, chief of the army general staff, considered the president so biased in favor of the Allies that he assumed that his peace proposal was "evoked by England." Most important, German officials realized that Wilson's peace terms were much more in line with Britain's than with their own, which included territorial annexations for the Central Powers in both the west and the east. Hence, judged Arthur Zimmermann, any involvement by Wilson in peace talks "would be detrimental to our interests" as it would put at risk "what we hope to gain from the war."[48]

As they spurned Wilson's mediation, the Germans also opted, after the Entente rejected their own call for a peace conference, to unleash their U-boats. They did so fully aware that their decision would probably lead to war with the United States. By this point, however, they dreaded a continued stalemate with the Entente more than they feared war with America. "America under Wilson's leadership is not friendly toward us," Adm. Henning von Holtzendorff, chief of the German admiralty, advised the kaiser on 9 January 1917. "Her entry into the war will not bring her any advantages and only extremely limited, and in no way decisive, advantages for the Allies." The United States, Vice Adm. Franz Ritter von Hipper reckoned in early February, "could not possibly work any harder against us in the future than it has already done to date." German military leaders also had contempt for America's small army and presumed that the U-boats would sink any American troop transports attempting to take it, or any enlarged force, to Europe. By the time America trained and organized an expeditionary force, moreover, the war would be finished, as the Germans expected the U-boats to force a British surrender within six months. With this estimate of the probable impact of American entry into the war and their belief that Germany could not win a protracted war of attrition with the Entente, the conclusion was clear: there was no compelling reason not to use their U-boat weapon in full and try to secure a quick win over their enemies.[49]

On the afternoon of Wednesday, 31 January 1917, a grave Bernstorff handed Lansing the announcement of Germany's renewed submarine campaign. Wilson was "sad and depressed" and shocked at the news. When Louis Lochner saw him on 1 February, the president looked "haggard and worried." He told House that he "felt as if the world had suddenly reversed itself; that after going from east to west, it had begun to go from west to east and . . . he could not get his balance." The most intense crisis yet in German–American relations was now upon him.[50]

The president should not have been surprised at this turn of events, however. Just as his program for international reform was highly problematic, so too was his diplomatic strategy for convincing the belligerents to accept it. As his preferred peace terms called for a retraction of Germany's power, and as he assumed that the Allies would eventually win the war, Wilson's diplomacy had aimed to persuade the Germans to accept defeat and the Allies to accept less than a decisive victory. He tried to attain these goals by helping the Entente's war effort while distancing himself from its war aims and criticizing, but not substantively impeding, its blockade. Wilson hoped that this policy would ensure—and hasten—Germany's recognition of its defeat, gain him influence with Britain, and maintain his image of neutrality in the eyes of the American public and Germany. Trusting the United States as a supportive friend, the British would see the wisdom of Wilson's appeal not to crush Germany. Respecting the United States as a neutral broker, the Germans would turn to Wilson to manage their retreat from the battlefield. The war would end in a "peace without victory," or, as Page more aptly called it, a "peace without conquest," and the task of building a new world free from power politics could then begin in earnest.[51]

Unfortunately for Wilson, his strategy of ostensible neutrality did not produce its intended results. As the following chapter discusses, at home it failed to satisfy either pacifists or Atlanticists, although Wilson did have some success in winning

support from the former. Abroad, Wilson's strategy contributed to a sharp deterioration in America's relationship with both Germany and Great Britain. The Germans saw the United States as, in essence, a de facto ally of the Entente. "At present," Bernstorff told House in late July 1915, "nobody in Germany believes in the
impartiality of the American Government." Under Wilson, the United States
armed the Allies, loaned them money, refused to challenge their starvation blockade, and repeatedly threatened Germany with a break in relations unless it restricted its use of its most effective maritime weapon against Britain, the submarine. Wilson also insisted that peace talks could only proceed on the basis of
Germany's giving up the chief negotiating card it had to play against the Allies,
namely its occupation of Allied territory. From a German point of view, Wilson
was not a neutral broker between the belligerents. He was instead balancing America's power against Germany in an effort to contain the Reich's territorial expansion
in Europe. He was an enemy.[52]

The British, in turn, viewed the United States as a power that shared their fear
of Germany but was too timid and selfish to shoulder the burden of actually fighting it. To use a term from international relations theory, the British saw Wilson's
America as a "buck-passer"—a state that "fully recognizes the need to prevent [an]
aggressor from increasing its share of world power but looks for some other state
that is threatened by the aggressor to perform that onerous task." The president, in
British eyes, sympathized with their basic aims in the war and allowed the blockade to go forward, but he also went out of his way to avoid war with Germany,
repeatedly made proposals that might have weakened Britain's stranglehold on
the Reich, criticized Britain's larger war objectives, and even threatened economic
retaliation if the British did not agree to open peace talks on his terms. Further,
Wilson gloated over America's ever-increasing power in public and embarked on
a military buildup threatening to Britain's supremacy at sea. Wilson was hardly a
reliable partner in world politics as far as the British were concerned. He might
not have been an enemy, but he certainly was not a friend.[53]

By late in 1915, the president realized that his policy of ostensible neutrality
was not working out as expected. In response, he promised the combatants that if
they agreed to his peace terms, the United States would join a collective security
league to uphold them. He also continually portrayed his policies as an expression of America's exceptionally moral, peaceful, and democratic character. These
declarations reflected Wilson's genuine beliefs about the exceptionalism of the
United States, but they were also aimed at persuading pacifists to support his
leadership and at convincing the belligerents, and especially the Allies, that they
need not seek to attain security through winning a decisive strategic advantage in
the war, that American power could provide security for them through a league
to enforce peace. Joining a league, Wilson assured them, would be the ultimate
manifestation of the unique character of the American people. It would be "the

opportunity for which they have sought to prepare themselves by the very princi-ples and purposes of their polity and the approved practices of their Government ever since the days when they set up a new nation in the high and honourable hope that it might in all that it was and did show mankind the way to liberty." Americans acted not out of narrow strategic calculations but out of a desire to serve mankind—so they could be trusted, as both mediators and as guarantors of a just settlement to end the war.[54]

However much Wilson believed in American exceptionalism and its implica-tions for international politics, his argument had little credibility with the Eu-ropeans. How could Britain take Wilson's words about American morality and trustworthiness at face value as British men died by the hundreds of thousands on the battlefield while the United States sat out the war? How could Germany believe him, when the United States acquiesced in Britain's blockade? "As matters stand," German leaders wrote Wilson in May 1916, "the German Government can not but reiterate its regret that the sentiments of humanity which the Govern-ment of the United States extends with such fervor to the unhappy victims of submarine warfare are not extended with the same warmth of feeling to the many millions of women and children who, according to the avowed intentions of the British Government, shall be starved and who, by their sufferings, shall force the victorious armies of the central powers into ignominious capitulation." Good in-tentions, declarations of moral and political superiority, and promises of future security guarantees could not obscure America's balancing and buck-passing be-havior, regardless of Wilson's expectations.[55]

Sensing this—perceiving, as he stated in August 1916, "in most of the European chancelleries, disinterested motives are incredible"—Wilson also tried to coerce the belligerents into accepting his peace terms. He threatened British leaders with economic and financial pain unless they went along with his mediation; he threat-ened the Germans with a diplomatic breach unless they restricted their subma-rine war; he threatened them both with the prospect of unprecedented American armament expansion unless they agreed to international reform. And he tried to bring political pressure to bear on them too, by appealing to their own public opinion to rally to his program.[56]

These threats did not do much to advance Wilson's goals. They further irritated and alienated the belligerents, as they underscored Wilson's refusal to consider international reform on any program of peace terms other than his own. They were not very credible either. Wary of practicing the tactics of power politics be-cause they contradicted his vision of international reform and risked generating militarism in America, the short-term threats, designed to force mediation and deter Germany's submarine attacks, were slow in coming and were not supported by any new military deployments. Consequently, they made little impression on either group of belligerents. The longer-term threat—the implied warning that the

United States would actively compete against the Europeans in any postwar arms races that developed—had no impact either, for similar reasons. Given America's history of antimilitarism, the widespread and powerful movement against even Wilson's modest program of military expansion, and Wilson's own repeated warnings about the dangers of European-style military preparedness for American democracy, it was not a believable threat. Absent international reform, the British and Germans probably concluded, the United States would most likely simply continue its traditional policy of relatively disarmed isolation. Finally, the idea of calling on liberals overseas to pressure their own governments emerged only in later 1916—too late to be effective.

The fundamental paradox of Wilson's national security strategy—the paradox of practicing power politics to end power politics—thus vitiated his diplomatic policies toward the belligerents no less than it undermined the plausibility of his peace program. Fixated on the goal of ending the balance of power in the name of avoiding a future of militarism for America, he hesitated to fully engage American power against Germany. That course, he perceived, would lead to the complete alienation of Germany from the project of international reform and the perpetuation of power politics by the Allies. Conversely, he feared German expansion and believed that international reform required containing Germany's power. This meant that he had to help the Allies fight the Germans, if only in a limited way. The result was a policy that produced the worst of all possible worlds. Wilson balanced his country's strength against Germany to a great enough degree to alienate it and put it on a collision course with the United States, but he failed to engage American power against the Reich enough to satisfy the British and so frayed America's relationship with them as well. Wilson's diplomacy was conducive neither to effective balancing, which would have aimed to defeat Germany quickly through active American intervention in the war, nor to buck-passing, which would have sought to avoid war with Germany altogether and let the Allies handle the threat themselves, nor to mediation for international reform, which would have required defending American neutral rights against both sides with equal forcefulness or abandoning them completely. From any angle, the president's diplomatic strategy failed to advance America's security interests.[57]

The failure of Wilson's diplomacy also had troubling implications for his vision of collective security. The Europeans saw the president's policy for what it was—an attempt to make the Entente suffer the cost and pain of balancing the power of Germany and to coerce both sides of belligerents into accepting his peace program. Confronted with the tactics of power politics, the Europeans responded in kind. The Allies tried to pass the buck back to the president by constantly calling on him to do more to confront Germany while the Germans tried to negate the power Wilson brought to bear against them. Neither side displayed any interest in Wilson's peace terms—the terms he described as vital preconditions for a

new international system. Why should they? Despite his rhetoric about American exceptionalism and about the war's illuminating every state's need for "a new
and more wholesome diplomacy" based on collective security, Wilson's national
security policies seemed little different from those of any other great power. His
actions made a mockery of his claim that the world was "upon the eve of a great
consummation" ending power politics. According to his theory of collective security, the war was supposedly underscoring the reality of a global interest in peace
and the urgency for nations to work together to end competitions for power. Yet
Wilson's own policies obviously increased America's share of world power, and
the president displayed no hesitation in manipulating that development to attain
his diplomatic goals. It was no wonder, then, that the Europeans rejected Wilson's
program for international reform—Wilson's actions made him look as little interested in it as they were.[58]

6

Debating Wilsonianism

The shortcomings of President Wilson's diplomacy toward the belligerents did not go unnoticed at home. Even liberal internationalists found aspects of the president's course hard to support. Nevertheless, criticism of Wilson's diplomacy did little to undermine support for the president's larger project of international reform. Relative to Wilson, the *New Republic* and the League to Enforce Peace, to differing degrees, favored more overt cooperation with Britain as the best way to advance toward collective security. This amounted to a different way of attempting to resolve the paradox of using the tactics of power politics to end power politics, not a rejection of the endeavor itself. Pacifists, in contrast, did criticize the logic underpinning Wilson's approach to the war. But they did not see the contradictory character of the president's diplomacy as reason to doubt the plausibility of international reform. Atlanticists, finally, berated Wilson for trying too hard to avoid war with Germany. This policy, they argued, threatened both America's immediate security and the cause of reform. Their criticisms of the president fell short of an outright rejection of Wilson's goal of collective security, however, leaving that objective, with all of its problems, as the focus of America's national security strategy.

Of the president's supporters, the *New Republic*'s editors' approach to persuading the belligerents to accept peace terms conducive to building collective security was probably the most similar to Wilson's. Having essentially the same views as the president about the dangers a triumphant Germany would pose to the United States and about the likelihood of an Allied victory in the war, the *New Republic* consistently endorsed policies favorable to the Allied war effort. In some ways, the editors wanted to provide even more support to the Entente than Wilson did. Thus they called on Wilson "to make a vigorous protest against the invasion of Belgium," supported perhaps by an American embargo of trade with Germany; opposed stopping American arms exports because it would favor the Germans, reward "militarism," and "would be regarded by the Allies as the most desperate treachery"; did not want to end the war while Germany occupied Allied territory in the west; demanded that Germany abandon submarine warfare altogether rather than just restrict it; and supported only pro forma protests against Britain's maritime system. All of these positions reflected the *New Republic*'s conviction that "the crushing of England and France would endanger our future" and its belief that, as a friend of Britain, the United States would have "a good chance of exerting a healing and moderating influence on international organization."[1]

Although the editors were disappointed with Wilson's failure to confront Germany over Belgium and the submarine issues more forcefully, they recognized that the president's posture toward the belligerents was like their own—and that such a pro-Allied policy carried with it the danger of alienating Germany. The Reich's submarine war zone declaration, they immediately concluded, was directed in part at the United States, "to scare American vessels away from waters in which they have a perfect right to be." America's arms sales to the Allies and Wilson's acquiescence in Britain's blockade angered the Germans, the editors believed. "It is easier to understand the present German bitterness against the United States," they observed shortly after the *Lusitania* attack, "when it is borne in mind that if we were to fight Germany we should be only doing in war what we are already doing in peace." In fact, despite Wilson's apparently successful negotiations with Germany over the submarine issue over the course of 1915–16, the *New Republic* assumed that sooner or later an incident would occur that would "compel our government to act" against the Reich. Given America's tilt toward the Allies and Germany's violent reaction to it, conflict between the two nations seemed inevitable.[2]

If war came, the *New Republic* believed, in common with Wilson, the results would undermine America's long-term security. Once aligned with the Allies, the United States would find it hard not to resist their demands upon Germany. "We should have to pool our resources with them," predicted the editors, and "agree not to make a separate peace" with the Reich. "We should be committed to their policies for the settlement of Europe with all the enormous consequences which that involves." America's "weight added to that of the Allies would certainly crush the great central empires," asserted the editors, which meant that the Allies would then be in a position to dictate whatever peace terms they wanted. At home, animosity toward German Americans, already noticeable to the editors in May 1915, would undoubtedly increase. "What is intolerance today would become persecution once war was declared," they feared. Democratic and constitutional norms would break under the pressure of war-induced domestic militarism. Meanwhile, aroused out of its usual "pacific" character, Americans would become "the most ruthless antagonists" toward Germany. A normally peaceful America would seek "to destroy its enemy completely," thus prolonging the war, reinforcing the Allied desire to dictate a peace according to the logic of balance-of-power politics, and ruining whatever chances existed for reforming the international system.[3]

The United States, then, faced a thorny dilemma. How could it reconcile a pro-Allied foreign policy with achieving the goal of international reform? Following Germany's attack on the *Lusitania,* the *New Republic* answered this question by urging that the United States frame whatever action it took against Berlin as "the placing of civilized sanctions behind international law." This could be done by reaching a "full and frank understanding with Great Britain" regarding that country's political aims in the war. In exchange for London's renunciation of a policy "which tended to convert the Quadruple Entente into a permanent conspiracy against the Central Powers" and its agreement to support a league of nations, the United States would overtly step up its naval and economic support for Britain's war effort against Germany. With an agreement securing Britain's support for nonvindictive peace terms and collective security, it was more likely that the Germans might still be won over to the cause of international reform, reasoned the editors, regardless of America's alignment against them.[4]

Similarly, during the *Sussex* crisis, the editors argued that the United States should respond to Germany's U-boat policy according to the principle, central to collective security theory, that neutrality in the face of any aggressor's violating international law was impossible. The administration should brand Germany an aggressor and announce "that we shall not only break off negotiations but aid her enemies until she agrees to abandon submarine warfare against commerce, until she agrees to evacuate Belgium, France, and Serbia, to indemnify Belgium, and to accept the principle that in the future all nations shall use their resources against the Power which refuses to submit its quarrel to international inquiry." Once the Germans submitted to this program, the United States would agree "to resume intercourse, and not furnish special aid to [Germany's] enemies." The United States would also help in maintaining European security and insist on equal treatment for Germany in international commerce.[5]

For the editors, this plan represented "a way of making the interests of America coincident with the interests of mankind." The United States would be taking action against Germany, probably in the guise of formally increasing material aid to the Allies and cooperating with their blockade. But it would avoid a "full-fledged partnership" with the Entente. It would maintain its freedom of action and withdraw its increased assistance to the Allies once Germany agreed to Wilsonian peace terms and promised to participate in a collective security regime. Hopefully Germany would embrace Wilson because it would see that it no longer had any hope of winning the war and because the president was acting not to assist the Allies in crushing the Reich but to attain a peace settlement consistent with international reform. The Allies, meanwhile, would realize that America had not given them a blank check with which to destroy the Reich; if they attempted to do so after Germany agreed to Wilson's peace program, Wilson would cut back on American assistance to them. This gave the Allies a strong incentive to agree to the president's peace terms too.[6]

Greater American military preparedness was a necessary component of the *New Republic's* diplomatic strategy. In part, the editors wanted military expansion because they thought that America was unable to defend the Monroe Doctrine and the nation's territorial integrity with its existing forces. They also saw moderate defense increases as a way to advance the Progressive ethos of substituting "a conscious social control for accident and confusion" in domestic policymaking. Finally, as noted in Chapter 3, the *New Republic* thought that America's preparedness would give a collective security organization the power it needed to deter war.[7]

Mostly, however, the editors endorsed preparedness because they wanted the means to intimidate Germany and Britain into accepting Wilson's peace program. "The President's only chance of receiving any comprehension from Germany," the editors argued in the aftermath of the *Lusitania* attack, "is by a dramatic threat." The administration needed to demand that Germany change its behavior or else the United States would mobilize its military and economic resources in favor of the Allies. Preparedness legislation gave credibility to such a threat. Even Wilson's relatively modest preparedness plan, the *New Republic* asserted in early 1916, "strengthened his . . . hand in his negotiations with the German government."[8]

At the same time, naval expansion implicitly threatened the British with a naval arms race if they refused to moderate their war aims against the Germans. The editors, indeed, worried that Congress would get carried away with naval building and enact a program aiming to overtake Britain's superiority, a course they believed would provoke Britain into a naval buildup of its own. Still, the editors recognized—and endorsed—the message the naval preparedness debate sent to the British. If Britain and the United States failed to reach an understanding on peace terms, they warned, the two countries "may be forced into the ruinous expense and suicidal folly of a competition in naval armament." Risky though it would be, America would compete against Britain if it had to. If Britain pursued power politics in Europe, the editors predicted, the United States would adopt a policy of "armed isolation" and, they implied, try to outbuild the British navy. Faced with this threat, the British would presumably be more likely to abandon their quest for a decisive victory over the Germans.[9]

In combination with the president's preparedness program, Wilson's conditional endorsement of a peace league also made plain the stakes the *New Republic* believed were at issue in the war. America was "potentially . . . the most powerful nation on earth" and was building itself into "a great military and naval Power." Its armed strength could be used in two ways. It could use it "to seek security in isolation," which would probably provoke an arms race between America and Europe. Alternatively, it could use its power to "defend an organization of mankind," which would provide security for all nations. Clearly the latter course was preferable for everyone, belligerents and America alike. But the United States would only choose it if all of the belligerents rejected balance-of-power politics in favor of a "peace without victory." If this demand had been ambiguous earlier in Wilson's diplomacy, it came into focus with the president's official endorsement of a peace league, as far as the editors were concerned.[10]

With the president's approach to the war now more clearly in line with their own, the editors enthusiastically supported Wilson's mediation efforts and believed he had some chance of success. "Our offer to join in a guaranty of the world's peace opens up the possibility of a quick and moderate peace," they predicted in June 1916. "To Germany it means security in return for the abandonment of aggression"—a deal the German people could hardly refuse, unless they were "incapable of learning anything." "It gives to the liberals of Europe a practical thing to work with" as well. Now liberals could say to their governments, "You tell us we must fight till the enemy is crushed, or there is no safety for our children. But to crush the enemy is to come near to crushing ourselves . . . here is a chance to organize security before we are shattered, and to guarantee that security with the untouched vigor of the richest people on earth. That is a better defense than anything you promise us." Wilson's December 1916 request that the belligerents state their peace terms, indeed, would allow liberals in Europe to triumph over their "tory" opponents, hoped the editors. Together with his offer of collective security, Wilson's call for war aims struck "a fatal blow at the ascendancy of the European reactionaries. Because of it the moderates will make peace."[11]

If Croly, Lippmann, and Weyl believed that they and the president had found a formula for reconciling support for the Allies with achieving an end to power politics, most of the leaders of the League to Enforce Peace addressed this key issue in a different manner. Relative to Wilson and the others, conservatives such as Marburg and Taft harbored less anxiety about how the Allies might exploit a decisive military defeat of Germany and were more doubtful that an autocratic Reich could be a trusted member of a collective security league. Marburg in particular concluded that international reform could only be achieved if a decisive defeat of Germany triggered a democratic revolution in that country. Taft, along with most of the rest of the LEP's leadership, preferred not to bet the viability of reform on internal developments in the Reich, however. Thus, the LEP officially envisioned a peace league open to all nations, regardless of their internal makeup. Nevertheless, Taft and most of his colleagues sympathized quite strongly with Marburg's line of argument, and they certainly wanted the Allies to inflict a decisive defeat upon the Reich.[12]

From Marburg's thinking it followed that the Allies were, in effect, already a league to enforce peace. If the United States truly cared about "decency in international conduct and . . . fair play and common justice," if it wanted to advance toward the goal of collective security in the most direct way possible, it needed "to act now as if the league were already in existence and to help discipline the lawbreaker." Benevolent neutrality toward the Allies did not go far enough in this direction, as far as Marburg was concerned. The United States had to intervene in the war militarily and throw in "its whole strength with the Allies." Intervention would shorten the war, Marburg maintained; it would hasten the day of Germany's defeat and internal democratization. It would also enhance the credibility of collective security because it would demonstrate America's commitment to act in defense of international agreements. Merely talking about a peace league could not show America's will to enforce collective security, "but here," with Germany's attack on Belgium, "is an opportunity to put our theory into practice." With the United States in the war against Germany, actively assisting others in speedily crushing an aggressor, "any league of peace proposed thereafter would then be regarded by the world as a much more real thing," which made it much more likely that the Allies would embrace it.[13]

Just as was the case with Marburg's view of the importance of German democratization to a league, most of the LEP's leaders inclined toward this argument without fully supporting it. Taft, for example, wanted to break relations with Germany after the *Lusitania* attack, fully aware that such an act might lead to war. "It may be that the attitude of Germany will ultimately require us, in defense of our honor and our interests," he advised Wilson, "to join the Allies and punish the ruthless spirit in her conduct of war which breaks every accepted law of war and every principle of international justice to neutrals." Taft also called for stepping up preparedness to show that America was ready "to insist upon our rights" and to defend itself "against invasion by any belligerent power." Indeed, by mid-1916, Taft decided that Wilson's policy on the submarine issue had "exposed this country to the charge of weakness and vacillation." On the other hand, Taft saw war as "a dreadful thing" and wanted to avoid it, and he, along with other LEP officials, remained concerned that too close an association with the Allies would alienate Germany from the whole project of international reform. Consequently, the LEP took no official stance on either intervening in the war or mediating an end to it. Essentially, the organization decided not to criticize Wilson's strategy for attaining a league while, at the same time, doubting it would work.[14]

In many ways, the Atlanticists' assessment of Wilson's diplomacy was not much different from Marburg's and Taft's. Although they had doubts about collective security theory and more faith than other leaders that power politics could maintain peace, Atlanticists did not attack the president for failing to balance America's power against the threat of German hegemony in Europe. Instead, they chiefly accused Wilson of endangering America's security by undermining its prestige and its national character. Wilson's approach to the war, they argued, was ruining the diplomatic credibility the United States needed to deter outside attacks, including attacks by Germany, and to pursue the goal of international reform—a goal they suggested they supported.

The president's decision to remain silent in the wake of Germany's rampage through Belgium was a central charge in this indictment, especially for Theodore Roosevelt. The Reich's actions, Roosevelt asserted, violated treaties, including the Hague conventions of 1899 and 1907 signed by the United States and the European powers, protecting civilian populations and guaranteeing Belgium's neutrality. Technically, it might be argued that the conventions did not obligate the United States to protest or act in some way against a violation of the agreements, although Roosevelt doubted this was the case. But by doing nothing in the face of Germany's obvious offenses against the treaties, the administration had for all practical purposes abandoned agreements ratified by the U.S. government. It had shown "bad faith" and acquiesced "in a wrong which we had solemnly undertaken to oppose."[15]

This behavior had grave consequences for American security. It conveyed weakness and "cowardice" to other powers, argued Roosevelt, and led them to view the United States with "contempt." In opting for "cold-blooded and timid indifference" toward "the gravest kind of international wrongdoing," Wilson had alienated potential friends and encouraged potential enemies. The president's course also undercut the credibility of international law, the incorporation of mankind's "progress of civilization" that Roosevelt and other Atlanticists believed contributed to world peace. By failing to protest against Germany's invasion of Belgium, Wilson brought the entire structure of international laws and treaties into disrepute and made it "an object of derision to aggressive nations." In this context, the notion of establishing some new kind of Hague treaty or peace league was not very believable, even though Roosevelt himself thought that creating one would enhance international security and the safety of the United States. "It is not merely ridiculous," Roosevelt scolded future LEP member Andrew Dickson White in November 1914, "it is wicked hypocrisy for us ever to talk of entering into another Hague convention unless we in good faith strive to secure the carrying out of the Hague conventions into which we have already entered."[16]

Indeed, to the degree that Wilson actually did take sides in the war, he appeared to seek the favor of the lawbreaker—Germany—and to hamper the cause of the defenders of the Hague conventions—the Allies. "We are not to protest when Belgium's rights are trampled under foot by the Germans," seethed Roosevelt in early 1915, "but are to make our first protest when England interferes with our sending copper to Germany to be used against the English and the Belgians." Britain's maritime system might not be entirely legal, Roosevelt conceded, but the administration forfeited whatever right it had to protest it when Wilson remained silent on Belgium. Given that silence, complaining about Britain's treatment of American shipping was "ignoble" and foolish, because all it did was alienate the side fighting for "the interests of civilization" in the war. The same could be said for Wilson's proposed ship purchase bill, which, Atlanticists argued, would provide Germany with much-needed cash and provoke the British into sinking or capturing the ships. Thus, if enacted, Wilson's proposal "would bring us very close to war not only with England alone, but with all her allies," an "unspeakable calamity" from the standpoint of Atlanticists.[17]

Roosevelt and Lodge specifically rejected the argument that Wilson's policies helped to position him as a mediator between the belligerents. "This is an idea which appeals to the thoughtless," jeered Roosevelt, "for it gratifies our desire to keep out of trouble and also our vanity by the hope that we shall do great things with small difficulty." Of course, if the war completely deadlocked, the Europeans might conceivably turn to Wilson as a mediator. But he would preside over the peace conference as a mere figurehead, with no influence over the peace settlement. Having stayed neutral in the face of Germany's violations of the Hague conventions, he could expect nothing more. "Under such conditions we shall be treated as we deserve to be treated," Roosevelt lectured, "as a nation of people who mean well feebly, whose words are not backed by deeds." The president's approach to the belligerents, Lodge concurred, amounted to "furtive meddling." It did not "place him in a very favorable light in the eyes of the world," Lodge confided to Roosevelt in January 1915, "nor do I think it will help Wilson in his desire to be the great pacificator and settle the war in Europe, for I am sure that by this time both sides heartily dislike him."[18]

The president's response to Germany's submarine warfare only intensified the Atlanticists' alarm over his policies. They watched in disbelief as Wilson warned Germany he would hold it to "a strict accountability" for the acts of its submarines and then, as Root put it, did "nothing" when German U-boats killed Americans. No policy could be more destructive of the credibility America depended upon for its security. Wilson's failure to respond to Germany's initial attacks upon the *Falaba* and the *Gulflight* simply encouraged it to continue its murderous behavior. The "men, women and children of the *Lusitania*," Roosevelt mourned, "were massacred because the German government believed that the Wilson administration did not intend to back up its words with deeds." The president's failure to take any action against Germany after the *Lusitania* attack, his statement about being "too proud to fight," and leaks from his administration indicating that his protests over the U-boat war were for domestic consumption, charged Atlanticists, all combined to invite still more German aggression against the United States, including more submarine attacks and subversive activities by its diplomats in America. The Germans, Root thought, "had learned to believe that, no matter how shocked the American Government might be, its resolution would expend itself in words. They had learned to believe that it was safe to kill Americans." Far from preserving America's safety, Wilson's "ultimatums that fail to ultimate" opened the nation up to attack. "We have not been following the path of peace," Root warned in February 1916. "We have been blindly stumbling along the road that continued will lead to inevitable war."[19]

The negative consequences of Wilson's diplomacy were exacerbated by his "entirely ineffective" military policy. "When our Government failed to make any provision whatever for defending its rights in case they should be trampled on," Root explained in early 1916, "it lost the power which a belief in its readiness and will to maintain its rights would have given to its diplomatic representations." It was no wonder, then, that Wilson's initial warnings to Germany to keep its submarine campaign within legal bounds had no effect. At the same time, America's lack of military preparedness made it futile for Roosevelt to promote his peace league, as his plan involved a pledge to make war on behalf of others. "It would be ludicrous to make such a promise until we have shown that we are willing to undertake defensive war on behalf of ourselves." Wilson's "sham-preparedness program" obviously failed to meet that standard, which meant that the United States would only discredit itself if it spoke up for a league now.[20]

Atlanticist criticisms of the president reached a climax in late 1916 and early 1917, as Wilson urged the belligerents to state their peace terms and move toward ending the war. "Peace without victory is the natural ideal of the man who is too proud to fight," scorned Roosevelt. The president was trying to rob the Allies of the decisive victory they were probably going to attain in the war, protested Atlanticists; Wilson asked "the world to accept a Copperhead peace of dishonor, a peace without victory for the right, a peace designed to let wrong triumph." Whatever his motives, neither group of belligerents wanted to follow the president's lead. By interjecting himself into their conflict, Lodge argued, Wilson risked alienating both sides—an unwise and dangerous policy. Finally, Wilson included a peace league and freedom of the seas as integral parts of a reformed world but yet again failed to do anything to oppose Germany's actions in Belgium and at sea. It was preposterous for Wilson "to mouth about standing for righteousness in the nebulous future" while doing nothing about it in the present. Wilson's "peace without victory" speech simply made America "an object of derision," an incredible nation whose threats and promises—the currency of its security—were worthless.[21]

Atlanticists did more than simply criticize the president, of course. They also put forward their own recommendations for how the United States should deal with the war. Most obviously, the day the war started Wilson should have stepped up America's military preparedness along the lines proposed by the Atlanticists. This would have put the United States in a position "such that every one knew our words would be made good by our deeds." Had Atlanticists been in power, they also would have officially condemned Germany's invasion of Belgium and responded instantly to Germany's initial submarine attacks. Specifically, they would have immediately protested against Germany's actions and perhaps seized German ships interned in American ports. Following the attack on the *Lusitania*, Roosevelt urged Wilson to seek "satisfaction" from Germany by "taking possession of all the interned German ships," forbidding all commerce with the Reich, and encouraging trade with the Entente. This stance, Roosevelt believed, would probably have resulted in war between the United States and Germany. But whether it did or not, such a course was necessary to maintain the diplomatic prestige Roosevelt considered vital to American security. Lodge and Root concurred. The latter condemned Wilson's "inaction" after the *Lusitania* sinking and later recalled that the United States should have entered the war as a result of the incident; the former favored positions similar to Roosevelt's. Atlanticists, in sum, preferred riskier steps than Wilson in response to Germany's U-boat attacks—steps that could easily lead to U.S. intervention into the war on the side of the Entente.[22]

Significantly, Atlanticists did not explain their recommended policies as a pro-Entente course, however. Clearly, their case against the president and their program of action against Germany implied that it was in America's interest for the Reich to lose the war. But they did not publicly describe this outcome as they did in private, as necessary to protect the Monroe Doctrine and America itself from attack. Instead, they criticized Wilson's approach to the war chiefly because of its negative impact on U.S. credibility, international law, prospects for a Rooseveltian peace league, and the moral character of the American people. As Lodge himself noted, he and Roosevelt were "very careful not to appear as championing one side against the other but have stood on the broad ground of Americanism." The consequences they identified with Wilson's policies were related to American security, of course, as they undermined America's ability to deter potential enemies and to contribute to the creation of a new system of international politics. But that was not exactly the same thing as charging the president with failing to ensure the defeat of a state with the potential power to threaten American supremacy in the Western Hemisphere.[23]

Atlanticists tended to avoid discussing the implications of German hegemony in Europe in part because they, along with virtually all other policy advocates, expected the Allies to win the war. Given this prevailing view, it made sense for Atlanticists to link their preferred policies to broad security concerns rather than to the threat of a German victory. The need to preserve U.S. credibility and prestige was a permanent interest that did not diminish because one side or the other might win the war. Even if the Allies prevailed, the need for American preparedness and for backing up words with deeds would still exist. If they had tied their military and foreign policy only to a hypothetical threat from a hegemonic Germany, in contrast, Atlanticists might have found their program lacking a rationale once Germany lost.[24]

Accusing Wilson of failing to guard America against the threat of German hegemony might backfire in another way. Even as he pinned his arguments for preparedness and "action" against Germany to general interests such as diplomatic credibility, Roosevelt saw that public opinion associated his recommendations with intervention in the war—something most Americans did not want to do. Demoralized by Wilson's "lofty" excuses for "nonaction," less than 5 percent of the public, in Roosevelt's estimation, agreed with his willingness to confront Germany more forcefully than the administration. Most people, he thought, saw him as "a truculent and bloodthirsty person" bent on war. Indeed, Roosevelt was so sensitive of the nation's overwhelming endorsement of neutrality that he at first even hesitated to call for Wilson to protest Germany's invasion of Belgium. "To make a verbal protest, unbacked by action, would be merely mischievous," he argued in October 1914. To be sure, he changed his mind on this point; by early November 1914 he decided that the cost to the credibility of the United States and international law from the administration's policy was too high to remain quiet about the issue. The fact that he waited at all, though, is revealing of the anti-interventionist environment with which Atlanticists had to contend.[25]

Ironically, pacifists probably at times felt almost as frustrated as the Atlanticists, as they watched Wilson adopt an approach to the belligerents they believed would imperil both America's safety and the cause of international reform. Pacifists, it will be recalled, identified American security with avoiding a war they considered irrelevant to American interests. Most of them also wanted to reform international politics on the basis of a noncoercive peace league, greater democratic control of foreign policy, armament limitation, and anti-imperialism. They desired this goal on moralistic rather than national security grounds, however. Finally, pacifists believed that a peace based on a "draw"—a peace designed to reestablish the status quo antebellum and to impress on the belligerents the futility of war—was the best basis for a reformed world free from power politics.[26]

Rigid neutrality was the most effective way to accomplish these objectives. By definition, neutrality kept the United States out of the war, thus serving America's primary security interest. It also set up American mediation of the conflict, and the sooner the war ended, the sooner risk of American involvement in it would disappear. Pacifists further believed that a mediated end to the war offered the best hope of achieving a peace based on the status quo antebellum. "If our nation is to remain neutral it must be indifferent as to the results of the war," Bryan reasoned; it had to "remain the sincere friend of ALL THE BELLIGERENTS, and thus become not only mediator but their accepted advisor in laying the foundation of a peace that shall endure."[27]

Pacifists disagreed with each other about the specific components of a proper neutrality policy, however. Bryan's views represented the dominant position, as well as the ambiguities involved with defining "neutrality." As best he could, Bryan strove to be neutral in spirit and according to international law and to resolve disputes between the United States and the belligerents peacefully, if necessary by sacrificing America's legal rights. Thus, three days after the war started, Bryan opposed any administration endorsement of American banks' lending money to the belligerents. While there was no "legal objection" to such loans, Bryan thought they would be inconsistent with Wilson's declared policy of neutrality and counter to the goal of hastening an end to the war. "I know of nothing that would do more to prevent war than an international agreement that neutral nations would not loan to belligerents," Bryan told Wilson. If loans were made to the various belligerents, "our citizens would be divided into groups," Bryan feared, and "money could not be furnished without expressions of sympathy" or without the development of a financial interest in the success of the combatants receiving the loan. Financial concerns lending the money would also use the press to promote their preferred belligerents, resulting in "our newspapers violently arrayed on one side or other, each paper supporting a financial group and pecuniary interest." These developments "would make it all the more difficult for us to maintain neutrality," Bryan predicted, "as our action on various questions that would arise would affect one side or the other and powerful financial interests would be thrown into the balance."[28]

In late September 1914, Bryan shifted his stance on this issue and decided that bank credits to belligerent governments were consistent with American neutrality. The French ambassador to the United States, Jean Jules Jusserand, convinced him that the loan ban was unfairly hurting the Allies—that it was unneutral in practice whatever its intention. Determined not to act in ways prejudicial to one side or the other and aware that private loans to belligerents were not unneutral under international law, Bryan agreed. In accord with his earlier thinking on loans, however, he continued to oppose the sale of belligerent government bonds to the American public. Private bank credit extended to the belligerents did not involve campaigns to arouse the public; loans offered for "popular subscription," in contrast, "would be taken up chiefly by those who are in sympathy with the belligerent seeking the loan." This distinction was meaningful to Bryan, easing his decision to accommodate Allied complaints about his loan policy.[29]

Significantly, when the administration dropped its disapproval of belligerent bond sales to the public in late 1915, Bryan, no longer Wilson's secretary of state, opposed the change. Regardless of their legality under international law, such loans impaired America's neutrality, Bryan argued, by creating an American financial interest in the success of one side in the war. For him, the sale of belligerent war bonds violated the spirit of neutrality—and that mattered more than legal technicalities.[30]

For similar reasons, Bryan recommended that the administration remain silent regarding Germany's invasion of and behavior in Belgium. It would be difficult to investigate the charges against the Reich, Bryan observed, "without danger of subjecting ourselves to severe criticism from the governments whose acts were investigated." Bryan also agreed with Lansing that Germany's violation of Belgium "does not affect American rights or interests, but those of the Belgians." The United States therefore had no right to protest it under the Hague conventions. Bryan saw no reason to judge Germany's motives either, given, as Lansing asserted, "it cannot be denied that national safety may justify a nation in violating its solemn pledges." Regardless of the legal and moral issues involved with the German attack on Belgium, Bryan was anxious to "avoid anything that can possibly bring us into collision with the belligerent powers." This factor, more than any other, caused Bryan to shy away from a protest against Germany's actions.[31]

Bryan's desire to remain impartial and avoid trouble with the belligerents informed his approach to American arms exports as well. Early on in the war, he agreed with State Department experts that the administration could not ban arms sales to the belligerents. According to the State Department, except in cases involving "civil strife" in Latin America, the United States had never imposed an arms embargo against belligerent states, nor had the Europeans. Germany itself formally acknowledged the legality of arms sales and, in any case, the executive branch had no authority to prevent them. Furthermore, in Bryan's opinion, congressional efforts to enact an arms embargo were motivated by a desire to help the Germans and hurt the Allies; their "*purpose*," Bryan stressed, " . . . is plainly to assist one party at the expense of the other." For all of these reasons, "any interference with the right of belligerents to buy arms here would be construed as an unneutral act." As such, Bryan opposed an arms embargo and worked hard to fend off resolutions in Congress to impose one.[32]

When it came to dealing with Britain's maritime system, Bryan agreed with Wilson's early policy of avoiding confrontations with London. He did so not out of any strategic calculation concerning America's interest in frustrating Germany's aims in the war, but because he saw threat making as an ineffective way to preserve a nation's rights; "appeals to friendship," in Bryan's view, worked better. The weak protest note of 26 December 1914 was consistent with this philosophy. It was a way to alert the British to their "mistake" in "unnecessarily arousing resentment among those interested in neutral commerce." It was precisely the lack of a threatening tone in the note that appealed to Bryan. "I think that it is the part of friendship to bring this matter to the attention of Great Britain," he advised Wilson, "in such a way as to lead to a careful consideration of the whole matter."[33]

As of early 1915, Bryan was basically satisfied with the administration's neutrality policy. He was concerned about domestic critics who charged Wilson with "partiality" toward the Allies, but overall he thought that their arguments were off base. He knew that British leaders felt that the United States was biased toward the Central Powers, because of the administration's silence on Belgium and its protests against the blockade, among other issues. Although he worried that the administration was in a "delicate position," as its actions could easily "irritate" either "our own people" or Britain, the criticism from both sides probably also reassured Bryan that Wilson was in fact steering a middle course between the belligerents. He was pleased as well that Wilson dealt with the frictions that developed with Britain with patient negotiations rather than confrontation—the tactic he saw as the surest way to maintain America's peace. Convinced that he and Wilson were essentially in agreement about how to deal with the war, Bryan therefore signed off on a detailed public defense of the administration's neutrality policy prepared by Lansing in late January.[34]

The president's initial response to Germany's submarine warfare campaign and to the intensification of Britain's blockade in March also met with Bryan's approval. Probably because it employed less forceful language than its original draft and was balanced by a protest note to the British against their use of the American flag to disguise their ships in the war zone, Bryan endorsed Wilson's "strict accountability" warning to Germany, sent on 10 February. Still, he worried that the war was entering a new and more dangerous stage, because of both the submarine announcement and what Bryan considered Britain's illegal attempt to starve Germany's civilian population into submission. To defuse the situation, Wilson and Bryan tried to convince Britain to "withdraw her objection to food entering Germany . . . in return for the withdrawal of the German order in regard to the war zone." This arrangement, Bryan hoped, would "clear the admosphere [sic]" and avert a U.S. confrontation with either belligerent. It would also emphasize America's neutrality because it essentially equated Germany's submarine warfare with Britain's food blockade. After this effort failed, Bryan supported the dispatch of a mild protest against the blockade, again hoping, as with the December protest, to assert U.S. rights but only "in the most friendly spirit." Finally, Bryan had little enthusiasm for confronting Germany over the submarine attack that killed an American in late March, as he feared a strong protest would look unneutral given the administration's relative inaction concerning Britain's blockade. When Wilson decided not to act on the incident, the secretary was no doubt relieved.[35]

The president's about-face after the sinking of the *Lusitania,* in contrast, alarmed and disturbed Bryan. By sending a threatening note to Berlin, Wilson revealed a strong bias in favor of the Entente. The Allies would surely applaud the note, Bryan wrote the president, "and the more they applaud the more Germany will be embittered because we unsparingly denounce the retaliatory methods employed by her without condemning the announced purpose of the allies to starve the non-combatants of Germany" and to use passenger liners to transport munitions. Bryan also noted Wilson's continued passivity concerning Britain's misuse of the American flag and its "unwarranted interference with our trade with neutral nations." Wilson's confrontation with Germany, he argued, would encourage London "not to make any concessions at all" on these issues. The administration's policies, Bryan implied—and stated bluntly in a cabinet meeting on 1 June—were not neutral. They were "pro-Ally." A firm stance toward Germany would simply highlight this fact. "Germany," warned Bryan, "can not but construe the strong statement of the case against her, coupled with silence as to the unjustifiable action of the allies, as partiality toward the latter."[36]

Wilson's demands, moreover, spoke the language of power politics, not peace. There were two ways to conduct international relations as far as Bryan was concerned: the "old system" of "force" that had "set the world at war" and a "new system" of "persuasion" that had yet to be fully practiced. "Force speaks with firmness and acts through the ultimatum," Bryan preached. "Persuasion employs argument, courts investigation and depends upon negotiation." As he interpreted Wilson's posture toward Germany, "It conforms to the standards of the old system rather than to the rules of the new." The president was practicing European-style politics, charged the *Commoner,* and he would have as much success in gaining his ends peacefully as the Europeans had had in July 1914.[37]

As an alternative to Wilson's policy of confrontation, Bryan recommended a reassertion of American impartiality toward the belligerents and unilateral American steps to de-escalate the crisis. As it protested Germany's submarine warfare, the administration should simultaneously renew its protest against Britain's maritime system. It should also signal Germany its willingness to have the dispute between the two nations investigated by an international commission for up to a year, as called for in the cooling-off treaties Bryan negotiated with several countries prior to the war. Finally, Bryan urged the administration to warn American citizens not to travel in the war zone on belligerent ships and to refuse port clearance to American passenger ships carrying munitions.[38]

When Wilson rejected these proposals in early June 1915, Bryan resigned as secretary of state. He then publicly advocated his program and added more recommendations to it. Most prominently, in early 1916, he lobbied for what became known as the McLemore-Gore resolutions. The ones introduced by Sen. T. P. Gore essentially prohibited American citizens from traveling on belligerent ships and stopped them from traveling on any vessel carrying war contraband; the resolution proposed by Rep. Jefferson McLemore withdrew the protection of the U.S. government from American citizens traveling on armed belligerent ships. In addition, Bryan now made it clear that in the event that a yearlong investigation of the submarine dispute between Germany and the United States failed to produce a peaceful settlement, the United States should postpone any action on the issue until after the war in Europe was over. If the United States then decided upon armed conflict with Germany, Bryan argued, at least "it would then be our own war" and not one bound up with that of the Allies. "God forbid that we shall ever tie ourselves to the quarrels, rivalries and ambitions of the nations of Europe," Bryan declared.[39]

To Bryan, his diplomatic agenda, not Wilson's, kept America truly neutral and thus offered the best hope of positioning the United States for mediation and for achieving international reform. The protest against Britain's blockade would "show Germany that we are defending our rights from aggression from both sides." Seeing America's impartiality and desire to treat both sides equally, Germany would be less likely to dismiss Wilson's protest and more inclined to have confidence in

the president as a peacemaker. Bryan viewed his proposals to submit the submarine dispute to an investigation and to restrict American travel in the war zone
in a similar light. This course, he argued, would "not only be likely to protect the
lives of some Americans and thus lessen the chances of another calamity, but
would have its effect upon the tone of the German reply and might point the
way to an understanding." The Reich, moreover, had accepted the principle of
investigation at the heart of Bryan's cooling-off treaties. Those treaties, signed by
the United States and thirty other nations by 1915, "commit us to the doctrine of
investigation *in all cases*," Bryan stressed to Wilson. The president had "no valid
excuse for not resorting to the plan." By employing it, Wilson could "emphasize
[its] value" and perhaps even "exert a profound influence upon the making of the
treaty between belligerent nations at the end of the war."[40]

Unlike Wilson, Bryan did not see U.S. diplomatic credibility riding upon a
willingness to confront Germany. The Reich's public warning to travelers that any
ship flying the British flag in the war zone might be attacked was not directed to
America, Bryan argued; it was not "a matter of offense" in his view. On the contrary, Bryan thought it "evidence of a friendly desire to evade anything that might
raise a question between Germany and the United States." The attack on the *Lusitania* did not alter Bryan's opinion. Nor did he believe Britain's behavior showed
hostility toward America. "Not one of these belligerent nations desires war with
the United States," Bryan asserted. Their actions were not aimed at intimidat-
ing the United States or influencing its policies. Rather, the belligerents were "so
mad at each other that, in their fight against each other, they forget that there is
anybody else in the world. . . . It is not intentional wrong that they do to us; it is
unintentional wrong." Even in the midst of the *Lusitania* crisis, Bryan maintained,
Germany's "tone" remained "friendly"; the Reich "is looking for a way out," Bryan
told Wilson on 3 June. Its apparent willingness to investigate various submarine
incidents indicated its desire to back away from a confrontation. All the United
States had to do was reciprocate, with Bryan's recommended actions, and a peaceful settlement of the controversy was certain. In short, the United States faced no
challenge to its security from Germany and had nothing to gain by provoking it
with ultimatums.[41]

Most other leading pacifists shared Bryan's general approach to neutrality issues and his uneasiness with Wilson's alignment of the United States with Britain.
"How long," Robert La Follette wondered in September 1915, "can we maintain a
semblance of real neutrality while we are supplying the Allies with munitions of
war and the money to prosecute war?" Taking Bryan's desire to avoid confrontations with the belligerents to its logical end, La Follette and most of his supporters
in the Senate wanted to embargo munitions exports, and La Follette specifically
raised the possibility of banning all trade with the combatants if necessary to avoid
war. Concerned about Wilson's pro-Allied bias, Edward Devine in the *Survey* also

called for an arms embargo, as did Irish and German American working-class organizations that agreed with much of the outlook on national security affairs held by the WPP and the AUAM. The latter two groups did not take a stand on an arms embargo, although the editors of the *Public,* who usually echoed their views, opposed one in part for the same reasons as Bryan. Whether an embargo occurred or not, however, most pacifists were attracted to Bryan's cooling-off principle as a way to deal with international disputes and to his proposals to restrict American travel in the war zone.[42]

The editors of the *Nation* chose a different tack. More so than other pacifists, the *Nation* supported Wilson's stance toward the belligerents, arguing that it was in fact genuinely neutral. Since both arms sales and loans to the belligerents were legal under international law, the *Nation* supported them as consistent with neutrality. In the journal's view, Britain's March 1915 intensification of its maritime system amounted to a declaration of a formal blockade, which rendered it legal too. Whatever friction remained between the United States and Britain over America's trade with neutral ports was minor and technical, and Wilson's mild protests were the appropriate way to deal with it. Germany's violations of the laws of cruiser warfare, in contrast, were a policy of "piracy" and "wickedness." Germany was trampling on "the law of nations and the law of God." Wilson had no choice, in the interest of upholding those laws, but to confront Germany in the manner he did. International law and the rights of humanity were "of more consequence than the changing aspects of the war," declared the *Nation,* because they offered hope of "a better world" once the war was over. "Indeed," the editors insisted, "it is the moral aspect of the entire stand of our Government in the controversy with Germany which overshadows every other."[43]

In common with other pacifists, however, the *Nation* opposed any military buildup to support what it viewed as a stand for moral ideals. Pacifists thought that any significant expansion of America's existing military establishment would lead to militarism at home and would be inconsistent with the goal of reforming the international system. When it came to America's diplomacy with the belligerents, they believed preparedness would destroy U.S. chances for mediating an end to the war. Wilson had succeeded in facing down Germany over the submarine issue, claimed the *Nation* in late 1915, solely by wielding "the moral power of the United States." Embracing preparedness would compromise that moral authority and ruin America's ability to speak for peace. As the editors argued in late 1914, when they first rejected calls for increases in America's armed forces, "how ineffective—how hypocritical—would be our appeal for peace, our offer of good services, . . . if we were to make that appeal fresh from new concessions to the armament ring." Indeed, worried Crystal Eastman of the AUAM in July 1915, increasing America's military preparedness "at a critical time like this, is most obviously playing with fire—it is inviting war upon us."[44]

Pacifists put forward their own version of preparedness as an alternative to Wilson's. If the president really wanted to support his diplomacy with enhanced national strength and avoid war too, he would focus on domestic social reform, not on a military buildup. "A nation composed of a few very rich, and many poor is already rotting at the core," thought Stoughton Cooley: "No amount of munitions, and no degree of enforced military training will save it." The Germans recognized this truth, added Frederic Howe—that was why they developed the most extensive program of social insurance and "state socialism" of any leading power prior to the war. They knew that being "efficient in peace" made them strong, as was demonstrated by their performance in battle. If the president wanted America to be in a "stronger position at home and abroad," he needed to pursue the "real preparedness of economic sanity and justice—not of militarism and aggression."[45]

"Real" preparedness, even if accompanied by a resolution of the submarine crisis with Germany, could not guarantee that America would avoid involvement in the war, however. Only an end to the conflict in Europe could do that. Pacifists therefore wanted Wilson to try to mediate an end to the war as soon as possible, without waiting for either group of belligerents to ask for it. The United States should act alone or, better yet, call for a conference of neutral nations to offer "continuous mediation" of the conflict. This proposal, advocated especially by Jane Addams and the WPP, expressed the pacifist belief that greater democratic control of foreign policy might advance peace. "With the military party in power in each country taking the censorship of the press into their hands," argued Addams, "the whole stream of communication which ordinarily makes for international public opinion in Europe has been stopped." A conference of neutral states, open to "different groups in the belligerent countries who have programs they wish to propose as a basis for negotiations" and to "experts" who would explore the issues involved in the war, would create an irresistible momentum for peace talks. It would "release the pent up public opinion" for peace among both neutrals and "the people of the belligerents." "Struggling liberal groups within the warring countries" would especially welcome a neutrals conference, as its recommendations would give them "an objective towards which to direct their governments." Last, a neutrals conference could also accelerate planning for international reform and present the belligerents with "an alternative to the . . . militaristic method of settling the dispute."[46]

The pacifists' dismay with Wilson's course, as well as their faith that the majority of Americans agreed with their views, led them to embrace various proposals to require a public referendum before war could be declared. Bryan called for such a measure soon after his resignation as secretary of state, and La Follette formally introduced his own version of it in the Senate in April 1916, during the *Sussex* crisis with Germany. Under his proposal, in the event that the United States broke diplomatic relations with another power, the Census Bureau would conduct an advisory referendum on the issue of war. The bill died in committee, but the general principle of a war referendum continued to appeal to pacifists as a way to exert democratic control over Wilson's foreign policy.[47]

The pacifists' willingness to endorse a measure as radical as the war referendum revealed the depth of their concern about Wilson's policies. Just as they perceived a disturbing similarity between Wilson's vision of collective security and the tactics of power politics, so too did most of them see the president's approach to the belligerents, at least until late 1916, as needlessly risky and provocative. His failure to protest against British and German violations of international law with equal fervor; his willingness to risk war with Germany over the submarine issue; his refusal to pursue "continuous mediation" through a neutrals conference, regardless of British objections; and his preparedness program all pointed to the same conclusion: Wilson's course was not consistent with the cause of international reform. His diplomacy contradicted it by recklessly throwing America's weight onto the Allied side of the scales of a balance of power directed at Germany. As Bryan suggested in noting Wilson's failure to apply the cooling-off principle in the crisis with Germany, Wilson in effect disowned fundamental precepts of international reform. He was embracing the "old system" of force and threat over promoting a new international order based on conciliation.

Liberal internationalists outside the administration, no less than Wilson, had difficulty constructing a plausible answer to the criticisms raised by the pacifists and Atlanticists. The *New Republic*'s strategy was to focus less on conciliating Germany and more on enticing the Allies into a commitment to end power politics. Wilson could do this, the editors argued, by offering to step up U.S. assistance to the Allies on a conditional basis. The United States would openly help their war effort, but only up to the point that Germany agreed to Wilsonian peace terms and a league of nations. If the Allies wanted to keep fighting to attain a peace even more destructive of German power, the United States would cut back on its aid and not join a league, leaving the Allies to deal with postwar security themselves. As the *New Republic* saw it, this program would demonstrate that America's overriding interest was in international reform, not in a continuation of power politics, even as the United States helped the Allies force a German withdrawal from Belgium and Europe.

The *New Republic*'s attempt to resolve the paradox of pursuing power politics to end power politics was no better than Wilson's, however. As the editors themselves observed, the president's existing neutrality policy gave the Allies access to American supplies while facilitating their blockade of Germany. As they repeatedly stated, such a policy made perfect sense given America's interest in preventing a German victory in the war. Why, then, should Britain make any concessions to the United States on peace terms in exchange for a marginal increase in American aid, especially when Wilson's existing policy was driving America toward war with Germany anyway? Croly, Lippmann, and Weyl had no answer to this question. Nor did they address the incredibility of threatening the Allies with a policy of "armed isolation" or the implausibility of Germany's trusting in a pro-Allied America brokering peace terms—problems with their policy that were identical to the ones bedeviling Wilson's.

The route to reform preferred by the League to Enforce Peace was less clear but just as problematic. Marburg believed that autocratic Germany would never genuinely embrace Wilsonian peace terms or international reform; it was pointless to try to conciliate such a brutal and untrustworthy regime. Attempting to do so hurt America's standing with the Entente, moreover, and undercut the credibility of America's commitment to collective security. As Marburg saw it, Wilson's method of reconciling the containment of German power with the goal of ending power politics would not work. The only way to advance reform, he argued, was for the United States to cast its lot with the Allies completely, decisively defeat Germany, and hope that a democratic revolution would then transform the Reich into a fit partner for a peace league.

Tempted though they were to agree with Marburg's analysis, most of the LEP's leadership refused to accept it. If the Reich did not become liberalized upon its defeat, the postwar peace league would not be a collective security organization, but an alliance aimed at the Germans. Power politics would not be reformed but perpetuated. It was more prudent, therefore, to maintain lines of communication with both Berlin and London and to be open to German membership in a league, without stating conditions about it. But at the same time, signaling its sympathy with the Allied goal of decisively defeating the Reich, the LEP did not endorse Wilson's mediation efforts. In the end, then, the LEP awkwardly straddled both Marburg's and Wilson's positions, leaving it without a coherent answer to the problem of how to defeat Germany and yet still involve it in a new world order based on collective security.

Combined with the perceptive criticisms of Wilson's diplomacy offered by pacifists and Atlanticists, the shortcomings of the policy prescriptions advanced by the *New Republic* and the LEP revealed grave weaknesses with the approach of liberal internationalists toward the war. Just as was the case with Wilson, neither the *New Republic* nor the LEP could figure out a viable diplomatic strategy for achieving the objectives bound up with the goal of reforming international politics. They could not do so because those objectives—containing Germany's power, preventing the Allies from crushing the Reich, and convincing the Germans to accept the legitimacy of a new world order based on the defeat of their ambitions—were incompatible with each other. Steps necessary to contain Germany lost the U.S. leverage with the Entente and alienated the Germans; policies designed to win the trust of Germany and threaten the Allies irritated Britain. This dilemma had another dimension too: the more the United States acted in ways consistent with the ideals of a reformed world, the less it could coerce either London or Berlin; conversely, if it behaved in a manner consistent with power politics, it undermined the credibility of international reform. Liberal internationalists could not devise a diplomatic strategy suitable for achieving their objectives, in short, because their objectives were contradictory.

Given the flaws in their diplomacy, as well as the problems with their peace terms and vision of world reform discussed in Chapter 3, one wonders how liberal internationalists managed to dominate the foreign and defense policy debates of 1914–17. Wilson's position as president and leader of the Democratic Party, of course, provides much of the answer. As Arthur Link and others have shown, Wilson was an unusually talented political leader. He was "a virtuoso and a spellbinder" at public speaking "during a period when the American people admired oratory above all other political skills." Within his first eighteen months in office, Wilson also compiled a remarkable legislative record, demonstrating a mastery of legislative and party politics rivaled by few American presidents. He completely dominated his party, as Link notes, to the point that in the later years of his term, he still remained in control of it "even when the country had turned against him and when he insisted upon policies that most Democrats thought were catastrophic." With such a leader as the chief spokesman for their program, and with the levers of the presidency in his hands, liberal internationalists had a decided advantage over their opponents.[48]

The ideas of liberal internationalists stood at the center of policy debates for more important reasons than Wilson's leadership, however. For the most part, their proposals held a commanding position because alternative national security strategies did not appear to be attractive options for the United States. One course, practicing European-style balance-of-power politics, made no sense at all to pacifists and liberal internationalists. They were certain that such a policy would never produce peace or preserve America's democratic way of life over the long term. It would instead make the United States the handmaiden of the Allies and doom it to a future of arms races, war, and militarism. As the Allies would probably prevail over Germany now and in the future, thus allowing America to escape the danger of having to face the Reich alone, there was no compelling reason to ally with them and risk paying the high costs of such a policy.

Atlanticists came the closest to endorsing a policy of preparedness and alliance with the Entente; certainly much of their analysis of international security affairs and of Wilson's diplomacy implied that an active engagement with balance-of-power politics was the most rational security strategy for the United States to adopt. But even they drew back from advocating it. Partly this was because they saw that most American leaders were averse to it. Because they desperately wanted to get America committed to their program of preparedness and because Germany would likely be contained by the Allies in any event, it made no political sense for

Atlanticists to buck the sentiment against balance-of-power politics and call for an alliance with Britain and France.

More significantly, though, Atlanticists themselves had doubts about the efficacy of a balance-of-power national security strategy. Shocked by the outbreak of the war, they began to question their pre-1914 faith that the balance of power and the limited but gradual growth of international law and morality worked together to produce peace. While they continued to call for greater military preparedness as the cornerstone of any national security policy, they also openly suggested that competitive armaments and mutual fears of preemptive attack had played a role in starting the war. At the same time, by calling for the creation of a Rooseveltian league to enforce peace, by suggesting that democratic reform in Germany would add to Europe's stability, and by attacking Wilson for undermining the credibility of international treaties such as the Hague conventions, they revealed a new willingness to emphasize that factors other than the balance of power could promote a more peaceful world. It was not simply domestic political calculations, then, that led them to call for international reform—it was a genuine wavering of confidence in balance-of-power politics as well. Consequently, they did not clearly articulate or defend a balance-of-power national security strategy for America.

Lacking a consistent strategic vision for America, Atlanticists came across in the nation's security debates as partisan militarists. Roosevelt's vitriolic denunciation of his opponents especially contributed to this image. Focusing less on his substantive ideas than his bombastic gibes, other policy advocates responded in kind. Roosevelt, charged Bryan, knew "no kind of glory except that which comes with brutish exultation over feats accomplished by brute force." No other American leader "has ever approached him in love of power for power's sake or in bloodthirstiness." The former president, thundered Bryan, was "a human arsenal, a dreadnought wrought in flesh and blood." To Roosevelt, observed the *Nation* in a review of a collection of the ex–Bull Mooser's national security speeches, "Americanism" evidently demanded that citizens "insult, taunt, and execrate the President of the United States and the Democratic party for all their words and acts." Gleefully noting his inconsistency on the issue of a protest on Belgium, the *Nation* scoffed that Roosevelt "is not a thinker, not a logician; he is a man of feeling." He was a "preacher," determined to "harangue" his flock into embracing the false idea that "the remedy for war is more war."[49]

With the case for a balance-of-power strategy so inconsistently and poorly presented, the only real alternative to collective security was apparently America's traditional approach to security—the course of relatively disarmed isolation from international political-military affairs. But this option had problems too. The growth of the preparedness movement, Wilson's success in getting Congress to enact significant defense increases, and the attacks by the belligerents on America's neutral rights all indicated that traditional isolationism might no longer be a viable national

security policy for the United States. Clearly events overseas frightened the American people, thus making them susceptible to militarism, and affected their nation's
sovereignty, thus making them vulnerable to war. Pacifists insisted that nothing
had changed, that greater armaments were not needed to protect America and that
America's international rights could safely be upheld with "moral power" only or
be abandoned. But while the majority of Americans probably still believed them,
growing numbers clearly did not.

As America's traditional policies of isolation appeared increasingly out of touch
with reality, liberal internationalists argued that America faced a choice. It could
try to reform international politics so as to end arms races, alliances, and war. Or
it could pursue *armed* isolation. The latter course had the virtue of avoiding one
aspect of power politics—alliances—and of preserving some degree of America's
freedom of action. But it could not provide immunity against arms races and war,
which meant that it was not likely to prevent America from succumbing to militarism at home. Only international reform could do that. International reform offered the *only* sure way to end the threat of militarism because it was the only national security strategy that promised to end balance-of-power politics. It was this
promise—and the hope of preserving American democracy that went along with
it—that drew American leaders to President Wilson's peace program, regardless of
all of its problems.

Indeed, aside from their differing assessment of the viability of traditional isolationism, pacifists and Wilson had much in common. After all, Wilson wanted
to stay out of Europe's fighting almost as much as they did. Both they and Wilson
wanted to mediate an end to the war before the Allies could win a decisive victory.
Both feared and loathed power politics and militarism. Thus, after his resignation, Bryan emphasized that he and Wilson "agree in purpose." Both of them, he
believed, prayed "with equal fervor" for a peaceful resolution of the submarine
dispute with Germany; they only differed "as to the means of securing it." Similarly, Stoughton Cooley of the *Public* questioned the logic of Wilson's effort to
entice Britain into a peace league with an increase of America's military power.
But Cooley understood the president's reasoning, declaring that Wilson "may be
credited with entire sincerity in seeking to oppose militarism by advocating an armament that will lead to disarmament." Wilson's blunt defense of his preparedness
program did not alienate the AUAM either. "Our interview with President Wilson
was satisfactory," Lillian Wald told the press after AUAM leaders visited the White
House in May 1916. They did not agree with the president's course, "but we know
at heart he is an anti-militarist." Privately, AUAM leaders reassured each other that
"the President had taken us into his intellectual bosom." The differences between
Wilson and the AUAM, they implied, were differences in degree, not in kind.[50]

Moreover, Wilson continually portrayed his peace program as an expression
of American exceptionalism and duty to humanity, using the same moralistic lan-

guage that had enormous appeal to the pacifists. When he summed up his late 1916 mediation bid and overall vision for world peace on 22 January 1917, declaring that America was born to "show mankind the way to liberty," pacifists responded enthusiastically. "I bring you on behalf of the American Union Against Militarism their profoundest gratitude for your noble speech," Wald wrote Wilson on 24 January. "It is a service to all humanity which it is impossible to exaggerate and we believe that its profound wisdom and philosophy will become more and more apparent as it recedes into the past." Bryan was equally ecstatic, even though he still opposed joining a coercive peace league. Wilson had made a "brave and timely appeal to the war-mad rulers of Europe," Bryan enthused in a letter to the president. "The basis of peace which you propose is a new philosophy—that is, new to governments but as old as the Christian religion, and it is the only foundation upon which a permanent peace can be built." United in their desire to end the war and end power politics, pacifists found it easy to overlook their differences with the president and cheer on his peace program.[51]

Still, their support for the president was highly conditional. To the degree that he could distinguish his program from traditional power politics, pacifists could rally behind the president. But their willingness to risk engagement with the balance of power was significantly less than Wilson's, because they viewed relatively disarmed isolation as still the best security policy for America. For them, international reform was a moral duty, but a duty America could and should abandon if fulfilling it exposed America too much to the dangerous currents of the existing international system. For Wilson, in contrast, as well as for other liberal internationalists, international reform was a vital necessity. "Isolation," to them, was an illusion; it really meant armed isolation, which in turn meant exposure to the dangers of arms races, war, and militarism. Risk taking in quest of reform—risk taking in the form of preparedness and coercive diplomacy—was therefore acceptable given the stakes involved for the United States. However paradoxical, America had no choice but to practice power politics to end power politics. For a moment, in January 1917, Wilson managed to convince pacifists to trust in his ability to resolve the contradictions inherent in this policy. How long he would be able to do so, however, was unclear.

7

Wilson at War

On 2 April 1917, a grim Woodrow Wilson entered the chamber of the House of Representatives and asked Congress to accept the war that Germany had "thrust upon" the United States. This development greatly complicated the president's efforts to end the system of power politics that he believed threatened America's free way of life. Once in the war, pressure grew to clarify the ambiguity surrounding exactly how collective security would work, but, perceiving political pitfalls in any plan he might propose, Wilson resisted doing so. At the same time, Germany's aggressive behavior made it much harder for the president to conceptualize how to achieve the containment and conciliation of the Reich he considered necessary for international reform. America's involvement in the war caused problems for Wilson at home as well, as it created an atmosphere of intolerance beneficial to Atlanticist critics of his peace program and made Wilson himself suspicious of pacifists who wanted more conciliatory treatment of Germany than he did. Fueled by his faith that American exceptionalism and the promise of collective security could overcome the ambiguities and contradictions in his peace program, however, Wilson remained committed to his goal of ending power politics. As the guns fell silent on the western front on 11 November 1918, he and the Allies were poised, he believed, "to set up such a peace as will satisfy the longing of the whole world for disinterested justice, embodied in settlements which are based upon something much better and much more lasting than the selfish competitive interests of powerful states."[1]

Wilson went to war fully aware that doing so could threaten his project for international reform. His fear that belligerency would ruin prospects for a "peace without victory" and derange and divide the American people caused him to strive to avoid war with Germany in 1915 and 1916. He continued to harbor these concerns after Germany's resumption of unrestricted submarine warfare. With the United States in the conflict, Wilson told journalist Frank Irving Cobb on 19 March, "Germany would be beaten and so badly beaten that there would be a dictated peace, a victorious peace." The chance for ending power politics would fade with such a victory. It meant, lamented the president, "an attempt to reconstruct a peace-time civilization with war standards. . . . There won't be any peace standards left to work with. There will only be war standards." Domestically, "illiberalism" would be required "to reinforce the men at the front." War fighting and maintaining America's political ideals were incompatible, in Wilson's view. "To fight you must be brutal and ruthless," the president insisted, "and the spirit of ruthless brutality will enter into the very fibre of our national life." Such bellicosity would complicate Wilson's ability to end the war with a moderate peace settlement, and, at home, Wilson thought, "the Constitution would not survive it." Militarism and chauvinism would engulf America if it went to war, Wilson feared, and destroy his opportunity to build a lasting peace abroad.[2]

Given these views, President Wilson did everything he felt he could do to avoid war, in spite of Germany's unrestricted submarine campaign. He hesitated to break relations with the Reich; he signaled the Germans that if they avoided destroying American ships in violation of international law, war could be averted; he tried to prod the Central Powers and especially Austria-Hungary into peace talks; he preferred "armed neutrality" to war, even after discovering Germany's attempt, in the infamous "Zimmermann telegram," to entice Mexico into fighting America; and, finally, he resisted going to war in the face of German submarines' destroying three American ships in mid-March. Wilson knew that American belligerency would greatly complicate his project for international reform, so he struggled mightily to find, in his words, a "loophole of escape" from it.[3]

In the end, he failed. Germany's "reckless and lawless" behavior, its evident determination to block whatever Wilson did to stay at peace "with some new outrage," convinced the president, by 20 or 21 March, that there was no alternative to war. Specifically, the Zimmermann telegram and the attacks on American shipping, on top of its intrigue in the United States and its rejection of Wilson's peace overtures, revealed that Germany's leaders, including its civilian leadership, wanted conquest, not a Wilsonian peace. The German government, the president declared in his war message, "entertains no real friendship for us and means to act against our peace and security at its convenience." It had shown itself to be "an irresponsible government which has thrown aside all considerations of humanity and of right and is running amuck." Such a regime obviously cared nothing for the program of peace and international reform that Wilson proposed to the world on 22 January 1917—the program that he felt would assure America of its national security. There was therefore no point in continuing to hope that Germany might show some restraint in its conduct and still opt, even at this late date, to support Wilson's vision of collective security.[4]

The longer the crisis went on, moreover, the more it became clear to Wilson that he stood at a crucial juncture in his relationship with the Allies. Fearful of

Germany's submarines, America's merchant ships stayed in port, something the British, Ambassador Page reported from London, interpreted as "the submission of our Government to the German blockade." Such a perception, Page warned, threatened to "interfere with any influence that we might otherwise have when peace comes." Conversely, U.S. belligerency, the president told Jane Addams, promised to give him "a seat at the Peace Table." Perceiving that the Allies were gaining the upper hand over Germany in the war, this desire—Wilson's wish directly to shape the peace settlement—was probably at a peak, and the only way to satisfy it, it seemed, was to enter the war.[5]

Indeed, "armed neutrality," the policy Wilson considered the most plausible alternative to war, seemed to offer few advantages as compared to belligerency. This option aimed to solve the problem of American merchant ships cowering in port by arming them and, ideally, by coordinating protection of them with other neutral states interested in continuing their trade too. The United States would not enter the war, thus avoiding all of the dangers associated with belligerency, but still actively protect its neutral rights, thus preserving the international credibility it needed to mediate a peace settlement based on international reform.[6]

Although Wilson endorsed this proposal and asked Congress to implement it on 26 February, he soon discovered that it too had practical problems. To be effective, Secretary of the Navy Daniels told the president, armed neutrality required cooperation with the Allies. Wilson would also have to allow American merchant ships to shoot submarines on sight inside the war zone, before the submarines fired first. These considerations, in Wilson's view, made "armed neutrality" look even less advantageous to America than outright belligerency. The United States would in effect be at war with Germany without admitting it, which would leave the Allies an opening to exclude the president from peacemaking. As Wilson told Congress, armed neutrality was "certain to draw us into the war without either the rights or effectiveness of belligerents." If he was going to incur the costs and risks of belligerency, Wilson wanted its benefits too, namely an ensured place at the peace conference. Armed neutrality could not guarantee that outcome, but an American declaration of war could.[7]

Ultimately, then, it was his quest for international reform, rooted in his conviction that American national security demanded an end to balance-of-power politics, that drew Wilson, however reluctantly, into "the most terrible and disastrous of all wars." Exactly how a new international system would work remained unclear, however. Concerned that proposing a specific enforcement mechanism for collective security might produce intense controversy at home and abroad detrimental to both the war effort and the goal of reform, Wilson avoided discussion of and planning for a peace league. He urged the French not to create a commission "to consider the feasibility, the form, and the objects of a Society of Nations"; refused to establish a British-American committee of experts to study the "machinery" of collective security; actively discouraged the League to Enforce Peace from discussing the details of a league in public; and opposed publication of the Phillimore report, Britain's plan for a league. "The minute you discuss details," Wilson observed to Louis Lochner, "the main issue is clouded and discussion diverted." The more nebulous the league, in other words, the easier to rally support for it.[8]

Rather than pinpoint an enforcement procedure for collective security, Wilson wanted to leave it "to develop of itself, case by case," after the league actually went into operation. This idea shaped the one written "covenant" for a league of nations that Wilson wrote prior to the end of the war. Completed in mid-August 1918, the draft guaranteed the political and territorial integrity of member states and threatened states that violated a specified arbitration process with an economic boycott and blockade. The draft lacked defined procedures for how the league would arrive at and implement its decisions, however. It was silent on the crucial issue of how league members would decide if a state had failed to submit to arbitration, to "carry out" an arbitral decision, or to refrain from commencing "hostilities" during a dispute. Nor did the draft indicate how the decision to order a blockade would be reached, how blockading forces would be organized, or how other league "action" for peace would be decided and executed. In short, Wilson's proposed league had no clear decision-making process at all—and thus no real means for enforcing its provisions.[9]

The president's confidence that the league's enforcement mechanisms would "naturally spring up" over time reflected more than just his political calculations and his pragmatism. His position also implied an intense faith in collective security theory—in the idea, explicitly asserted in the draft covenant, that "any war or threat of war, whether immediately affecting any of the Contracting Powers or not, is . . . a matter of concern to the League of Nations and to all the Powers signatory hereto." If this proposition were true, if all nations had an equally vital stake in peace everywhere, then the league's lack of enforcement mechanisms did not matter very much. Once nations had recognized their interdependence with a covenant to safeguard each other, they would find a way to uphold it. "The establishment of a league of nations," Wilson lectured a visiting Swiss scholar, "is in my view a matter of moral persuasion more than a problem of juridical organization. . . . When men of good will, of whatever country, come to understand their true common interests, the most redoubtable obstacles which bar the route to the establishment of a new international order will have been surmounted." The shared interest of the league's members in peace around the globe would make the league work, not the fine print of any constitution.[10]

Logically, this vision of international reform had to include the Germans. A league of the United States and the Allies, formed during the war, "would inevitably be regarded as a sort of Holy Alliance aimed at Germany," Wilson argued. It would "be merely a new alliance confined to the nations associated against a common enemy." Such an organization would contradict the theory that a collective interest in peace existed among "all nations." It could not be considered a collective security organization, which meant that the existing system of power politics would persist.[11]

Yet after the events of early 1917, the Reich seemed less suitable than ever to be a partner in a peace league. Not only had it forced the United States into the war, it now appeared bent on throwing "a broad belt of German military power and political control across the very center of Europe and beyond the Mediterranean into the heart of Asia." Revealing in public what he had long expressed in private, Wilson in June 1917 declared that if Germany's plans succeeded, "America will fall within the menace. We and all the rest of the world must remain armed, as they will remain, and must make ready for the next step in their aggression." With a German victory, the world would be "dominated a long age through by sheer weight of arms and the arbitrary choices of self-constituted masters, by the nation which can maintain the biggest armies and the most irresistible armaments—a power to which the world has afforded no parallel and in the face of which political freedom must wither and perish." America's future as a free society, secure from arms races and militarism, was directly threatened by Germany's now unambiguous quest for world power.[12]

Faced with such an enemy, Wilson had to rework the terms he intended to serve as the basis for international reform. Before April 1917, it will be recalled, the president had been willing to base peace on a return to the status quo antebellum (with the exception of creating an independent Poland), disarmament, and the establishment of a peace league. But now, given its treachery and evident lust for conquest, Wilson wanted to alter "the *status quo ante* out of which this iniquitous war issued forth, the power of the Imperial German Government within the Empire and its widespread domination and influence outside of that Empire." The president began to express this goal soon after America entered the war, but he gave his most comprehensive statement of it on 8 January 1918, in his famous Fourteen Points Address to Congress. This program, among other things, called for the Central Powers to evacuate all of the territory they occupied in the war; implied that they would have to pay reparations to "restore" Belgium, France, and other nations; indicated that Alsace-Lorraine should be returned to France; demanded the creation of an "independent Polish state" with "free and secure access to the sea"; and vaguely suggested redrawing the frontiers of Italy and the Balkan states. The thrust of the president's platform was clear, even if the details were not: his preferred peace settlement envisioned both indemnities and territorial annexations of one sort or another at the expense of Germany and its allies.[13]

Wilson's determination "to restrict German power for evil in the future" expressed itself with particular forcefulness in his policies toward the Reich's key ally, Austria-Hungary. The latter, Wilson was convinced, was "the vassal" of Berlin, used by the Germans to advance their own ambitions. From February 1917 to about March 1918, the president tried to pry the Austrians from Germany's grasp by promising them peace talks on the basis of only minimal territorial losses around the periphery of the Austro-Hungarian Empire. If the dual monarchy was broken apart, Wilson warned French ambassador Jusserand, parts of it might want to unify with Germany on grounds of ethnic kinship. The resulting "Germanic nucleus would be great, and its power even more redoubtable, since we cannot foresee what sort of counterweight Russia could offer." A few months later, Wilson added that autonomy for "the races forming the Austro-Hungarian agglomeration" would be "the greatest obstacle to the consolidation of the *Mitteleuropa* bloc," as the non-German elements of the empire would "act as a check upon the German policy of the country and prevent Vienna from submitting docilely to Berlin's orders." By April 1918, once it seemed evident that the Austrians would not defect from their ally, Wilson switched policy and supported the dismemberment of the Austro-Hungarian state as a way to sever its links to the Reich. To deal with the problem of a rump Austria unifying with—and strengthening—Germany, the administration, as the war came to end, was considering simply not allowing any Austro-German union to take place, regardless of whether or not such a position violated the principle of self-determination. After all, as Secretary of the Interior Franklin Lane pointed out to Wilson, a union would amount to such a gain for Berlin that it "would leave the Germans victors after all."[14]

Similar considerations of power lay behind Wilson's approach to Alsace-Lorraine. On the one hand, the president had good cause not to support the transfer of the two provinces from Germany to France. Doing so might embitter the Germans against the peace treaty, thus poisoning prospects for international reform. Weary from three years of brutal warfare, the French, Wilson thought in August 1917, might not desire the return of the provinces "enough to make it a *sine qua non* of peace," in any case. In addition, the people of Alsace-Lorraine might not want to be returned to France; children spoke German in the provinces, Wilson claimed; France could conceivably lose a referendum on reclaiming the territory. Finally, the American people, in Wilson's estimation, were wary of fighting for the territorial aims of the Allies. All of these factors pointed to the same conclusion: the president should avoid making the return of Alsace-Lorraine to France a U.S. war aim.[15]

Yet Wilson included the restitution of Alsace-Lorraine in the Fourteen Points. Although he struggled with how to word the demand to minimize the chance of offending the Germans or American public opinion, he insisted on including it in his list of war aims over the initial objections of Colonel House. He even underscored its importance by putting it in the same point (point 8) that demanded Germany free and restore the French territory it invaded in 1914. This had been a

nonnegotiable part of Wilson's peace program since the start of the war; by placing Alsace-Lorraine alongside it, the president actually reduced his maneuvering
room on the issue.[16]

Wilson's sense that Germany had done an injustice to France in taking the provinces in 1871 partly explains his decision to make their return a war aim. Given his
lack of certainty as to the political desires of the people of Alsace-Lorraine, however, what mattered more to Wilson was the unambiguous fact that taking Alsace-
Lorraine from the Germans would weaken them and strengthen the French. British foreign minister Balfour stressed this point in a memo he sent Wilson in May
1917, as did Sidney Edward Mezes, David Hunter Miller, and Walter Lippmann in a
paper read closely by the president in January 1918. By shifting the provinces back
to France, Balfour argued, "you would further increase the population of France
relative to the population of Germany, which undoubtedly must make for the equilibrium of Europe, and because it makes for the equilibrium of Europe, makes also
for the peace of the world." Since 1871, Balfour continued, Germany had found
ways to exploit Lorraine's iron deposits "to an extent which makes them a very
formidable adjunct to Germany's industrial power." Together with its coal deposits, Alsace-Lorraine's iron played an important role in giving Germany in 1914 "a
greater power of producing munitions . . . than the whole of the rest of the world
put together." Transferring Alsace-Lorraine to France could significantly reduce
the Reich's capability for aggression.[17]

To impose terms as detrimental to Germany's power as those of the Fourteen
Points, Wilson recognized that he needed to inflict a decisive military defeat on
the Reich. The United States would not stay on the defense as a belligerent, Wilson promised in his war message. It would instead "exert all its power and employ
all its resources to bring the Government of the German Empire to terms." The
president backed up this threat by building up and then sending an American
expeditionary force to France, mobilizing the country for war, and sending military and economic aid to the Allies. If necessary, he declared on 14 June 1917, the
United States might send "millions" of men into battle to crush autocratic Germany's armed forces.[18]

The president's new emphasis on limiting the Reich's power and subduing its
armies did not mean he had given up on the task of conciliating Germany. It did
mean that that chore—vital to attaining Wilson's strategic objective of ending power
politics—became even harder to manage than it had been prior to April 1917. In
grappling with this crucial issue, Wilson focused more intently than ever on assessing the relationship between German democratization and prospects for international reform. On the one hand, he thought Germany's people were more pacifically
inclined than their autocratic rulers. "It was not upon their impulse that their government acted in entering this war," Wilson perceived. "It was not with their previous knowledge or approval." Germany's popularly elected parliament, the Reich-

stag, approved of and financed the war, according to Wilson, because the German people mistakenly believed that the Allies, and, after April 1917, America, wanted to destroy the Reich. The Germans wanted "emancipation from fear" as much as Americans did. In fact, argued the president, while the "spirit of freedom" did not suit "the plans of the Pan-Germans," it could nevertheless "get into the hearts of Germans and find as fine a welcome there as it can find in any other hearts."[19]

On the other hand, however, Wilson had serious doubts about the disposition of Germany's masses and their elected representatives. Rather than repudiate their government's conquests, they seemed excited by them. If Germany's leaders could hold onto their gains, Wilson predicted publicly in June 1917, "they will have justified themselves before the German people; they will have gained by force what they promised to gain by it." To be certain, in July 1917, the Reichstag, by a decisive 212–126 majority, passed a peace resolution vaguely echoing the so-called Petrograd formula, a proposal by the All-Russian Congress of Soviets for a peace settlement based on national self-determination, no annexations, and no indemnities. But the Reichstag majority had little reaction when the kaiser's ministers seemed interested in the peace resolution solely as a device to entice Russia into signing a separate peace treaty with the Central Powers. Significantly, even though in October 1917 the Reichstag majority, for the first time, had had a hand in the kaiser's appointment of a new chancellor, Count Georg von Hertling, the German government continued to use the peace resolution as a way, in Wilson's words, "to lead the people of Russia astray" and secure a peace leaving Germany in control of eastern Europe. The government and the majority leaders, indeed, were "in harmony with regard to both foreign and domestic issues," reported the State Department in November. Far from reining in the autocracy, the Reichstag majority, even as it grew more assertive, seemed complicit in the regime's intrigues in the east in late 1917.[20]

Even more alarming, the autocracy's machinations were successful. On 15 December 1917, a few weeks after the Bolsheviks took power in Russia, the Central Powers and the Russians signed an armistice; formal peace talks commenced on 22 December at Brest-Litovsk. On 9 January 1918, after the Allies had rejected participation in the talks, the Germans in effect declared that they no longer felt bound by the peace resolution and demanded extensive concessions from Russia as the price of a settlement. When the Russians refused, fifty-two German divisions resumed their advance in the east, meeting little resistance. The Soviets then met the Reich's demands, signing the treaty of Brest-Litovsk on 3 March. Under its terms, Russia lost sovereignty over its Baltic provinces, Poland, and Belarus. The Central Powers would decide the fate of those areas "in agreement with their population." Russia also gave up its claims to Finland, the Ukraine, and the Caucasus. In other provisions, Russia had to disarm its navy, demobilize its army, and reimburse the Central Powers for maintaining prisoners of war. All told, Russia lost about one-third of its prewar population (55 million people), one-third of its agricultural land, 54 percent of its heavy industry, 33 percent of its railway systems, 73 percent of its iron ore output, and 89 percent of its coal mines. On 5 March, Rumania also signed a preliminary treaty with the Central Powers, agreeing to give up territory to Bulgaria and to grant future economic concessions to the Reich. Finalized in the Treaty of Bucharest on 7 May, these concessions, in the words of one historian, "reduced Rumania to the position of a vassal state of Germany." Much the same could be said of virtually all of eastern and southeastern Europe.[21]

For the most part, the Reichstag majority either supported or acquiesced in the Reich's aggressive policies in the east. Although the suspension of negotiations at Brest-Litovsk in mid-January had contributed to a wave of protest strikes in Germany supported by the Social Democratic Party (SPD), the largest party in the Reichstag, there was no outcry on the home front when German troops swept deeper into Russia in February. The socialists, Samuel Gompers and William English Walling told Wilson, had no desire "to relinquish German domination over Germany's present allies, nor her economic domination over Russia and all surrounding small nations." When the Reichstag majority debated the German government's demands upon Russia later in the month, Matthias Erzberger, a key leader in the majority coalition and in the pivotal Catholic Zentrum, proclaimed his support for them. The proposed terms were compatible with the Reichstag peace resolution, he insisted. Even though German troops occupied the region, so long as Germany avoided outright annexation of Russia's border areas and organized them according to the principle of self-determination, Erzberger argued, "the peace treaty falls completely within the framework of our Resolution." Others in the majority coalition agreed; only SPD leader Philipp Scheidemann suggested that Brest-Litovsk contradicted the peace resolution. Pleased that the war had apparently ended in the east, however, the SPD did not vote against the treaty when it came up for ratification in March, opting to abstain instead. It passed overwhelmingly, with the support of both conservatives and the nonsocialist parties of the Reichstag majority. Only the radical Independent Socialist Party, the USPD, voted against it. When the Treaty of Bucharest came up for ratification in June, even the SPD voted for it. The ideals of the peace resolution, it appeared, had been abandoned in favor of the fruits of conquest.[22]

Brest-Litovsk, as well as the opening of a massive offensive by Germany on the western front on 21 March 1918, perplexed and frustrated the president. "The amazing thing to my mind is that a lot of German people that I know like the government they have been living under," Wilson confided to a group of reporters a few weeks after receiving a State Department memo describing the political situation in Germany. "It took me a long time to believe it; I thought they were bluffing." He still thought there were "genuine liberal elements in Austria and even in Germany who sincerely wish to follow democratic ideals," he told British diplomat William Wiseman, "but . . . they are too small a minority to have any influence at present on the peoples, as a whole." Like it or not, most of Germany's people evidently shared at least some of the hunger for conquest that animated their autocratic leaders.[23]

Wilson's ambivalent view of Germany's people caused him to see the democratization of the Reich as offering only a partial solution to the problem of conciliating the Germans. Between August 1917 and January 1918, Wilson made it clear that even if Germany established a new government responsible to the Reichstag rather than to the kaiser, no peace process could begin unless the Germans accepted his peace program as the basis for a settlement. The United States would "regard the war as won," Wilson declared in December, "only when the German people say to us, through properly accredited representatives, that they are ready to agree to a settlement based upon justice and the reparation of the wrongs their rulers have done." Moreover, the president expected Germany's autocrats to fall only if their armies suffered military defeats. "If they fall back or are forced back an inch," Wilson predicted, "their power both abroad and at home will fall to pieces like a house of cards. . . . If they fail, their people will thrust them aside." Thus, to end the war, not only would a democratic Germany have to embrace Wilson's peace terms, but also it would be doing so, Wilson assumed, in the context of a balance of power on the battlefield that had radically shifted in favor of America and its friends.[24]

The president also expected a clear military victory, coupled with Germany's democratization, to abate the aggressive impulses of the German people. Prior to April 1917, Wilson had hoped that frustrating the war aims of all the belligerents would purge them of desires to gain conquests by war. Now, much more fixated on Germany's behavior alone, he thought of the proper "psychological basis" of a lasting peace in a very different manner. The more the Germans specifically suffered through the experience of a decisive defeat in the war and the toppling of their government, the better, Wilson suggested in a private conversation in August 1917, as it would make them unwilling to support aggression in the future. "There would be, there," Wilson believed, "a guarantee much more serious . . . than all the declarations which could be obtained from Germany and written in the peace treaty."[25]

Still, because Wilson saw some sectors of German opinion as pacific in character and because he believed that "a steadfast concert for peace can never be maintained except by a partnership of democratic nations," German democratization would allow him to take positive steps to conciliate the Reich. If the Germans implemented domestic political reforms and accepted his peace terms, then, Wilson promised, he could commence peace talks with them; he could have, as he put it, "intelligent dealings" with representatives of the Reichstag majority concerning the details of his Fourteen Points. A democratic Germany would also gain full membership in a postwar league of nations. America, Wilson assured Germany, believed that "peace should rest" upon all peoples' "equal right to freedom and security and self-government and to a participation upon fair terms in the economic opportunities of the world,—the German people of course included, if they will accept equality and not seek domination." If Germany democratized, in short, it would still be reduced in power and punished, but Wilson could reach out to it with the hand of friendship too, which would greatly enhance the chances for international reform.[26]

If Germany failed to dismantle its autocratic system, reconciling with it would be more problematic, but not impossible. Prior to the Brest-Litovsk treaty, when Wilson had some hope that he could entice Germany's democrats into taking power, the president warned that not only would he not negotiate with the Reich's autocratic leaders, but he also "might" not admit them "to the partnership of nations which must henceforth guarantee the world's peace." And, he added, it "might be impossible . . . to admit Germany to the free economic intercourse which must inevitably spring out of the other partnerships of a real peace." The president hoped this discrimination would be temporary; in time, he suggested in December 1917, it would "cure itself, by processes which would assuredly set in." Here Wilson no doubt hoped that eventually a defeated Germany would democratize, recognize the justice of his peace program, and demonstrate its good faith to the new international community. When it did so, it would be welcomed into the new world order.[27]

After Brest-Litovsk, as his disillusionment with Germany's democrats intensified and the likelihood of having "to sign peace with the Military Party in Germany" increased, Wilson clarified his policy for how to deal with Germany's autocracy if it still ruled in Berlin at the end of the war. First, he more openly contemplated the prospect of having to invade German territory in order to coerce the Germans into accepting his peace terms. He would never buy concessions in the west by allowing the Germans "a free hand in Russia and the East," Wilson vowed in April 1918, because that would leave Germany with an empire powerful enough to "overawe" Europe. He would not seek peace with Germany's autocrats "by any kind of bargain or compromise" because all they wanted was conquest. They could obtain peace only by unconditionally accepting his terms. To be sure, Wilson had "no desire" to invade Germany, given how harmful that would be to his chances for conciliating the Reich. But, "if they oblige us to march triumphantly into Berlin," he swore to journalists on 8 April 1918, "then we will do it if it takes twenty years."[28]

Once Germany's autocratic government was beaten into submission, Wilson continued to anticipate having to use economic coercion to ensure that it signed and carried out the peace treaty Wilson and the Allies dictated to it. But by September 1918, wary that this approach might make reconciliation with the Germans impossible, Wilson no longer suggested that a defeated Reich would be excluded from the league of nations. The league, Wilson argued, had to be established at the time of the peace conference, when the Germans were present, and the league's constitution "must be a part, . . . in a sense the most essential part, of the peace settlement itself"—the settlement the Germans would sign. The league, Wilson asserted on 27 September, "cannot be formed now. If formed now, it would be merely a new alliance confined to the nations associated against a common enemy." It would make the league, Wilson noted privately, "a group formed to maintain [a] balance of power"—exactly the opposite of the kind of world order the president associated with American security. To attain his goal of ending power politics, Wilson recognized, Germany—even autocratic Germany—had to be "invited to join the family of nations, providing she will behave according to the rules of the Society."[29]

Including the Germans in the league would not only ensure its congruence with the logic of collective security but also make any coercion that might be necessary to ensure that they behaved consonant with international reform. Once the league was established, any economic warfare directed against the Germans would be transformed from an instrument to benefit an "economic alliance" into a tool to uphold the peace settlement and collective security. In a treaty based on the Fourteen Points and including within it the league, Wilson explained, there could be "no special, selfish economic combinations," as those would violate the ideal of a settlement "consistent with the common interest of all." But the moment the treaty was signed and Germany, as a signatory, was included in the league, "the power of economic penalty by exclusion from the markets of the world" would be "vested in the League of Nations itself as a means of discipline and control." The Allies and the United States, if they chose to coerce the Germans with a postwar economic boycott, would not be attacking an enemy. They would be acting as guarantors of collective security *against a fellow league member,* against "parties to the peace whose promises have proved untrustworthy." To Wilson, such action would represent not a contradiction of international reform but a fulfillment of it.[30]

Ideally, any postwar coercion of the Germans would not last very long. Even if Germany's autocracy was still in place at the end of the war, Wilson continued to assume that its failure on the battlefield would mark the beginning of the end of its days. Sooner or later, Germany's democrats would overthrow it. As was the case before Brest-Litovsk, Wilson hoped that the pain and suffering sure to accompany defeat would also have a salutary effect on the German people. Given their evident approval of Germany's aggression in the east, indeed, the transforming impact of a defeat in the war became more important to Wilson than ever. "The German people," Wilson affirmed to Sir William Wiseman in late August, "must be made to hate war, to realize that no military machine can dominate the world today." Once democratized and purged of their aggressive inclinations, the Germans would likely not just follow the peace treaty imposed upon them but embrace it.[31]

As he had prior to America's entry into the war, Wilson tried to enhance the attractiveness of his peace terms by portraying them as a product of American exceptionalism. "We have no jealousy of German greatness," Wilson avowed in his

Fourteen Points Address, "and there is nothing in this programme that impairs it. . . . We do not wish to injure her or to block in any way her legitimate influence or power." Instead, Americans were acting only as "an instrument in the hands of God to see that liberty is made secure for mankind." Unlike other nations, Americans had "no selfish ends to serve," Wilson asserted in his war message. "We desire no conquest, no dominion. We seek no indemnities for ourselves, no material compensation for the sacrifices we shall freely make." The principles underlying Wilson's peace terms were "bred" in the American people, but they were also "the principles of a liberated mankind." Possessed of a unique character that made it the champion of universal ideals of liberty, the United States was thus positioned "to do an unprecedented thing" if the Germans would accept its program: "To base peace on generosity and justice, to the exclusion of all selfish claims to advantage even on the part of the victors."[32]

If the president's approach to the problem of harmonizing America's war against Germany with the goal of ending power politics was complicated, so too were his policies toward the Allies. No less than before America's entry into the war, Wilson deeply distrusted the Entente. While the president and the Allies now agreed on the need to avoid any sort of compromise peace with "the present rulers of Germany," they still differed as to what a final peace settlement should look like. The president was especially wary of Italy's territorial demands; Allied sphere-of-influence agreements "relative to Asia Minor"; British, French, and Japanese desires to take Germany's colonies and concessions in Africa and Asia; Britain's opposition to free seas; and Allied, and in particular British, determination "to smash German trade permanently" after the war. The president was also probably aware of—and, if he did know about it, certainly opposed to—French wishes to limit or end German sovereignty over the Rhineland. As Wilson told the French ambassador, he wanted a "scientific peace," not a settlement of territorial dismemberment "that would create new Alsace-Lorraines." Finally, Wilson perceived that the Allies had different ideas about a league of nations than he did and that they, unlike him, wanted to exclude Germany from any postwar international security organization that was created. From multiple angles, the Allies, Wilson emphasized to House in July 1917, "*have not the same views with regard to peace that we have* by any means."[33]

Allied war aims undermined Wilson's peace program in two ways. First, the more the Allies appeared to be aiming to secure selfish strategic and economic advantages from the war, the more they might force German liberals and leftists to rally around the autocracy in self-defense while alienating Russia and the Left in the West from the war effort. If Germany's will to fight increased while that of the Allies diminished, the war would obviously be harder for Wilson to win, if it could be won at all. Allied war aims also endangered Wilson's agenda for international reform for the same reason they had prior to April 1917: if implemented, they would alienate both Germany and America from the cause of building a new world order. "Responsible statesmen must now everywhere see, if they never saw before," Wilson asserted in his reply to the pope's peace appeal, "that no peace can rest securely upon political or economic restrictions meant to benefit some nations and cripple or embarrass others, upon vindictive action of any sort, or any kind of revenge or deliberate injury." The wrongs Germany committed must be righted, the president conceded in December 1917. "But they can not and must not be righted by the commission of similar wrongs against Germany and her allies." Trying to dismember or humiliate Germany would create within it a "desire for revenge," ruining chances for a lasting peace treaty. The American people too would recoil from such a settlement. "Their object was a stable peace and they did not believe that a stable peace could be based upon aggression," Wilson warned the British. They would not tolerate any terms contrary to those suggested by the president's Fourteen Points; they would not countenance "debating and seeking to reconcile and accommodate what statesmen may wish, with their projects for balances of power and of national opportunity." Americans would only embrace a settlement meeting Wilson's definition of "impartial justice." Otherwise, the president suggested, they would turn their backs on Europe and on international reform and seek security as best they could on their own.[34]

However much the Allies posed a danger to his goal of ending power politics, though, Wilson needed them. He could not maintain military pressure on Germany without them. Nor could he build collective security without their cooperation. Somehow, then, Wilson had to get the Allies to fight the war and yet abandon their own war aims in favor of his.[35]

The president met this challenge in part by signaling that he might make a separate peace with Germany unless the Allies agreed to his peace program. He refused to sign any of the treaties the Allies had signed with each other, including the one pledging each of them not to make a separate peace with the Reich; avoided sending American representatives to inter-Allied conferences for as long as possible; made it clear that he did not feel bound by decisions of the Allied Supreme War Council; failed to consult in any substantive way with Allied leaders on any of the major addresses he made concerning his peace program; and tried, especially in September 1918, to identify his program with the aspirations of the Allied peoples rather than the Allied governments. He even pointedly refused to refer to the United States as an "allied" power, insisting on calling America an "associate" of the Entente instead. As he declared in his Fourteen Points Address, his terms were "the only possible programme" for peace. Once Germany accepted his program, he implied, America's war would be over. What the Allies chose to do at that point was up to them.[36]

The president hoped, of course, that if they reached that juncture, the Allies would opt to join him in crafting a just peace settlement conducive to establishing collective security. But to increase the chances they would, he tried to ensure that he would be able to exert leverage over them at the peace conference. The deployment and use of U.S. combat troops in France had much to do with Wilson's ability to secure this goal. After an extended debate within the administration lasting from February to June 1917, the president decided to raise an army through conscription, send troops to France at a rate of 120,000 a month, and have them complete their training behind Allied lines before going into battle as an independent army under the command of Maj. Gen. John J. Pershing. He rejected suggestions by the Allies for "a large number of smaller *units* which they could feed promptly into their line as parts of their own organizations in order to maintain their man power at full strength." As Gen. Tasker Howard Bliss pointed out to Wilson, the Allied plan could mean that the United States might have a million men in France and yet not have its own army. That was unacceptable to the president. Instead, he opted to create a "separate and distinct" U.S. force he could use to intervene in the war decisively, at a time of his own choosing, with maximum military and political effect. He then maintained this policy until the end of the war with only minimal modifications, despite enormous pressure from the Allies, especially during the German offensive of spring 1918, to brigade American infantrymen with the Entente's armies.[37]

In addition to positioning his military forces to maximize his diplomatic influence, Wilson also anticipated coercing the Entente into accepting his peace program at the end of the war. The war aims of the Allies diverged from his own, Wilson told House on 21 July 1917, but he had a plan to deal with them. "When the war is over we can force them to our way of thinking," Wilson predicted, "because by that time they will, among other things, be financially in our hands." A few months later, the president reiterated this idea to his cabinet. The Allies might want to set up "selfish trade arrangements" against Germany after the war, but the United States could stop them. "This country will have money & can compel the nations to measure up to our standard or not be given credit," Daniels recorded Wilson asserting. "We must impose these American views upon Europe for the good of all."[38]

Concerned about provoking disagreements with the Allies that could imperil the war effort against Germany, Wilson did not openly attempt to force the Allies to endorse his peace program in 1917 and 1918. But he did subtly remind them of the power America could exert over them. Despite British warnings in late June 1917 that an Allied "financial disaster" was "imminent" unless the United States provided "immediate help," Wilson let Secretary of the Treasury William McAdoo drag his feet on issuing them loans. The Entente's financial difficulties were not resolved, in fact, until late August. The president also did not ask Congress to suspend the building of battleships started under the 1916 navy program—the same program that promised America naval equality with the British by the early 1920s. He made this decision despite British protests that the ships were taking up resources better devoted to the construction of destroyers and other craft for antisubmarine warfare.

Britain even promised Wilson naval assistance in the event Japan ever attacked the United States, if the administration would abandon its capital shipbuilding in favor of destroyer construction. The president rejected this deal, telling Wiseman that the United States wanted "to play a 'lone hand,' and not commit herself to any alliances with any foreign power." With these statements and actions, and with measures designed to help America compete with Britain in world markets, Wilson underscored his ability to adopt policies detrimental to Allied interests after the war.[39]

The president balanced his threatening posture toward the Allies with an effort to avoid confrontations with them. He refrained from announcing his war aims in public until January 1918, as he perceived any discussion of peace terms was "full of dynamite" for America's relations with the Entente. When he finally did present his peace program in his Fourteen Points Address, he went out of his way to praise Lloyd George's statement of terms, delivered on 5 January 1918 in Caxton Hall. "There is no confusion of counsel among the adversaries of the Central Powers," Wilson asserted, "no uncertainty of principle, no vagueness of detail." This last claim was not really true, as several of Wilson's Fourteen Points, including especially the ones on territorial issues, lacked specifics. Ambiguity worked to Wilson's advantage, however: the more he focused on general principles, the easier it was to sidestep all of the questions that might cause a break between America and its "associates" in the struggle against Germany. As the president noted to Wiseman in a discussion of how to keep "working men" committed to the fighting, the key was to keep "firmly and constantly to the front certain very simple truths about the war." Getting into details on peace terms risked conflict, at home and abroad, so Wilson refused to talk about them.[40]

Ultimately, Wilson relied on the hope of security offered by a league of nations to entice the Allies to cooperate with him. Thus, when Italian leaders complained to Wilson that his proposed terms concerning their territory ignored their defense concerns, the president tried to reassure them by pointing to the promise of collective security. The league's "mutually defensive pledges," Wilson told the Italian ambassador, "would render strategic considerations such as those affecting the Adriatic much less important." America was looking out for the true interests of the Allies, Wilson likewise promised the British. He "would not assent to a peace inimical to them." The United States itself sought "no material advantage of any kind" in the war; all it wanted was a lasting peace for all. Therefore the Allies should have faith in America, regardless of differences over war aims, and abandon "the great game, now forever discredited, of the balance of power."[41]

Wilson's plea for trust was aimed with particular emphasis at Russia, whose revolutionary turmoil posed particularly difficult choices for the president as he sought to defeat Germany and manage his complex relationship with the Allies. The Bolshevik Revolution of November 1917 and Russia's subsequent peace treaty with Germany at Brest-Litovsk threatened to negate the Allied blockade of the

Reich and thus prolong the war, spur leftist and pacifist opposition to the war in the Allies and America, and tempt Japan into invading Siberia on the pretext of denying Germany access to the region's resources and munitions stockpiles. A Japanese invasion, Wilson thought, would do little to hurt Germany, but it might drive the Russians even more into Germany's arms, discredit the moral authority of the Allies, undermine the credibility of his claim to be fighting for international reform, and increase the power of a Japanese state he distrusted. Trying to dissuade Japan from such a course, though, irritated the Allies, who were anxious to protect Siberia from the Germans, and angered the Japanese to the point that Britain feared they might switch sides in the war. At the same time, Wilson was at a loss as to how to reinvigorate Russia's war effort, especially with the Bolshevik regime in power—a regime claiming to represent the Russian Revolution and yet one Wilson considered, because of its ideology, its evident willingness to work with Germany, and its lack of firm control over large parts of Russia, basically illegitimate.[42]

Confronted with a "kaleidoscopic" minefield of political problems in Russia, Wilson focused on frustrating Germany's efforts to secure gains in the east—gains that posed the greatest immediate threat to achieving his peace program—at the least possible risk and cost to the war effort in the west and to the principle of allowing Russia to work out its political future without outside interference. Soon after the United States entered the war, the administration mounted a propaganda campaign in Russia to convince the Russians to keep up their fight against Germany and to reassure them of American aid and the justice of America's war aims. In late 1917 and early 1918, Wilson also authorized covert financial assistance to anti-Bolshevik forces in southern Russia who appeared interested in resisting the Germans. Nothing much came of this effort, but it was soon followed, in June 1918, by the dispatch of some 4,500 American troops to Murmansk, a port near the northern harbor of Archangel. This action was designed to deny Germany military supplies sent by the Allies to Russia in 1917, to show cooperation with the Allies at a time when the issue of brigading American troops on the western front was causing strain in the alliance, and to rally either Bolshevik or anti-Bolshevik forces in northern Russia to battle the Germans. None of these steps guaranteed the reestablishment of an eastern front against the Reich, but they at least offered a chance of complicating Germany's efforts to consolidate its gains in the east.[43]

Wilson's decision to intervene in Russia militarily was not confined to Murmansk and Archangel for long. In July 1918 the president also decided to send seven thousand American troops to Vladivostok. Primarily, he acted because of reports he received, beginning in late March and then increasingly after mid-June, indicating that anti-German, anti-Bolshevik forces were gaining momentum in Siberia and were battling ex-German and Austrian prisoners of war allied with the Bolsheviks. Most importantly, Wilson gradually came to believe that a force of roughly forty thousand Czechoslovakian troops, who had served in Russia's army prior to the Bolshevik seizure of power and who were now, in the spring of 1918, spread out along much of the Trans-Siberian railroad, were resisting "perhaps 20,000 Austrian German prisoners armed by Soviet government and commanded by German officers." The Czechs wanted Allied military assistance in this struggle and, indeed, considered themselves part of the Allied coalition fighting the Central Powers. As the Supreme War Council further described the situation on 3 July, the Czechs were rallying anti-Soviet, anti-German Russians to resist German domination of Siberia and opening up an opportunity for the Allies "to gain control of the railways through the whole of Siberia as far as the Urals." By aiding the Czechs "against German and Austrian prisoners," Wilson hoped to block easy German access to Siberian resources, fend off the possibility of large-scale Japanese intervention without offending Tokyo's sensibilities, and, as he put it, "steady any efforts at self-government or self-defence in which the Russians themselves may be willing to accept assistance."[44]

Once the Russian intervention was under way, Wilson almost immediately became disenchanted with it, as he saw that it was doing little to hurt Germany. Confounding the administration's expectations, Japan unilaterally almost doubled its troop commitment to Siberia in late July, the Czechs encountered stiff Russian resistance in securing the Trans-Siberian railroad and demanded more aid, and the British commander in Archangel seemed more interested in suppressing Bolshevism than in inspiring the Russians to fight the Germans. As Wilson laconically noted in mid-September as he read reports about the northern ports, "The situation is not at all what it was anticipated it would develop into." Wanting to focus on the western front, not on what increasingly looked like a distracting quagmire in the east, Wilson decided in late September 1918 not to send any additional troops to Russia beyond those already dispatched and to restrict the theater of operations of American forces in Siberia. In the administration's view, "bloodshed and anarchy" were engulfing Bolshevik Russia and, for the sake of the war effort against Germany, the United States needed to limit its exposure to it.[45]

The president's primary goal of coercing Germany into accepting his peace terms affected how he dealt with the American home front no less than it influenced his Russian policy. Wilson went to war anxious that belligerency might unravel American democracy and unleash a spirit of ruthlessness threatening to his conception of a just peace. Once actually in the war, however, this concern was quickly overshadowed by a fear that too many Americans were either indifferent to his peace program or actively supportive of terms more favorable to Germany. Americans needed to be "fanned into an active enthusiasm" for battle, Wilson agreed with a friend of Lansing's in June 1914. Particularly in the Midwest and Far West, he saw, people did "not yet understand fully why we are in the war, and that we must 'see it through.'" He perceived that Germany had an extensive covert operations network working to stir up trouble inside America too, to the point of worrying, in February 1917, that the Germans had a plot to assassinate him. More significantly, the president had grave concerns about leftist and liberal attraction to a "premature peace" based on the Petrograd formula. Somehow, Wilson had to find a way to arouse the public to support fighting for his peace program while avoiding a militarized state.[46]

In addressing this challenge, Wilson chose to concentrate government repression on those he considered soft on Germany rather than on those, like Theodore Roosevelt, who favored harsh terms for the Reich. This was not an easy decision for the president. As the next chapter discusses, Atlanticists loudly criticized the administration for not fighting the Central Powers more vigorously and for failing to stand forthrightly for an unconditional surrender by Berlin. As Walter Lippmann and Herbert Croly pointed out to Wilson, cracking down on the pacifist left while doing little against "militarists like Mr. Roosevelt" emboldened the latter, and they, as much as the former, were not in sympathy with Wilson's war aims. The president himself was irritated with Roosevelt's attacks on his policies and, by September 1918, clearly wished to do something to silence him.[47]

But he felt that his hands were tied. With the nation battling a foe Wilson repeatedly described as brutal and treacherous, how could the administration try to repress people who were, in Croly's words, "irreconcilable pro-war enthusiasts"? After all, the whole point of the government's censorship and propaganda policies was to shore up support for Wilson's policy of fighting Germany. Albert Sidney Burleson, Wilson's postmaster general and censor in chief, clearly saw the situation this way. When the president asked him why the administration went after socialist critics of the war but not Roosevelt, Burleson replied that nothing Roosevelt said indicated "disloyalty to the Government." However much their war aims differed from Wilson's and undermined the president's peace program, Burleson could not act against them because "Mr. Roosevelt and others of like kidney have the reputation of being extreme advocates of extermination of the Central Powers." Once at war, in other words, Wilson found it impossible to direct repression in any direction other than to his left—toward people, Lippmann observed, who often supported the general concept of international reform.[48]

In addition to censoring leftist critics of the war and flooding the country with prowar propaganda, Wilson used a variety of other coercive policies at home to ensure that he could bring Germany to terms. Invoking "the principle of universal liability to service," he persuaded Congress to raise his armies through conscription. He sharply expanded the government's powers over the economy, through varying degrees of price controls, labor regulations, and the construction of government-owned shipyards. He stepped up taxes on corporate profits and personal incomes, acquired the power to reorganize executive agencies and departments at his own discretion, and prohibited the use of edible grains for distilled beverages.

Most dramatically, in late 1917, the federal government took over direct control of America's vast railroad system.[49]

The president did not think that his repressive and coercive measures corrupted American democracy. The draft embodied the "great idea," the president declared on Registration Day, "that in a democracy the duty to serve and the privilege to serve falls on all alike." Selective service also allowed the government to allocate manpower efficiently and with as little disruption to the economy as possible, which Wilson believed would help preserve "standards of labor" and "enforcement of the Child Labor Law"—progressive achievements the president associated with democracy. Indeed, the administration included Samuel Gompers, the head of the American Federation of Labor, on the Advisory Commission of the Council of National Defense and successfully pushed for many pro-labor provisions in its war contracts. In Wilson's view, his wartime labor measures had given workers "a new dignity and a new sense of social and economic security."[50]

The president also tried to limit the government's use of legal coercion to achieve its mobilization goals and to avoid expanding the federal bureaucracy. In most areas of the economy, the administration relied on publicity campaigns, private persuasion, and the voluntary cooperation of consumers, business, and labor to get its way. By supporting the Sedition Act of 1918, the administration thought that it could prevent mob violence against antiwar dissenters while fending off proposals to increase the War Department's role in counterespionage efforts and to subject civilians to court-martial by the military. Similarly, Wilson saw the Justice Department's use of the American Protective League—a semiprivate vigilante organization—as an alternative to creating a new government intelligence bureau to operate at home and abroad, in effect, a central intelligence agency. In whatever sphere, the economy or internal security, mobilizing America "on a volunteer basis," Wilson argued, was "the finest possible demonstration of the willingness, the ability, and the efficiency of democracy, and of its justified reliance upon the freedom of individual initiative."[51]

The growing momentum to pass a woman's suffrage amendment to the Constitution no doubt reinforced Wilson's confidence that fighting Germany was not destroying American democracy. "The services of women during this supreme crisis of the world's history have been of the most signal usefulness and distinction," the president announced in 1918. "The war could not have been fought without them, or its sacrifices endured." Because the struggles involved with the war democratized national service, women should share in democracy's duties and benefits too, Wilson argued. "We have made partners of the women in this war," he asserted to the Senate. "Shall we admit them only to a partnership of suffering and sacrifice and toil and not to a partnership of privilege and right?" Although the suffrage amendment was not approved by Congress until 1919, its passage by the House of Representatives in January 1918 lent added credibility to the president's claim that

even while at war, Americans remained committed to their democratic ideals—
that the battle against Germany had become, in Wilson's words, "a peoples' war."[52]

Most basically, Wilson's peace program tempered the militaristic pressures unleashed by the fighting overseas. Defeating German aggression served America's
own security needs, a goal in accord with traditional power politics. But it also
advanced the cause of international reform, which enhanced the security of all
nations. The goal of collective security thus transformed the war from a selfish
enterprise into one consistent with America's historic mission to serve others and
with American democracy. America's involvement in the conflict showed "to all
mankind," Wilson argued, that "we did not set this government up in order that
we might have a selfish and separate liberty, for we are now ready to come to your
assistance and fight out upon the field of the world the cause of human liberty."
Because Americans had "no selfish ends to serve" in the war, they could "fight
without passion and . . . observe with proud punctilio the principles of right and
fair play we profess to be fighting for." A war for international reform, a war to
end self-seeking power politics, could not regiment or corrupt Americans. "In
this thing," in its service to all in building collective security, "America," Wilson
claimed, "attains her full dignity and the full fruition of her great purpose."[53]

In late 1918, the climax of Wilson's struggle to set the stage for international reform finally appeared at hand. With their armies in the west exhausted and over-
extended after three failed attempts to shatter the Allied front, Germany's top military and political leaders decided that the Reich had to reorganize its government
and move to end the war. With the acquiescence of the Reichstag's leaders, the
kaiser appointed Prince Max of Baden as chancellor, replacing Hertling. Significant although incomplete democratic reforms were quickly put into effect, and a
new cabinet, made up mostly of representatives from the Reichstag majority bloc,
including members of the SPD, took office. After agonizing for several days over
when exactly to make an armistice request of the United States, the new government sent off a note to Wilson on the night and early morning of 4–5 October.
Signed by Prince Max, it asked for an immediate armistice and peace negotiations
on the basis of the Fourteen Points and Wilson's "subsequent pronouncements."[54]

The president hesitated to respond to the German government's note. At first
glance, the note presented Wilson with a chance to end the war in a manner most
conducive to international reform: through talks with a democratizing German
government, without the need for a costly invasion on German soil that might
reduce the Reich, in the words of one report Wilson received, to "utter ruin." But
grasping the hand Germany extended had risks as well. As editorials Wilson read
on 7 October pointed out, there was no guarantee that Germany's democratic
reforms would continue to develop or even remain in place. William Bullitt in
the State Department, in fact, believed that "the reins of power still remain in

the hands of the Kaiser and the military authorities." The president also doubted that Germany had really been militarily defeated—a condition he had long associated with the advent of genuine German democratization. Finally, Wilson knew that press editorials and opinion in the Senate strongly opposed any peace negotiations with the Reich. The American people, as House summed up his view of public opinion in his diary, were "war mad." They wanted to beat Germany to its knees and force a "complete surrender" by Germany's leaders.[55]

On 8 October, Wilson finally decided not to reject the German note but to put military and political conditions on continuing an exchange. Before any "discussions" of peace could begin, Germany had to concede that negotiations would only deal with "the practical details" of applying the Fourteen Points, to withdraw its forces "everywhere from invaded territory," and to make clear who exactly the imperial chancellor spoke for. These terms allowed Wilson to claim that he was not violating his own public commitment not to bargain with Germany's autocracy, even though he was responding to its note. More importantly, if the Germans accepted his preconditions for talks, the president would have the military security he needed to impose his program on the Reich whether it democratized or not. As Wilson told his aide, Joseph Tumulty, the day he composed the first draft of his note, if he could accept the German initiative, "the war will be at an end, for Germany cannot begin a new one." In Wilson's mind on 7–8 October, Germany's evacuation of Allied territory would render it incapable of restarting the war. The president could then engage in limited negotiations with its democratizing government—an important step toward reconciliation with the Germans—while holding the military high ground.[56]

Events after Wilson dispatched his note to Berlin, however, led him to toughen his stance toward the Germans. The Republican-led clamor for the Reich's "unconditional surrender" if anything intensified; whipped up by eighteen months of the administration's own propaganda campaign, one supporter told the president, Americans wanted "the Kaiser and his family . . . swept from power." More troubling, Wilson discovered that his demand for a German withdrawal from occupied territory would not give him the military security he wanted against the Reich. A simple military evacuation, Wilson learned from General Bliss on the evening of 8 October, might allow the Germans to "retire to . . . strong positions behind the Rhine with their armies and armaments and supplies intact" while they delayed withdrawing troops in the east. Then they could bargain with the Allies to try to salvage their gains from Brest-Litovsk. Allied military and political leaders made essentially the same point to the administration the next day and demanded that any armistice include, among other provisions, the disarmament of the enemy under strict time limits, the surrender of war supplies stored in the Rhineland, the surrender of the German naval base at Heligoland, the evacuation of Alsace-Lorraine, and the occupation by the Allies of five strategic points in the provinces. Finally, despite their peace initiative and internal political reforms, the Germans seemed as brutal and devious as ever, as one of their submarines sank a passenger steamer on 10 October, killing nearly two hundred civilians, and their reply to Wilson's first note, sent two days later, suggested that they wanted a cease-fire without any crippling conditions imposed on their armies.[57]

Wilson responded to these developments in his second note to Germany, sent on 14 October. Rather than just demanding a German withdrawal from all invaded territories, the president now emphasized, first, that "the process of evacuation and the conditions of an armistice are matters which must be left to the judgment and advice of the military advisers of the Government of the United States and the Allied Governments." Second, an armistice would not be considered as long as Germany's armed forces sank passenger liners at sea and destroyed civilian property on land as its armies retreated. Finally, the president suggested, more pointedly than he had in his first note, that Germany's government still possessed an "arbitrary power" that Wilson had pledged America to destroy. The Germans needed "to alter" this power as "a condition precedent to peace, if peace is to come by the action of the German people themselves." Otherwise, the 14 October note implied, peace would arrive only by the action of America and the Allies, without any German participation in it at all.[58]

The president's new conditions for an armistice were tailored to meet both his domestic and international needs. First, the military's prospective terms gave Wilson the "definitive victory" in the war he wanted; as he told the Germans, he insisted on "absolutely satisfactory safeguards and guarantees of the maintenance of the present military supremacy of the armies of the United States and the Allies in the field." This standard of military security would be met, though, without an extensive occupation of the Reich. One naval base and five strategic points in Alsace-Lorraine might be taken and Germany largely disarmed in the west, but no Allied army would have to fight its way to Berlin. To Wilson, such terms would avoid "undue humiliation" of the Germans while preventing them from "taking advantage of [the] armistice to reform their forces and better their position." The Germans would be defeated and under Wilson's control but not so abased and deranged that international reform could not proceed. At the same time, the president's deference to Allied military authorities allowed him to resist Republican pressures for an invasion of the Reich without appearing weak—an important consideration with congressional elections crucial to his diplomatic prestige only weeks away.[59]

Wilson's second note to Germany also revealed a shift in his posture on negotiations. Given its apparent attempt to manipulate an armistice to its military advantage and given his continuing doubts as to the extent of its democratic reforms, Wilson no longer planned to have any discussion with the German government over the practical details of the Fourteen Points. Stripped of much of its armament in the west and under limited, but strategically significant Allied occupation, no government of Germany would be in a position to negotiate with Wilson and the Allies over anything. At most, Wilson told William Wiseman, the Germans should be allowed to attend the peace conference after the armistice "to state their case." Otherwise, the conference would smack of traditional power politics; without the Germans there, it would look like America and the Allies were "dividing the spoils amongst ourselves." "The same thing applied to the League of Nations," Wilson added. "Germany ought to be present when the League of Nations is constituted." Whether or not this meant that Wilson still planned to admit Germany to the league was not clear. But if the Germans did not further alter their government, as indicated in Wilson's note, it would be hard for the president, for domestic political reasons, even to allow them into the peace conference. With the kaiser still on his throne, Wilson could not have any contact with Germany during the writing of the peace treaty; with the kaiser gone and the autocracy further enfeebled, Germany could at least plead its position at the conference and might still get into the league, which was a much better outcome from the standpoint of reconciling with it.[60]

The approach that Wilson developed in his second note to Germany—and the rationale behind it—continued in his third message to Berlin, sent on 23 October. If anything, the president's distrust of Germany's new government, and, consequently, his determination to incapacitate its military capability, deepened. Presented with an intercepted German cable revealing a scheme by the Germans to keep troops in the east while they secured an armistice in the west, Wilson thought that he discerned "the old Prussian trickery and deceit." Germany's constitutional changes remained unratified as well, and at home calls for the Reich's unconditional surrender persisted. Meanwhile, Allied military experts refined the conditions that they wanted to make a renewal of the war by Germany impossible. As Wilson learned between 18 and 22 October, they now contemplated the occupation of Alsace-Lorraine, the surrender of some of Germany's navy, partial German disarmament on the western front, and, perhaps, the occupation of the Rhineland. The president fully digested this information; leaving the armistice terms to "military men," he told his cabinet on 22 October, "might include leaving all heavy guns behind, and putting Metz, Strasburg, etc., in the hands of the Allies, until peace was declared." Although Wilson was growing concerned that the Allies were "getting to the point where they were reaching out for more than they should have in justice," such terms were still in line with the policy that Wilson developed in his second note: he wanted to avoid a full-scale invasion of the Reich while rendering it powerless to resist him.[61]

Thus, in his note of 23 October, Wilson explicitly demanded that any ceasefire leave Germany militarily prostrate. The military advisers of the United States and the Allies would draft the armistice, and it had to put the West "in a position to enforce any arrangements that may be entered into and to make a renewal of hostilities on the part of Germany impossible." The only armistice Wilson would accept was one that gave the Allied coalition "the unrestricted power to safeguard and enforce the details of the peace to which the German Government has agreed." More bluntly than in his second note, Wilson also declared that Germany's political reforms had fallen short of establishing a parliamentary democracy and, to the degree it had "partially" changed, there were no guarantees that the changes were permanent. As far as he was concerned, Wilson charged, "the power of the King of Prussia to control the policy of the Empire is unimpaired." If the United States had to deal with the existing regime now or in the future, the president warned, "it must demand, not peace negotiations, but surrender." The best that Germany could hope for, as was the case on 14 October, was to be allowed to comment on the peace treaty and to have a chance at league membership, and even those privileges were dependent on further changes in its government.[62]

With the dispatch of Wilson's notes of 23 October to the Germans and the Allies, the center of action concerning an armistice shifted to Paris, the seat of the Supreme War Council. The "terms of the armistice," the president cabled Pershing on 28 October, "should be rigid enough to secure us against renewal of hostilities by Germany but not humiliating beyond that necessity, as such terms would throw the advantage to the military party in Germany." He repeated the same formula to House, who arrived in Paris as Wilson's representative on 25 October, although with a different rationale for it. He was certain, he told the colonel, that "too much success or security on the part of the Allies will make a genuine peace settlement exceedingly difficult if not impossible." Wilson continued to want the Germans militarily reduced to the point that they could not recommence fighting, in short, but not so humiliated that they rallied to the autocracy or completely collapsed into chaos.[63]

Drawing this line proved hard to do. At the time of House's arrival in Paris, the president contemplated terms that, at a minimum, significantly disarmed Germany in the west and allowed the Allies to occupy strategic points in Alsace-Lorraine. These terms themselves, General Bliss told Wilson on 24 October, essentially said to Germany, "Surrender, and we will then do as we please." Nevertheless, the top French military leader, Marshal Ferdinand Foch, wanted even more "drastic" terms, Bliss reported. Foch "demanded that the Germans should retire at the rate of 30 kilometers per day until they reached a line 50 kilometers east of the Rhine and that they should surrender to the Allies four bridge heads on the Rhine to be occupied by the Allies"—terms Bliss considered "humiliating" to the Germans and sure to require a "league of armed nations" to uphold. Wilson at first sympathized with this analysis; on 28 October, in a cable to General Pershing, he questioned the need for any occupation of either Alsace-Lorraine or the Rhineland, likening the latter to "practically an invasion of German soil." Yet on the same day, in a cable to House, Wilson seemed confused as to what to do, as he thought the position of generals Haig and Pétain was "safer than Foch's," even though Haig wanted to occupy Alsace-Lorraine and Pétain called for possessing both the provinces and the "possession of such bridge heads on the eastern side of the Rhine by the Allies as may be necessary to ensure their control of that river." Trying to cripple Germany and yet not humiliate it was such a contradictory task that even Wilson seemed perplexed by it.[64]

In the event, Wilson decided to go along with Foch's terms, as well as with demands that Germany surrender 160 submarines and "intern" much of its surface navy at neutral or Allied ports, pending final disposition at the peace conference. He did this despite knowing that Lloyd George had doubts concerning the occupation of the Rhine bridgeheads and despite warnings from Bliss that the Allies were trying to write "approximate Peace Terms in the Armistice." Wilson agreed with terms he feared might be excessive because, at bottom, there was no alternative to them given the president's desire to render Germany incapable of restarting the war. As one student of the armistice has pointed out, "Any armistice able to prevent Germany's renewing hostilities could not be 'moderate and reasonable.'" Bliss saw total German disarmament as an alternative to occupying the Rhineland, but that course had problems too. It would still amount to "a complete surrender on the part of Germany," Bliss admitted, and, Wilson may have feared, it would make it impossible for Germany's new government to defend itself against the Far Right or the Far Left. Bliss's proposal thus offered no better way to apply Wilson's armistice preferences than did Foch's terms. The president desired both "the unrestricted power to safeguard and enforce" the peace against Germany and terms easy enough to conciliate the German people. But he wanted the former more, so he agreed to put the latter at risk.[65]

The president more readily agreed to an Allied demand to append a reservation to their acceptance of the Fourteen Points as the basis for the peace treaty. Reported by House on 30 October, this statement asserted that "compensation will be made by Germany for all damage done to the civilian population of the Allies, and their property . . . by land, by sea, and from the air." Wilson had long indicated that he thought Germany should pay some sort of indemnity for the damage it caused to the nations it invaded; as the Allies pointed out, the president himself had called in the Fourteen Points for invaded territories to be "restored." Germany had to pay for the wrongs it had committed and Wilson wanted its power reduced. Forcing Germany to pay reparations could help accomplish both of these goals.[66]

Other aspects of the Allied position during the deliberations at Paris deeply alarmed Wilson, however. On the same day that House told the president of the Allied stance on reparations, he also revealed that the British would not accept the second of the Fourteen Points, freedom of the seas, because, in Lloyd George's words, "it takes away from us the power of blockade." France and Italy, House added, also had objections to the Fourteen Points and were "not at all in sympathy" with the idea of a peace league. Unlike the case with the military and naval terms the Allies wanted, Wilson reacted immediately to this news, authorizing House to tell Allied leaders he would not participate in a peace settlement lacking freedom of the seas and a league of nations. Wilson also applauded House's threat to the British that if they did not relent on the free seas issue, "their policy would lead to the establishment of the greatest naval program by the United States that the world had ever seen." As negotiations continued, the president urged House to repeat this threat; tell the British, he cabled on 4 November, that if they did not accept the principle of freedom of the seas, "they can count upon the certainty of our using our present great equipment to build up the strongest navy our resources permit, as our people have long desired."[67]

The president reacted so strongly to the Allied statements because they went to the core of his vision for world reform. Military security against Germany was also central to his program, but the differences between Wilson and the Allies on that score were minimal. In contrast, Britain's refusal to endorse Wilson's free seas principle had ominous implications for international reform. It implied that Britain contemplated building and maintaining its own naval power for its own block-ades against its own enemies, as if the league and its responsibility for disarmament and collective security did not exist. "We are pledged to fight not only to do away with Prussian militarism," Wilson reminded House on 30 October, "but militarism everywhere." Naval blockades were to be used to uphold collective security, to enforce, specifically, economic sanctions against league-designated aggressors. Allowing blockades to be employed by a great power outside the league's authority would defeat the whole purpose behind creating a league of nations in the first place—and a peace without a viable league of nations, Wilson told House, "would be without any guarantee except universal armament which would be intolerable."[68]

Neither Wilson nor the Allies wanted their coalition to fall apart as it stood poised on the brink of victory, however. On 30 October, Lloyd George offered to accept the Fourteen Points as the basis for the peace treaty, with one reservation on reparations and one stating that Britain reserved "complete freedom" on interpreting freedom of the seas at the peace conference. Wilson replied that he wanted the principle of freedom of the seas accepted, but he also recognized that the term needed further definition, as did the meaning of a blockade, "in view of the many new circumstances of warfare developed by this war." The British stood by their reservation on the issue but told House in writing on 3 November that they were "willing to discuss the freedom of the sea in the light of the new conditions which have arisen in the course of the present war." Wilson accepted this statement as the only way available to resolve the crisis. Aided by French leader Georges Clemenceau, in an apparent payback for House's support of Foch's military terms, the colonel meanwhile got the Allies to agree to the rest of the Fourteen Points, including the league of nations, without reservation. The Allies, House exulted to the president on 5 November, "are now committed to the American peace programme."[69]

As the Allied-American armistice negotiations reached their climax, Wilson warily observed the continued development of Germany's new government. He remained skeptical of the Reich's democratization, despite its ratification in late October of constitutional amendments making its government fully responsible to the Reichstag. He did not publish a memo the Germans sent him detailing their constitutional changes, and the administration's fourth note to them, directing them to contact Foch to receive the armistice terms, was addressed to the "Imperial" German government, just as his earlier messages had been. The president still expected to invite them to the peace conference and to be allowed into the league of nations, but nothing of substance would be discussed with them. New constitution or not, true negotiations with Germany remained out of the question.[70]

The president did not explain his position, but his reluctance to embrace Germany's government probably reflected the same views he had held of the Germans earlier, when he sent them his second and third notes. Having received a report of German plans to unleash their submarines if peace talks broke down, he may have agreed with Lansing that Germany's "military regime" still held some power, that it had not been fully eliminated. Wilson may also have concurred with the opinion of Lester Woolsey, a legal expert that Lansing asked to review the Reich's constitutional changes. Any constitution could be changed, Woolsey suggested. The only real guarantee of a permanent democracy lay in its people's good faith in it—a commitment he thought the German people lacked. A certain evaluation of Germany's democratization, in other words, was impossible, as one could never truly know if the Germans had genuinely committed themselves to it or not. In any event, the ratification of Germany's new parliamentary constitution left President Wilson unmoved—*nothing* the Germans did with respect to liberalizing their government seemed to satisfy him.[71]

A few days after he dispatched his last note to the Reich, Wilson wondered if even allowing the Germans to attend the peace conference would be impossible. Between 3 and 7 November, revolution spread rapidly across Germany, and, on 9 November, Prince Max resigned as chancellor and announced that the kaiser had abdicated. A new provisional government of socialist "people's commissars" took power, chaired by SPD leader Friedrich Ebert. Wilson learned of the initial revolutionary disturbances on 6 November, then received from Bullitt the next day a more detailed report on them, emphasizing the government's effort to combat Bolshevik agitation. In part, Wilson welcomed news of the revolution, telling Homer Cummings on 8 November that perhaps, finally, the Germans "had shaken off the imperialistic rule and the military autocracy." But he also worried about anarchy and Bolshevik-like "madness" engulfing Germany—"excesses" that could prevent it from participating in the peace conference. By 11 November, as he announced the armistice to Congress, Wilson had concluded, first, that he should speed humanitarian relief to the Central Powers to conciliate their peoples and fend off radicalism and, second, that he needed to await developments before deciding how to deal with them in peacemaking. If necessary, he resolved, he and the Allies would simply make a peace for the Germans—"a peace that will justly define their place among the nations, remove all fear of their neighbors and of their former masters, and enable them to live in security and contentment when they have set their own affairs in order."[72]

Whether the president would achieve that goal or not remained to be seen. What was clear, though, was that America's participation in the war sharply intensified the contradictions involved with Wilson's national security strategy. As he conceived it, international reform in part depended on both limiting Germany's power and conciliating it. Trying to accomplish this paradoxical task prior to April 1917 had been hard enough. Once the United States entered the war on the Allied side, it became almost impossible. Because Germany had attacked American ships, intrigued with Mexico to form an anti-American alliance, rejected Wilson's mediation efforts, and continued to pursue conquests in Europe, the president's suspicion of it hardened into implacable hostility. He became more determined than ever to defeat the Reich and to reduce its power to a level below that of 1914—so much so, indeed, that he embarked on a risky intervention in Russia in large part to make sure that Germany would have no chance to make any gains from the war. He also wanted Germany's people to suffer in their defeat so that they would be deterred from aggression in the future. But at the same time, he continued to perceive that international reform could not proceed if the war left Germany a broken, embittered nation. These conflicting goals posed a difficult dilemma for the president: the more he focused on rolling back Germany's power, the less likely he could conciliate it; the more he tried to appease it, the less likely he could defeat it in the war. More so than ever after April 1917, then, Wilson's strategy to secure America's future was inherently problematic.

Germany's democratization seemed to offer one way out of this predicament. The German people, in Wilson's estimation, were not obsessed with dominating their neighbors or with conquest. A parliamentary government would be unlikely to engage in aggression and would be more trustworthy than Germany's autocracy in its diplomacy. It would also be willing, Wilson hoped, to repudiate the kaiser's wrongs, make restitution to his victims, and allow territorial readjustments in the interests of justice and collective security. If they were convinced that their military masters had led them into disaster, and if they were assured of just and fair treatment by the West, the German people would seize power, stop fighting, and genuinely embrace Wilson's peace program. Germany's power would be controlled, but its people would be partners in international reform.

But this solution to the German problem was always more apparent than real. For all of his proclaimed faith in the peaceful character of the German people, Wil-

son consistently had doubts about them. His belief that they would support the autocracy if it delivered on conquests; his dismay with their ratification of the Brest-
Litovsk treaty; his statements, before and after Brest-Litovsk, that they needed to
suffer pain in order to realize the futility of aggression; and his fear they might
degenerate into Bolshevik-like anarchy all suggest that Wilson, deep down, trusted
the German people only marginally more than he did their autocratic leaders.
They were different than their military masters—but it was a difference in degree,
not in kind. Hence the peace terms the president offered them were essentially the
same as those offered to Germany's autocracy, especially after March 1918.

Even if Wilson had fully trusted the German people, it quickly became apparent during the armistice negotiations that assessing the extent and permanence
of political reform in Germany was very hard to do. In his third note to Berlin,
Wilson found himself in the awkward position of conceding that Germany's government had "partially" changed and now spoke for the Reichstag but insisting
that it was still under the military's control too, apparently because its constitutional proposals had not yet been ratified. Even after the Reichstag approved the
new constitution, Wilson still seemed to think that the new parliamentary system
was somehow illegitimate or transitory. This was not an irrational position for
him to adopt. After all, America did not have agents inside Germany carefully
monitoring its democratic reforms. Newspaper reports and the State Department
analyses of events inside Germany were speculative and sketchy. And, as Lansing's
legal expert pointed out, any constitution the Germans wrote up could always
be changed. Fundamentally, how could Wilson really be certain that Germany
might not one day revert to an autocratic state? He couldn't, so he proceeded with
demanding strict military security against the Germans despite their assurances
that they had changed. Without admitting it to himself, he largely sacrificed conciliating Germany for controlling it.[73]

To be certain, Wilson saw his peace program as more conciliatory toward the
Germans than the terms preferred by the Allies. Highlighting his differences with
the Entente could both underscore this point, thus helping to woo the Germans
into embracing his program, and put pressure on the Allies to modify their war
aims. But with Wilson determined to defeat and control Germany, he could not
pursue this tactic very far. Appealing to Allied leftists to agitate for a revision of
the Entente's peace terms could backfire if they became too conciliatory toward
the Reich and called for something like the Petrograd formula. Openly exerting
leverage on the Allies could give the Reich an opening to drive a wedge in the coalition against it and cause intense controversy at home with the Republicans. It
could imperil the whole war effort. Thus, although the president tried to strike a
threatening pose with them, with his not-so-veiled threats to make a separate peace
with Germany, to out-build their navies and merchant marines after the war, and
to curtail the flow of financial aid they received from America, he never actually

provoked a showdown with the Allies over war aims. He came close during the armistice negotiations but settled for their agreement to make the Fourteen Points the basis for the peace treaty and for Britain's meaningless commitment "to discuss" freedom of the seas at the peace conference. As Wilson himself acknowledged, the "practical details" of the Fourteen Points remained open for negotiation; the real confrontation with the Allies over peace terms, if there would be one, was deferred for a later date. In theory the president had leverage over the Allies and needed to use it to get them committed to his program and to make his terms more palatable to Germany. But in reality, while the war was on, he could not afford much daylight to appear between himself and the Entente governments.[74]

Similarly, as Wilson had feared in March 1917, once the United States engaged in actual warfare to defeat power politics and the threat of militarism, its domestic liberties came under severe strain and Wilson had to repress pacifists who either opposed the war or wanted a peace based on the Petrograd formula. The president believed that he kept wartime repression and regimentation to within acceptable limits, especially by encouraging voluntarism, but even he publicly admitted that "the mob spirit" had emerged in "many and widely separated parts of the country." By the time of the armistice negotiations, Wilson noted such "intolerant hatred of Germans" among the public that he feared "American Prussianism" was engulfing the nation. One of his top political advisers, indeed, considered Republican demands for Germany's unconditional surrender to have been one of the controlling factors behind the Democrats' loss of the 1918 congressional elections. Again, this outcome was hardly a surprise given Wilson's need to whip up support at home for the war and for stringent terms against the Germans. But predictable or not, the wartime intolerance that Wilson fostered further narrowed his already limited ability—or willingness—to include substantive steps toward reconciliation with Germany in his peace program.[75]

Given his wartime desire for extensive limits on Germany's power, Wilson counted on the promise of collective security to reconcile the Germans—and the Allies and liberals at home and abroad—to his peace program. But the war further revealed the dubiousness of collective security theory—the notion that all nations had a vital stake in peace everywhere. If this idea was correct, selfishly competing to enhance one's own security at the expense of others was irrational, as true safety derived from acting according to the international community's collective interest in peace. Indeed, prior to April 1917 Wilson had hoped to underscore the futility of power politics by arranging a peace settlement that frustrated the Allies almost as much as the Germans. But once he plunged America into the fighting, Wilson obviously focused more on defeating and punishing Germany than he did on frustrating the Allies. At the same time, the behavior of America and the Allies during the war indicated that they cared about their power relative to each other almost as much as they cared about defeating Germany. Wilson distrusted Britain, France, Italy, and Japan, after all, because he saw in their respective war aims that each had its own selfish agenda for maximizing its power and security. And he, in turn, was evidently ready to hedge against a failure to come to agreement with them on war aims by hoarding America's military power as much as he could and by continuing parts of the 1916 naval program. Yet somehow, with the end of the war, a peace league based upon mutual recognition of interdependent security was supposed to spring into being and competitive power politics come to an end. If the behavior of the great powers during the fight against Germany was any indication, however, such an expectation was wildly optimistic.

Regardless of the evidence indicating that his program was deeply flawed, Wilson saw no reason to abandon it. For one thing, he managed to avoid confronting some of its contradictions and problems by not engaging them. Aware that getting too specific about his preferred peace terms might alienate the Germans and the Allies and cause division at home, he kept his Fourteen Points as vague as possible. Aware that any detailed proposals about how a collective security regime would enforce its decisions would raise protests at home and abroad, he actively discouraged substantive planning for a league and did little himself. So long as his goals remained abstract, so long as they could be summed up as simply a "world . . . made fit and safe to live in," it was easier for the president to maintain domestic and international support for them. This political imperative, though, also gave Wilson a handy excuse for turning away from the hard task of translating his program into a viable international structure for peace—a task that might have forced him to reconsider its efficacy.[76]

More fundamentally, President Wilson thought that American exceptionalism would allow the United States to overcome any obstacle blocking the path to international reform. He deeply believed that America was the "chief interpreter to the world of those democratic principles which we believe to constitute the only force which can rid the world of injustice and bring peace and happiness to mankind." He spoke, he asserted on 27 September 1918, for the "plain workaday people" everywhere who wanted an end to the balance of power. Certain that America stood for universal values beneficial to all, Wilson could feel confident that whatever coercion he did overseas or at home would be recognized, and accepted, as a temporary evil for a greater collective good, not as a selfish bid for power by the United States or by his administration. Seeing himself and America as the instrument of an international yearning for justice and peace, Wilson believed as well that any dispute over peace terms or the league's machinery would ultimately be overcome. There was no need, then, to worry about the contradictions and ambiguities in his program. Such matters were mere details, easily mastered by the will of America's good intentions.[77]

Abroad, however, Allied statesmen were largely unimpressed with Wilson's claim to be an exceptional spokesman for humanity. They were irritated by Wilson's unilateralism, especially when the president replied to Germany's armistice notes without consulting them, and by his assumption of moral superiority over them. Wilson's attitude, Wiseman observed in September 1918, "has tended to become more arbitrary, and aloof, and there are times when he seems to treat foreign governments hardly seriously." Given the vast discrepancy between the casualties suffered by the Allies and those by America in the fighting—total American combat deaths as of 6 April 1918, for example, were 163, while British casualties from 21 March to 7 April 1918 were 115,868—it is not surprising that Wilson's "associates" resented his attempts to dominate peacemaking. From their point of view, Wilson was hardly in any position to suggest, as he did on 27 September 1917, that his peace terms represented the true yearnings of the masses and theirs did not.[78]

Neither British nor French leaders had a high regard for the substance of Wilson's peace program either. They had grave doubts about the workability of collective security; no nation, Lloyd George thought, would give up any national sovereignty to a peace league. Britain and France did pay lip service to the idea of international reform in public, recognizing its popular appeal, but their own respective sketches of a league assumed that it would essentially be a continuation of the wartime coalition against Germany. As for Wilson's Fourteen Points, the Allies considered them sufficiently vague that they could agree to them and still achieve their own strategic war aims. The president's peace program, as Lloyd George's secretary put it, was "mostly verbiage and [would] have to be interpreted in fact by the light of the situation and the determination of the different parties concerned."[79]

Finally, the British did not see Wilson as a consistent opponent of power politics, regardless of his proclaimed support for international reform. Fully aware that their massive losses on the western front were sapping their nation's strength, the British badly wanted the United States to get more into the fighting; for London, the point of brigading American troops with British forces was to preserve British manpower and thus help Britain to preserve its power for the peace conference. Wilson's refusal to do anything but minimal brigading indicated that the president was willing to risk losing the war in order to build his own army—an army British leaders feared would give the United States a predominant role in peacemaking. "What Bliss calls the God-damned American programme is going to f—— up the whole show," fumed one senior British general at the height of the brigading controversy. To the British, in other words, Wilson was trying to do to them what they were trying to do to him: pass the buck for fighting the Germans to maximize his nation's power for his diplomacy.[80]

The president's naval policies before and during the armistice negotiations also undercut his credibility as an international reformer. Sir Eric Geddes, Britain's first lord of the admiralty, bluntly gave his reaction to the administration's course as the war came to an end. Its decision to continue to build capital ships during the war and its insistence that no prejudgment be made about the disposition of Germany's warships prior to the peace conference indicated its intentions clearly enough to him. Wilson, Geddes argued, wished to create a new sea power, alone or in combination with others, that would be "the equivalent of, or greater than, the sea power of the British Empire." "In other words," Geddes emphasized, "he is pursuing the 'Balance of Power' theory, which has hitherto so much influenced European policies, and is applying it in sea power only to world politics." Wilson's actions spoke louder than his words—and his actions made him look like a traditional practitioner of power politics.[81]

The Germans were more willing to take the president's peace program seriously—but only so long as it benefited Germany. When Wilson first proclaimed the Fourteen Points, many of the leaders of the Reichstag majority thought that they could serve as the basis for a peace treaty, provided that they left all of Germany's territory intact, including Alsace-Lorraine. Matthias Erzberger in particular also saw a league of nations in Germany's security interests, assuming that it was based on a negotiated peace between equals. Even during the armistice exchanges in October 1918, when Wilson essentially demanded Germany's surrender despite its democratic reforms, Erzberger and the SPD's cabinet leader, Philipp Scheidemann, continued to hope that the president would ultimately deliver a liberal peace for them. Desperate to grasp any possibility that Germany might escape serious penalties for the war, Germany's leaders, despite their shock at Wilson's stance on armistice terms, convinced themselves that the Fourteen Points might be manipulated to their own advantage and that Wilson, having proclaimed that international reform depended on a peace of justice, would help them. If he did not, he would reveal himself to be a hypocrite.[82]

Wilson's efforts during the war to reconcile the contradictions in his peace program therefore had very mixed results. Germany and the Allies had committed themselves to making the Fourteen Points the basis of the peace treaty, but the Points were so vague that they all expected Wilson's program to work in their favor. Germany's armed forces had been defeated, its power reduced, and its autocracy destroyed, but whether or not it would be conciliated depended, at least in part, on Wilson's satisfying a German interpretation of the Fourteen Points—something he had no intention of doing. The Allied-American coalition remained intact, but Allied leaders were more interested in practicing traditional diplomacy than in advancing international reform, and many of them saw Wilson not as the avatar of collective security but as an aggressive promoter of his own nation's power and influence. And at home, the president's wartime foreign and domestic policies marginalized his opponents and dominated the political center of national security debates. But it was an illusory consensus, even as Wilson managed to reinforce the nation's fear of power politics and militarism. "The war thus comes to an end," Wilson announced to Congress after reading out the armistice terms against Germany—but his struggle to achieve his national security goals still had a long way to go.[83]

President Woodrow Wilson, c. 1916. Library of Congress, Prints and Photographs Division [reproduction number LC-USZ62-107577].

Woodrow Wilson and William Jennings Bryan, 25 January 1913. Library of Congress, Prints and Photographs Division [reproduction number LC-USZ62–68294].

Right: Crystal Eastman and Amos Pinchot, c. 1914. Library of Congress, Prints and Photographs Division [reproduction number LC-DIG-ggbain-21959].

Far right: Jane Addams, 1914. Library of Congress, Prints and Photographs Division [reproduction number LC-USZ62-10598].

Below left: Hamilton Holt, c. 1915. Library of Congress, Prints and Photographs Division [reproduction number LC-DIG-ggbain-27968].

Below right: William Howard Taft, c. 1915. Library of Congress, Prints and Photographs Division [reproduction number LC-USZ62-11453].

Theodore Roosevelt, c. 1908. Library of Congress, Prints and Photographs Division [reproduction number LC-USZ62–93318].

Elihu Root, c. 1914. Library of Congress, Prints and Photographs Division [reproduction number LC-USZ62–37254].

Henry Cabot Lodge, c. 1916. Library of Congress, Prints and Photographs Division [reproduction number LC-USZ62–36185].

The American Commission to Negotiate Peace, Paris, 18 December 1918: from left to right, Col. Edward M. House, Robert Lansing, Woodrow Wilson, Henry White, and Gen. Tasker Howard Bliss. Library of Congress, Prints and Photographs Division [reproduction number LC-USZ62–80161].

Extent of Central Powers' expansion, 1918.

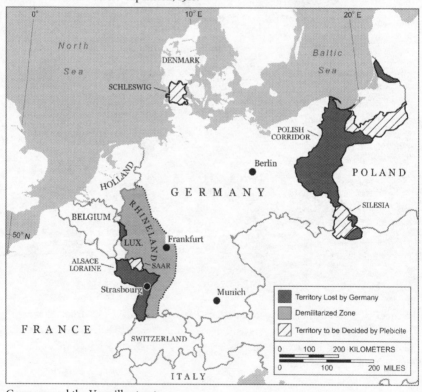

Germany and the Versailles treaty.

Territory held by the Central Powers, end of 1915.

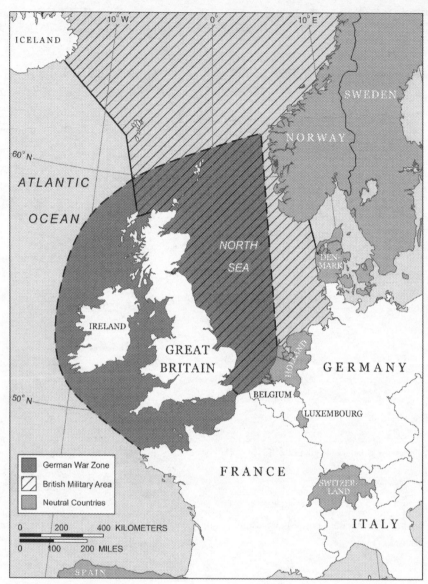

The war in the North Atlantic.

8

National Security Debates, 1917–18

At first glance, America's entry into the war appeared to rally a divided country to President Wilson's program for international reform. Significant numbers of pacifists embraced the president's logic concerning national security affairs while Atlanticists expressed fears of militarism if Germany won the war and endorsed the general concept of a league of nations. These manifestations of support for Wilson's national security views were conditional and tenuous, however. Neither former pacifists nor Progressive supporters of liberal internationalism could pinpoint the peace terms they thought should form the basis for a league, although they stressed that Germany had to be allowed into the organization and receive equal opportunities in the world economy. Nor could they explain exactly how a league should be run, although they emphasized that its institutions needed to have democratic representation. In contrast, Atlanticists and conservative liberal internationalists thought that a league had to begin by excluding and punishing Germany, and the LEP viewed democratic representation within a league as unimportant. At the same time, members of the LEP were divided among themselves concerning how a league should function. Overall, the war experience increased the desire of most of America's leaders to escape from power politics, but the leading proposal for doing so, the establishment of a collective security regime, remained as vague and problematic as ever.

To be sure, the reaction of liberal internationalists to Germany's resumption of unrestricted submarine warfare was clear enough. The Reich's government, they argued, had rejected the president's vision of international reform in the most violent possible way, revealing itself to be an "international criminal." It was murdering American citizens and terrorizing America's lines of communication to the Allies, to the nations that at least partly shared Wilson's peace aims and that historically had helped America preserve the security of the Western Hemisphere. Germany's submarine campaign would "probably" fail to defeat the Entente, conceded the *New Republic's* editors, but there was a chance it might succeed—a chance America could not afford to take. If Germany won the war, the United States would find itself frightened and alone in a hostile world. "In its fear it will arm," predicted the *New Republic,* "until its territory is spotted with camps and its shores bristle with guns and battleships, and its armament will be dictated by a spirit and employed for a purpose which will be most injurious, perhaps even fatal to American liberalism." Recoiling from accepting the heightened risk of such a future, where the only alternative to arms races and militarism would be to submit to German dictation, liberal internationalists agreed that America had no choice but to fight.[1]

They had differences, however, when it came to adjusting their peace program to America's new status as a belligerent. One response came from the *New Republic's* editors (and former editors, as Walter Lippmann, e.g., left the journal to work for the War Department), usually supported by Hamilton Holt's *Independent.* In a major shift of opinion from their pre-1917 views, Herbert Croly and his colleagues, soon after America entered the war, began to oppose any peace based on the status quo antebellum. Earlier, they had associated a status quo ante peace with Germany's dominance of central and southeastern Europe, "Middle Europe" as they called it, and had accepted such an outcome to the war as the necessary price for winning the Germans over to the cause of international reform. But now, given Germany's renewed aggressiveness in the war, the editors concurred with President Wilson that German hegemony over Middle Europe amounted to hegemony over the entire continent and so would condemn America to a future of arms races and militarism. To Lippmann, indeed, Wilson's June 1917 explanation of the danger of German domination of Middle Europe was "the most adequate and searching expression of the meaning of this war that has yet been uttered." To remove this threat, the peace settlement had to be based on Wilson's Fourteen Points—terms clearly at odds with the status quo antebellum.[2]

More broadly, the Reich's aggressive behavior after 1 February 1917 led the *New Republic* to reject the kaiser's autocratic government as a negotiating partner. The autocracy was completely insincere in its claim to have an interest in Wilson's peace program; all it really cared about was conquest and domination over others. If it stayed in power, the peace settlement ending the war would have to be "determined to a considerable extent by military considerations and would consist in large measure of material guarantees." At worst, suggested the editors, such a program might involve crushing Germany's armies, invading its territory, demanding an unconditional surrender, and then imposing a peace that left Germany and Austria defenseless, politically isolated, stripped of territory, and economically strangled. At a minimum, the *New Republic* agreed with Wilson, if Germany's autocracy remained in place, the United States had to dictate peace terms to it and possibly exclude it from equal economic treatment after the war. This policy, summed up by the president in his annual message to Congress and endorsed by the *New Republic* four days later, seemed like the only approach the United States could take with a regime as pernicious as the Reich's.[3]

If autocratic Germany could not be a full partner in building a new world order, however, the *New Republic* doubted that the existing system of unstable power politics could ever be ended. The force of a genuine collective security organization had to be "wielded by the community on behalf of a commonly agreed law . . . which shall assure fair and equal treatment to all alike." Smashing and physically controlling Germany would violate that standard. "If we start with 'strategic frontiers,' that do violence to nationality," argued the editors, "or economic exclusions to the disadvantage of states that have no colonies, we shall be attempting to crystallize inequity." A collective security league would be viewed as "a broken reed," and statesmen would trust in "secret arrangements" to provide for their safety. More specifically, to have any hope of maintaining their ascendancy over the Reich, the United States and the Allies would have to pursue the "permanent military organization of the world." America's future would be one of "armament, militarism, economic nationalism and power politics." Sooner or later, whatever alliance was set up to control Germany would fall apart, assumed the editors, and the German people would find a way to recover their strength and launch what for them would be "a war of liberation." Thus, for international reform to succeed, the Germans had to embrace the peace settlement: "If the defeat of German aggression is to be final," the editors stressed, "every possible attempt must be made to persuade the German people eventually to acquiesce in it."[4]

Like Wilson, Croly and his colleagues saw the democratization of Germany as an attractive and yet problematic way to achieve a peace settlement conducive to conciliating the Germans. On the one hand, Germany's people and the Reichstag did not control Germany's foreign policy, the *New Republic* asserted, and they supported the war primarily out of fear of foreign aggression. If the Reichstag took power, it could probably be trusted to work sincerely with the United States in negotiating a peace based on Wilson's terms and in building a league of nations. On the other hand, the *New Republic* also had doubts about the pacific character of Germany's masses. Germany's people were easily swayed by patriotic emotions, and the Reichstag, the editors noted, stood by the autocracy so long as it enjoyed success in the war, even if that success involved conquering other nations. More than once, in fact, the editors implied that they suspected Germany's most popular political party, the Social Democrats, of insincerity in renouncing aims of conquest. Even if the peaceful intentions of Germany's democrats could be granted, Germany's leaders might establish a "pretend democracy" as a way to gain a moderate peace settlement and then, at some future date, resume their aggression. Although the editors thought such a scenario unlikely, they acknowledged that it was a possibility. Despite all of the hopes they placed in German democratization as a way to save international reform, the editors conceded, "there is . . . no way of guaranteeing . . . the future civility of a democratized Germany."[5]

In 1917, the *New Republic* hoped that stalemate on the western front and assurances by the Allies of fair treatment to a democratized Germany would be enough to spark German democratic reform and negotiations to end the war. But Germany's advance into Russia, the Brest-Litovsk treaty, and the great German offensive in the west in early 1918 all eroded the journal's faith in the political strength and character of the Reich's democrats. Germany's "military party" was now "in the ascendant," lamented the editors in March. "Their Russian successes have renewed their hold upon the state." Weaning Germany's democrats from the autocracy now required a decisive military victory by the America and the Allies, the editors concluded by August. They also made less of a distinction between how democratic Germany and autocratic Germany should be treated at the end of the war. Determined to prevent a peace league from becoming a traditional balance-of-power alliance, the *New Republic* insisted in the summer of 1918 that even autocratic Germany had to be admitted to a postwar league of nations and, so long as it behaved, not be discriminated against in international trade. Almost as distrustful of a democratic Germany as an autocratic one, however, the editors asserted that any German government, democratic or not, would have to receive a "dictated" peace. Whatever happened in Germany, a league would go forward—but only on U.S. terms.[6]

The *New Republic* confirmed this posture during the armistice negotiations in October and November 1918. Regardless of Germany's democratic reforms, the editors approved of armistice terms they described as leaving the Germans "beaten and prostrate." Germany had to disarm as a condition of a cease-fire because whatever the disposition of Germany's new government, the army might refuse to follow its commands. Occupying the Rhineland and Alsace-Lorraine made sense because the United States had to make it impossible for Germany to renew the war. Demanding that Germany agree in principle to pay for war damages it caused was necessary too given the German peoples' unwillingness or inability to stop the Reich's campaign of conquest. "For the future peace of the world," lectured the editors, "it is necessary that it should be demonstrated, once and for all, that this policy does not pay."[7]

The *New Republic* did not see its heightened concern with limiting Germany's power in the summer and fall of 1918 as an abandonment of the goal of a peace of reconciliation. "The problem is not to destroy but to change [Germany]," reiterated the editors as they cheered on Wilson's armistice negotiations, "to lead her people away from the worship of military strength." The armistice terms were consistent with this objective because they fell short of demanding an unconditional surrender by Germany's new government. Recognizing that Germany had begun to reform its autocracy, Wilson, perceived the *New Republic,* refused to march to Berlin and dictate terms on German soil. The editors assumed the president planned ultimately to admit democratic Germany into the postarmistice peace conference where, at the least, it would obtain equal economic rights and entry into the league of nations. They claimed that the military and occupation provisions of the armistice did not "prejudice the decision of any essentially political problem," except perhaps for Alsace-Lorraine, which the editors conceded was going to be transferred to France. Indeed, they added, the German government should welcome the "laming" of Germany's army, because it gave the new regime "assurance against a military coup d'etat." The armistice terms might be "harsh," but they remained in line with the *New Republic*'s strategy of using "military chastisement as an agency of human reconciliation."[8]

Although the leaders of the League to Enforce Peace shared the *New Republic*'s goal of reconciling with Germany and including it in a peace league, most of them rejected the *New Republic*'s strategy for accomplishing this objective. Under the impact of the submarine crisis and America's entry into the war, they abruptly lost their faith that a democratic Germany could be a fit member of a peace league anytime soon. Since at least Germany's unification in 1871, Taft and other LEP spokesmen now argued, the imperial regime had pounded into the German people an ideology of "unmitigated national egoism." Naturally submissive to authority and impressed by the Reich's rise to power in the late nineteenth century, Germany's people "surrendered their souls to Prussia." Glorifying state power and brute strength, they lost all sense of morality and developed a "hatred and contempt for the people of other lands." The autocracy's success in the war, particularly in Russia, reinforced this attitude and its accompanying thirst for conquest. The pathology of Germany's wolfish nationalism could not be explained merely by pointing to the character of its autocratic leaders. The root of the problem instead lay in the "moral degeneration" of the entire German population.[9]

It followed that democratizing Germany would do little to make it an acceptable member of a league of nations. "National democracy helps not at all," William English Walling asserted at the 1918 LEP convention, "with an aggressive megalomaniac nation." According to Taft and his supporters, democratic political reform in Germany was just one step on a long road of psychological rehabilitation. To prepare the way for Germany's eventual admission to the league, the United States and the Allies had to inflict a crushing military defeat upon the Reich, march to Berlin, and demand an unconditional surrender, regardless of whether Germany's government democratized. Justice required that Germany pay for its crimes, and, more importantly, only the shock of defeat could trigger the moral regeneration of Germany's people. "Nothing but force," bellowed Taft, "can cure the brutality and ruthlessness of force." Total victory in hand, the Allied coalition should then dictate peace terms featuring indemnities, territorial adjustments at Germany's expense, the complete disarmament of the Central Powers, and, Taft implied, economic discrimination against them. Once the Germans demonstrated their moral awakening by carrying out these terms, then and only then could they be considered truly democratic and suited for membership in the league. This process might take a long time; Walling thought it would take "years or decades." However long it took, the point of the enterprise was to punish and transform the Germans, to chastise them and get them to show repentance for their sin of aggression.[10]

Liberal internationalists diverged on the relationship of the Allies to international reform no less than they did on the issue of reconciling with Germany. Except for a brief period in early 1918, when British prime minister David Lloyd George gave a major speech that seemed to echo Wilson's peace program, liberal internationalists frequently debated about how to deal with the problem of getting the Allies to commit themselves to ending power politics. Theodore Marburg of the LEP, Holt, and the New Republic's editors thought that the way to address this issue was to form an initial league of nations before the war ended. It would be easier to commit the Allies to the concept of collective security and to resolve differences over war aims now, they reasoned, while the Allied coalition had a common enemy. Moreover, argued frequent New Republic contributor Norman Angell, the Allies pursued selfish strategic objectives because they did not believe that a peace league would ever become a reality. That skepticism had to be dispelled by actually creating a working league or it might not be possible ever to convince the Allies to abandon their "scramble for individual power."[11]

Most leaders of the LEP disagreed with this analysis. Trying to create a wartime league might simply "emphasize the differing interests of the Entente," thought John Bates Clark, and hurt the war effort. And if an American-Allied league was formed, even with assurances that it would be expanded to include a reformed Germany later, its alliance-like character might permanently alienate the Germans from the whole project of international reform. For most of the LEP, the way to manage differences with the Allies over war aims was either to assume that victory over Germany would swing the Allies behind a league or to hope that America's power and Wilson's prestige among liberals overseas would be enough to compel the Entente to submit to the president's program.[12]

Russia, the most troublesome member of the coalition against Germany, also provoked debate among liberal internationalists. To the New Republic, the Entente's failure clearly to embrace Wilson's peace terms was a chief factor behind revolutionary Russia's disaffection from the war, a disastrous development that rallied Germany's people to the autocracy and threatened to prolong the fighting for years. When the Bolsheviks made peace with Germany in early 1918, the New Republic's editors reacted in much the same way as Wilson did. They hoped that Lenin's government would fall but were wary of any large-scale and direct American action to overthrow it, because that might mean involvement in a civil war and might alienate Russia from the administration's peace program. They also favored limited intervention in Russia, however, to spur Russian resistance to Germany and fend off an Allied-Japanese invasion that the editors were sure would totally discredit the goal of ending power politics. In contrast, members of the LEP thought that assurances of America's willingness to fight Germany, rather than a public discussion of war aims, would keep Russian resistance alive. As Russia collapsed and left the war, Taft and other LEP leaders blamed Bolshevik collusion with Germany and called for massive intervention in Russia to re-create an eastern front. In their view, Japan was a loyal supporter of America's war aims while the Bolsheviks were simply "tools of the German high command." Sending 200,000 or more troops to Russia to fight the Bolsheviks and the Germans was therefore not counter to the goal of international reform but consistent with it.[13]

As they struggled with determining how to use the war to advance toward the league of nations, liberal internationalists uncomfortably watched how the conflict transformed America's domestic life. In general, they agreed with President Wilson's approach to the home front. Most of the public was apathetic about the war, they perceived, and a "considerable minority" of pacifists, socialists, and German sympathizers actively opposed it or wanted an inconclusive peace that left Germany with too much power. The administration had no choice but to engage in some amount of repression to combat this minority, just as it also had a right to assert some measure of authority over the economy and manpower in order to mobilize the nation to fight. Despite the coercive character of the government's domestic policies, liberal internationalists agreed that the war stimulated American democracy to some degree. The draft might be "autocratic, unfair, and ruthless," admitted the *New Republic*, but it also avoided dividing the country into "heroes and stay-at-homes," was a "valuable experience in organized cooperation," and brought diverse men together to learn from each other's experiences. More broadly, the objective of ending power politics—the aim of safeguarding democracy through collective security—lay "at the very core of American national morale in relation to the war." It uplifted America's democratic spirit above whatever repression and intolerance existed at home, inspiring Americans to meet the test of war without succumbing to militarism.[14]

Still, in different ways, liberal internationalists were uneasy with Wilson's domestic policies. Croly and his colleagues at the *New Republic* were alarmed by the administration's crackdown on antiwar dissent and its promotion of "exclusively vindictive and coercive" war propaganda. The government's stance was politically counterproductive, warned the editors, because it threatened Progressive support for the war and divided public opinion "into fanatical jingoism and fanatical pacifism" opposed to Wilson's war aims. Even more troubling, the administration supported legislation, the Espionage Act, that the *New Republic* considered unconstitutional. In addition, while the editors often asserted that mobilization policies benefited labor and advanced the Progressive ideal of greater public control of the economy, they sometimes betrayed anxiety about growing state power. Creating an "economic dictatorship," they worried, could easily "degenerate into a hideous instrument of tyranny if continued unchanged after the war." The "new national economy" had its positive aspects, but it potentially had a very dark side as well.[15]

Conservatives at the LEP reversed the priority of these concerns: they rarely expressed opposition to the administration's censorship policies while clearly fearing the implications of the federal government's authority over the economy. "Never in the history of this country has the President had such vast and unlimited power as he has today," exclaimed Taft in October 1918. The initial version of the Overman Act, which allowed Wilson to reorganize executive departments without consulting Congress, looked especially dangerous. It gave Wilson "dictatorial powers," charged Taft, and amounted to "fighting Kaiserism with Kaiserism." The former president later approved of a more moderate bill, but he never lost his suspicion that Wilson tried to use the wartime emergency to acquire illegitimate powers. He also suggested that the war stimulated the administration's antibusiness, prolabor proclivities and, more generally, organized labor's desire to attack the rights of private property. America's constitutional checks and balances would probably safeguard free enterprise, Taft hoped, but he nevertheless worried that the postwar period would bring experiments in government power sure to have "disastrous results."[16]

Whatever the domestic damage done by the war, liberal internationalists were willing to tolerate it as long as American belligerency produced international reform. A league of nations, Lippmann reiterated in October 1918, was "the foundation of the whole diplomatic structure of a permanent peace." Neither the *New Republic* nor a new pro–collective security lobbying group organized by Croly and other Progressives, the League of Free Nations Association (LFNA), had much to say about how a peace league would function, however. The league's success chiefly depended, in their view, on the peace settlement "remedying the conditions, economic and other, which lead to division and conflict." They also reaffirmed their faith in the basic premise of collective security, shared by the LEP too, "that under modern conditions of warfare neutrality is an impossible position." When it came to the actual organization of the league, Croly and his colleagues were mostly concerned with preventing the development of "an immense bureaucratic union of Governments." Calling for a "democratic union of peoples," they urged an end to secret diplomacy and the establishment of "genuinely democratic parliamentary institutions in the League." But how these institutions—or any other organ of the league—would identify and act to discipline aggressors was left unclear. On these crucial issues, both the *New Republic* and the LFNA were silent.[17]

The League to Enforce Peace had a markedly different conception of a peace league compared to the LFNA. Unlike the latter, the LEP did not make any official comment about the need for a league to be based on a peace settlement that avoided economic and strategic discrimination against the defeated powers. Such a settlement was important to Holt and Marburg, but Taft and most other LEP spokesmen, it will be recalled, did not see harsh treatment of Germany as at all incompatible with building a collective security organization. Similarly, whereas the LFNA dwelled on the need for a league to have parliamentary representation in it, the LEP did not, although its "Victory Program" of November 1918 did call for a league to have a "representative Congress" to codify international law and consider how to advance peace and progress.[18]

What really absorbed—and divided—the LEP was the problem of determining the scope and operation of a league's organs of collective security. By the end of the war, most LEP leaders decided that a league should have the power to enforce the decisions it made on "justiciable" issues (i.e., questions relating to the interpretation of treaties or international law). This marked a shift from their pre-1917 position that a league should simply compel a hearing of international disputes. The 1918 Victory Program hinted than a league should enforce its recommendations concerning political controversies too, and it called for "an administrative organization" with vague powers to monitor international relations. Marburg disagreed with all of these provisions. He applauded the idea of enlarging a league's scope, but he doubted that governments would join such a powerful organization. If they did, they might not honor their commitments to it. Trying to go beyond the LEP's original proposals, Marburg thought, would wreck "the whole program." The LEP split over how a league should implement its decisions as well. A significant minority, led by Marburg, proposed that "an absolute majority" of a great power–dominated "international council" have the power to determine if a member had violated the league's conflict resolution rules and should face military sanctions. The LEP's executive committee rejected this idea, however, and approved a draft treaty that left unstated the voting procedure of the "executive body" charged with identifying and dealing with aggressors. In this respect, at least, the LFNA and the LEP concurred with each other: neither group could explain how a peace league's enforcement procedures would work.[19]

Despite their divisions and problems, the ranks of liberal internationalists grew during the war, infused with converts from pacifism. This development did not occur immediately. During the submarine crisis of early 1917, pacifists overwhelmingly argued that the United States should not enter the war against Germany. "We run no danger of invasion," emphasized an ad hoc peace committee including Amos Pinchot, Randolph Bourne, and Max Eastman. Driven by desperation exacerbated by America's favoritism toward Britain, Germany lashed out at the Entente as best it could, and America unfortunately got in the way. Going to war over such "incidental" injuries made no sense to the pacifists. It would ruin whatever chance the United States had to mediate a peace without victory by allowing

Britain to inflict a crushing defeat on the Reich and by inflaming the military spirit of the German people and rallying them to their autocracy. "Besides losing our opportunity to serve the world," added the AUAM, "we should lose the best of our possessions—democracy and individual liberty." Belligerency meant conscription and the loss of civil liberties: "It means dictatorship," the AUAM declared. Rather than enter the war, the United States should waive its neutral rights, keep Americans out of the war zone, and try to work out some sort of accommodation with the Reich. Most pacifists also endorsed armed neutrality as an alternative to belligerency, especially if the United States pursued it in cooperation with other neutrals. Such a policy, they argued, would maintain America's position as a neutral mediator and presage the formation of a league of nations. Certain that the vast majority of Americans opposed war while only "Wall Street" wanted one, pacifists insisted, finally, that a popular war referendum precede any declaration of hostilities by Congress. Democratic control of foreign policy, they believed, offered the best chance of stopping America's march toward the abyss.[20]

Once Congress actually voted for war, the pacifists' united front crumbled. Some, like Max and Crystal Eastman, hesitated to fall in line behind the president until Wilson's proclamation of the Fourteen Points and Germany's advance into revolutionary Russia. Others—including the editors of the *Public;* Stephen Wise, Paul Kellogg, and Lillian Wald of the AUAM; Lucia Ames Mead and Carrie Chapman Catt of the WPP; the editors of the *Nation;* and William Jennings Bryan— shifted toward Wilson's position on national security affairs more rapidly. In part, they did so in an attempt to maintain their influence with the administration. But they had substantive reasons for changing their stance as well. In contrast to their views of 1915 and 1916, many pacifists increasingly perceived that Germany's autocratic leaders planned the war and pursued war aims far more sweeping and sinister than the Entente's. Germany's autocracy wanted to dominate Europe, and, in a sharp break with their previous views, many pacifists thought it might succeed. "Until very recently," noted the editors of the *Public* in June 1917, "practically all discussion of the war in this country has taken for granted the ultimate defeat of Germany." But now, with its submarines prowling the seas and its armies seemingly planted for good in Russia and France, "it is possible to visualize a Germany no longer kept within bounds by the British fleet, her rulers flushed with victory, dominating Western Europe as Rome dominated the Mediterranean." Far from being too exhausted or distracted by its European rivals to continue its aggression, a Reich with hegemony over Europe would seek to extend its power to the Western Hemisphere. This might be a "distant" threat, conceded the *Nation,* but it was a real one, and, if Germany did win the war, Wilson was right to point out that America would have to militarize itself in self-defense. To the pacifists who swung behind the president in the spring and summer of 1917, the war had become "a war of defense, to protect all that makes the world a decent place to live in."[21]

The conversion of many leading pacifists to liberal internationalism did little to clarify the key issues surrounding the achievement of Wilson's peace program. In general, most of them echoed the *New Republic*'s views on Wilson's foreign and domestic policies, while some, like the editors of the *Public* and Stephen Wise, occasionally tilted more in the direction of Taft's positions. Although former pacifists endorsed the LFNA's conception of international reform, they sometimes also offered alternative ideas. The LFNA and the LEP both associated disarmament with a reformed world, for example, but they portrayed it as a long-term goal. The point of a peace league was "not to surrender arms, but to combine them." Only after the league proved itself as a peacekeeping organization could plans for arms limitation go forward. In contrast, the *Nation,* even though one of its editors helped to form the LFNA, argued that disarmament was "the prerequisite to the reorganization of the world on sane lines and to the establishment of the League to Enforce Peace." The *Public*'s Stoughton Cooley was a leading figure at the LFNA too, but, unlike the LFNA's statement of principles, his journal considered ending "tariff walls" to be crucial to a lasting peace. Free trade would promote international good will, prosperity, and liberty and democracy within nations. Without it, a league would have to rely on threats of force to preserve peace; with it, claimed Louis Post, the league's conflict resolution edicts could become "self-executing." Such arguments only further clouded the question of how a collective security organization would actually work.[22]

Not all pacifists migrated into the ranks of liberal internationalists after April 1917. Most of the Socialist Party continued to oppose the war on grounds similar to those advanced by the pacifists in early 1917, and a new pacifist group, the People's Council, emerged in the spring of 1917 to advocate national security views consistent with the prewar pacifist outlook. Robert La Follette persisted in his pacifist stance as well.[23]

But the most interesting and revealing of the persistent pacifists was Randolph Bourne, a young intellectual who had worked with Pinchot and Max Eastman on an antiwar publicity campaign during the submarine crisis. His argument against Wilson's decision to intervene in the war assumed, like the pacifist case prior to 1917, that it was not possible for Germany to establish a hegemonic power over Europe threatening to the United States. When Germany unleashed its submarines, Bourne admitted, "the safety of the seas, the whole Allied cause, seemed suddenly in deadly peril." But America could have defused this danger through a policy of armed neutrality. This course would have convinced the Germans that their sea campaign would fail, which meant that they could not win the war. The way then would have been open to a negotiated peace, "the most hopeful possible basis for the covenant of nations." The Germans probably would have ended up holding "Mittel-Europa," Bourne predicted, but he thought that the Reich's dominance over the region would not last. "There are strong democratic and federalist forces at work in the Austro-Hungarian monarchy," he asserted in August 1917. The peoples of central and southeastern Europe would resist "Prussian enslavement," particularly since a czarist Russia no longer existed to threaten them. And with the war killing large numbers of Germany's upper-class leaders, democracy was sure to come soon to the Reich itself in any case. "In this light," declared Bourne, "it is almost immaterial what terms are made."[24]

Wilson's policy of trying to destroy Germany's position in Middle Europe by force, applauded by the New Republic, ruined any hope of international reform, contended Bourne. At home, America's "significant classes" fastened "a semi-military State-socialism on the country," easily whipped up most of the masses into a prowar mob eager to crush Germany, and repressed what little active dissent remained. Abroad, Wilson's strategy became "indistinguishable from that of the Allies," which led the German people, fearful for their very existence, "to cling even more desperately to their military leaders." Prospects for German democratic reform—Wilson's preferred route to a negotiated settlement and a peace league—thus faded away, lost in the blood and smoke of a prolonged war. Even if Germany did democratize at the point of America's guns, Bourne doubted that it would be a peaceful state. On the contrary, "A Germany forced to be democratic under the tutelage of a watchful and victorious Entente would . . . be a constant menace to the peace of Europe." For Bourne, trying to reform power politics by practicing power politics was a doomed enterprise. Unlike the New Republic, he gibed, he "had not the imagination to see a healed world-order built out of the rotten materials of armaments, diplomacy and 'liberal' statesmanship."[25]

In contrast to the pacifists, Atlanticists did not react to American belligerency by reassessing their national security strategy and dividing their ranks. Roosevelt, Root, and Lodge instead saw Wilson's decision to enter the war as vindication of the ideas they had promoted since 1914. The president's neutrality policies, they argued, had bred an "overweening contempt" in Germany for the United States, to the point where German leaders released their submarines from restraint because they believed that America lacked the will and capability to respond. Wilson had to go to war because otherwise he would have completely destroyed what was left of his nation's diplomatic credibility, thus exposing America to a future of endless challenges to its interests. The president said as much himself in his War Message of 2 April 1917, Roosevelt charged. "His message bears out all I have said for the past two and a half years, and condemns all he has said and done for those two and a half years."[26]

Failure to join the fight against Germany might have led to a German victory in the war—a prospect that continued to frighten Atlanticists. More publicly and in more detail than they had prior to 1917, they spelled out how a German win would threaten the United States. If the Reich could hold onto its dominating position in Central and eastern Europe, eventually it would overawe the western Europeans and achieve hegemony over the whole continent. It would then challenge the Monroe Doctrine. The United States would never be able to deter such an attack on its vital interests "unless," Roosevelt asserted, "we ourselves became a powerful militarist state with every democratic principle subordinated to the one necessity of turning this nation into a huge armed camp." Roosevelt stressed that he was not talking about a program of universal military training here, a type of peacetime preparedness he still advocated. He meant "a nation whose sons, every one of them, would have to serve from three to five years in the army, and whose whole activities, external and internal, would be conditioned by the fact of the necessity of making head, single-handed, against Germany." America's free way of life would be doomed in such circumstances. The "conditions of modern war make it impossible for democracy to keep itself always prepared for defense against attack," explained Root, "and to continue its free democratic institutions." When it came to the stakes involved with defeating Germany, at least, Atlanticists and liberal internationalists spoke with one voice.[27]

At times, they also sounded similar in their desire to have Germany's people transform the Reich's government into a democracy. Lodge, for example, described the war in April 1917 as one between "free popular government" and "military autocracy represented by the Prussian system." Roosevelt echoed his friend, asserting that "the only way to make sure the future of liberty is to secure the complete overthrow of the Germany of the Hohenzollerns." While this statement was somewhat vague, it could easily be interpreted to mean that Roosevelt viewed the democratization of the Reich as a crucial way to enhance the security of the postwar world. Roosevelt even implied that if Germany's people managed to "separate themselves" from their government and repudiated it, they would merit less "condemnation" than would otherwise be the case. German democratization, it seemed, would not only make the world safer but also allow the Germans to escape harsh treatment at the hands of the Allied coalition.[28]

Yet however much they hinted at this conclusion, Atlanticists never actually embraced it. They argued that Hohenzollern rule had "completely debauched the German people" and that the vast majority of Germans, including those in the SPD, "eagerly supported the German autocracy in its course of international robbery and murder." Regardless of whether Germany democratized, the war had to end with a "peace of overwhelming victory" by the United States and the Allies. Outlined in some detail by Lodge and Roosevelt, the Atlanticists' preferred peace terms included restoring Belgium; transferring Alsace-Lorraine to France; peeling off Austrian territory for Italy; creating a "large Poland" with access to the sea; restoring Montenegro, Serbia, and Rumania "to full power and independence"; breaking up the Austro-Hungarian and Turkish empires; transferring northern Schleswig to Denmark; removing all German control over any part of Russia and the Baltics;

and allowing Britain and Japan to keep the colonies they had seized from the Reich. Atlanticists also strongly implied that they wanted Germany to face economic discrimination after the war and pay heavy reparations to the victors.[29]

These terms aimed to deter Germany from future aggression by limiting its power and by making its people feel the pain of losing the war. Thus, when Lodge presented his list of peace terms, he specifically detailed the strategic advantages they would give the Allies over the Reich. "Our business is to put her back into a padded cell within her own boundaries," Lodge declared, "where the Germans can do anything they please to each other but out of which they cannot again rush forth upon an innocent and unoffending world." Roosevelt endorsed this reasoning and added that Germany needed to be taught a lesson it would never forget. "The surest way to make them keep the peace in the future," he avowed, "is to punish them heavily now."[30]

Suspicious of Wilson's commitment to winning a complete victory over the Reich, Atlanticists remained wary of the president's plans for a postwar peace league. Any collective security organization that included Germany was out of the question as far as they were concerned. It was absurd, scoffed Roosevelt, "to enter a league in which we make-believe that our deadly enemies, stained with every kind of brutality and treachery, are as worthy of friendship as the Allies who have fought our battles for four years." The only peacekeeping league that made sense to him was one involving "a pledge by the present Allies to make their alliance perpetual, and all go to war again whenever one of them is attacked." Joining such an alliance—or any league for that matter—could never be "a substitute" for America's own national preparedness, Roosevelt added. For Wilson to suggest that it could be, by calling for arms reduction in his Fourteen Points Address, was dangerous in Roosevelt's eyes. Preparedness based on universal military training still offered the best, most democratic means of both preserving American security and enabling America to serve others overseas. Finally, Roosevelt and other Atlanticists found the broad principles Wilson often linked with a lasting peace, such as promoting self-determination or lowering trade barriers, to be vague, impossible to fulfill in practice, or simply wrong. Most of Wilson's peace principles, scorned Lodge, were "mere words and general bleat about virtue being better than vice."[31]

Despite these criticisms of Wilson's vision of international reform, Atlanticists avoided directly attacking the fundamental assumptions of collective security and, indeed, continued to suggest that they supported the concept on some level. To be sure, Roosevelt did indirectly attack the idea of nations' having an overriding stake in peace everywhere, as he stated at one point that guaranteeing the political independence and territorial integrity of other states could involve America "in war over matters in which we had no interest whatever." And whenever he discussed a league, Roosevelt was careful to say that America should make no promises that it could not or should not keep. He did not elaborate on what promises he had in mind, however. Roosevelt sounded more directly supportive of a league when he attacked Wilson for undercutting the credibility of collective security by failing to ask Congress to declare war on Germany's allies, Turkey and Bulgaria; reendorsed his own collective security plan as "sound doctrine"; proclaimed his "delighted . . . support" for "the movement for a League to Enforce Peace, or for a League of Nations," so long as it only supplemented American preparedness; and indicated he would support Germany's future membership in a league if it "repented" for its crimes. The skepticism Roosevelt expressed for Wilson's concept of collective security, then, was more than counterbalanced by statements lending credence to it.[32]

Atlanticists mirrored their ambivalence about a peace league in their reaction to Wilson's domestic policies. If anything, they wanted even harsher repression of antiwar dissenters than the president did. They approved of Wilson's economic mobilization measures, and they claimed that participation in the war uplifted the American peoples' "spirit of sacrifice and service." But the domestic impact of the war nevertheless troubled Atlanticists. Wilson, alleged Roosevelt, used the censorship powers granted to him by Congress "to reward the Administration's personal or political supporters and punish the Administration's personal or political opponents." The administration-sponsored Sedition Act of 1918 needlessly enhanced Wilson's power to dictatorial dimensions, Roosevelt complained. "It is a proposal to make Americans subjects instead of citizens," he warned. "It is a proposal to put the President in the position of the Hohenzollerns and Romanoffs." Together with the wartime controls on the economy, Wilson's apparatus of repression had "set aside" the Constitution and, Lodge feared, put America on the road toward "State socialism." Unless America reversed course soon, its domestic freedoms could very well be lost forever, crushed in the grip of "an executive authority unprecedented in scope and absolutism."[33]

For all of their criticisms of the president, neither Atlanticists nor persistent pacifists offered much of a credible alternative to Wilson's wartime policies or, more broadly, to the approach toward national security affairs offered by liberal internationalists. Bourne's critique of American intervention in the war rested on his belief that a German-dominated Middle Europe either would not last or would be rendered strategically irrelevant by German democratization. But he presented little evidence to support this argument, beyond suggesting that the Russian Revolution would give the peoples of Middle Europe the confidence they needed to rebel against the Germans. Revolutionary Russia might just as well frighten neighboring states and push them into German arms, however; it might cause the Germans to tighten their hold on their conquests still more; and it might simply open the door to further German advances in the east, as indeed it did in early 1918. Bourne's own analysis of foreign policy decision making in wartime America also belied his faith in the pacific character of a democratized Reich. Germany, presumably, had its own "significant classes" enthralled by war, just like America did, and, just like in America, presumably they could manipulate and coerce the masses into supporting whatever foreign policy they wanted. The grounds for thinking that German hegemony over Middle Europe would be brief or inconsequential were thus shaky—and if that expectation was wrong, Bourne's antiwar position collapsed.

Atlanticists certainly made what seemed like cutting attacks on the president, with their cries for unconditional surrender, permanent preparedness, and peace terms openly discriminatory against Germany. But their statements that democratic Germany would merit less "condemnation" than Germany's autocracy, their talk of a repentant Germany one day joining a peace league, and Roosevelt's explicit endorsement of the League to Enforce Peace all sounded a different tune. Ultimately, the Atlanticists sounded just like Taft. Indeed, Roosevelt privately and publicly reconciled with Taft in 1918, on the basis of supporting universal military training, a peace league, and all-out war against the Germans. The two men even issued statements together urging voters to return a Republican Congress and denouncing the Fourteen Points and Wilson's autocratic impulses at home. Atlanticists, it seemed, had joined the conservative wing of liberal internationalism.[34]

A number of different factors lay behind the Atlanticists' muddled position during the war. They were eager to keep the Republican Party unified for the 1918 congressional elections, and downplaying their opposition to a league was one way to accomplish this goal. As William Widenor implies, they may also have seen a postwar league of America and the Allies as the only politically feasible way to get permanent UMT enacted and to continue the wartime alliance against Germany. Talk of a peace league that might one day include Germany, finally, might weaken the Reich's will to fight; it was good wartime propaganda.[35]

Again, though, one gets the sense that Atlanticist gestures in support of a collective security league reflected more than just tactical political considerations. As noted earlier, even before America entered the war, Atlanticists had advocated a peace league in part because they wanted to invigorate the international moral code they thought helped to stabilize balance-of-power politics. After April 1917 the cost of the war to the United States—and the need to put force behind righteousness—became clearer to them than ever before. For one thing, the war touched both Roosevelt and Lodge personally, with one of Roosevelt's sons killed in combat while Lodge's son-in-law died in an army training camp. For the first time, Atlanticists also saw firsthand how modern warfare enhanced the power of the state and led policymakers to violate the Constitution. Militarism had been an abstract and distant threat in their view prior to 1917. Now they had actually experienced it—and it alarmed them. Such pain and fear no doubt enhanced the Atlanticists' genuine attraction to a league along the lines of Roosevelt's 1914 plan, including eventually a democratic and materially weakened Germany.[36]

Whatever their motives, Atlanticist comments about a league, German democracy, and the dangers of a wartime absolutist state all lent support to the arguments put forward by liberal internationalists. At the same time, as in the pre-1917 period, their harsh rhetoric castigating Wilson for America's prewar "broomstick preparedness" and trumpeting the need to "beat Germany to her knees" seemed so blindly supportive of the existing system of power politics that their warnings about the incredibility of the collective security program were drowned out. "Many of us were shocked at the peace terms put forth by Senator Lodge," confided Carrie Chapman Catt to Wilson in September 1918. "He had much of the substance, but the spirit of humanity was not there. There was none of the thrill, the exaltation which your exposition of our aims produces." The editors of the *Public* had the same reaction. Lodge's war aims were "unexceptional," but his "frank . . . acceptance of an outlook dominated by force must cause astonishment wherever Americanism has meant a liberalizing and unselfish spirit."[37]

With pacifists offering a risky response to the German threat and Atlanticists inconsistently raising questions about Wilson's policies while endorsing a peace league, liberal internationalists consolidated their dominant position in American national security debates. But their argument for how the United States could secure its free way of life in the modern world continued to suffer from grave weaknesses. First, they still found it impossible to explain clearly how they planned both to control Germany's power and conciliate it—the two crucial preconditions to international reform that they had identified prior to America's entry into the war. Progressive liberal internationalists—namely the *New Republic*'s editors, former pacifists such as Paul Kellogg, and the LEP's Hamilton Holt—were stymied by this dilemma because they could not bring themselves to trust the pacific character of Germany's democrats. Had they been able to do so, they might have formulated peace terms that simply called for a return to the status quo antebellum and an inclusive peace league if Germany democratized. Because they worried that Germany's democrats might be animated by desires for conquest and that a German democratic revolution might not prove to be permanent, however, they wanted to reduce Germany's power for aggression more extensively, regardless of the character of its government. As Bourne trenchantly observed, this sharply raised the risk of enraging the Germans and turning them into a permanent threat to the peace of Europe.

Conservative advocates of collective security, as well as some socialist LEP members such as William English Walling, had a more coherent view of the relationship between peace terms and international reform than the Progressives did. But they had their own problems. Because they saw the German people as utterly corrupted by Germany's autocratic government, they were determined, like the Atlanticists, to invade Germany and force it to surrender unconditionally whether it democratized or not. They implied that they had little concern if Germany lost territory and population in the peace settlement or if it faced economic discrimination by the victors. Harsh terms were necessary to limit Germany's power, impose just penalties for its wrongdoing, and, most importantly, induce a genuine repudiation of aggression by its people. Defeated and punished, Taft predicted, "the scales will fall from their eyes, and with clearer vision they will see that he whom they have ignorantly worshipped is the devil and not God." Once that happened, they could be welcomed into a league of nations; punishment to trigger redemption, in other words, was now the necessary precondition to reconciling with the Germans and salvaging international reform.[38]

But what if the German epiphany did not occur? Taft and his supporters had no answer to this question. They did not even bother to try to answer it. But wasn't it likely that the German people would feel embittered and betrayed by the punishment meted out to them, especially because they had constantly been told that their autocratic government was the real culprit in the war and not them? The *New Republic*'s editors thought so; trying to grind Germany into the ground, they argued, would "prevent her moral recovery." And if the Germans were antagonized by their treatment, then the league would remain an anti-German alliance. Power politics—the same power politics the LEP believed would lead to arms races and war—would persist. Betting on Germany's redemption through suffering to win the prize of international reform was a long shot at best—but Taft refused to acknowledge this reality, let alone discuss it.[39]

A convincing explanation of how a collective security league would actually be administered remained elusive as well. Progressives in the LFNA considered some sort of parliamentary representation in the league crucial to its success, whereas the LEP did not. Ex-pacifists who had joined the ranks of liberal internationalists saw disarmament and free trade as efficacious international reforms in and of themselves, an idea rejected by both the LFNA and the LEP. The LEP, meanwhile, divided over the proper scope of a peace league, with some members urging that it only compel a hearing of disputes and others wanting rulings on legalistic issues enforced. Most important, neither the LFNA nor the LEP was able or willing to describe exactly how a league of nations should arrive at and enforce its decisions.

This omission was all the more striking given that many liberal internationalists urged that a league be formed immediately, while the war was still going on. They perceived that the Allies wanted strategic safeguards against Germany—safeguards perhaps even beyond what Taft wanted—because the Allies did not think an effective league would ever become a reality. They were therefore anxious to establish a wartime league to show the Allies that it did in fact exist and that seeking selfish strategic advantages was no longer necessary. But even as they made this proposal, liberal internationalists refused to say how a wartime league should operate, apparently because they weren't sure or worried that whatever they said might cause division among the Allied coalition and sink their idea. The Allies, then, were being asked to forego vital security interests in order to lend credibility to an organization that might fall apart if it were subjected to detailed scrutiny.

Fundamentally, liberal internationalists outside the administration, in common with Wilson, simply trusted that one way or another, a league could be made to work. The interdependence of the modern world, "the almost universal feeling on the part of the common people of the world that the old diplomacy is bankrupt," and the unique ability of America to speak "for a higher ideal and a broader justice" compared to other nations would all combine to turn a peace league into a workable enterprise. It did not matter if the details of how this would happen were unclear. "The absolutely indispensable condition of success of a new international order is faith in its possibility," preached the *New Republic*. "So long as men believe that a thing is impossible," added Norman Angell, "that belief of itself renders the belief true; just as the contrary belief would render the contrary true." The way liberal internationalists described it, a peace league could be brought into existence through sheer force of will.[40]

It had to be. Despite the fact that the peace terms necessary for a league were contradictory and vague, despite the ambiguity over how a league would operate, it had to be a viable policy objective, because the alternatives—isolated security or endless power politics—still looked like paths to arms races, war, and militarism. The war's domestic impact, indeed, underscored to liberal internationalists the fragility of democracy in an insecure international environment. Try as they did to see positive aspects to the domestic scene, they were obviously disturbed at the repressive, bureaucratic character of the wartime state, so vividly described by Bourne. And, overseas, the destructiveness of modern weapons all too graphically suggested that a second general war could be catastrophic. "Civilization as we know it," declared Lawrence Lowell at the 1918 LEP convention, "has reached a point where it must preclude war or perish by war, and war can be precluded only by a conquest of the world by a single power, or by an organization of many nations to prevent its recurrence." As the former was not a realistic goal, the latter objective had to be achieved. In November 1918, as the fighting on the western front finally ended, liberal internationalists placed their hopes in Wilson to attain it.[41]

9

Wilson and the Versailles Treaty

President Wilson's strategy for safeguarding America from a future of arms races, militarism, and war met its ultimate test during and after the Paris Peace Conference of 1919. In intense, often acrimonious negotiations, Wilson and the leaders of the Allies produced a single document, the Versailles treaty, which contained both the Covenant of the League of Nations and the peace terms ending the war with Germany. This achievement did not resolve the contradictions and ambiguities plaguing the president's national security strategy, however. The Versailles treaty permanently restricted Germany's power, punished it for causing the war, and excluded it from the League for the foreseeable future. Yet at the same time, Wilson and the Allies acknowledged Germany's democratic revolution and proclaimed it "a great hope for peace." Similarly, the League Covenant assumed that an international system based on a competition for power would produce another war and that all nations had a vital stake in peace everywhere. But the League began operation as an alliance directed at Germany, contained escape clauses allowing nations to avoid participation in the enforcement of collective security, and seemed to exempt the Monroe Doctrine, as defined by the United States, from its jurisdiction. As was the case prior to 1919, Wilson expected America's power and moral exceptionalism to alleviate the contradictions in his peace program. This solution depended on the United States actually demonstrating its supposedly exceptional character in practice, however—something President Wilson continued to find impossible to do.[1]

The challenges facing Wilson at Paris centered above all on Germany. The overthrow of the Reich's imperial government in November 1918 had done little to solve the riddle of finding a way to control Germany's power while conciliating its people, the riddle that Wilson believed had to be solved in order for international reform to succeed. If anything, political conditions in Europe and America at the end of the war magnified the difficulties involved with this problem. One new development that complicated the issue was an upsurge of Bolshevik agitation in Germany in the months immediately after the armistice, from December 1918 to March 1919. Bolshevism thrived on human misery, Wilson perceived, and harsh peace terms, combined with postwar Germany's economic dislocation, might allow the radical Left to come to power in Berlin. Once this happened, Germany might degenerate into "anarchism," or, as David Lloyd George told the president, it might ally with Bolshevik Russia and try to build "a vast red army under German instructors and German generals." In either case, the task of reconciling with the German people would have to be put aside in favor of imposing sweeping physical controls on the former Reich—if a peace treaty could be signed at all.[2]

Yet however much the threat of Bolshevism reinforced Wilson's long-standing desire to avoid "excessive demands" upon the Germans, he worried even more about unregenerate militarism in the postwar German republic. No less than at the time of the armistice, Wilson distrusted the Germans, suspecting them of harboring aggressive desires. In mid-February 1919, for example, Wilson worried that Allied and American military demobilization could make it hard "to compel the Germans to accede to our demands." Delay in imposing disarmament terms upon the Germans "might lead them to a false sense of self-confidence, and the German Government's forces might consolidate in a way which is not at present possible to forecast, and the ancient pride and boastfulness of Germany might gain a new lease of life." In late February and again in mid-March, Wilson suggested that republican Germany hungered for conquest in eastern Europe just as much as had the kaiser. "It must not be forgotten that Germany's ambitions had always leant towards the South and East," he observed in a discussion on demilitarizing the Rhineland, and he wanted to know "whether sufficient thought had been given towards ensuring the safety of those regions against future German aggression." In late January Wilson indicated Germany could not be trusted for at least "a generation." The president repeatedly expressed similar views in April, May, and June—views which implied that building a new system of international security had to rest primarily on containing Germany's power and deterring it from aggression, not on conciliating it.[3]

Similar crosscurrents structured Wilson's relationship with Allied leaders. Their agreement to base the peace treaty with Germany on the Fourteen Points did not allay the president's suspicions of them. They wanted "to get everything out of Germany that they can," he charged, to get a peace not of justice but of "loot or spoliation." Such demands would have to be resisted, as they would embitter the Germans and undermine the chances for a lasting peace. Conversely, Wilson could ill afford to alienate the Allies lest they abandon his project for a league of nations. Breaking up the alliance over a disagreement on peace terms might also encourage Germany to resume its aggression. Finally, Wilson perceived that public opinion in the Allied nations wanted to make Germany "pay the cost of the war," an impossible demand. In December 1918, Lloyd George's coalition swept an electoral landslide partly on the basis of calls to "strip Germany as she has stripped Belgium." A few days later, Clemenceau won a resounding vote of confidence in France's Chamber of Deputies after delivering a strong defense of balance-of-power politics. These developments suggested that if Wilson pushed too hard for lenient terms for Germany, Lloyd George and Clemenceau could fall from power and be replaced by leaders even more hostile to Wilson's program than they were.[4]

The president's own political situation in the United States also complicated his calculations concerning Germany. The Republican electoral victory in November 1918 meant that the GOP, led by Henry Cabot Lodge, would control the United States Senate and thus the ratification process for whatever peace treaty Wilson brought home. The public in general, moreover, appeared "excited and superheated and suspicious" to Wilson and hostile to any easy treatment of the Germans. The president's Progressive supporters, however, expected a treaty based as minimally on considerations of power as possible. Here too, then, Wilson's political needs pushed him in opposite directions when it came to determining how to strike just the right balance between controlling and conciliating the former Reich.[5]

The president responded to these conflicting perceptions and pressures by erring on the side of caution in his posture toward the Germans. Containing and punishing Germany, he decided, had to take precedence over building a process of reconciliation. This is not to argue that Wilson ignored the latter goal in his deliberations at Paris. As we shall see, he did not. As he had in the armistice negotiations, however, he tended to subordinate it to the objective of weakening Germany's capability and disposition to pursue aggression. In so doing, he hoped to diminish the chances of a future war breaking out in Europe that could involve the United States and to provide an international environment conducive to collective security and arms limitation. At times, to be sure, Wilson did make concessions to the Allies that produced peace terms harsher than he would have liked. In these cases, which chiefly involved reparations, the Rhineland, and the Shantung settlement, the president valued holding the wartime alliance together more than getting his way on the particular issue at stake. But most of the time, Wilson preferred stringent terms against Germany in any event, which helped to minimize conflicts with his colleagues.

This preference emerged clearly in the president's stance on military and territorial issues. In discussions about the disarmament terms, which required Germany to permanently reduce its army to 100,000 men, largely stripped it of heavy weapons, outlawed its air force and submarines, and forced it to surrender most of its warships, Wilson expressed concern about how to enforce the provisions but otherwise had no problem with them. "Our principle safety," Wilson was certain, "will be obtained by the obligation which we shall lay on Germany to effect complete disarmament." To secure France's border with Germany, Wilson supported the permanent demilitarization of the Rhineland, including a strip of territory on the right bank of the Rhine, and, even before the peace conference began, agreed to France's annexation of Alsace-Lorraine. In the east, determined not to leave Poland so weak that it might be "foredoomed to vassalage" under Germany, Wilson strongly supported detaching Danzig from German sovereignty and creating a Polish corridor to the sea that he noted included almost 2 million Germans. Consistent with this view, in June 1919, he resisted allowing a plebiscite in Upper Silesia, a region rich in resources slated to shift from Germany to Poland. Wilson also opposed Austrian unification with Germany, at least for the foreseeable future, because it "would mean that the new Germany would be one of the most powerful countries in Europe"; readily agreed to Italy's annexation of the strategic south Tyrol region bordering Austria; and raised no objection to Czechoslovakia's claim on its Bohemian frontier with Germany, the Sudetenland, at least in part because of economic and security concerns raised by the Czechs.[6]

The president's desire to punish Germany, distinct from his desire to weaken it, tended to emerge chiefly in nonmilitary and nonterritorial matters. Most significantly, it appeared in the negotiations between Wilson and the Allies over reparations. Regardless of the differences the president had with Clemenceau and Lloyd George over the details of this problem, Wilson assumed that German "aggression" had caused damages to the Allies that had to be made good. The Germans had committed crimes in starting and prosecuting the war; it was just that they pay for their behavior. Thus, when the French made extensive claims on the Saar largely on the grounds that Germany had willfully destroyed coal mines in northern France at the end of the war, Wilson gave them a sympathetic hearing. He objected to the annexationist aspects of their program, but he had "no difficulty" with France receiving "compensation in kind, . . . if possible, in the Saar region." Justice demanded nothing less, and Wilson worked diligently in March and April to find a way to transfer the Saar's coal to France as reparation for Germany's destruction of the French mines.[7]

Equity for the Allies was not the only thing on Wilson's mind as he insisted that Germany make amends for its aggression. He also wanted to impose penalties on the former Reich to deter its people from ever supporting an aggressive war again. This aim was one reason why Wilson resisted putting the kaiser on trial for criminal acts. The kaiser had not violated criminal law in authorizing Germany's attack on Belgium, Wilson believed. He and the German nation had instead broken international law, and "up to now," Wilson argued, "the responsibility for international crimes has been solely a collective responsibility." Putting the kaiser on trial might undercut Germany's collective guilt for the war. "What I want to avoid is leaving to historians any sympathy whatsoever for Germany," Wilson explained to the Allies. "I want to consign Germany to the execration of history and to do nothing to allow it to be said that we went beyond our rights in a just cause." The point of any proceeding against the kaiser should be to underscore not his individual criminality but Germany's "supreme offense against international morality and the sanctity of treaties" and, in so doing, vindicate international law. "What I seek is the severest lesson," Wilson declared in early April. He wanted to brand unprovoked aggression an "unspeakable crime" and, as Lansing advised, to make "an example for the future . . . to those who would by committing a similar act plunge the world into war."[8]

Excluding Germany from the League of Nations offered Wilson another way to punish the former Reich and deter it from future aggression. "Germany's present chaotic state," the president resolved in early December 1918, "would make it necessary to put her on probation, as it were, until she showed herself fit for reception into the League." The German nation needed to prove that it had "a responsible, decent government" and a "sincere intention to observe its international obligations" before it could gain entry into the world's new collective security organization. Until then, it would be marked as an outlaw, which could only add to the opprobrium Wilson thought it deserved. Having suffered the pain of such a public shaming, hopefully the Germans would think twice about ever acting in a criminal manner again.[9]

While barring Germany from League membership was itself a punishment, it also gave the Associated powers (the Allies and the United States) license to impose other penalties on the former Reich. Given Germany's "abuses" in running its colonies, Wilson asserted in January, everyone agreed that they should not go back to its control. They should instead go to a "trusteeship by the League of Nations" where Germany, not being a member, would have no say over them at all. Germany's exclusion from the League meant too that it would not enjoy "equitable treatment" for its commerce, a privilege for League members proposed by Wilson and written into Article 21 of the draft Covenant in mid-February. A few weeks later, Wilson concurred in his economic team's advice to make no provision for Germany's right to equal trading conditions in the commercial sections of the peace treaty. When combined with Germany's lack of League membership, this omission in effect invited the Associated powers to discriminate against the Germans in international trade—a severe penalty in Wilson's view, judging from the statements he had made about it during the war.[10]

Despite Wilson's disposition toward tough peace terms for Germany, at times he went along with Allied proposals to punish or weaken the Germans not because he agreed with them but because he wanted to hold the wartime alliance together. In negotiations to set the amount and payment of Germany's reparations liability, Wilson wanted the final terms to be consistent with the armistice agreement, which had limited reparations to "all damage done to the civilian population of the Allies and their property" and to state a fixed total of Germany's liability based on its capacity to pay over a thirty-year time frame. Such terms would honor

America's November 1918 promise to Germany and produce a reasonable sum that the Germans would accept and endeavor to pay. The stability of the settlement, in turn, would encourage private American investors to lend money to Germany and to the Allies, money the Europeans needed to finance their reconstruction from four years of fighting. Clemenceau and especially Lloyd George, however, felt enormous domestic political pressure to make Germany pay the full cost of the war. As Wilson's financial experts told him in mid-February, the Allied position represented "a definite and fundamental difference of opinion" with his views and, they implied, threatened the unity of the Allied-American coalition.[11]

In response to this crisis, Wilson made significant concessions to the Allies. He agreed to a reparations settlement that asserted Germany's moral responsibility for all war costs, recognized that Germany did not have the resources to pay such costs, and deferred the determination of Germany's actual liability and how it would be paid to an American-Allied Reparation Commission, which would decide these issues no later than May 1921. Meanwhile, Germany had to make initial reparations payments, in gold and in transfers of a variety of economic assets, totaling 20 billion gold marks (roughly $5 billion).[12]

Parts of this package were easier for Wilson to accept than others. He had little trouble agreeing to Article 231, the provision declaring Germany's responsibility for "causing all the loss and damage" suffered by the Allies as a result of its "aggression" in the war. This statement completely accorded with Wilson's view that Germany launched a premeditated war of conquest in July 1914. But the president felt uneasy about failing to state a fixed amount Germany would owe, especially as this might inhibit banks from lending Germany any money. With Allied leaders "against a lump sum . . . because they are afraid to tell their people the truth about the amount they can get out of Germany," Wilson felt that he had little choice but to go along with deferring the final reparations liability to the Reparation Commission. "Either the figure which we might fix would terrify the Germans," Lloyd George argued, "or it would be impossible for M. Clemenceau and me to get public opinion to accept it." And if Clemenceau or Lloyd George fell from power, even more hawkish leaders might replace them, making it harder for Wilson to hold the wartime alliance—and the nucleus of the League of Nations—together.[13]

The imperative to maintain some degree of unity with the Allied governments also drove Wilson to make concessions to France on Rhineland security that appeared to run counter to his vision of international reform. Confronted with French demands to detach the Rhineland from German sovereignty and to occupy it indefinitely with an inter-Allied military force—demands Wilson believed would foster an undying desire for a war of revenge in the Germans—the president offered to join Britain in pledging "to come immediately to the assistance of France so soon as any unprovoked aggression against her is made by Germany." Wilson also agreed to inter-Allied military occupation of the Rhineland and four bridgeheads across the river for up to fifteen years. If the Reparation Commission found that Germany was refusing to observe its reparations obligations or if the Associated powers decided that "the guarantees against unprovoked aggression by Germany"—that is, the American and British security treaties with France—were insufficient for France's safety, the occupation could be extended. These provisions implied that the League of Nations, Wilson's agency of international reform, was somehow not up to the job of ensuring France's security—an implication clearly threatening to Wilson's goal of ending power politics and an implication that Wilson tried hard to counter.[14]

The president's decisions to offer France a security treaty and to accept potentially prolonged occupation of the Rhineland were painful for him to make. He made them because the French obviously felt extremely vulnerable to a German attack and because Clemenceau faced strident demands from inside his own government to get physical guarantees to protect France from the German threat. France's supreme military leader, Ferdinand Foch, and its president, Raymond Poincaré, both personally pressed Wilson on Rhineland security, and both made their opposition to Clemenceau's compromises on the issue abundantly clear. He had to have at least a partial fifteen-year occupation of the Rhineland and the bridgeheads, Clemenceau told House, if he hoped to fend off Foch's opposition and sustain himself in the Chamber of Deputies. To keep Clemenceau in power, to avoid losing a leader who was willing to sacrifice France's demand for a separate Rhenish republic sure to poison prospects for a lasting peace, Wilson believed he had to meet the French premier's pleas for concessions at least halfway.[15]

Even as the president worked to maintain unity with his wartime partners and to punish and control Germany, he did not ignore the goal of conciliating the German people. He tried to attain this objective chiefly by interlacing the peace settlement with the League of Nations so as to mask or soften peace terms detrimental to the Germans. Thus the American and British security guarantee to France had to be recognized by the League's Executive Council "as being consistent with the Covenant," which meant to Wilson that the security pact was "not an alliance with anybody." Similarly, the League, not France, would administer the Saarland while the French exploited the coal resources of the region; permanent control over Germany's disarmament fell to the League, not the Allies; Danzig became not Polish but a "free city" under the protection of the League; Germany's colonies were not annexed by the victors but transferred to mandates "acting on behalf of the League of Nations"; and the assembly of the League, not the Associated powers alone, would decide when Germany would be granted admission to the new international society of states. All of these measures, as well as others, signaled that the peace terms were not instruments of selfish national advantage but part of a larger effort to end power politics for all. When combined with Wilson's reiterations of American selflessness and exceptionalism, hopefully they would alleviate the sting of the treaty's terms and make it easier for the Germans to accept the new world order.[16]

As Wilson struggled at Paris to find just the right balance between controlling, punishing, and conciliating Germany, he also had to translate his vision of a world based on collective security into a constitution for a league of nations. In the weeks just before the peace conference opened, Wilson reaffirmed the conception of the league he had expressed during the war. Agreements and pledges should be asserted in "general form" to boycott nations that failed to submit disputes to the league for a hearing and to guarantee the political sovereignty and territorial integrity of member states. While both large and small powers should each have one vote, most of the actual machinery of the league should be left to develop out of experience. To make the league a reality, what mattered was the commitment of nations to the theory of collective security. "War," Wilson emphasized, "must no longer be considered an exclusive business. Any war must be considered as affecting the whole world."[17]

In the actual negotiations that produced the draft Covenant of 14 February 1919, however, the president took positions that appeared to show a lack of faith in collective security theory. He went along with the principle that any action by the League could only be taken by a unanimous vote, not including the parties to a dispute. He added a new provision that the Executive Council would only "advise" how members should fulfill their obligation to preserve each other's political independence and territorial integrity. He watered down the article on economic sanctions, leaving it, in the words of his legal advisor, David Hunter Miller, "vague and uncertain" how the League would determine if a boycott should be implemented. He fended off French proposals to create an "international force" to verify arms limitation agreements and to provide organized planning for the League's military actions against aggressors, proposals France considered crucial to making the League something more than "a screen of false security." Finally, Wilson opposed efforts to specify how the League would determine if a member had any treaties or obligations inconsistent with the Covenant.[18]

In part, Wilson adopted these positions because he wanted to placate Britain, whose support he considered vital for making the League viable, and because he thought they would facilitate ratification of the Covenant by the Senate. But he also betrayed a wariness to commit the United States in advance to act against aggression anywhere in the world. America's Constitution forbade him from making such commitments, he claimed, and no one in the United States wanted "American troops . . . liable to be ordered to fight at any moment for the most remote of causes." In fact, Wilson asserted, "no nation will consent to control." Nations, in other words, including the United States, wanted to be free to judge for themselves whether it was in their interest to respond to aggression—a proposition directly at odds with the theory that all nations had a vital stake in peace everywhere.[19]

President Wilson continued to retreat from the basic premise of collective security during talks to revise the draft Covenant in March and April 1919. Advised that changes to the draft were necessary to gain Senate ratification of the treaty, Wilson worked in the League of Nations Commission to make the unanimity rule explicit, to exclude domestic matters from the League's jurisdiction, to provide a right to withdraw from the Covenant, and to specify that nothing in the Covenant affected "the validity" of the Monroe Doctrine. He also again successfully resisted French efforts to create an international "organism" to do military and naval inspections and planning for the League.[20]

To varying degrees, these positions all ran counter to the axiom that warfare anywhere threatened the interests of all the world's nations. The unanimity rule implied that a nation might not agree with others that a conflict demanded a response by the League. The domestic exclusion provision suggested that wars arising from a domestic matter, such as immigration policy, somehow did not threaten world stability, although conflicts arising from international issues did. But how could a collective interest in peace exist regarding one kind of dispute but not another? Similarly, if it was imperative for states to work together to safeguard their common stake in peace, why did the United States want an option available to withdraw from the Covenant? "If a League were to be established at all," the French argued in response to the withdrawal provision, "the foundation should be firm. . . . It was a question of founding a new system of international relations." And did not the reference to the Monroe Doctrine imply some sort of exemption for America from the terms of the Covenant? The Monroe Doctrine amendment, Leon Bourgeois feared, would create "two groups of States under the Covenant: the United States on the one hand, and the European States on the other." Perhaps, his colleague Fernand Larnaude added, the United States "might some day assert that this doctrine forbade some act of intervention decided upon by the other members of the League." As the amendment was "the only one which concerned a particular country," it was "out of harmony with the rest of the document." It undermined the fundamental idea that a collective interest in peace existed and could be relied on to produce a collective response to any aggression anywhere.[21]

In his own interpretation of the amended Covenant, Wilson paradoxically asserted that it was consistent with collective security theory and yet still left the United States "an absolute control over all the actions and measures of the League." He found it hard to make a case for this contradictory position. As he pondered how to formulate the Monroe Doctrine amendment, he told Gov. Samuel McCall that he hoped to find a way to frame it so that the League would "leave to us the single responsibility of safeguarding territorial integrity and political independence of American states." But when asked in the League of Nations Commission if the Monroe Doctrine would "prevent League action in American affairs," Wilson "replied in the negative." His amendment, he defensively asserted, "was nothing but a recognition of the *fact* that [the Monroe Doctrine] was not inconsistent with the terms of the Covenant." Later, when he was in the United States trying to get the peace treaty ratified, Wilson took the opposite position. The Covenant's reference to the Monroe Doctrine, he explained, meant "that the United States will look after it and won't ask the permission of anybody else to look after it." In line with this view, the president implied that under the amended Covenant, the United States would not submit to arbitration or inquiry by the League any issue the United States declared fell under the Monroe Doctrine. In the vote on the treaty in November 1919, Wilson also tacitly supported a reservation explicitly stating that as far as the United States was concerned, the Monroe Doctrine was "not in any way impaired or affected by the Covenant of the League of Nations and is not subject to any decision, report or enquiry by the council or assembly." How this could be squared with the president's assertion in Paris that "the Covenant would take precedence over the Monroe Doctrine" was ambiguous, to say the least.[22]

Wilson's analysis of the provision excluding domestic matters from the League was equally confused. According to his repeated statements, the domestic exclusion section of Article 15 meant that the League would not take up "such matters as immigration, tariffs, and naturalization." He also eventually supported a reservation to the treaty asserting that no member nation was required to submit to the League "any matter which it considers to be in international law a domestic question." In March 1919, however, and again in September, Wilson argued that nothing could be discussed in the League concerning any members' domestic affairs "*unless* something is occurring in some nation which is likely to disturb the peace of the world." In addition, in response to concerns that Ireland would be off-limits for action by the League because Britain considered it a domestic issue, Wilson disagreed and pointed to Article 11 of the Covenant. "Any threat of war, whether immediately affecting any of the Members of the League or not," this provision stated, "is hereby declared a matter of concern to the whole League, and the League shall take any action that may be deemed wise and effectual to safeguard the peace of nations." Here again Wilson embraced two irreconcilable positions: he wanted to exclude America's domestic matters from the League's jurisdiction, but he believed in a collective interest in peace everywhere too, which meant that the League should take action on any issue, domestic or not, that might lead to war.[23]

The president also had difficulty explaining the provision for economic sanctions against violators of the League's conflict resolution procedures. He never clarified the issue of how its members would decide to implement the sanctions, simply describing them as "automatic." If a violation of the League's arbitration and conciliation provisions occurred, "we would have no choice" but to implement a boycott of the violator immediately; doing so was a "legal obligation" under the Covenant, and "in a legal obligation there is no element of judgment." At the same time, though, Wilson argued that the Covenant did not impinge on Congress's constitutional authority to declare war. "Nothing could have been made more clear to the [Peace] Conference," Wilson assured the Senate Foreign Relations Committee, "than the right of our Congress under our constitution to exercise its independent judgment in all matters of peace and war."[24]

But wouldn't the imposition of an "absolute economic boycott" against a nation amount to war? Wilson himself suggested it would. Arguing that the threat of a boycott was a powerful deterrent against aggression, Wilson called economic sanctions "an infinitely more terrible instrument than war." The boycotted state would be "hermetically sealed by the united action of the most powerful nations in the world"; no people, goods, or communications would be allowed to enter or leave it. Although Wilson tried to dub such a boycott a "peaceful" action, obviously it would involve a blockade—and under international law a blockade was an act of war. Wilson also noted that the boycott would be "deadly" and implied that it would starve the targeted nation's people, just as the blockade during the war had "brought Germany to her knees." If the boycott was the robust, automatic penalty against violators of the Covenant that Wilson said it was, then it *had* to undermine Congress's war powers. Yet Wilson, against all logic, claimed that it did not.[25]

The president was only marginally more cogent in his interpretation of Article 10. As stated in the Covenant, Article 10 read: "The Members of the League undertake to respect and preserve as against external aggression the territorial integrity and existing political independence of all Members of the League. In case of any such aggression or in case of any threat or danger of such aggression the Council shall advise upon the means by which this obligation shall be fulfilled." In explaining the meaning of this article to the Senate Foreign Relations Committee, Wilson described it as "a very grave and solemn moral obligation." It asserted a general principle or "general promise" by the members to protect each other against aggression. But the article left it up to each member to decide for itself in each case if aggression was actually involved. Unlike the "legal obligation" involved with instituting a boycott against violators of the League's conflict resolution provisions, there was no automatic sanction attached to Article 10. Instead, "There is involved the element of judgment as to whether the territorial integrity or existing political independence is invaded or impaired." Unless the United States was a party to the issue in question, its representative had to agree with the other members of the council before any advice about how to fulfill Article 10 could be given. "And the unanimous vote of the Council," Wilson stressed, "is only advice in any case. Each government is free to reject it if it pleases." Congress was thus left free to judge for itself whether the case in question was "one of distinct moral obligation" under Article 10 and required an American response.[26]

This interpretation accorded with Wilson's view of the American-French security treaty, which he described as essentially an extension of the Covenant. The security pact, Wilson argued, "leaves us free to judge ourselves whether it is a case of crying 'Wolf! Wolf!' or really an unprovoked movement of aggression." Similarly, in agreeing to Article 10, the United States endorsed the principle that aggression was illegitimate and that the League's members had a duty to respond to aggressors. But because the Covenant allowed Americans to decide for themselves when and how in practice they would fulfill these obligations, "we cannot," Wilson promised, " . . . be drawn into wars that we do not wish to be drawn into."[27]

By emphasizing the limited nature of the commitments involved in Article 10, Wilson yet again backhandedly suggested that collective security theory was wrong. On one occasion in explaining Article 10, in fact, Wilson remarked that America did not want to be "drawn into every little European squabble" under its terms, and he doubted it would. "If you want to put out a fire in Utah, you don't send to Oklahoma for the fire engine," he reasoned. If trouble arose in the Balkans, the Europeans would deal with it. America would not get involved "unless the flames spread to the world." But the League was founded upon the notion, proclaimed Article 11, that "any war or threat of war, whether immediately affecting any of the Members of the League or not, is . . . a matter of concern to the whole League." A nation in a collective security regime supposedly viewed any war, anywhere as a threat. Waiting to see if the conflict "spread" before acting to contain it was consistent with power politics, not a new world order.[28]

Wilson further underscored the League's departure from the precepts of collective security by implying that the organization was an alliance against Germany in all but name. The new nations created by the peace treaty, he noted, lay directly in the path of territory that Germany wanted to dominate. "If the nations of the world do not maintain their concert to sustain the independence and freedom of those peoples," Wilson warned, "Germany will yet have her will upon them." The Germans, in fact, hoped that the United States would not join the League because "the arrangement" against it would then collapse. To be certain, Wilson also claimed that the League was "the combination of all against the wrongdoer" and a "method of common counsel with regard for the common interests of mankind," and was not, therefore, an alliance. But with the Germans excluded from the League and Wilson describing it as the chief bulwark against their future aggression, this argument did not sound very convincing.[29]

The contradictory and ambiguous character of the Covenant did not prevent Wilson from characterizing it as "an absolute reversal of the principles of the old system," however. To the president, the League's revolutionary character chiefly derived from America's commitment to its precepts of collective security, even if that commitment was only general in nature. Under the Covenant, and in particular under Article 10, the United States pledged itself to the principle that settling disputes by force, without a hearing, was wrong and that aggression—the strong preying on the weak—was wrong too. This meant in each case violations of the Covenant appeared to occur, the United States was required to take notice and to assess the situation in question, in consultation with the other members of the council. Under existing international norms, Wilson pointed out, "no nation has the right to call attention to anything that does not directly affect its own affairs." Article 11 of the Covenant gave the United States that right; the conflict resolution provisions (Articles 12–13 and 15–16) and especially Article 10 *obligated* the United States not just to pay attention to all cases of impending or actual war but to pass judgment on them. The Covenant thus created, as Wilson described it, "an attitude of comradeship and protection among the members of the league, which in its very nature is moral and not legal."[30]

America's adoption of this "attitude" gave the League the ability to deter potential aggressors and thus to move the world away from power politics and toward a lasting peace. Because Wilson believed that the modern world was interdependent and that a "community of interest" existed in maintaining peace, he assumed in most cases that the opinion of the members would agree about whether or not the "moral obligation" to protect states against aggression had become operative. He took it "for granted that in practically every case the United States would respond." Even if other nations hesitated at first to do their duty under Article 10, Wilson was confident that they would ultimately follow the U.S. lead. Both before and after the peace conference, Wilson repeatedly claimed that other nations had an "absolutely unquestioning confidence . . . in the people of America" and looked to America for "guidance." World leaders "knew, above all things else, what America stood for," Wilson asserted. They knew that Americans were "the champions of liberty throughout the world" and that America, "because it draws its blood from every civilized stock in the world," was "created to be the mediator of peace." They knew too of America's rising economic strength in the world, and respected it. "America is going to grow more and more powerful," Wilson anticipated, "and the more powerful she is, the more inevitable it is that she should be entrusted with the peace of the world." Thus, despite the apparently weak provisions of the Covenant, any potential wrongdoer would know that the United States was obligated to judge its behavior. "And no nation is likely to forget," Wilson argued, "that behind the moral judgment of the United States resides the overwhelming force of the United States." The rest of the world would no doubt concur in America's judgment, which meant that the power available to confront an aggressor would be magnified manyfold. If Germany "had known that there was a possibility of that sort of concurrence," Wilson lectured the Senate Foreign Relations Committee, "she never would have dared to do what she did." A future potential aggressor would never dare to act either.[31]

If the United States for some reason failed to join the League, the balance of power would again dominate international politics. The world, Wilson warned, "would experience one of those reversals of sentiment, one of those penetrating chills of reaction, which would lead to a universal cynicism." Feeding on the resulting disorder, Bolshevism might spread across Europe, and the Bolsheviks, according to Wilson, were "a little group of men just as selfish, just as ruthless, just as pitiless, as the agents of the Czar." They were a Prussian-like "amateur autocracy" who were as much of a threat to peace as the autocratic authorities in Berlin who had launched the war in 1914. In the absence of the League, Germany would intrigue with the Bolsheviks, too, to try to dominate Russia and reopen "her road to the East and to the domination of the world." Inevitably, "all nations will be set up as hostile camps again." Power politics would return with a vengeance, Wilson predicted. "The military point of view will prevail in every instance, and peace will be brought into contempt."[32]

The return of international anarchy and balance-of-power politics would immediately threaten the United States. Other nations would blame America for destroying the League and would deeply resent its behavior. The United States would be "looked upon with suspicion and hostile rivalry everywhere in the world." At the least, the Allies would set up an economic "combine" against the United States to force down the price of American exports and to shut it out of their own export markets. Such a trade war could only damage America's economy, Wilson argued. It would not cripple the United States given America's relative economic self-sufficiency compared with the Europeans, but it would hurt the nation's economic prosperity to some degree. Simply on the grounds of material self-interest, as Wilson told businessmen in Los Angeles, if America rejected the League, "you lose your game, you do not win."[33]

Whatever commercial pain America suffered in a world of renewed power politics paled in comparison to the damage its democratic way of life would suffer. Viewed as a hostile rival by the Allies, considered as, in effect, a traitor to the anti-German cause and to the cause of world peace, the United States would vastly have to expand its national defense forces. If Americans stood alone in the world, as they would without a League of Nations in existence, then "we must be physically ready for anything to come," exclaimed Wilson. "We must have a great standing army. We must see to it that every man in America is trained to arms. We must see to it that there are munitions and guns enough for an army that means a mobilized nation." America's military power would have to be "kept up to date" and "ready to use" in an instant too, which required "a concentrated, militaristic organization of government," complete with secret planning agencies and "a spying system" to keep watch on all of America's potential enemies. A "military class" would have to be created to manage this new defense establishment, taxes raised to pay for it, and the economy reoriented to serve it. "All of that is absolutely antidemocratic in its influence," cried Wilson. "You would have a military government in spirit if not in form." As he explained in a pro-League address in Kansas City: "If you are

determined to be armed to the teeth, you must obey the orders and direction of
the one man who can control the great machinery of war. Elections are of minor
importance, because they determine the political policy, and back of that political
policy is the constant pressure of the men trained to arms, enormous bodies of
disciplined men around them, unlimited supplies of military stores, and wonder-
ing if they are never going to be allowed to use their education and skill and ravage
some great people with the force of arms. That is the meaning of armament." As
Wilson had argued since the first year of the war, "Political liberty can exist only
when there is peace." In a world dominated by the fear and arms races of power
politics, America's freedoms would die, suffocated by the scourge of militarism.[34]

Wilson's national security strategy charted a deeply problematic course for America's future safety, however. By the standards of traditional power politics, the Versailles treaty put prudent and enforceable limits on Germany's strength and, more
so than other treaties imposed on defeated nations, held out some promise of future reconciliation. But when measured against Wilson's standards of justice and
international reform, the treaty fell short, especially in the eyes of the Germans.
They had their own idea of what constituted a lasting peace—and their definition,
not surprisingly, did not weaken Germany nearly as much as Wilson's did. In
early 1919, they believed that a treaty embodying Wilson's program would restrict
reparations to repairing physical war damage in Belgium and northern France;
minimize German losses in the east to Polish populated areas only, and even then
any territorial transfers had to be ratified by an affirmative vote of two-thirds of
the population of the district in question; transfer Alsace-Lorraine to France only
after a plebiscite; leave the Saarland and the Rhineland unquestionably under
German sovereignty; turn over Germany's colonies to the League, with Germany
receiving a mandate to administer at least some of them; allow Germany's union
with Austria; and grant Germany immediate entry into the League of Nations.
This program obviously differed from Wilson's, but the Germans argued that it
was fully consistent with the Fourteen Points.[35]

    When they examined the draft treaty in May 1919, the Germans were stunned.
"This shameful treaty has broken me," one of the German peace delegates moaned
on the night of 7 May, "for I had believed in Wilson until today." "All those who
were hopeful that America would give the world a new evangel of Brotherhood
have been cruelly deceived," despaired a leading German pacifist, Count Max
Montgelas. The treaty had a "crushing" effect on German public opinion, reported
Charles Dyar in Berlin in a message to the American peace commission. "The
German people did not expect such peace terms. . . . The shock to them is all the
more terrific because they were consistently encouraged in the notion that peace
on the basis of President Wilson's principles would not establish Germany's guilt
and the necessity of atonement and reparation. . . . The Allies have gone back on

their solemnly pledged word, it is said, and President Wilson has proven himself the greatest hypocrite in history."[36]

Angry and bitter at what they saw as the president's betrayal, the Germans paid no attention whatsoever to the conciliatory provisions Wilson built into the treaty. Instead, they immediately resolved to resist all of the treaty's terms. "Let no man believe that a German who, at the risk of the heaviest moral and material sacrifices, has fought the spirit of militarism in his own country," vowed Montgelas, "will ever submit to foreign brutality." Chancellor Scheidemann, on behalf of the Weimar government, denounced the treaty as "unbearable, unrealizable, and unacceptable." Every party except the Independent Socialists supported this statement. In their official responses to the treaty in Paris, Germany's peace delegates echoed it too. "The more deeply we penetrated into the spirit of this Treaty," they protested to the Associated powers in late May, "the more convinced we became of the impossibility of carrying it out. The exactions of this Treaty are more than the German people can bear." Eventually, Germany did decide to sign the treaty, but it did so, its government declared, under duress and "without . . . abandoning its view in regard to the unheard of injustice of the conditions of peace."[37]

If Wilson's linkage of international reform with treaty terms aiming simultaneously to weaken, punish, and conciliate the Germans had the unfortunate effect of utterly alienating Germany, it also undercut the legitimacy of Germany's democrats. They had trusted Wilson to deliver a peace treaty ending power politics; they had identified themselves with Wilson's program of international reform. But the president had instead produced a treaty clearly designed in large measure to contain and hurt Germany, a treaty that most Germans saw as an instrument of oppression. Forced to sign it, Germany's democrats now appeared to the German people not as agents of a lasting peace but as failures or, worse, traitors. The political consequences for them—for the liberal and leftist parties "on whom the future of the Weimar Republic depended"—were devastating. The upper and middle classes in particular, in the words of one historian, "identified the democratic Republic with the external humiliation of Germany," and the moderates in those social strata who had been willing to give Weimar a chance turned against it. In elections in June 1920, the leading pro-Weimar parties lost 8 million of the 19 million votes they had received in early 1919. The Far Left and the militaristic, nationalistic Right, conversely, the enemies of German democracy, made significant gains.[38]

Germany's denunciations of the treaty left Wilson in an impossible situation. His national security strategy assumed that the Germans would embrace his definition of a fair peace treaty, even if it hurt Germany, because, at bottom, they believed in American exceptionalism as much as he did. When they instead angrily denounced the treaty as incompatible with the Fourteen Points, the president was left with the choice of trying new measures to conciliate them or focusing on maintaining the limits on German power prescribed in the treaty. He had no interest in the first option because German criticisms of the treaty simply confirmed to him that "their minds have been debased by a false philosophy," a "dream of conquest and oppression," and that it might take longer than he had hoped for them to re- pent for their crimes. Loosening up controls on their power and removing some of the penalties imposed on them before they had done that—before they had really had a "change of heart"—was too risky. It could merely encourage the Germans to recommence their aggression.[39]

But with Germany defeated and set on a democratic path, punishing Weimar and limiting its power looked more contradictory than ever to the goal of ending power politics. "If we continue to sit in the enforcement of this peace," Herbert Hoover worried in mid-April 1919, "we will be in effect participating in an armed alliance in Europe," exactly the opposite of what Wilson wanted to do to safeguard America's future. Even before the treaty was signed, members of the American and British peace delegations were invoking Wilson's stated objective of interna- tional reform to justify weakening some of its most crucial enforcement provi- sions, including the occupation of the Rhineland. Wilson, to be sure, defeated most of these last-minute attempts to appease the Germans. But the fact that they were made at all revealed how Wilson's constant attacks on power politics eroded the will of the Associated powers to enforce their own peace settlement against Germany—even as Germany's hostility to the treaty made their determination to uphold it crucial to a stable peace.[40]

As the president's emphasis on the necessity of international reform weakened Britain's and America's will to enforce the treaty, it also contributed to tensions within the coalition arrayed against the former Reich. In early August 1919, for example, Wilson threatened to withdraw the French security treaty from Senate consideration if France refused to establish League mandates in the Middle East, as Wilson believed the French had agreed to do in Paris. Irritated with British and Italian behavior in the region as well, Wilson groused to Lansing that he was almost inclined to withdraw from the League "when it is composed of such in- triguers and robbers." In the name of upholding his principles of justice and a new world order, Wilson also continued to protest against Japan's claim on Shantung and Italy's on Fiume, two demands raised at the peace conference that Wilson believed violated the peace principles of the Fourteen Points. By February 1920, Wilson was so agitated over the Fiume issue that he accused the Allies of return- ing to the "old order" of world politics. If they persisted in their behavior, he de- clared, he would abandon the Versailles treaty altogether and let the Allies try to enforce it themselves. This was not an idle threat: at the end of 1919, in an effort to drive home to the Senate the consequences of rejecting the League, Wilson with- drew American representatives from the various commissions associated with the peace treaty. Over French protests, he even withdrew the American Peace Com- mission from the Supreme Allied Council. Finally, in March 1920, Wilson clashed with France after he publicly claimed that "a militaristic party" controlled French policy and privately protested France's methods for enforcing the reparations provisions of the peace treaty, methods Wilson suggested bordered on illegitimate power politics. A coalition of great powers had been necessary to defeat Germany and, most likely, would be necessary to contain it in the future as well. But by the spring of 1919, Wilson, waving the banner of international reform, was putting that winning coalition under strain.[41]

In the end, then, Wilson's national security strategy enraged the Germans, undermined their democratic leaders, and weakened the willingness and ability of the Associated powers to preserve the restraints they had put in place to prevent Germany from launching a second world war. This negative outcome might have been mitigated to some degree had the League of Nations been a viable instrument of international reform. The Covenant, after all, contained provisions to deter and if necessary defeat any aggressor, including Germany. And, as Wilson suggested, sooner or later Germany would gain entry into the League, and when it did, it would be treated as an equal, which would no doubt diminish its hostility toward the peace treaty. Thus a workable League might render the problems with Wilson's German policy largely moot.

But the Covenant, as we have seen, was itself problematic. Its weak and vague provisions for enforcing collective security, including an apparent exemption of the Monroe Doctrine from the League's jurisdiction, implied that the whole idea of a collective interest in peace everywhere in the world was illusory. Wilson denied this charge, arguing that America's commitment to the Covenant, combined with its exceptional moral authority and prestige, would make collective security credible. Ultimately, just as he depended on American exceptionalism to reconcile the Germans to the peace treaty, American exceptionalism would also make the League a working reality, regardless of the loopholes and ambiguity of the Covenant.

Wilson's behavior toward the Allies during and after the peace conference, however, belied his claims about America's unique character among nations, exactly as it had earlier during the war. As the president himself admitted, the United States was not alone in working to ensure that the League council could not order a member into battle without its consent. "America is not the only proud nation in the world," Wilson noted to a luncheon audience in San Francisco. "I can testify from my part in the councils on the other side of the sea that the other nations are just as jealous of their sovereignty as we are of ours." Indeed, Wilson boasted, "the only difference between some of them and us is that we could take care of our sovereignty, and they couldn't take care of theirs." All nations wanted the freedom to look after their own interests in their own way, Wilson suggested—especially the United States.[42]

The United States was also little different from other nations in its willingness to use coercion to get its way in negotiations. In addition to an attempt to exert financial leverage over Italy during the standoff over Fiume, Wilson threatened the Allies with an American arms buildup if they did not make concessions to his peace program. When the Allies at first refused to agree to a mandate system for the colonies of the defeated powers, Wilson argued that their stance would turn the League into "a laughing stock" and bring the system of "competitive armaments" back into world politics. "In that case," he warned, "the United States would have to have a greatly increased navy and maintain a large standing army." The president told reporters in December 1918 that if Britain refused to agree to arms limitation planning under the League, "the United States should show her how to build a navy." Faced with intransigence from the British, he asserted, America was ready "to meet any program" of naval construction they attempted. To back up this threat, Wilson asked Congress to authorize a second three-year naval building program to accelerate the naval expansion already approved in 1916. In April, Wilson did tell the British he would withdraw support for the new naval bill, but only "if the kind of peace is made for which we are working and which will include a League of Nations." The United States wanted a new world order dependent on American exceptionalism, but in order to get one it was willing to use a traditional tactic of power politics, the threat of an arms race, against its own supposed allies.[43]

This threat was implicit as well in Wilson's warnings that he would sign a separate peace with the Central Powers if he did not get agreement on his preferred peace terms. Deployed most dramatically in his negotiations with France over the Saarland and with Italy over Fiume, and again in early 1920 over multiple issues, Wilson's declared willingness to abandon the Allies meant that he was ready, if necessary, to sacrifice the League of Nations rather than be a party to an unjust peace treaty. As a world without the League would be a world of competitive power politics, with a rapidly arming America, whenever Wilson threatened to turn his back on the Allies, he was also, in effect, threatening to arm against them.[44]

Such threats were made to attain international reform, of course. According to Wilson, America always had the best interests of the world at heart; it was "the only idealistic nation in the world" dedicated to disinterested service and equal rights for all nations. But at Paris Wilson refused to reduce the war debts the Allies owed the United States, despite the obvious hardships they had endured to achieve victory and despite America's sitting on the sidelines for more than two years while they fought the Central Powers alone. Congress opposed any debt reduction, and, Wilson complained, "America has grave difficulties of her own." Rather than focus on war debts, the president advised, the Allies should promote Europe's economic recovery by lowering their reparation demands on the Germans. Similarly, when confronted with protests from the smaller nations at Paris about some of the provisions of the draft treaty, Wilson dismissed their criticisms, asserting that they would have to trust the Big Four to do the right thing for them. After all, Wilson lectured, the great powers had won the war, and "in the last analysis the military and naval strength of the Great Powers will be the final guarantee of the peace of the world." America and the Allies had the power to write the peace treaty however they wanted, and the weaker nations would just have to accept that reality.[45]

The traditional character of much of Wilson's statecraft—and the striking contrast it presented to his claims of American exceptionalism—did not go unnoticed by other leaders at the peace conference. If the United States really trusted in the League of Nations, observed Lloyd George, it would not continue its naval building program. Continuing to build would turn the League into "a mere piece of rhetoric." Robert Cecil, the administration's chief British collaborator in negotiations to draw up the Covenant, agreed, seeing it as "unreasonable for Wilson to build a large Navy and insist on everybody else joining the League of Nations." On the Shantung issue, the Chinese government noted, Wilson and the Allies had simply favored the strong over the weak in letting Japan keep its gains. They had betrayed Wilson's "lofty principles" to keep Japan happy, regardless of what happened to China. Colonel House caught the prevailing mood in Paris on 31 May, the day of Wilson's "great power" discourse to the smaller states. Given the sharp difference between the president's remarks and his vision of a reformed world, House confided to his diary, "one can see why the question is so constantly asked whether his talk means anything at all." If the president was not careful, House worried, "the feeling of distrust for him will become universal."[46]

Wilson's apparent hypocrisy at Paris was nothing new. It reflected the contradiction at the core of his approach to national security affairs. Since at least late 1914, the president believed that power politics in general and Germany's power in particular threatened American democracy. These two beliefs were logically at odds with each other. Fear of Germany's power implied that the United States should balance against it, through military preparedness and an alliance with the Entente. But fear of power politics implied that the United States should avoid arms buildups and keep aloof from the Allies. In theory, establishing a system of collective security could resolve this dilemma by creating a world in which German power would be contained without power politics. But this apparent solution had little substance in reality. To create the atmosphere of security necessary for America and the Allies to trust in a peace league for their protection, international reform had to begin by limiting Germany's power and punishing it for its criminal behavior. For the foreseeable future, "collective security" really meant an armed alliance directed against the Germans—a logical contradiction. To escape from this quandary, Wilson tried to build the promise of long-term reconciliation into the peace treaty and to avoid terms he thought smacked too much of Allied self-aggrandizement. But pursuing these measures involved bullying and coercing the Allies, which threatened both the spirit of collective security and the image of American exceptionalism on which Wilson thought the League depended to work. Ultimately, Wilson appeared hypocritical to both the Germans and the Allies, which seriously diminished the chances for long-term containment of Germany and for creating a viable League. As the problems with the Covenant revealed, moreover, the latter goal was dubious in any event. The president's national security policies thus led to a strategic dead end—and the only alternative strategy available, as Wilson portrayed it, was armed isolation.

10

National Security Debates, 1918–20

Both products of President Wilson's negotiations at Paris—the treaty terms dealing with Germany and the Covenant of the League of Nations—provoked intense controversy in the United States. To persistent pacifists and many Progressive supporters of collective security, the Versailles treaty went too far in containing and punishing Germany. The treaty reflected an Allied desire to dominate Europe and increase their empires, these critics charged, and it would perpetuate power politics. From this perspective, the League was essentially an alliance sure to involve the United States in wars to preserve the Allies' ill-gotten gains. The League to Enforce Peace and most of the League of Free Nations Association, in contrast, either defended the treaty or argued that the League of Nations could redeem it. Although their interpretation of the Covenant was as confused as Wilson's, they insisted that the League was a viable instrument of international reform. Atlanticists, meanwhile, directly attacked collective security, calling it unrealistic and dangerous to American interests. But they failed to rally support for an American-Allied entente as an alternative to the League, opting instead to work with Republican supporters of collective security to attach reservations to the treaty that strictly limited America's obligations under the Covenant. Had it not been for Wilson's objection to the reservation on Article 10, the reserved treaty would have been ratified—an outcome revealing how the president's view of power politics and international reform still dominated national security debates, even as the Versailles treaty itself was defeated.

Of the factions engaged in the fight over the treaty, the pacifists were the most convinced that "discarded diplomats of the old school" had prevailed in Paris. Led now by Oswald Garrison Villard and the editors of the *Nation,* who withdrew the support they had given Wilson during the war; a reinvigorated Robert La Follette and a handful of insurgent Republicans in the Senate such as George W. Norris and Asle J. Gronna; and Max and Crystal Eastman, although they were increasingly absorbed by events in revolutionary Russia, pacifists denounced the treaty as "a peace of undisguised vengeance." At most, Villard suggested, Germany should have been required to cede Alsace-Lorraine, to lose its colonies temporarily to a league, to demilitarize the Rhineland, to disarm, and to "make good" damage it had caused in Belgium and France. But the treaty went well beyond those terms. By stripping away territory that rightfully belonged to Germany, allowing Japan to take over German concessions in China, excluding Germany from the League, imposing excessive reparations, and forcing Germany to disarm without any corresponding disarmament by the Allies, the treaty made a "mockery of that sanctified formula of 14 points." It was shaped not by Wilson's peace program but by the secret treaties of the Allies, and so it aimed to advance Allied imperialism while permanently destroying Germany as a great power. A product of cynical strategic calculations and naked greed, the treaty was nothing less than an "international crime."[1]

Pacifists blamed Wilson for this awful outcome to the war. Either the president had purposefully abandoned his program of international reform in favor of allying America to the imperialism of the Allies or, more likely, he was too weak and incompetent to stand up to Allied pressure to compromise his principles. The president should have demanded the abrogation of the Entente's secret treaties while the war was still on, argued the Nation's Lincoln Colcord, but instead he arrogantly believed that "he would be able single-handed to offset them at the Peace Conference." He never should have let the conference negotiations take place in secret and, once it was clear what the Allies wanted to do to Germany, he should have publicly denounced them and gone home. Wilson foolishly left himself in the position of "playing a lone and secret hand," unwilling or unable to rally the world's "plain people" to his program. It was the president's own fault that the war ended "with bitterness and hatred as well as with colossal hypocrisy."[2]

Given the character of the peace treaty and Germany's exclusion from the League of Nations, the League could not be an agency of international reform. It was simply part of the "old, old scheme" of power politics, scorned La Follette, "modified a little, to fit the times." The League was "an alliance among the victorious governments . . . by which their conquered enemies may be kept in subjugation and exploited to the uttermost." Not only would the League enforce the "spoils-grabbing compact of greed and hate" against Germany, but also it would maintain the existing "economic and political status quo" around the world and crush radical movements such as Bolshevism that challenged imperialism. As members could hardly ignore Article 10 without turning the League into "a mere aggregation of warring factions," La Follette perceived, once the United States signed on to the Covenant it would find itself yoked to the imperial oppression and strategic self-interest of the Allies. "Senators, if we go into this thing," La Follette warned, "it means a great standing Army." The League would put the United States "perpetually in a state of war, so that no new principle will need to be invoked in order to suppress any publication offensive to the administration, or to imprison any citizen whose criticism of the Government is offensive to Federal officeholders." It would entrap America in an unreformed international system certain to kill its democratic way of life.[3]

The pacifist analysis of the Versailles treaty implied that Germany was no longer a threat to American security. Convinced that a democratic Germany was sure to be peaceful, pacifists displayed little interest in punishing the former Reich or controlling its power. If anything, their preferred peace terms might actually increase Germany's potential military power to a level beyond that of 1914. Although they did not spell out the exact peace terms they thought were appropriate, pacifists indicated that Germany ought to be allowed to unify with Austria, annex the Sudentenland, join the League, enjoy equal access to world markets, and tie its future arms reductions to comparable arms reduction on the part of the Allies. The *Nation* also appeared to want the Rhineland occupation and German reparations payments strictly limited. This program was not one that conveyed any apprehension of a future German menace to Europe or America. On the contrary, it suggested that whatever danger Germany had posed to the world had passed along with the kaiser's rule; it was time, the *Nation* appeared to believe, to welcome democratic Germany back into the ranks of the world's great powers.[4]

To be sure, pacifists did concede or imply that the United States had an interest in Europe's security and stability. But they suggested that interest was small, especially as Germany's autocracy was defeated and dismantled. After all, according to the *Nation,* even the War Department recognized that America's geographic position made it virtually invulnerable to invasion by Germany or any other major power. It would be preferable from America's standpoint if Europe did not degenerate into chaos, but even if it showed signs of doing so, the United States would not be well served by involving itself in the Old World's political-military affairs. The United States, declared the *Nation's* editors in March 1920, "will not be a party any further to schemes for destroying Germany, or to alliances such as in the past have paved the way to war. It will not knowingly aid the imperialistic plans of Great Britain or France or Italy any more than it will aid those of Germany." If the Germans ever resumed their aggression in the future, it appeared that pacifists, as they had in 1914, would count on the Allies to handle that problem on their own, without any help from the United States.[5]

With these views in mind, pacifists called on the Senate to reject the Versailles treaty. Rather than continue down a road sure to lead to armaments, war, and militarism, the United States could and should detach itself from power politics and advance international reform on its own terms. It should reduce its own armaments as an example to others and, La Follette prescribed, join the League only if its member states abolished conscription, limited arms expenditure, provided for a popular referendum before going to war, renounced the economic exploitation of League mandates, and endorsed the right of revolution for all peoples, including those living in colonial empires. The editors of the *Nation,* for their part, called on the Allies to revise the peace treaty in Germany's favor. They also wanted America to restore "freedom of economic opportunity" at home by breaking up monopolies and "working out a democratic organization within industry itself," to urge other nations to do the same, and to adopt free trade. "With these established," the editors confidently predicted, "the rise of a league of nations would be automatic, and the perpetuation of a war would be inconceivable." But even if these democratic world reforms failed to materialize, the editors saw no reason to change America's posture of lightly armed isolation. "The United States can go on with its national life," they asserted, "calmly awaiting the day of a sound international order and an honest league of nations without having to be armed to the teeth."[6]

A new figure in the forefront of pacifist ranks, Republican senator William E. Borah of Idaho, echoed nearly all of these arguments. From 1914 through 1918, to be certain, Borah at times sounded less like a pacifist than an Atlanticist, as he called for a naval buildup to support a vigorous defense of America's neutral rights, voted in favor of war with Germany to uphold America's honor and diplomatic credibility, and demanded an unconditional surrender from the Reich. Still, even in this phase of his career, Borah expressed elements of the pacifist outlook on national security affairs. Despite the war against Germany, Borah defended the wisdom of America's traditional aloofness from European political and military affairs. He joined "no crusade" to spread democracy or remake the world, he declared in 1917. "I seek or accept no alliances; I obligate this Government to no other power. I make war alone for my countrymen and their rights, for my country and its honor." Focused on this narrow definition of the meaning of the war, Borah paid little attention to how German dominance of Europe might affect the United States, and he did not perceive that America might have an interest in helping the Allies contain Germany's power over the long term. Indeed, he distrusted the Allies and did not think the United States had any significant stake in their territorial aims in the war.[7]

Once Germany surrendered and democratized, Borah agreed with the view of the peace treaty, the League, and American foreign policy put forward by the *Nation* and La Follette. He particularly attacked collective security theory. No nation, he argued, would in practice ever submit any matter of any consequence to a peace league for judgment, nor would any state allow its armed forces to be ordered into battle by any international agency. Nations would not implement any economic boycott against an aggressor unless it was to their advantage to do so either. "There is no such thing as friendship between nations as we speak of friendship between individuals," lectured Borah. "Nations and peoples act from self-interest." Those who believed that nations perceived a vital stake in peace everywhere were in error, according to his analysis; their plans for the League were based on "an imaginary world."[8]

Because the League could not really be an organ of international reform, it had to be something else—namely a tool created by the Allies to force the United

States to serve their strategic and imperial interests. Signing the Covenant and remaining faithful to it meant "the transferring, if not legally, in effect, the power to declare war from the Congress of the United States to some tribunal over which the people themselves who must fight the battles and pay the taxes have no control." It meant "renouncing the doctrine of Washington and the entering of the politics and alliances of Europe . . . [and] the abandonment of the Monroe Doctrine and permitting Europe to interfere in the affairs of the western continent." In Borah's eyes, such a policy certainly benefited the Allies, as they could draw the United States into the work of policing Europe and protecting their empires. But it made no sense at all for America, given that America had no vital interest in either upholding the European peace settlement or in defending imperialism.[9]

In fact, entanglement in the League would destroy America's free way of life, especially as involvement in the war, in Borah's estimation, had already eroded it. The twisted logic of collective security, as Borah understood it, was to use "force to destroy force, conflict to prevent conflict, militarism to destroy militarism, war to prevent war." If it became involved with the League, America would have to increase its armaments and engage in conflicts around the globe, just as it was now engaged in an intervention in Russia to destroy Bolshevism. The League, thundered Borah, "is Prussianism, extended, amplified, denationalized." Becoming an armed, aggressive policeman overseas would teach Americans to value force and repression over reason and law, with devastating results for their domestic liberties. American political institutions might appear to remain intact, Borah conceded, "but when you shall have committed this Republic to a scheme of world control based upon force, upon the combined military force of the four great nations of the world, you will have soon destroyed the atmosphere of freedom, of confidence in the self-governing capacity of the masses, in which alone a democracy may thrive." For the sake of its own democratic values, and to preserve its ability "by precept and example, through influence and counsel, to continue her lead . . . in the world struggle for free government," the United States had to reject the League completely and rededicate itself to its own national ideals.[10]

If Borah's emergence as a powerful voice against the League helped to revitalize pacifism after the war, so too did the *New Republic*'s disillusionment with Wilson's diplomacy. Much more so than the president, the *New Republic*'s editors believed in the peaceful disposition of Germany's new democratic government. "Of the three possible Germanys—Junker, Ebert, or Sparticide," wrote Walter Lippmann upon his return to the *New Republic* in March 1919, "there can be no doubt that Ebert's is the one with which the world can best live at peace." The goal of the Associated powers should therefore be to prop up Germany's democracy with moderate peace terms, something they had committed themselves to doing during the war. "President Wilson," the editors reminded their readers in early 1919, "is pledged in the most unequivocal and irrevocable way to obtain for a democratized Germany the same security, the same independence and the same opportunities for growth which other free nations enjoy." As the Germans had overthrown their autocracy and as the *New Republic* saw no reason to doubt Weimar's peaceful intentions, Wilson had to follow through on his promises and "work for an ultimately contented and restored Germany."[11]

When the editors read the Versailles treaty, they were appalled. The treaty, they cried, was an "inhuman monster" created "in the spirit of the traditional diplomacy of Europe." Its terms were "less in accord with the Fourteen Points than was the peace of Brest-Litovsk." Specifically, the editors objected to the Japanese acquisition of German concessions in Shantung, which they argued should go to the Chinese; the suspension of German sovereignty over the Saarland; the apparently sweeping powers of the Reparation Commission, which they claimed gave the Allies "a dictatorship over the industrial system out of which Germany is to pay"; the exclusion of Germany from the League, which they assumed meant that the Germans would face discriminatory treatment in world trade; the lack of a fixed sum of reparations; the banning of a German union with Austria; the lack of German self-determination in the Sudentenland, the Tyrol, and German-speaking areas assigned to Poland; the open-ended character of the Rhineland occupation; and, finally, the "one-sided disarmament" of the former Reich. "Under such a peace," the editors exclaimed, "the German nation must disintegrate." At the very least, the treaty gave the Germans "too many good reasons for feeling themselves thoroughly abused." It sent exactly the wrong message to the German people, teaching them "that a defeated democracy suffers no less than a defeated autocracy. . . . [I]t teaches, not that crime has its penalties, but that defeat is something to be avoided." Far from initiating a process of reconciliation and international reform, the treaty confirmed that the cynical logic of power politics still ruled the globe.[12]

Tied to such a settlement, the League was nothing more than an alliance certain to drag America into the efforts of the Allies to dominate Europe. Even before the publication of the peace terms, the *New Republic*'s editors were critical of the draft Covenant for its lack of an "inter-parliamentary assembly" to ensure that the League was "an association of peoples" as well as of governments. They were also wary of Article 10, calling it "one of those grand generalities behind which every opponent of change can barricade himself." Once the editors saw the peace treaty for Germany, they became convinced that the Covenant was an "instrument of competitive imperialist nationalism." Under it, the United States would be committed "to preserving the status quo against anything that diplomacy can manipulate into the appearance of aggression." The United States would become a pawn in the strategic machinations of Britain and France, as they sought to uphold their unjust and unworkable settlement against Germany.[13]

Unwilling to accept the costs and risks of participation in the League-cum-alliance with the Entente, the *New Republic* called for ratification of the Versailles treaty with the reservation that America would not commit itself to enforce all of its peace terms. The United States should become, in effect, a limited, consulting member of the League, with full freedom of action to deal with international affairs however it wished. With America's guarantee to uphold the peace treaty removed, argued the editors, the Allies would have no choice but to appease the Germans and revise the peace treaty. Wilson's decision to stick with the Allies in Paris "gave them a sense of security which they have used in order to press to the limit demands they would not have dared to make under other circumstances," contended the editors. "With nothing but their own force to rely upon," the Allies would see "the folly of permanently subjugating Central Europe." The movement for treaty revision would be further spurred, the *New Republic* believed, by the advancing fortunes of the Allied Left: "The time limit is approaching," the editors confidently asserted, "when a more liberal France and a more liberal England will prefer peace in Europe to an ultimately disastrous attempt at what never yet has succeeded in all history." Once liberalism triumphed and the treaty was revised, a true "League of Free Nations" would then emerge, including Germany, and the United States could safely commit itself to uphold collective security.[14]

This argument constituted a remarkable turnabout for Croly and his fellow editors. Up until the publication of the peace treaty, they had always insisted that insecurity drove the Allies to seek strategic advantages over Germany. America's commitment to a peace league, they had argued in 1916, would alleviate that dynamic by giving the Allies the promise of safety through international reform rather than through power politics. The editors made the same case in 1917 and 1918, when they suggested that forming a wartime league of nations would help induce a moderation of Allied war aims. For similar reasons, Croly and the Progressives at the LFNA, in November 1918, had demanded that the League be the first order of business at the peace conference. "If, as in the past, nations must look for their future security chiefly to their own strength and resources," they argued, "then inevitably, in the name of the needs of national defence, there will be claims for strategic frontiers and territories with raw materials which do violence to the principle of nationality." But now, confronted with a peace treaty reeking of strategic calculations despite the existence of the Covenant, the *New Republic* suddenly decided that making the Allies feel more insecure would lead them to abandon power politics in favor of international reform. The United States needed to leave Europe in order to save it—a complete reversal of the *New Republic*'s earlier views.[15]

To further confuse matters, the editors also implicitly accepted a reservation to the Covenant that they themselves said undermined collective security theory. Exempting the Monroe Doctrine from the League's jurisdiction, the *New Republic* argued in mid-April 1919, contradicted the "lesson of the war"—the idea that all nations had a "common interest . . . in the preservation of peace." It would invite other nations to exempt their own spheres of interest from the League's authority too, destroying any possibility of a collective security regime ever emerging. "When all nations insist on protecting themselves by methods agreeable only to themselves and refuse to discuss those methods with the other nations," declaimed the editors, "they are all condemned to a common insecurity—the kind of insecurity which creates and necessitates purely military alliances" and other "suicidal" policies like endless military preparation. Yet once the *New Republic* resolved to oppose any American guarantee of Europe's security, the journal quickly lost interest in fighting an exemption for the Monroe Doctrine. By late September, the editors were fully behind all of the Lodge reservations to the Covenant, including one declaring that the United States alone would interpret the doctrine and would not submit to the League any matter related to it. Spheres of interest might contradict collective security theory, but the *New Republic* supported one for America anyway.[16]

Despite the editors' support for ratification of the treaty with reservations, their overall response to the Versailles treaty mirrored that of the pacifists. In urging the United States to renounce any obligation to uphold the treaty's terms, the editors assumed that the nonaggressive nature of Germany's democracy and the growing liberalization of the Allies would make for peaceful treaty revision regardless of the persistence of anarchy in world politics. They also implicitly expected the Allies to be able to contain Germany by themselves, without any American help, if for some reason the Germans decided to overturn the treaty by force. Finally, the editors appeared to think that whatever happened in Europe, at least for the foreseeable future, America could safely scale back its military forces, as they opposed the administration's plans for postwar defense increases. Together, these ideas amounted to a de facto endorsement of the pacifist policy of modestly armed isolation as the best route to safeguarding America's future.[17]

Most liberal internationalists, as well as Progressives such as Jane Addams who had been lukewarm supporters of President Wilson during the war, did not join in the *New Republic*'s abrupt lurch toward pacifism. One faction, including most of the League of Free Nations Association and the Woman's Peace Party, William Jennings Bryan, Hamilton Holt, and Theodore Marburg, supported Wilson's stance on the peace treaty with varying degrees of enthusiasm. Another group, represented by most of the LEP and a collection of so-called mild reservationists in the Senate who largely echoed Taft's views on national security affairs, also shared Wilson's outlook on the treaty in many ways but, unlike the president, were eager to put conditions on American membership in the League. Regardless of their orientation, however, both sets of liberal internationalists had trouble articulating a coherent interpretation of the Covenant. In some respects, indeed, their analysis of collective security was even more contradictory than Wilson's.[18]

To the faction sharing President Wilson's reluctance to attach reservations to the Senate resolution ratifying the Versailles treaty, the advance of international reform represented by the Covenant outweighed whatever shortcomings existed in the peace terms imposed on Germany. For some, this calculation was a close call. Both the LFNA and the WPP objected to the peace settlement on grounds similar to those of the *New Republic*. But most members of the two organizations decided that rejecting the treaty or attaching formal reservations to it would, in Paul Kellogg's words, "scrap the hope of the world that inheres in the covenant" and thrust nations back into the maelstrom of the balance of power. Directly attacking the *New Republic*'s claim that America's refusal to enforce the peace treaty would cause the Allies to abandon power politics, pro-LFNA Progressives replied that "precisely the opposite is what has always happened in the past. The more lowering and insecure the future, the more those in power have been impelled to grab everything in sight." Rather than embark on a futile attempt to isolate America from the chaos that would inevitably engulf Europe if the League was crippled, the United States should ratify the treaty while pointing out its problems in a separate resolution and trust that the League, under American leadership, would soon revise the peace terms to bring them more in line with the Fourteen Points.[19]

Liberal internationalists anxious to ratify the peace treaty also perceived that some of the proposed reservations to the Covenant contradicted its basic premise. None of the LFNA's proposed "declarations of interpretation" had anything to do with exempting the United States from the obligations of Article 10 or the Monroe Doctrine from the League's jurisdiction, for example. Such reservations "in the direction of national self-interest," Kellogg declared, "would be out of joint with our whole professions." Similarly, Marburg thought that such reservations exuded "mistrust and selfishness" on the part of America. They struck at the "mutual confidence and respect" essential to "the spirit of the League." If the United States renounced its obligations under Article 10, the League would become a "voluntary institution" incapable of deterring aggressors; if the United States demanded an exemption for the Monroe Doctrine, other states would reserve their own vital interests as well, undermining the whole concept of collective security and thus striking "at the very heart of the Covenant." No collective security regime could accommodate its members' declaring exemptions from its obligations and still hope to remain an agency of international reform.[20]

Yet even the most ardent supporters of the Covenant were unable to articulate a consistent view of the meaning of its terms or how reservations might affect them. Like Wilson, Holt argued that, under Article 10, "it is inconceivable that [the League council] will recommend that the United States send her troops to any part of the world except where we have a direct interest or our proximity makes us the logical policeman." This view, which was echoed by Marburg, implied that some conflicts or wars were not of America's concern—a contention at odds with collective security theory. Holt also, reluctantly, ended up accepting a reservation exempting the Monroe Doctrine from the League's authority in order to get the treaty ratified, even though he implied that it was destructive to the Covenant. The

LFNA likewise ultimately went along with all of the Lodge reservations, despite the organization's initial posture that such qualifications were utterly incompatible with the spirit of the League. Finally, Marburg, who probably did the most detailed analysis of the Covenant, had an ambiguous view of the League's authority over domestic matters. He suggested that the League did not have the "positive power to interfere in the internal affairs of its members," but, at the same time, it did have the right "to take notice" of "internal conditions" threatening to peace and to "invite" the government concerned to use the League's "tribunals of inquiry." The authority to turn the League's spotlight of publicity on a state's internal affairs apparently did not constitute a "positive power" to Marburg. But it was not clear why it didn't, especially as the League's cooling-off procedures were premised on the notion that public exposure of disputes put forceful pressure on the parties to resolve them peacefully.[21]

Liberal internationalists who supported reservations to the Covenant early on offered still other interpretations of the peace treaty. With the exception of the Shantung settlement, which most of them considered unjust treatment of China, proreservationist liberal internationalists did not have any problem with the peace terms imposed on Germany. The German people had to be "cured" of their lust for conquest, Taft argued, and only severe punishment could accomplish that goal. Because Germany appeared to be "an unrepentant international criminal," moreover, the reduction of its potential and actual military power was "reasonable self-defense" and, in the long run, would pave the way for Allied arms limitation. Unlike the Progressives of the LFNA and the WPP, then, Taft and the mild reservationists in the Senate in general agreed with President Wilson's approach toward the Germans at the peace conference.[22]

Their endorsement of collective security theory was more qualified, however. Although they continued to proclaim their faith in it, Taft and the mild reservationists in the Senate made statements directly contrary to its basic tenets. They insisted that the League was not an alliance but, in their next breath, described it as anti-Bolshevik and, even more so, as a combination against the Germans. Taft explicitly hoped that Germany would not be admitted to the League "for a long time," asserted that the League would protect new European states created "to constitute bulwarks against a revival of German power," and conceded the possibility that nations not allowed into the League might form a "warlike . . . rival league of nations." Senator Le Baron Colt, similarly, argued that the League was "absolutely necessary to secure the peace of the world by the enforcement of the terms of peace." It would be "dishonorable," he added, "to desert France, England, and Italy in this critical hour" by failing to agree to the Covenant. The League was so much like an alliance, in fact, that Porter J. McCumber, another leading mild reservationist in the Senate, openly worried that the exclusion of Germany might perpetuate power politics. "This covenant," he warned in June, "should not be so drawn or arranged as to compel other nations to unite and thus divide the world into hostile camps." Why the existing treaty would not have precisely that result, though, given its exclusion of Germany and Russia, was not clear.[23]

Proreservationists also had a contradictory posture concerning America's stake in conflicts in "distant countries." In accord with Wilson, Taft usually argued that the League council would not call on the United States to help suppress conflict in regions where it lacked a direct interest. "The Council," Taft promised, "would not attempt to draw the United States in until the trouble growing out of the disturbance bade fair to involve world consideration." In the Senate, Irvine L. Lenroot, Frank Kellogg, and Albert Cummins were blunter in asserting that America did not have a compelling interest in preserving the security of nations around the globe. "We are undoubtedly interested in preventing Germany from again becoming a world menace and in maintaining the stability of certain nations which have been formed through the results of this war," Kellogg observed. "But to perpetually guarantee the territorial integrity and existing political independence of every nation in the world in distant continents is quite another proposition." He doubted that the American people or their elected representatives would support interventions in remote disputes, and he suggested that he would agree with their refusal to do so.[24]

Clearly, these positions ran counter to the premise of collective security, that all nations, including the United States, had a vital interest in any threat to peace, anywhere. Those who were against American intervention "into a war in the causes of which we are not directly concerned," A. Lawrence Lowell of the LEP asserted, were really "ultra-pacifists, for they shrink from using the force necessary to prevent war in the world." They were effectively traitors to the cause of collective security. "If we believe in preventing war we must use the means necessary to do so," insisted Lowell. "We must be willing to risk a small sacrifice to insure against a larger one." Significantly, Taft himself, in contrast to what he usually said, stated in January 1919 that events in supposedly "remote" regions such as the Balkans could affect American security, so the United States should be willing to agree "to make a small war in order to suppress a world war." Trying to draw lines between conflicts not immediately related to America's interests and those of relevance to world peace made no sense under collective security theory—yet many liberal internationalists tried hard to draw them.[25]

This basic contradiction—voicing support for collective security theory while rejecting commitments based on it—can be seen even more clearly in the reservation program put forward by Lenroot and others in the Senate and supported by Taft and most of the LEP. In their final form, as produced by negotiations held chiefly between Lodge, Lenroot, and Kellogg, the most crucial Lodge reservations specified that the United States would be the "sole judge" as to whether it had fulfilled all of its international obligations and obligations under the Covenant prior to withdrawing from the League; that it would not submit to the

League any question it decided lay within its domestic jurisdiction, including immigration matters and the tariff; that it alone would interpret the Monroe Doctrine and would not submit to the League any question that it believed depended on or related to it; and, finally, that the United States would assume "no obligation to preserve the territorial integrity or political independence of any other country . . . under the provisions of article 10."[26]

These reservations blatantly flew in the face of collective security theory. The LFNA, Holt, and Marburg all recognized this fact. "The reservations proclaim a desire on our part to be relieved of the common obligation which effective co-operation requires," lamented Marburg. They appeared to be based not on the notion of a collective interest in peace but on a belief that nations pursued their own specific security interests above all others. Lenroot made this implication explicit at one point. The League council was a "political body," he noted in July, as he called for a reservation on domestic issues. "Each member of the council will be seeking advantage for his own government." Based on this assumption, the reservations made perfect sense. Because nations competed for advantage and power against each other, the United States needed to take care to protect its vital interests, such as its hegemony over Central America and control over its immigration policies, from interference by the League. It needed to avoid squandering its resources in conflicts not of its own concern too. It needed, in short, to pay attention to preserving or enhancing its own power relative to the power of others—a position totally at odds with the claim that nations should value peace around the world more than anything.[27]

The illogical posture of Taft's supporters toward the Covenant was perhaps most graphically revealed in an exchange between McCumber and Walter Edge, another mild reservationist, on 17 November, days before the first vote on the treaty. At issue was a proposal by a vociferous anti-League senator, James Reed, to exclude from the League's jurisdiction any question the United States declared affected "its honor or its vital interests." Denouncing Reed, McCumber argued that his proposed reservation made a mockery of the whole idea of a peace league; it would "undo" America's longtime efforts to promote arbitration and its current attempt "to make a world-wide contract between all nations." Edge then spoke out against Reed as well, but from a different angle. There was no need for Reed's reservation, he argued, because, having gone over the Covenant "with a fine-tooth comb, endeavoring to ascertain every section or article . . . whereby the interests of our country might be seriously impaired to its disadvantage," the Senate had agreed to a package of reservations that left America's vital interests and honor "amply protected and taken care of." The reservationist program, in other words, exempted all of America's vital interests from the League's authority—something that would undo the very goal of international reform that Edge, McCumber, and the rest of their group claimed they believed in.[28]

. . .

Atlanticists were more forthright in their skepticism of collective security theory. The idea of a peace league, Lodge acknowledged in December 1918, was "captivating and attractive. Everybody would like to bring about a world condition in which wars would be impossible." But pious wishes could not obscure the fact that, in any peace league, the details would be absolutely vital in assessing its efficacy. In Lodge's view, a league could be either "an exposition of vague ideals and encouraging hopes, or it must be a practical system." If it was going to be "practical and effective," it had to have "authority to issue decrees and force to sustain them." To Lodge, that meant any effective league would have to have the power to order into action the armed forces of its member states to uphold collective security. "Let us be honest with ourselves," pleaded Lodge. "It is easy to talk about a league of nations and the beauty and necessity of peace, but the hard practical demand is, Are you ready to put your soldiers and your sailors at the disposition of other nations?" If not, a league would lack the power to enforce its commands and would be nothing more than a sham league, an illusion. If so, then a nation would be giving up much of its national sovereignty. Avoiding this issue would not make it go away; for Lodge, it went "to the heart of the whole question" of a league.[29]

Most likely, thought the Atlanticists, the Covenant created an incredible international security regime. "'Europe has a set of primary interests which to us have none or a very remote relation,'" Root approvingly quoted George Washington. Although the "Old and the New Worlds" had become more intimate since the 1790s, Atlanticists believed that Washington's axiom was still essentially valid. "The people of the United States have no direct interest in the distribution of territory in the Balkans or the control of Morocco," Root asserted, "and the peoples of Europe have no direct interest in questions between Chile and Peru, or between the United States and Columbia [sic]." In fact, Europeans and the United States were on opposite sides when it came to the Monroe Doctrine and were "bound to look at questions of emigration and immigration from different points of view, and under the influence of different interests." The world war revealed important common interests between the Allies and America, but, Lodge added, "such wars as that are, fortunately, rare." For the most part, the League benefited the Europeans while putting America's safety at risk. "There is no gain for peace in the Americas to be found by annexing the Americas to the European system," Lodge calculated. If confronted with a choice between intervening in a conflict remote from their own interest or preserving their own peace, Root believed that the American people would always choose the latter; they would always abandon their supposed stake in peace around the globe in favor of protecting their own lives and treasure. The premise of collective security, then, was simply wrong. Consequently, if the United States signed off on the Covenant, "the worst possible thing for the peace of the world would happen—that the United States should have made a solemn treaty and should break it."[30]

Of course, it was possible, as Wilson argued, that the League would ultimately leave it up to each nation to decide whether an international crisis rose to the level of a true threat to world peace, in which case one could refuse to take action in a dispute and would not be breaking faith with the Covenant. But if that were true, replied the Atlanticists, then the League would lack the ability to deter potential aggressors. If League members could escape the obligations of collective security and still not be in breach of the Covenant, they would do so, suggested Atlanticist senator Frank Brandegee. Such a League would not have deterred Germany from war in 1914 and could not provide any real degree of security for its member states. It would be "like a rope of sand," sure to collapse the moment nations turned to it for aid. Root concurred; Wilson's idea that "moral obligations" were somehow both optional and superior to legal obligations struck him as "curious and child-like casuistry," as well as "false, demoralizing and dishonest." If the precise obligations under the Covenant were unclear, moreover, the League would just generate international disputes rather than solve them. "Misunderstandings as to terms are not a good foundation for a treaty to promote peace," intoned Lodge. In his view, Wilson's tortured explanation of America's obligations under Article 10 amounted to saying that nations could break treaties whenever they wanted—an attitude "fatal not only to any league but to peace itself."[31]

Despite seeing the League as, at bottom, "a pipe dream," Atlanticists did not forcefully present an alternative to it or to the pacifist policy of lightly armed isolation. To be sure, they did indicate their preference for a national security strategy based on the principles of power politics. They applauded the peace treaty for weakening the Germans and strengthening the Allies, urged that America continue its naval buildup and institute universal military training, and called for establishing some sort of "entente" between the United States and the Allies. Atlanticists saw two ways to achieve the latter objective. The first, embodied in a resolution put forward by Sen. Philander Knox, involved ratifying the peace treaty separately from the Covenant and declaring that the United States would henceforth consult with the Allies regarding any future threat to Europe's peace. Alternatively, Atlanticists wanted to ratify the French security treaty that Wilson had signed in Paris, so long as Article 3, which stated that the treaty would come into and remain in force only with the approval of the League council, was removed. To Atlanticists, deterring a German attack on France was a cornerstone of American security—and either Knox's "new American doctrine" or the French security treaty would make that interest clear to the world.[32]

Yet over the course of 1919, Atlanticists spent relatively little time promoting this program. Instead, they focused on limiting America's obligations under Wilson's League of Nations. Roosevelt led the way in the weeks before his death on 6 January 1919, as he promoted a plan in which a peace league would settle minor disputes between its members but have no jurisdiction over a nation's vital "spheres of interest." Similarly, Root's response to the League Covenant, revealed in public letters in March and June 1919, endorsed the concept of a collective interest in peace and the desirability of arms control but rejected Article 10 and any obligation to submit "purely American questions" to the League's authority. Lodge embraced Root's views. Working with Lenroot and other mild reservationists in the Senate, he reworked the wording of Root's proposals, added new ones, and then supported ratification of the Versailles treaty with his reservations in votes in November 1919 and March 1920.[33]

As Atlanticist leaders lent qualified support to the League, they also reinforced the prevailing aversion to power politics. One of the most startling aspects of the League, Lodge charged, was that "it is not a league of peace; it is an alliance, dominated at the present moment by five great powers, really by three, and it has all the marks of an alliance." It dealt primarily with "political conditions, not judicial questions"; its decisions would be made by "political appointees whose votes will be controlled by interest and expedience"; and, worst of all, "its decisions are to be carried out by force." Arranged as an alliance, the League would do little for peace, Lodge argued; it would make for war instead. The world had learned, Root agreed, that "alliances do not prevent war, but merely vary the combination of the warring elements." Article 10, creating "an independent alliance for the preservation of the *status quo*," would fail to promote peace, just as the combinations prior to 1914 had failed to prevent war. "It is a throw-back to the old discredited alliances of the past," complained Root. "It speaks a language of power, and not the spirit of progress." These statements, in combination with their endorsement of the goal of "general disarmament" and their continuing denunciations of the "dictatorship" the president created at home during the war, made the Atlanticists appear to link power politics with war and militarism almost as much as Wilson and the pacifists did.[34]

The Atlanticists' glorification of Washington's advice against involvement in Europe's political affairs likewise buttressed the pacifist stance on national security strategy. "Washington was not only a very great man but he was also a very wise man," declared Lodge. By following the policies of Washington and Monroe, America had built its strength and rose to greatness. "The fact that we have been separated by our geographical situation and by our consistent policy from the broils of Europe has made us more than any one thing capable of performing the great work which we performed in the war against Germany," Lodge asserted. America's power to serve others rested on its independence and its ability "to reduce to the lowest possible point the foreign questions in which we involve ourselves." From this point of view, a national security policy of political-military isolation was not only viable but a necessity.[35]

As was the case in the past, the Atlanticists' unwillingness to fight vigorously for a national security strategy oriented toward power politics reflected a variety of factors. Partly it was a product of political calculations: all indices of public opinion suggested that the American people wanted the peace treaty, with the Covenant, ratified in some form. In addition, the two chief Atlanticist alternatives to the Covenant—Knox's "new American doctrine" and the French security treaty divorced from the League—threatened Republican unity and garnered no support from Wilson and the Democrats. Given the animosity toward power politics expressed by pacifists and liberal internationalists, Atlanticists may also have seen the League as the only way to maintain a political relationship with the Allies and help them to keep Germany contained. Finally, as they had prior to 1919, Roosevelt, Lodge, and especially Root all recoiled from "the horror of the war" and seemed uneasy with the prospect of naked power politics, divorced from any international moral code, shaping the postwar world. They longed for civilization to resume its orderly progress; they wanted a peace league that would be both practical and, in Roosevelt's words, "a real step forward." However much they scorned Wilson's League of Nations, it appears likely that they nevertheless saw in its basic principles the beginnings of a better world.[36]

The debate over the Versailles treaty thus revealed and reinforced the Wilsonian national security strategy that had begun to dominate American political circles after August 1914. To varying degrees, nearly all American leaders portrayed alliances and armaments as inherently unstable and threatening to America's domestic way of life. At the same time, relatively few opposed making American participation in the League of Nations, in one form or another, central to America's approach to international security affairs. The final votes on the Versailles treaty, in November 1919 and March 1920, graphically illustrate this point. Fully 80 percent of the Senate voted for the treaty, with Republicans in general supporting ratification with reservations and most of the Democrats favoring unreserved approval. Only 20 percent of the Senate rejected the treaty altogether, irrespective of whatever reservations were attached to it. Perceiving this breakdown, the "irreconcilables" were amazed when Wilson's Democrats and Lodge's reservationists failed to reach a compromise on the treaty. "It is the most ridiculous and laughable situation I have ever encountered," Hiram Johnson chortled after the November vote. He knew how stunning the outcome was given the overwhelming support expressed for some kind of American participation in collective security.[37]

Had it not been for Wilson's opposition to the Lodge reservation on Article 10, the treaty almost certainly would have been ratified. Wilson himself ended up tacitly endorsing reservations on withdrawing from the League and on excluding domestic matters and the Monroe Doctrine from its authority. Democrats in the Senate agreed with the substance of those reservations as well. As early as August 1919 they had reconciled themselves to a "mild" reservation on Article 10 too, which confirmed that Congress could reject the advice of the League council to use force to uphold the article's provisions without putting America in breach of the treaty. By November some of them were willing to accept Lodge's "strong" reservation on Article 10; by March 1920 the president's field marshal in the Senate, Gilbert Hitchcock, had to struggle to prevent a majority of his Democratic colleagues from embracing it. Only Wilson's threat to refuse to complete the process of ratification if the treaty passed with the Article 10 reservation held them in line. As Thomas Bailey put it aptly, the president engaged in "the supreme act of infanticide," snuffing out the consensus around a limited commitment to collective security born of his vision of a reformed world order.[38]

Why did he do it? Wilson did have substantive reasons for his actions. The reservation to Article 10 finalized between Lenroot's group and Lodge began with the words "The United States assumes no obligation to preserve the territorial integrity or political independence of any other country . . . under the provisions of article 10." To Wilson, that language destroyed America's promise under Article 10 to pass judgment on all apparent acts of aggression and to provide leadership to the world in invoking, when the United States deemed it appropriate, the principle of collective security. What the reservation proposed, Wilson maintained on 24 September, was that "we should make no general promise, but leave the nations associated with us to guess in each instance what we were going to consider ourselves bound to do. . . . It is as if you said: 'We will not join the league definitely. . . . We will not promise anything, but from time to time we may co-operate.'" The reservation meant that America could totally ignore acts of aggression and take no stand on them at all if it so desired. As far as Wilson was concerned, it thus released America from officially recognizing the principle of collective security and, in so doing, struck at "the very heart and life of the Covenant itself."[39]

In addition, from the start of the ratification battle, Wilson feared that if he went along with reservations to the treaty, other nations would demand reservations too, and the whole treaty would then have to be renegotiated. The president was not alone in this opinion: David Hunter Miller, one of Wilson's key advisors on the Covenant, voiced it in June 1919, just before Wilson returned home from Paris, and Hamilton Holt asserted it in the *Independent* throughout most of the fight over the treaty. Similarly, Wilson may have worried in August that if he agreed to allow reservations to be attached to the treaty, domestic opponents of the Covenant would endlessly demand more and more objectionable qualifications neither he nor other nations could ever accept.[40]

Still, it is hard not to conclude that the decline of Wilson's health in the summer and fall of 1919 played the decisive role in preventing ratification of the treaty. On 18 July, Wilson confided to William Wiseman that he thought political realities might force him to agree to reservations, including ones to Article 10 and on the Monroe Doctrine. This was a sound judgment by the president, as it was clear by mid-July that the mild reservationists in the Senate would not vote for the treaty unless reservations were attached to it. The wise course for Wilson to pursue at this juncture was to negotiate with Lenroot's group on the wording of the reservations, to keep them as mild as possible. On 19 July, however, Wilson suffered what the editors of his papers term "most likely a small stroke." His behavior thereafter became increasingly erratic. Until early September, he pronounced himself open to "interpretive" reservations so long as they were not included in the resolution of ratification—a position unacceptable to the mild reservationists. During this same period, mid-July to late August, he failed to participate in meaningful negotiations with Lenroot's group, engaging in fruitless personal appeals to them to change their stance on reservations instead. On 25 August, angry at the Senate Foreign Relations Committee's approval of an amendment to the treaty radically changing the section on Shantung, Wilson abruptly shifted tactics and resolved "to go to the people" and give the Senate "a belly full" of a fight over the treaty. Although he shortly thereafter confidentially wrote up his own reservations to offer if he needed them to get the treaty passed, Wilson's irrational decision to go on an extended speaking campaign effectively ended whatever chance the president had to shape a compromise with the mild reservationsists. Mistakenly thinking he could whip up public opinion against them, he pushed the mild reservationists into the waiting arms of Lodge.[41]

Once out on his speaking tour, a grinding marathon of forty speeches over twenty-one days, Wilson's health rapidly deteriorated, with disastrous consequences for the treaty. On 26 September the president, his blood pressure "running out of control," broke down, and he returned to Washington. A few days later, on 2 October, Wilson suffered a massive stroke that left him almost totally incapacitated for more than a month. By early November, the president had recovered to a marginal degree, but his political judgment was now even more impaired than it had been in August. Unwilling to accept that he simply did not have the votes to get the treaty ratified without the reservations Lodge had written up with Lenroot's group, Wilson fixated on the destructive language he saw in the reservation on Article 10. He rejected the pleas of his advisors to settle for minimal changes to the reservation or to accept it in order to ratify the treaty; he gave no support to last-minute efforts at compromise; and he ignored the point, made by Taft and others, that even if the reservation essentially negated Article 10, the conflict resolution provisions and the declaration of collective security in Article 11—parts of the Covenant Wilson himself had repeatedly said were as important to peace as Article 10—were still intact. It is hard to imagine that a healthy Wilson would have adopted such a posture—or would have lost control over the writing of the reservations in the first place. But the president was a shadow of his former self after 2 October 1919. Consequently, even though Wilson's approach to American national security clearly dominated debates over the Versailles treaty, the treaty itself failed. America stood alone, confronting a world in which anarchy and power politics still reigned supreme.[42]

Conclusion

Following the defeat of the Versailles treaty in March 1920, the stalemate between President Wilson and the Senate Republicans continued, as both sides anticipated that the elections of 1920 would settle the issue. But the drift of opinion toward a national security strategy of moderately armed political isolationism was clear. Hoping his position on the League would be vindicated in the upcoming election, Wilson continued to distance the United States from the Allies, who were struggling to wrap up outstanding issues from the peace conference and begin enforcing the treaty's terms against the Germans. Lodge and Root, meanwhile, found their control over Republican foreign policy slipping away to Borah, as they decided for the sake of party unity not to press for a platform plank endorsing either ratification of the Covenant with reservations or Knox's "new American doctrine." Instead the Republican platform in 1920 vaguely supported the creation of a new "international association" while applauding "the time-honored policies of Washington, Jefferson, and Monroe." At the same time, neither Republicans nor Democrats showed any enthusiasm for an expansive postwar military policy, pushed largely by army leaders in the War Department and Republican senator James W. Wadsworth Jr., featuring an army of around 300,000 men and a program of universal military training. The latter provision was dropped from the final bill, and, revealingly, Congress only appropriated funds for an army of fewer than 200,000 soldiers. By March 1921, when Warren Harding took the oath of office as president, the consensus in favor of a strategy of limited American commitment to collective security had collapsed.[1]

Many historians have bemoaned this denouement to the national security debates that absorbed America during World War I. Even qualified American membership in the League, John Milton Cooper Jr. suggests, might have helped to build "a strong collective security system" after the war and, perhaps, have averted the breakdown of the Versailles system in the 1930s. Whatever his "flaws and missteps," Cooper argues, "Wilson was right." His "vision of order," his vision of a new international system based on collective security, was the wise one for America and the world. The alternative, Cooper declares, was a chaotic world of "ethnic and national conflicts, genocides, and world wars."[2]

Such arguments ignore the profoundly flawed character of the collective security program. The premise of collective security—the idea that all states had an overriding stake in peace throughout the world—appeared to require a state to intervene in international disputes around the globe, regardless of the relevance of those conflicts to its own immediate interests. As both pacifist and Atlanticist critics of collective security pointed out, such a policy could easily require a massive military establishment, subvert Congress's war powers, and leave America in a constant state of warfare overseas. Liberal internationalists backhandedly conceded these dangers, as they trumpeted collective security theory and yet insisted that America would not get involved in "distant wars" under the League and demanded the League not have any authority over the Monroe Doctrine. Moreover, many liberal internationalists, including especially Wilson, constantly berated the Europeans for failing to abandon their own selfish scrambling for strategic advantage, implying that other nations did not really believe in collective security theory either.[3]

The means to establish a collective security regime were also inconsistent with the notion that war had become the real enemy of all nations. From the moment it began, the project of ending power politics depended, first and foremost, on shifting the distribution of power in the world against Germany and in favor of America and the Allies. Before a peace league could be established, liberal internationalists argued from 1914 to 1917, at the very least, Germany had to give up its wartime gains. From 1917 to 1918, they wanted Germany's power reduced still more, to a level below what it possessed at the start of the war. Although they could never agree exactly how much to reduce Germany's strength, they all wanted the Germans contained. To make sure that Germany carried out the treaty terms designed to weaken it, most liberal internationalists demanded it be kept out of the League indefinitely. For all appearances, then, war was not the main threat to civilization in the modern world. Germany was the true danger, and the League, supposedly the vehicle for ending power politics, looked a lot like an alliance to marshal the power of the victors against their defeated foe.

President Wilson's vision for building a new world order included another problematic element: the notion that spreading democracy would contribute to the efficacy of collective security and thus to a lasting peace. Again, liberal internationalists incessantly promoted this idea, especially after 1917, but in practice they demonstrated a lack of faith in it. It was, after all, an inherently uncertain proposition. As Wilson and his supporters recognized, the masses could easily become belligerent over insults to national honor, anxious to protect national interests from potential attack, or excited about pursuing conquests or tokens of national prestige. Even if one granted that "aggression is the work of a minority," it was unclear what type of democratic organization of society or government could prevent an aggressive minority from asserting itself. Sometimes liberal internationalists described the Allies as democratic, for example, but on other occasions—usually whenever the Allies did something in opposition to American policy—they did not. "I have spent twenty years of my life lecturing on self-governing states, and trying all the time to define one," Wilson confessed in Paris, but "I haven't been able to arrive at a definition." He was reduced to claiming, "I recognize one when I see it," but he could not explain how. His position on when exactly Germany became a trustworthy democracy was consequently highly unstable, much to the dismay of the Germans. At first he suggested that the creation of a new German government responsible to the Reichstag would do it, then he decided that the Reich's constitutional reforms had to be duly ratified, and then, in the end, resolved that the true test of Germany's democratization lay not in its political structures but in its willingness to comply with the peace treaty. Ultimately, regardless of how they viewed Germany's democratization in 1919, the advocates of collective security still wanted the former Reich's power limited and controlled—implying that they distrusted it whether it was democratic or not.[4]

One could argue that whatever the problems with it, Wilson's project for international reform was a politically expedient way to rouse Americans out of isolationism and commit the United States to doing what was necessary to protect its security, namely, helping maintain peace in Europe. The idea of collective security, from this perspective, essentially operated as a device to mask active American involvement in power politics from a public that probably would not otherwise have endorsed such a policy. Even if Wilson did not consciously think of his national security strategy in this way, had the treaty been ratified, America, for all practical purposes, would have been pledged to uphold European security against the Germans.[5]

This argument seriously misinterprets the nature of Wilson's strategy. Regardless of their attention to the problem of containing Germany's power, liberal internationalists always wanted to conciliate Germany too, because if the Germans never accepted their defeat, international reform would never become a reality. In large measure, Wilson and his supporters counted on American exceptionalism—America's supposedly unique ability to stand for and embody ideals of justice, democracy, and progress—to woo Germany into embracing a new world order built on its loss in the war. But the character of the peace terms to be imposed on Germany obviously mattered as well, which was why liberal internationalists tried to make sure the peace settlement, in Wilson's words, did not "injure" Germany's "legitimate influence or power." Where to draw the line between a "legitimate" and "illegitimate" reduction of Germany's strength was never clear, however, and over the course of 1914–19, Wilson and the *New Republic*'s editors in particular drew it in different places at different times. When Wilson finally settled on a package of terms at Paris, the Germans, in part because Wilson's promises of "justice" had led them to expect better treatment, bitterly denounced it. As the *New*

Republic immediately concluded, reform could only proceed if that anger was quelled, which meant that Germany would have to be appeased, presumably by softening the terms of the treaty. If the Allies resisted appeasement, they, not Germany, would be the enemy of international reform. And, as Wilson himself repeatedly warned, if the Allies wanted to practice power politics, America would abandon them in favor of a policy of armed isolation. Far from committing Americans to Europe, then, liberal internationalism made American involvement in Europe highly conditional. Only if the Allies agreed to do whatever America said was necessary for attaining international reform—an end based on a dubious theory of international relations and on peace terms apparently subject to the whim of German emotions—would the United States help to preserve Europe's security.[6]

Indeed, the arguments put forward by liberal internationalists made it very unlikely that Americans would ever think clearly about how to protect their interests, in Europe or elsewhere, in a rational manner. Convinced that the existing system of great power politics was inherently unstable and that endless participation in it would militarize America's domestic political economy, they believed that the United States had to change the system or isolate itself from it as much as possible. The former course was deeply problematic in both its ends and means. As for isolationism, liberal internationalists rightly perceived that America could not in fact isolate itself from the effects of major crises within the existing international system. Faced with a general war overseas or the prospect of confronting a powerful, hostile state, Americans were clearly willing to contemplate military measures they saw as potentially threatening to their free way of life. Isolationism sooner or later meant armed isolation—a policy with the virtue of independence of action but the vice of militarism at home. Neither national security strategy offered by Wilson and his supporters—and by Atlanticists and pacifists to varying degrees as well—thus made any sense as a way to preserve America's physical safety and the health of its democratic institutions.

Yet the framework of thinking about national security affairs produced by the debates during World War I persisted. In the 1920s, pacifists, Wilsonians, and Republican policymakers disagreed about the degree of America's isolation from the dangers of world politics and about how to pursue international reform. But few questioned the axioms that the balance of power inevitably led to war, that power politics could and should somehow be ended, and that active involvement in power politics by the United States would ruin its democracy. In the 1930s, as Germany and other nations violently challenged the international order established at Versailles, Americans sharply divided into camps favoring either economic cooperation with collective security efforts overseas or a policy of armed isolationism. By the later part of the decade, though, as Germany became ever more aggressive, Wilson's ideas about national security even more clearly dominated defense debates. "Democracy cannot thrive in an atmosphere of international insecurity," Franklin Roosevelt declared in mid-1937. "Such insecurity breeds militarism, regimentation and the denial of freedom of speech, of peaceful assemblage and of religion." The threats from overseas were not simply confined to Germany or Japan. Americans had to master one "simple but unalterable fact in modern foreign relations between nations," FDR lectured a radio audience in 1939. "When peace has been broken anywhere, the peace of all countries everywhere is in danger." Once Germany and Japan were totally defeated, Roosevelt promised, America would then work for an international system where the "four freedoms" existed "everywhere in the world" and armaments were reduced "to such a point . . . that no nation will be in a position to commit an act of physical aggression against any neighbor"—a new world order of "general security."[7]

Not even the advent of the Cold War shattered the core ideas about power politics and militarism that lay at the center of American thinking about national security affairs. As Melvyn Leffler has shown, American leaders during the Truman administration sought to contain the Soviet Union largely because they believed that if the Soviets dominated Eurasia, the United States, for its own protection, would be forced to turn itself into a heavily armed "garrison state" devoid of economic and political freedoms. Leffler argues that to make containment work, the United States realized it needed to revive Western Europe and co-opt the latent power of Germany and Japan into an American-dominated Western coalition. To accomplish these tasks, in turn, America had to pursue policies, such as boosting economic recovery in Germany, that alienated the Soviets and risked war. The United States also had to ensure that the decaying colonial empires of the Western Europeans remained out of the Soviet orbit so that their resources could help Europe's economic and military recovery. These imperatives, according to Leffler, quickly drove America into undertaking a global policy of containment, backed by an extensive conventional and nuclear arms buildup.[8]

The logic of containment that Leffler describes is compelling. But to explain American policies more completely, one needs to recognize how they reveal the endurance of long-held Wilsonian views about national security. First, the goal of American policymakers was not simply to contain the Soviets. American leaders believed that eventually, if the West thwarted Soviet expansionism, the Soviet state would collapse from within or transform itself into a government, as George Kennan put it, willing to express its aspirations "only in peaceful and friendly associations with other peoples." In other words, President Truman and his advisors assumed that with victory in the Cold War, the world would enter, in Truman's words, a "new era" of peace. Given the deeply ingrained aversion of American leaders to power politics, this new era would presumably rest not on the endless maneuvering of the balance of power but instead on some sort of American-led collective security system composed of democratic states and institutionalized in the United Nations.

Just as in the two world wars, the ultimate threat to American security during the Cold War was not really a specific country but the system of power politics itself.[9]

The all-encompassing, militarized character of the Truman administration's containment policy also reflected two key Wilsonian assumptions about international relations. One held that arms races and the logic of military preemption dominated the operation of the existing system of power politics; the other, that to build collective security, America had to respond in some way to all cases of aggression everywhere in the world. Determined not to be vulnerable in the existing order while equally dedicated to creating a new one, American leaders during the Cold War treated all threats, from the Viet Minh in Indochina to the Soviet Union in Europe, as vitally important, and they met those threats largely with military means. Like Wilson, they practiced power politics to end power politics—except they did so with a global reach and an obsession with military coercion never exerted before.

Finally, Wilson's approach to national security affairs gave Cold War policymakers some confidence that implementing containment around the globe would not lead to militarism at home. The way Wilson and his supporters described it, policies of military preparedness, coercive diplomacy, and war overseas could safely be pursued, at least in the short run, so long as they were tied to the goal of international reform. Linked to the vision of a new world order based on collective security and democracy, a massive American military establishment would not corrupt America's freedoms but protect them from the certain destruction they would face if power politics continued forever. In addition, along with Theodore Roosevelt and the Atlanticists, liberal internationalists promoted the notion that the character traits supposedly stimulated by military training—traits of hard work, self-sacrifice, and patriotism—invigorated democracy and thus worked to offset the dangers that a large-scale professional military establishment posed to the Republic. The threat of militarism would not go away as America did what was necessary to reform the international system, but that threat could be managed, assuming America never simply embraced the existing system and acted like a traditional European great power.[10]

With the end of the Cold War in 1991, many American leaders eagerly looked forward to the transformation of international politics they had long anticipated. "Not since 1945," President George H. W. Bush announced as the Soviet Union crumbled, "have we seen the real possibility of using the United Nations as it was designed: as a center for international collective security." Predictably, however, the end of the Cold War did not end the anarchical structure of the international system or the power politics that went with it. Nations continued to compete for power, to build armaments, and to engage in coercive diplomacy to attain their strategic objectives. The Soviet Union disappeared, but a new world order based on collective security failed to materialize.[11]

American leaders have responded to this outcome in ways that reveal the continuing influence of Wilsonian ideas about national security affairs. Nearly all of them assume that multipolar, balance-of-power politics are inherently unstable and must somehow be ended. Liberals tend to believe that this goal can best be furthered by strengthening institutions of collective security such the United Nations, fostering international trade, and promoting the spread of democracy. Conservatives, while they agree on the last two policies, appear to have given up on the first one as a means for ending the balance of power. But this does not mean that they have abandoned this goal. They would agree, rather, with Lawrence Lowell's comment at the 1918 LEP convention that "war can be precluded only by a conquest of the world by a single power, or by an organization of many nations to prevent its recurrence." As the latter strategy has failed, conservatives—and especially neoconservatives in the Republican Party—appear to have embraced the former alternative. As the Defense Department's 1992 draft Defense Planning Guidance statement summed up this strategy, "We must account sufficiently for the interests of the advanced industrial nations to discourage them from challenging our leadership or seeking to overturn the established political and economic order. . . . We must maintain the mechanisms for deterring potential competitors from even aspiring to a larger regional or global role." A revision of the statement also stressed the need for the United States to maintain a wide lead in military capability over other nations, to act unilaterally if necessary to protect its interests, and not to allow any nation it decided was hostile to dominate any region of importance. The goal of this strategy, in other words, is to convince nations such as Germany, India, and China not to behave—or even want to behave—like independent great powers. They should trust America to look after their interests on their behalf while, at the same time, the United States intimidates all states into accepting the existing distribution of power in the world. The balance of power will end not through collective security but because the only real power will be the United States.[12]

Few Americans argue that neither the liberal nor the conservative approaches to preserving American national security will work. Certainly few politicians or political commentators suggest that balance-of-power politics are inevitable in a world of independent nation-states and that American democracy is best preserved not by trying to escape from this reality but by recognizing it. One is hard-pressed, indeed, to hear anyone of prominence in American political circles define a hierarchy of specific national interests in the world, articulate a strategy to protect those precise interests, and identify allies who can share the burden of that strategy. Nor is it easy to find American leaders who caution that while the spread of democracy around the globe may be a positive development, the United States cannot assume it will significantly alter the competition for power between nations. In these most basic and disturbing ways, Wilsonianism dominates America's discourse about national security affairs at the dawn of the twenty-first century just as it did nearly one hundred years ago.

Notes

Abbreviations

Annals	*Annals of the American Academy of Political and Social Science* 66 (July 1916)
CR	*Congressional Record*
EBG	Edith Bolling Galt Wilson
EMH	Edward Mandell House
FDR	Franklin Delano Roosevelt
FRUS	*Foreign Relations of the United States*
HCL	Henry Cabot Lodge
HCL-TR	Henry Cabot Lodge and Charles F. Redmond, eds., *Selections from the Correspondence of Theodore Roosevelt and Henry Cabot Lodge, 1884–1918*, 2 vols. 1925; rpt., New York: Da Capo, 1971
HD	House diary
KAS	Ralph Stout, ed., *Roosevelt in the Kansas City Star: War-time Editorials*. Boston: Houghton Mifflin, 1921
LEP	*Enforced Peace: Proceedings of the First Annual Assemblage of the League to Enforce Peace, Washington, May 26–27, 1916*. New York: League to Enforce Peace, 1916
LEP 1918	*Win the War for Permanent Peace*. New York: LEP, 1918
LFM	*La Follette's Magazine*
Mantoux	Arthur S. Link and Manfred F. Boemeke, trans. and eds., *The Deliberations of the Council of Four (March 24–June 28, 1919): Notes of the Official Interpreter, Paul Mantoux*. 2 vols. Princeton, N.J.: Princeton Univ. Press, 1992
NR	*New Republic*
NSL	*Proceedings of the National Security Congress under the Auspices of the National Security League, Washington, January 20–22, 1916*. New York: National Security League, 1916
NYT	*New York Times*
OGV	Oswald Garrison Villard
PPAFDR	Samuel Rosenman, ed., *Public Papers and Addresses of Franklin D. Roosevelt*, 13 vols. New York: Russell and Russell, 1950–69
PWW	Arthur S. Link et al., eds., *The Papers of Woodrow Wilson*, 69 vols. Princeton, N.J.: Princeton Univ. Press, 1966–94

RLF   Robert La Follette
SUM   Fred L. Israel, ed., *The State of the Union Messages of the Presidents, 1790–1966,*
             3 vols. New York: Chelsea House, 1967
TMdoc   John H. Latane, ed., *Development of the League of Nations Idea,* 2 vols. New
             York: Macmillan, 1932
TN   *The Nation*
TR   Theodore Roosevelt
TRLET   Elting E. Morison, ed., *The Letters of Theodore Roosevelt,* 8 vols. Cambridge,
             Mass.: Harvard Univ. Press, 1951–54
WHPL   Burton J. Hendrick, ed., *The Life and Letters of Walter H. Page,* vol. 3. New York:
             Doubleday, Page, 1925
WHT   William Howard Taft
WHTE   James F. Vivian, ed., *William Howard Taft: Collected Editorials, 1917–1921.* New
             York: Praeger, 1990
WHTP   Theodore Marburg and Horace E. Flack, eds., *Taft Papers on the League of Na-
             tions.* 1920; rpt., New York: Kraus, 1971
WJB   William Jennings Bryan
WW   Woodrow Wilson

Full citations for all sources in the endnotes appear in the select bibliography.

Introduction

1. Diary of Dr. Grayson, 4 Dec. 1918, *PWW* 53:315–16n4, and 315–16.

2. See, e.g., Lloyd E. Ambrosius, "Woodrow Wilson and George W. Bush: Historical Comparison of Ends and Means in Their Foreign Policies," 509–43.

3. I have arrived at these shorthand labels for the groups I am discussing with some difficulty—no such label for groups holding complex ideas about American national security policy is really satisfactory. "Pacifists" was chosen for the first group chiefly because they were often called by that term in the political debates of the time. Indeed, pacifist leaders themselves sometimes used the term to describe their general aversion to the use of force to solve international disputes. It is important to note, though, that few pacifists actually completely rejected the use of violence to achieve political ends. As this book explores, some of them ended up supporting American involvement in the war. I chose "liberal internationalists" to describe the second group because historians have increasingly used this label to denote President Wilson's perspective on American foreign relations. As I argue later, because I think conservatives in the LEP shared much of Wilson's perspective on national security affairs, I have included them under the "liberal internationalist" label. The term "Atlanticist" is taken from an article by Priscilla Roberts. She uses it to describe the same group I examine—the leaders clustered around Theodore Roosevelt—and I think it captures one of their key ideas, namely their interest in building some sort of security relationship between the United States and Britain. See Roberts, "The Anglo-American Theme: American Visions of an Atlantic Alliance, 1914–1933." I am indebted to Lloyd Ambrosius for his thoughtful comments on how to name the three groups, and in particular for his suggestion to use the term "liberal internationalists" for the Wilsonians.

4. For authors who emphasize the role of missionary exceptionalism in Wilsonian diplomacy from a sympathetic point of view, see John Milton Cooper Jr., *The Warrior and the Priest: Woodrow Wilson and Theodore Roosevelt;* Thomas J. Knock, *To End All Wars: Woodrow Wilson and the Quest for a New World Order;* and Arthur S. Link, *Woodrow Wilson.* See also Edward H. Buehrig, *Woodrow Wilson and the Balance of Power;* Frederick S. Calhoun, *Power and Principle: Armed Intervention in Wilsonian Foreign Policy;* Klaus Schwabe, *Woodrow Wilson, Revolutionary Germany, and Peacemaking, 1918–1919: Missionary Diplomacy and the Realities of Power;* and Tony Smith, *America's Mission: The United States and the Worldwide Struggle for Democracy in the Twentieth Century.* For scholars with a more critical perspective, see Lloyd E. Ambrosius, *Woodrow Wilson and the American Diplomatic Tradition: The Treaty Fight in Perspective;* Norman A. Graebner, *America as a World Power: A Realist Appraisal from Wilson to Reagan;* George F. Kennan, *American Diplomacy;* and Robert E. Osgood, *Ideals and Self-Interest in America's Foreign Relations: The Great Twentieth-Century Transformation.* For works stressing both missionary exceptionalism and trade concerns, see Ross Gregory, *The Origins of American Intervention in the First World War;* N. Gordon Levin Jr., *Woodrow Wilson and World Politics: America's Response to War and Revolution;* Carl Parrini, *Heir to Empire: United States Economic Diplomacy, 1916–1923;* and William Appleman Williams, *The Tragedy of American Diplomacy.* For authors who emphasize concerns about militarism and national power in Wilson's diplomacy more so than those previously mentioned, see David M. Esposito, *The Legacy of Woodrow Wilson: American War Aims in World War I;* Melvyn P. Leffler, *The Elusive Quest: America's Pursuit of European Stability and French Security, 1919–1933;* Frank Ninkovich, *The Wilsonian Century: U.S. Foreign Policy since 1900;* and Daniel M. Smith, *The Great Departure: The United States and World War I, 1914–1920.*

1. Militarism and Power Politics, 1914–17

1. "A Memorial to the President of the United States by the American Union against Militarism," c. 8 May 1916, *PWW* 36:632. Some pacifists did support minor enhancements of America's armed forces. See Chapter 2 of this volume. On the 1914 military, see John Whiteclay Chambers II, *To Raise an Army,* 75.

2. Crystal Eastman, "War and Peace," *Survey* 37 (30 Dec. 1916): 363; J. H. Dillard, "Militarism and Human Progress," *Public* 18 (24 Dec. 1915): 1239; Stoughton Cooley, "Military Democracy," *Public* 19 (2 June 1916): 505–6; "The Universal Military Service Cure-all," *TN* 102 (11 May 1916): 511.

3. Cooley, "Military Democracy," 506; OGV, "Shall We Arm for Peace?" *Survey* 35 (11 Dec. 1915): 296–97, and "Preparedness Is Militarism," *Annals,* 218–19.

4. OGV, *Preparedness,* 17, 16; Jane Addams, "The Revolt against War," *Survey* 34 (17 July 1915): 356.

5. Charles Jefferson, "Why Not Take This Step?" *LFM* 6 (3 Oct. 1914): 4; Eastman, "War and Peace," 364; Amos Pinchot, "Preparedness," *Public* 19 (4 Feb. 1916): 112; WJB, "Shall Militarism Devour the Farm?" *Commoner* 16 (Jan. 1916): 3.

6. Samuel Danziger, "Adequate Defense," *Public* 17 (11 Dec. 1914): 1177. See also RLF, "Take the Profit Out of War," *LFM* 7 (Feb. 1915): 2.

7. "A Colloquy with a Group of Antipreparedness Leaders," 8 May 1916, *PWW* 36:639; "Memorial to the President," 632; Stoughton Cooley, "Undermining Liberty," *Public* 19 (21 July 1916): 676; "Swinging Around the Circle against Militarism," *Survey* 36 (22 Apr. 1916): 96.

8. WW, "An Annual Message to Congress," 8 Dec. 1914, *PWW* 31:421–23.

9. See WW, "An Address on Preparedness to the Manhattan Club," 4 Nov. 1915, *PWW* 35:167–73; Chapters 2, 3, and 5 of this volume.

10. WW, "Address on Preparedness to the Manhattan Club," 169–70; WW, "Remarks to the Gridiron Club," 11 Dec. 1915, *PWW* 35:340–41. For UMT and Congress, see James Hay to WW, 8 Feb. 1916, *PWW* 36:141–42; and WW to Lindley Miller Garrison, 10 Feb. 1916, *PWW* 36:162–64.

11. WW, "An Address in St. Louis on Preparedness," 3 Feb. 1916, *PWW* 36:118; WW, "An Address on Preparedness in Kansas City," 2 Feb. 1916, *PWW* 36:104; "Colloquy with a Group of Antipreparedness Leaders," 643.

12. WW, "An Address in Des Moines on Preparedness," 1 Feb. 1916, *PWW* 36:82; WW, "An Address in Pittsburgh to an Overflow Meeting," 29 Jan. 1916, *PWW* 36:40; WW, "An Address in Milwaukee on Preparedness," 31 Jan. 1916, *PWW* 36:60; WW, "Address in Des Moines on Preparedness," 82.

13. WW, "An Address in New York on Preparedness," 27 Jan. 1916, *PWW* 36:13.

14. WW, "Remarks at a Luncheon in New York," 17 May 1915, *PWW* 33:210; "Colloquy with a Group of Antipreparedness Leaders," 643–44.

15. Herbert Croly, "The Effect on American Institutions of a Powerful Military and Naval Establishment," *Annals*, 158–59, 161. See also Chapters 2, 3, and 6 in this volume.

16. Walter Weyl, *American World Policies*, 8, 137–38, 9–10, 137–38, 8. See also "Poltroons and Pacifists," *NR* 5 (22 Jan. 1916): 293. *NR* also favored government manufacture of munitions. See editorial, *NR* 4 (30 Oct. 1915): 319–20.

17. "The Newer Nationalism," *NR* 5 (29 Jan. 1916): 319; "The Plattsburg Idea," *NR* 4 (9 Oct. 1915): 247–48. See also Samuel Gompers, *NSL*, 200–201; Simeon Larson, *Labor and Foreign Policy: Gompers, the AFL, and the First World War, 1914–1918*, 68–73.

18. "Plattsburg Idea," 248; "Newer Nationalism," 319–21.

19. "Preparedness," *Independent* 83 (20 Sept. 1915): 379; "Preparation for National Defense," *Independent* 83 (15 Nov. 1915): 250; Edward Filene, *LEP*, 44. For WHT, Marburg, and Lowell, see Knock, *To End All Wars*, 62; *TMdoc*, 1:114; WJB and WHT, *World Peace: A Written Debate between William Howard Taft and William Jennings Bryan*, 118; WHT in *NYT*, 26 June 1916, 20. See also Chapters 2, 3, and 6 in this volume.

20. For an example of laughter at the threat of munitions makers, see HCL, *NSL*, 365–66. For an example of the Atlanticists' faith in expert military advice, see TR, *Fear God and Take Your Own Part*, 85, 94. For summaries of the Atlanticist defense proposals, see TR, *Fear God*, 84–108; HCL, *NSL*, 357–66; Elihu Root, *NSL*, 245–47.

21. TR, *NYT*, 15 Nov. 1914, 5:5; TR, *NYT*, 8 Nov. 1914, 5:1.

22. Luke E. Wright, *NSL*, 95; TR, *Fear God*, 99, 100, 104–5, and 103–7, passim; TR, *NYT*, 29 Nov. 1914, 5:5. See also TR, *The Foes of Our Own Household*, 231–49, 258–70.

23. Elihu Root, in Robert Bacon and James Brown Scott, eds., *Addresses on International Subjects by Elihu Root*, 443; HCL, "Force and Peace," 9 June 1915, in HCL, *War Addresses, 1915–1917*, 39–40; TR, *Fear God*, 99.

24. "For a Peace Conference of Neutral Nations," *Survey* 33 (6 Mar. 1915): 598; "The Week," *TN* 100 (28 Jan. 1915): 95; OGV, "The United States and the Peace Treaty," *North American Review* 201 (Mar. 1915): 382; WJB, "Making the Issue Clear," *Commoner* 15 (July 1915): 1.

25. WJB, "Peace Day," *Commoner* 14 (Oct. 1914): 15; WJB, "The War in Europe and Its Lessons for Us," *Commoner* 15 (Nov. 1915): 14; WJB, "The Real Issue," *Commoner* 15 (June 1915): 3.

26. Charles Jefferson, "Military Preparedness: A Peril to Democracy," *Annals*, 232; Lucia Ames Mead, "America's Danger and Opportunity," *Survey* 35 (23 Oct. 1915): 90; Danziger, "Adequate Defense," 1177.

27. Frederic C. Howe, *Why War?* 64, 63, 109, 5, 64, and 3–160, passim.

28. Ibid., 154–55, 83, 155, 83, 98 (emphasis dropped), 110.

29. Ibid., 310, 311, 312.

30. Platform of the Woman's Peace Party, 10 Jan. 1915, reprinted in Mary Louise Degen, *History of the Woman's Peace Party*, 41 and 40–41, passim; RLF, "Hold Fast to Real Patriotism," *LFM* 8 (May 1916): 2; OGV, "United States and the Peace Treaty," 387. See also WJB, "Labor's Interest in Peace," *Commoner* 15 (July 1915): 8. On male aggression, see Emmeline Pthick Lawrence, "Motherhood and War," 5 Dec. 1914, in John Whiteclay Chambers II, ed., *The Eagle and the Dove: The American Peace Movement and the United States Foreign Policy, 1900–1922*, 46–49; Harriet Hyman Alonso, *Peace as a Women's Issue: A History of the U.S. Movement for World Peace and Women's Rights*, 60–61; Barbara J. Steinson, *American Women's Activism in World War I*, 6, 9–10.

31. WJB, "The Meaning of the Flag," *Commoner* 15 (July 1915): 13; "On Being Practical," *TN* 103 (3 Aug. 1916): 102; "The Larger Effects," *TN* 100 (20 May 1915): 553; Edward Devine, "Humanity, Security and Honor," *Survey* 34 (7 Aug. 1915): 432. On anarchy, see Kenneth Waltz, *Theory of International Politics*, and John Mearsheimer, *Tragedy of Great Power Politics*.

32. David Starr Jordan, "The Minimum of Safety," *Survey* 34 (1 May 1915): 115–16.

33. WW, "An Address to the Senate," 22 Jan. 1917, *PWW* 40:536, 539.

34. WW, "A Luncheon Address to Women in Cincinnati," 26 Oct. 1916, *PWW* 38:531; HD, 30 Aug. 1914, *PWW* 30:462; WW, "Address to the Senate," 22 Jan. 1917, 538; WW, "Luncheon Address to Women in Cincinnati," 531. On international law, see WW, "The First Draft of the Second Lusitania Note," 3 June 1915, *PWW* 33:328; "An Appeal to the President," *NR* 6 (22 Apr. 1916): 303; A. Lawrence Lowell, *LEP*, 176–77. See also Chapter 2 in this volume.

35. WW, "Address to the Senate," 22 Jan. 1917, 538; WW, "Address in New York on Preparedness," 13; Thomas Raeburn White, *LEP*, 26. See also Weyl, *American World Policies*, 113–14; Walter Lippmann, *The Stakes of Diplomacy*, 83. Even before the war broke out, Wilson worried about the European arms race, as he sent Colonel House to Berlin and London to try to broker an arms reduction treaty. See Link, *Wilson*, 2:314–18.

36. "An Interview with Henry Noble Hall," 31 Oct. 1916, *PWW* 38:569; WW, "A Commencement Address at the United States Military Academy," 13 June 1916, *PWW* 37:214; Robert Latham Owen to WW, 13 Nov. 1915, *PWW* 35:201; WW to Owen, 15 Nov. 1915, *PWW* 35:205; Frederic Howe to WW, 9 June 1916, *PWW* 37:180; and WW to Howe, 15 June 1916, *PWW* 37:230. For the Pan-American Pact, see WW, "A Draft of a Pan-American Treaty," 16 Dec. 1914, *PWW* 31:472.

37. "Whom the Gods Would Destroy," *Independent* 79 (10 Aug. 1914): 195; *TMdoc*, 1:60; Weyl, *American World Policies*, 138, 137; "Financial Imperialism," *NR* 7 (17 June 1916): 161. See also Lippmann, *Stakes of Diplomacy*, 106; Gompers, *LEP*, 104, 106–7, 109–10; Sondra R. Herman, *Eleven against War: Studies in American Internationalist Thought, 1898–1921*, 73.

38. HD, 30 Aug. 1914, *PWW* 30:462–63; "A Memorandum by Herbert Bruce Brougham," 14 Dec. 1914, *PWW* 31:459; HD, 3 May 1916, *PWW* 36:597. See also WW to WJB, with enclosure, 12 May 1915, *PWW* 33:176; WW to EBG, c. 23 Aug. 1915, *PWW* 34:298–99; "Colloquy with a Group of Antipreparedness Leaders," 648; WW, "An Unpublished Prolegomenon to a Peace Note," c. 25 Nov. 1916, *PWW* 40:69. On views of Russia, see "A Communication:

The War as We See It," *NR* 6 (26 Feb. 1916): 103; Link, *Wilson*, 3:205–6; *TMdoc*, 1:5; Herman, *Eleven against War*, 67–68.

39. "Why America Exports Arms," *NR* 3 (10 July 1915): 242; Croly, "The Meaning of It," *NR* 4 (7 Aug. 1915): 10; "Timid Neutrality," *NR* 1 (14 Nov. 1914): 7; "Germany's Real Offense," *NR* 3 (22 May 1915): 54–55; "An End to Rival Armaments," *Independent* 79 (17 Aug. 1914): 228; *TMdoc*, 1:3. See also Henry F. Pringle, *The Life and Times of William Howard Taft*, 2:872; Samuel Gompers, *Seventy Years of Life and Labor: An Autobiography*, 189.

40. WW, "A Draft of a Peace Note," c. 25 Nov. 1916, *PWW* 40:71. See also WW, "An Address in Milwaukee on Preparedness," 31 Jan. 1916, *PWW* 36:57.

41. Lippmann, *Stakes of Diplomacy*, 96, and see 80–83, 107–8, 113–14, 124; Weyl, *American World Policies*, 19, 113–14, and see 76–77, 107–11, 237, 247–48.

42. Hamilton Holt, "The Way to Disarm: A Practical Proposal," *Independent* 79 (28 Sept. 1914): 428 and 428–29, passim; A. Lawrence Lowell, "A League to Enforce Peace," *Atlantic Monthly* 116 (Sept. 1915): 392; Edward Filene, *LEP*, 48; Theodore Marburg, *LEP*, 130.

43. WW, "Unpublished Prolegomenon," 68.

44. Ibid., 69; WW, "Address to the League to Enforce Peace," 27 May 1916, *PWW* 37:115. On Mexico, see Knock, *To End All Wars*, 9; WW, "Democracy and Efficiency," c. 1 Oct. 1900, *PWW* 12:12–13.

45. Stockton Axson, *Brother Woodrow*, ed. Arthur S. Link, 231; Link, *Wilson*, 2:279; HD, 6 Nov. 1914, *PWW* 31:274. See also WW, "The Modern Democratic State," c. 1–20 Dec. 1885, *PWW* 5:63, 70–71; WW, "A Lecture on Democracy," 5 Dec. 1891, *PWW* 7:352–56; Lloyd E. Ambrosius, *Wilsonianism: Woodrow Wilson and His Legacy in American Foreign Relations*, 27; Ido Oren, "The Subjectivity of the 'Democratic' Peace: Changing U.S. Perceptions of Imperial Germany," 173; John M. Mulder, *Woodrow Wilson: The Years of Preparation*, passim.

46. *TMdoc*, 1:110–11. For *NR*, see Walter Lippmann, "Insiders and Outsiders," *NR* 5 (13 Nov. 1915): 35; "What Is Opinion?" *NR* 4 (18 Sept. 1915): 172.

47. TR to George Walbridge Perkins, 6 Apr. 1916, *TRLET* 8:1029; TR to Hugo Münsterberg, 8 Aug. 1914, *TRLET* 7:795; TR to Frederick Scott Oliver, 22 July 1915, *TRLET* 8:956.

48. TR, *SUM*, 3:2165; Root, in Bacon and Scott, *International Subjects*, 143; TR to Cecil Arthur Spring Rice, 1 Nov. 1905, *TRLET* 5:63; TR to Elihu Root, 23 July 1907, *TRLET* 5:725. On the Moroccan crisis, see also TR to John St. Loe Strachey, 22 Feb. 1907, *TRLET* 5:596. On Japan, see TR to Eugene Hale, 27 Oct. 1906, *TRLET* 5:473–75; Richard W. Leopold, *Elihu Root and the Conservative Tradition*, 60–62; and Howard K. Beale, *Theodore Roosevelt and the Rise of America to a World Power*, 326–32.

49. Root, in Robert Bacon and James Scott, eds., *Miscellaneous Addresses by Elihu Root*, 277, 276, 277, 278; Root, in Bacon and Scott, *International Subjects*, 156, 127, 170–71, and see 163–64. See also Leopold, *Elihu Root*, 74; Herman, *Eleven against War*, 23–33, 38–39; David Jayne Hill, *NSL*, 27.

50. TR, "World War," *Outlook* 108 (23 Sept. 1914): 177; Root, in Bacon and Scott, *International Subjects*, 403, 394–95; TR, "World War," 177; Root, in Bacon and Scott, *International Subjects*, 419. See also HCL, *War Addresses*, 265, 277.

51. TR, *SUM*, 2:2038, 3:2163, and see 2:2038–39, passim, 3:2224–25. On arms races, see TR to Edward Grey, 28 Feb. 1907, *TRLET* 5:600–601; Root, in Bacon and Scott, *International Subjects*, 138; HCL, *Speeches and Addresses, 1884–1909*, 187–92.

52. TR, *SUM*, 2:2037; TR, *The Strenuous Life*, 32; TR, *SUM*, 2:2139.

53. TR, *SUM*, 2:2061, 2:2037, 3:2223, 3:2162. See also Root, in Bacon and Scott, *International*

Subjects, 129–44, passim. See also Herman, *Eleven against War,* 23–42; Beale, *Theodore Roosevelt,* 336–54; Martin David Dubin, "Elihu Root and the Advocacy of a League of Nations, 1914–1917," 439–42; Frank Ninkovich, "Theodore Roosevelt: Civilization as Ideology," passim.

54. TR, *Addresses and Presidential Messages of Theodore Roosevelt, 1902–1904,* 121; TR, *SUM,* 2:2132–33, 3:2162; HCL, quoted in William C. Widenor, *Henry Cabot Lodge and the Search for an American Foreign Policy,* 137, and see 137–41, passim; TR, *SUM,* 2:2039.

55. TR, *NYT,* 27 Sept. 1914, 4:1; TR, "World War," 169; TR to Albert Apponyi, 17 Sept. 1914, *TRLET* 8:820; Root, in Bacon and Scott, *International Subjects,* 391; HCL, *War Addresses,* 30, 31, and see 29–31, passim.

56. TR to Hugo Münsterberg, 8 Aug. 1914, *TRLET* 7:794; TR, *NYT,* 11 Oct. 1914, 4:3; TR to Hugo Münsterberg, 8 Aug. 1914, *TRLET* 7:795. For Root and Lodge, see Philip Jessup, *Elihu Root,* 2:313, 375; Root to A. Lawrence Lowell, 10 Feb. 1916, in World Peace Foundation, *Pamphlet Series* 6 (June 1916), 3; Root, in Bacon and Scott, *International Subjects,* 395; HCL, *War Addresses,* 252.

57. TR, *Fear God,* 79; TR, *NYT,* 8 Nov. 1914, 5:1; TR to Rudyard Kipling, 4 Nov. 1914, *TRLET* 8:830. See also HCL, *CR,* 63d Cong., 3d sess., 15 Jan. 1915, 1610; Hill, *NSL,* 25–26; Root, in Bacon and Scott, *International Subjects,* 434–35; HCL, *War Addresses,* 127–35.

58. TR to Münsterberg, 3 Oct. 1914, *TRLET* 8:823; TR to Lee, 22 Aug. 1914, *TRLET* 7:810; TR, "World War," 171, 170–71; TR to Lee, 17 June 1915, *TRLET* 8:936.

59. John Jay, Alexander Hamilton, and James Madison, *The Federalist Papers,* 69–70; *Congressional Annals,* 16th Cong., 2d sess., 8 Jan. 1821, 775–76. See also Ross A. Kennedy, "Uncertain Security: American Political Ideology and the Problem of Militarism, 1890–1941," chap. 1; Jay, Hamilton, and Madison, *Federalist Papers,* 45–54, 60, 65, 67–71, 172, 257–58, 260.

60. *CR,* 57th Cong., 2d sess., 16 Dec. 1902, 355; *CR,* 56th Cong., 2d sess., 5 Dec. 1900, 75. See also Kennedy, "Uncertain Security," chap. 2.

61. TR to William Allen White, 7 Nov. 1914, *TRLET* 8:835, 836, and 835–40, passim. On the Adamson Act and the Keating-Owen Act, see TR to Lyman Abbott, 2 Sept. 1916, *TRLET* 8:1112. See also Cooper, *Warrior and the Priest,* 248–50; "Newer Nationalism," 319–21.

2. National Security, 1914–17

1. WJB, "Peace Day," 15; OGV, "United States and the Peace Treaty," 383. See also RLF, "The Duty of Neutral Nations," *LFM* 7 (Mar. 1915): 7.

2. WJB, "A False Philosophy," *Commoner* 15 (July 1915): 7; "The Week," *TN* 99 (10 Dec. 1914): 676. See also RLF, "Imprudent Graft," *LFM* 8 (Sept. 1916): 2; "Committee to Fight 'Huge War Budget,'" *Survey* 35 (1 Jan. 1916): 370.

3. RLF, "Imprudent Graft," *LFM* 8 (Sept. 1916): 2; Charles T. Hallinan, "Putting Pins in Preparedness," *Survey* 35 (26 Feb. 1916): 632; "Let Us Have the Truth," *TN* 101 (25 Nov. 1915): 615.

4. "A True American Voice," *TN* 99 (10 Dec. 1914): 679; "Anti-Preparedness Committee," *Public* 19 (14 Jan. 1916): 34. See also Lucia Ames Mead, "Compulsory Military Service," *Public* 19 (8 Dec. 1916): 1166; Stoughton Cooley, "A Second Class Navy," *Public* 19 (30 June 1916): 603.

5. Cooley, "Second Class Navy," 603; OGV, *Preparedness,* 4. On the open door, see "For a Peace Conference of Neutral Nations," 598; Pinchot, "Preparedness," 112–13; Howe, *Why War?* 337.

6. "A Woman's Peace Party Full Fledged for Action," *Survey* 33 (23 Jan. 1915): 434; Crystal Eastman letter, *NR* 3 (24 July 1915): 313; WJB, "Wasting Time," *Commoner* 15 (Aug. 1915): 5; WJB, "Our Duty," *Commoner* 15 (Aug. 1915): 5; WJB, "Wasting Time," 5. See also "Towards the Peace That Shall Last," *Survey* 33 (6 Mar. 1915): pt. 2.

7. Sir Cecil Arthur Spring Rice to Sir Edward Grey, 3 Sept. 1914, *PWW* 30:472; *TMdoc*, 1:7; "America to Europe, August, 1916," *NR* 7 (29 July 1916): 321; "Not Our War," *NR* 3 (5 June 1915): 109; "America to Europe, August, 1916," 321. See also WHT in *NYT*, 20 Apr. 1916, 5. For other early examples of WW's expressing anxiety about a German victory, see Axon in Link, ed., *Brother Woodrow*, 193; EMH to WW, 22 Aug. 1914, *PWW* 30:432–33; and WW to EMH, 25 Aug. 1914, *PWW* 30:450; WW to Grey, 19 Aug. 1914, *PWW* 30:403; HD, 30 Aug. 1914, *PWW* 30:462; Spring Rice to Grey, 8 Sept. 1914, *PWW* 31:14. WW on only one occasion expressed a lack of fear about the consequences of a German victory. See HD, 4 Nov. 1914, *PWW* 31:265; see likewise "If Germany Wins," *NR* 4 (11 Sept. 1915): 141–42.

8. WW to EMH, 4 Aug. 1915, *PWW* 34:79; HD, 15 Dec. 1915, *PWW* 35:359. On WW's fear of German military bases, see HD, 4 Nov. 1914, *PWW* 31:265–66. For another Gerard report, see Lansing to WW, 4 Aug. 1915, *PWW* 34:83. On the submarine war, see WW to EBG, 19 Aug. 1915, *PWW* 34:258; WW, "An Address to a Joint Session of Congress," 19 Apr. 1916, *PWW* 36:506–10. See also Holt, "Way to Disarm," 427; C. Roland Marchand, *The American Peace Movement and Social Reform, 1898–1918*, 40–41, 151–59; Pringle, *Taft*, 2:737–39, 873, 927–29; Buehrig, *Wilson and the Balance of Power*, 106–7, 112–23.

9. *TMdoc*, 1:4; Walter Hines Page to WJB, 15 Oct. 1914, *PWW* 31:159–60; HD, 25 Nov. 1914, *PWW* 31:355, and 15 Oct. 1915, *PWW* 35:70–71; Link, *Wilson*, 3:636; HD, 29 Mar. 1916, *PWW* 36:380. See also Lansing to WW, 12 Nov. 1915, *PWW* 35:194; WW to Lansing, 1 Mar. 1916, *PWW* 36:233–34; HD, 8 Oct. 1915, *PWW* 35:43. Wilson had concerns about German ambitions in Latin America even before the war. See OGV, diary, 14 Aug. 1912, *PWW* 25:24. For another sign of WW's fear of any German presence in the Western Hemisphere, see Link's discussion of the administration's 1915–16 effort to purchase of the Danish West Indies in *Wilson*, 5:80–83. For the views of other liberal internationalists, see "The Next Step," *NR* 3 (31 July 1915): 323; "Why Do We Arm?" *NR* 4 (30 Oct. 1915): 323–24; "An Alliance with Great Britain," *NR* 5 (20 Nov. 1915): 56–58; WHT in *NYT*, 20 Apr. 1916, 5.

10. WW, "Address in New York on Preparedness," 11; WW, "Address in Milwaukee on Preparedness," 62; WW, "An Annual Message on the State of the Union," 7 Dec. 1915, *PWW* 35:297–98.

11. HD, 25 Nov. 1914, *PWW* 31:355, 3 Dec. 1914, *PWW* 31:385, and 22 Sept. 1915, *PWW* 34:506; Spring Rice to Grey, 8 Sept. 1914, *PWW* 31:14. One can see still more evidence of WW's consistent desire that Germany lose the war in his stance on peace terms, which from late 1914 onward always supported Allied demands that Germany give up its control of Belgium and northern France. See Chapters 4 and 5 of this volume.

12. HD, 28 Nov. 1915, *PWW* 35:259, 260, and 15 Dec. 1915, *PWW* 35:356.

13. WW to Grey, 19 Aug. 1914, *PWW* 30:403; "Memorandum by Herbert Bruce Brougham," 459.

14. Theodore Marburg, "Now Is the Appointed Time," *Independent* 80 (26 Oct. 1914): 126; editorial, *NR* 2 (20 Mar. 1915): 163–64; "Alliance with Great Britain," 57; "Communication: War as We See It," 102. See also Pringle, *Taft*, 2:932, 934.

15. WW to EBG, 18 Aug. 1915, *PWW* 34:242–43. See also "If We Enter the War," *NR* 6 (22 Apr. 1916): 305; "Enter Italy," *NR* 3 (22 May 1915): 55–56; "Terms of Peace," *NR* 8 (9 Sept. 1916): 131; Frank Simonds, "Why Germany Must Lose," *Independent* 84 (15 Nov. 1915): 262; "The

Prospect of Peace," *Independent* 88 (25 Dec. 1916): 512; Pringle, *Taft*, 2:872; HD, 28 Sept. 1914, *PWW* 31:94–95, and 3 Dec. 1914, *PWW* 31:385; William Joel Stone to WW, 25 Mar. 1916, *PWW* 36:366 and 366–68, passim; WW to Stone, 28 Mar. 1916, *PWW* 36:374; EMH to Sir Edward Grey, 11 May 1916, *PWW* 37:21; and WW to EMH, 12 May 1916, *PWW* 37:24.

16. Quotes from Paul Guinn, *British Strategy and Politics, 1914–1918*, 122, 171.

17. "The War as We See It," *NR* 6 (26 Feb. 1916): 103; EMH to WW, 22 Aug. 1914, *PWW* 30:432; and WW to EMH, 25 Aug. 1914, *PWW* 30:450. See also *TMdoc*, 1:5, 2:714.

18. WW to WJB, 14 Apr. 1915, *PWW* 32:520; EMH to WW, 1 June 1916, *PWW* 37:134; Lippmann, *Stakes of Diplomacy*, xiii–xiv. See also Link, *Wilson*, 3:193–95, 267–308.

19. "Memorandum by Herbert Bruce Brougham," 459; "From the Diary of Chandler Parsons Anderson," 9 Jan. 1915, *PWW* 32:45. David Esposito misses this evidence and overstates Wilson's concerns about Russia. See Esposito, *Legacy of Woodrow Wilson*, 4, 15, 17, 91, 134.

20. "Memorandum by Herbert Bruce Brougham," 459; WW, "Unpublished Prolegomenon," 69; EMH to Grey, 11 May 1916, *PWW* 37:21; and WW to EMH, 12 May 1916, *PWW* 37:24; *TMdoc*, 1:96, and see 95–96, passim; see also *TMdoc*, 1:104, 115, 145–46; Guinn, *British Strategy and Politics*, 122. The LEP even considered sending WHT to London to convince the Allies to commit themselves to a peace league rather than focus solely on postwar power politics. See *TMdoc*, 1:118, 145–46, 183, 195–96, 201–2, 215. For *NR*'s concerns about the Allies, see Croly, "The Structure of Peace," *NR* 9 (13 Jan. 1917): 289; "War at Any Price," *NR* 5 (27 Nov. 1915): 85.

21. WW, "Unpublished Prolegomenon," 69. See also WW, "Address to the Senate," 22 Jan. 1917, 536; WW, "Luncheon Address to Women in Cincinnati," 531; "War at Any Price," 85; Croly, "Structure of Peace," 289; Croly, "Meaning of It," 10–11. Taft also predicted that the persistence of Europe's current alliance structure would lead to another war. See WJB and WHT, *World Peace*, 93.

22. Edward A. Filene, *LEP*, 37; WW, "A Nonpartisan Address in Cincinnati," 26 Oct. 1916, *PWW* 38:541; WW, "An Address in Washington to the League to Enforce Peace," 27 May 1916, *PWW* 37:113; WW, "Annual Message to Congress," 8 Dec. 1914, 423; WW to WJB, 7 Jan. 1915, *PWW* 32:25; WW, "An Address in Chicago on Preparedness," 31 Jan. 1916, *PWW* 36:66–67; WW, "Address in Milwaukee on Preparedness," 57. See also Link, *Wilson*, 3:76, 82, 91–104, 161–70, 616–25; Thomas Raeburn White, *LEP*, 25; Philip H. Gadsden, *LEP*, 146–47; Lowell, "League to Enforce Peace," 399–400; "The End of American Isolation," *NR* 1 (7 Nov. 1914): 9; editorial, *NR* 1 (5 Dec. 1914): 1.

23. "Colloquy with a Group of Antipreparedness Leaders," 646; "The Declaration of Interdependence," *Independent* 89 (5 Feb. 1917): 202. See also Gompers, *LEP*, 105–6.

24. "Alliance with Great Britain," *NR* 5 (20 Nov. 1915): 57; WW, "Unpublished Prolegomenon," 67; WW to EBG, 9 Aug. 1915, *PWW* 34:140; HD, 15 Oct. 1915, *PWW* 35:72n3; WW, "Draft of a Peace Note," 70; WW, "Luncheon Address to Women in Cincinnati," 531. For Page's letter on air strikes, see Page to WW, 23 July 1915, *PWW* 34:20. See also "'Preparedness' for What?" *NR* 3 (26 June 1915): 189.

25. Weyl, *American World Policies*, 152, 59–60, 162–82, 186–89, and see also 107–11, 214–15. *NR*'s discussions of trade and security issues never mentioned anything about trade's being vital to America's economy. See, e.g., "China Pays," *NR* 3 (15 May 1915): 30; "The Higher Imperialism," *NR* 3 (5 June 1915): 110–11; "Alliance with Great Britain," 56–58; "Aggressive Pacifism," *NR* 5 (15 Jan. 1916): 263–65; "Pan-Americanism Defined," *NR* 5 (15 Jan. 1916): 265–66; "Com-

munication: War as We See It," 100–104. Holt did not express any concern about "open doors" and America's fundamental well-being when he discussed security either. See "End to Rival Armaments," 228; "Peace without Vengeance," *Independent* 79 (21 Sept. 1914): 396; "Declaration of Interdependence," 202. Filene and Gompers worried about a postwar tariff war, but most speakers at the 1916 LEP convention did not mention trade issues when discussing postwar power politics. See *LEP*, 24–26, 30–32, 42–45, 96–100, 106–8, 115–22, 175–81. See also *WHTP*, 46–52; and Lowell, "League to Enforce Peace," 392–400.

26. WW, "Speech of Acceptance," 7 Aug. 1912, in John Wells Davidson, ed., *A Crossroads of Freedom: The 1912 Campaign Speeches of Woodrow Wilson,* 33; Levin, *Woodrow Wilson and World Politics,* 26. For a WW summary of his proexport program, see WW, "An Address in Baltimore to the Grain Dealers' Association," 25 Sept. 1916, *PWW* 38:262–70.

27. David M. Kennedy, *Over Here: The First World War and American Society,* 345; WW, "Remarks on the Business Outlook," 25 June 1914, *PWW* 30:210 and 210–12, passim; WW, "Remarks at a Press Conference," 1 June 1914, *PWW* 30:129 and 128–29, passim; WW, "Luncheon Address to Women in Cincinnati," 528.

28. WW to Champ Clark, 10 Dec. 1914, *PWW* 31:448; WW, "Annual Message to Congress," 8 Dec. 1914, 416 and 416–18, passim; WW to William Joel Stone, 17 Jan. 1915, *PWW* 32:134n1; WW to Nancy Saunders Toy, 4 Feb. 1915, *PWW* 32:191. Wilson also removed language from a proposed 1916 Democratic Party platform plank calling trade a "vital element in our domestic prosperity." See William Cox Redfield to WW, with enclosure, 3 June 1916, *PWW* 37:160; and WW, "A Draft of the National Democratic Platform of 1916," 10 June 1916, *PWW* 37:194.

29. Luke E. Wright, *NSL,* 90; TR to Nicholas Murray Butler, 24 Sept. 1907, *TRLET* 5:806; TR to WHT, 22 Dec. 1910, *TRLET* 7:190; Beale, *Theodore Roosevelt,* 38. See also Widenor, *Henry Cabot Lodge,* 97–98.

30. HCL, *NSL,* 368; TR, *Fear God,* 76, 81, and see 76–101, passim; HCL, *NSL,* 359–60, and see 357–69, passim.

31. TR to Münsterberg, 3 Oct. 1914, *TRLET* 8:823. See also TR to Münsterberg, 8 Aug. 1914, *TRLET* 7:795; TR to William Sheffield Cowles, 27 Oct. 1911, *TRLET* 7:423; Beale, 81–171; Widenor, *Henry Cabot Lodge,* 158–59; Leopold, *Elihu Root,* 59–60.

32. Quoted in Widenor, *Henry Cabot Lodge,* 188, 217; William L. Marbury, *NSL,* 226, and 220–27, passim; Henry Wise Wood, *NSL,* 163, and see 162–63, passim. See also Root, in Robert Bacon and James Brown Scott, eds., *The United States and the War: The Mission to Russia, Political Addresses by Elihu Root,* 20–22.

33. Root, in Bacon and Scott, eds., *International Subjects,* 442, 443, and see 391–93. See also TR, *Fear God,* 82; Bacon, *NSL,* 60–65.

34. TR to Spring Rice, 18 Feb. 1915, *TRLET* 8:890, and see 890–91, passim. See also TR to Arthur Hamilton Lee, 7 June 1916, *TRLET* 8:1053; TR in *NYT,* 29 Jan. 1917; TR to St. Loe Strachey, 1 Jan. 1917, *TRLET* 8:1139; HCL, *Senate and the League of Nations,* 273–75; Root, in Bacon and Scott, eds., *United States and the War,* 25–26; Widenor, *Henry Cabot Lodge,* 195, 249, 251; Jessup, *Elihu Root,* 2:316–17; Leopold, *Elihu Root,* 114; John A. Garraty, *Henry Cabot Lodge: A Biography,* 307. On TR's opposition to dismembering Germany, see TR to Münsterberg, 3 Oct. 1914, *TRLET* 8:824; TR to Münsterberg, 2 Nov. 1914, *TRLET* 8:826; TR, *NYT,* 11 Oct. 1914, 4:3. Lodge and Root almost certainly shared TR's opposition to dismembering Germany. Widenor notes their close association in foreign policy matters and that

Lodge and TR profoundly agreed on foreign policy issues. See his *Henry Cabot Lodge,* 193, 197. Lodge also praised TR articles that included TR's opposition to destroying the German nation. See HCL to TR, 20 Jan. 1915, *HCL-TR,* 2:452.

35. TR, *NSL,* 85; TR, *NYT,* 29 Nov. 1914, 5:5; Luke E. Wright, *NSL,* 90–91, and see 89–91, passim; HCL, *NSL,* 368; Root, in Bacon and Scott, eds., *United States and the War,* 324. See also *NSL,* 19, 26–27, 147, 194–97, 308–14; John Patrick Finnegan, *Against the Specter of a Dragon: The Campaign for American Preparedness, 1914–1917,* 4, 38.

36. "Claude Kitchin's Statement on the Nation's Preparedness—He Gives Facts," *Commoner* 15 (Dec. 1915): 10.

37. "Mr. Kitchin's Letter on Preparedness," *Commoner* 15 (Nov. 1915): 10. On German aggressiveness, see, e.g., Pinchot, "Preparedness," 112.

38. "The 'Preparedness' Flurry," *TN* 99 (3 Dec. 1914): 647; WW, "Address in Pittsburgh on Preparedness," 32; "Colloquy with a Group of Antipreparedness Leaders," 645.

39. WJB, "The Duty of a Friend," *Commoner* 16 (Feb. 1916): 1; OGV to WW, 30 Oct. 1915, *PWW* 35:142; "Colloquy with a Group of Antipreparedness Leaders," 636; "A Memorial," c. 8 May 1916, *PWW* 36:633; "Colloquy with a Group of Antipreparedness Leaders," 646, and *PWW* 36:636–37, passim.

40. Charles T. Hallinan, "The New Army Law," *Survey* 36 (17 June 1916): 309; Lillian Wald, in *Preparedness for National Defense: Hearings,* 64th Cong., 1st sess., 1916, pp. 1030 and 1029–30, passim; Hallinan, "New Army Law," 309; Cooley, "Second Class Navy," 603; "Memorial to the President of the United States," 633; OGV, "Preparedness Is Militarism," 223 and 218–23, passim.

41. WJB to WW, 19 Sept. 1914, *PWW* 31:56; "Woman's Peace Party Full Fledged for Action," 434. For more on the pacifist view of terms for ending the war, see Chapter 3 in this volume.

42. Edward Devine, "Ourselves and Europe, II: Enduring Peace," *Survey* 37 (18 Nov. 1916): 158. See also "The Cup of Bitterness," *TN* 100 (20 May 1915): 553–54; Cooley, "President Wilson's Peace Note," *Public* 20 (5 Jan. 1917), 5–6. WJB foresaw a draw in the war. See "The Way Out," *Commoner* 15 (July 1915): 6.

43. For a discussion of why Atlanticists chose to play down their fears of Germany, see Chapter 6 in this volume.

3. The Vision of Collective Security, 1914–17

1. WW, "Address in Washington to the League to Enforce Peace," 114. For WW's talk with EMH about consultations, see HD, 30 Aug. 1914, *PWW* 30:462. On a prewar EMH tip to Europe to promote disarmament, see Link, *Wilson,* 2:314–18. On the early stages of the preparedness movement in Congress and on WW's concern that it could lead to militarism, see, respectively, Link, *Wilson,* 3:137–38; WW, "Annual Message to Congress," 8 Dec. 1914, *PWW* 31:421–24. By mid-December 1914 WW had begun formulating ideas about a collective security scheme for Europe modeled on one for the Western Hemisphere. See HD, 16 Dec. 1914, *PWW* 31:469. For *NR*'s early thoughts on a league, see "Pacifism vs. Passivism," *NR* 1 (12 Dec. 1914): 7. The inspiration for the LEP can be traced in part to Holt, "Way to Disarm," 427–29.

2. WW, "An Address in Omaha," 5 Oct. 1916, *PWW* 38:348; WW, "Nonpartisan Address in Cincinnati," 541; *WHTP,* 79; "Appeal to the President," 304.

3. WW, "Draft of the National Democratic Platform of 1916," 196, and see 195–96, passim; WW, "Address in Washington to the League to Enforce Peace," 114–15, and see 116; Talcott Williams, *LEP,* 84. See also "The Note as Americanism," *NR* 9 (30 Dec. 1916): 230; "Mr. Wilson's Great Utterance," *NR* 7 (3 June 1916): 103; *TMdoc,* 2:722; *LEP,* 189. The terms "league" or "league of nations" will only be capitalized when referring to the League of Nations created at Paris in 1919, unless the term is capitalized in the primary source itself.

4. WW, "Address to the Senate," 22 Jan. 1917, 534; WW, "Address in Omaha," 348; Thomas Raeburn White, *LEP,* 22, and 22–23, passim; WW, "Address in Washington to the League to Enforce Peace," 114. WW had endorsed the "cooling-off" concept as a way to settle disputes before the war broke out, as he supported Secretary of State Bryan's effort to negotiate bilateral treaties providing for signatories to submit all disputes to investigation for a period of six months or one year. See Link, *Wilson,* 2:280–83. See also "Appeal to the President," 304; "A League of Peace," *NR* 3 (26 June 1915): 190–91.

5. WW, "Address in Washington to the League to Enforce Peace," 116; WW, "Address to the Senate," 22 Jan. 1917, 535. For *NR,* see "Appeal to the President," 304; "Mr. Wilson's Great Utterance," 103; Croly, "Structure of Peace," 288–90; "League of Peace," 190–91.

6. See *TMdoc,* 2:704–8, 711–12, and 1:39, 61, 212–13; *LEP,* 14–19, 132–33; 138–39; *WHTP,* 108, 121. On the legalistic focus of the prewar peace movement, see Marchand, *American Peace Movement,* 32–69.

7. WW, "Address to the Senate," 22 Jan. 1917, 539; *TMdoc,* 1:67–68. See also Lansing to WW, 24 Nov. 1915, *PWW* 35:247; "Alliance with Great Britain," 56–58; "Aggressive Pacifism," 263–65; "Pan-Americanism Defined," 265–66; *TMdoc,* 1:77–78, 2:705, 721–23, 728–29, 731; *WHTP,* 120–21. On WW's initial ideas about international reform, see HD, 16 Dec. 1914, *PWW* 31:469–70; Richard Heath Dabney to WW, 1 Jan. 1915, *PWW* 32:4–5; WW to Dabney, 4 Jan. 1915, *PWW* 32:10–11. On this issue and on WW's late 1915 decision regarding a global league, see also Chapter 5 in this volume. Foulke did manage to get the LEP to use vague language in its program to try to ensure that a league's judicial tribunal could not declare the Monroe Doctrine a "justiciable" issue. See Dubin, "Elihu Root," 443.

8. *WHTP,* 49, and 47–49, passim; WW, "Address to the Senate," 22 Jan. 1917, 535; "The Enforcement of Peace," *Independent* 80 (12 Oct. 1914): 43; Marburg, *LEP,* 138; White, *LEP,* 20. See also Weyl, *American World Policies,* 244; "Terms of Peace," 131.

9. WW, "Address to the Senate," 22 Jan. 1917, 535; WW, "Remarks to the Associated Press in New York," 20 Apr. 1915, *PWW* 33:38; WW, "Address in Washington to the League to Enforce Peace," 114.

10. *WHTP,* 117, 79, and see 78–79, passim; "Alliance with Great Britain," 58, and 56–58, passim. See also Lowell, "League to Enforce Peace," 400.

11. WW, "Address in Pittsburgh on Preparedness," 34, and see 28; WW, "Address in St. Louis on Preparedness," 115; "A Colloquy with Members of the American Neutral Conference," 30 Aug. 1916, *PWW* 38:115; WW, "Address on Preparedness to the Manhattan Club," 169; WW, "Democracy and Efficiency," 12–13; WW, "An Address in Cleveland on Preparedness," 29 Jan. 1916, *PWW* 36:48; WW, "Commencement Address at the United States Military Academy," 215; WW, "Address in Chicago on Preparedness," 72; WW, "Commencement Address at the United States Military Academy," 214. For Wilson's comments on the American

political system, see WW, "An Address to the Federal Council of Churches in Columbus," 10 Dec. 1915, *PWW* 35:335; WW, "Address in Pittsburgh on Preparedness," 28. See also Link, *Revolution, War, and Peace*, 6–7. For an example of *NR* echoing WW, see "Appeal to the President," 304. *NR* also saw U.S. policy toward Mexico in the 1840s as aggressive, but the editors blamed it not on American democracy but on "a slave-owning oligarchy." See "The Wisdom of the Wise," *NR* 14 (9 Feb. 1918): 43. For the LEP, see White, *LEP*, 27.

12. WW, "Address to the Senate," 22 Jan. 1917, 537, 536–37, 537. For more on the open door and trade, see WW to WJB, 23 Nov. 1913, *PWW* 28:586; WW, "A Speech in Long Branch, New Jersey, Accepting the Presidential Nomination," 2 Sept. 1916, *PWW* 38:137.

13. *TMdoc*, 1:108; White, *LEP*, 18. See also *TMdoc*, 2:722. The LEP did not mention the open door in its program, and it did not come up for discussion in the key organizational meetings that developed the LEP platform. See *TMdoc*, 2:703–17.

14. Link, *Revolution, War, and Peace*, 8, and 8–11, passim; Ambrosius, *Wilsonianism*, 24, 25, and 22–27, passim. I am indebted to Professor Ambrosius's excellent discussion here for my sense of Wilsonian self-determination. For more on Wilson's view of imperialism, see WW, "An Address on Latin American Policy in Mobile, Alabama," 27 Oct. 1913, *PWW* 28:450–51; Edward G. Lowry, "What the President Is Trying to Do for Mexico," Jan. 1914, *PWW* 29:92–97; Link, *Wilson*, 4:350–56. See also Knock, *To End All Wars*, 25–26. On Wilson and race relations in the United States, see, e.g., Link, *Wilson*, 2:246–54; Knock, *To End All Wars*, 24; Cooper, *Warrior and the Priest*, 210–11. On Wilson and the Philippines, see WW, "Democracy and Efficiency," 17–19; Link, *Wilson*, 4:350–55.

15. Weyl, *American World Policies*, 276, 277, and 276–79, passim; "League of Peace," 191; Lippmann, *Stakes of Diplomacy*, 95, and 87–159, passim; "League of Peace," 191.

16. On government control of munitions, see WW, "Draft of a Pan-American Treaty," 472. The proposal did not appear in WW's two major addresses concerning his reform vision, however. See WW, "Address in Washington to the League to Enforce Peace," 113–16; and WW, "Address to the Senate," 22 Jan. 1917, 533–39. WW later dropped the idea from his Pan-American treaty proposal. See WW, "A Draft of the Pan-American Pact," 3 May 1916, *PWW* 36:595–96. For a different interpretation of WW and the issue of democratic control of foreign policy, see Knock, *To End All Wars*, passim; and Smith, *America's Mission*, 84–88, 94. For *NR*, see editorial, *NR* 4 (30 Oct. 1915): 319–20; "League of Peace," 190–91; "Mr. Wilson's Great Utterance," 102–4; Croly, "Structure of Peace," 287–91; "Taking the Referendum Seriously," *NR* 10 (24 Feb. 1917): 92. The LEP's official program contained nothing about democratic control of foreign policy. See *LEP*, 189–90; *TMdoc*, 1:60.

17. Lowell, "League to Enforce Peace," 400; *WHTP*, 116. See also "Colloquy with a Group of Antipreparedness Leaders," 645–46; "Mr. Wilson's Great Utterance," 103; "Roosevelt and Righteousness," *NR* 9 (13 Jan. 1917): 282–83; William H. Wadhams, *LEP*, 157–58; Holt, *LEP*, 54–56; White, *LEP*, 26; *TMdoc*, 1:113. Knock oversimplifies the LEP's position on disarmament. See his *To End All Wars*, 57.

18. WW, "Address to the Senate," 22 Jan. 1917, 539, and see 533–39, passim. On WW, see also "Memorandum by Herbert Bruce Brougham," 458–59; diary of Chandler Parsons Anderson, 9 Jan. 1915, *PWW* 32:44–45; EMH to WW, 15 Feb. 1916, *PWW* 36:180n2; and see HD, 6 Mar. 1916, *PWW* 36:262; and EMH to Sir Edward Grey, 7 Mar. 1916, *PWW* 36:266. For details on the exchanges between WW and the Allies on peace terms, see Chapters 4 and 5 in this volume. For *NR*, see "Peace without Victory," *NR* 9 (23 Dec. 1916): 201; "War as We See It," 102–3; "Appeal to the President," 304; "America Speaks," *NR* 9 (27 Jan. 1917):

340–42; "The Will to Believe," *NR* 9 (13 Jan. 1917): 285. For the LEP, see *TMdoc*, 1:95–96, 104, 115, 214, 219–20, 251–52, 257; Pringle, *Taft*, 2:872, 934; "Peace without Victory," *Independent* 89 (5 Feb. 1917): 203. The sorts of terms LEP leaders had in mind can probably best be seen in the Allied war aims statement of early 1917. See William Graves Sharp to Lansing (Allied War Aims Statement), 10 Jan. 1917, *PWW* 40:439.

19. On Germany, see Chapter 2 in this volume; for views of the international system, see Chapter 1.

20. "Colloquy with a Group of Antipreparedness Leaders," 648; "Appeal to the President," 304.

21. WW, "Unpublished Prolegomenon," 68; "War as We See It," 102.

22. *TMdoc*, 1:181; WW to Robert Lansing, 19 Dec. 1916, n. 1, *PWW* 40:277; WW to Lansing, 19 Dec. 1916, *PWW* 40:276. See also *TMdoc*, 1:23; 2:703–06.

23. *TMdoc*, 1:4, 160.

24. *TMdoc*, 1:208, and see 207–8, passim, 2:714. Lowell was also wary of creating a league out of the Entente. See Herman, *Eleven against War*, 75–76.

25. WW to Lansing, 19 Dec. 1916, *PWW* 40:276–77; WW, "Address in Washington to the League to Enforce Peace," 116; WW, "Address to the Senate," 22 Jan. 1917, 539; *TMdoc*, 1:221, and see 220–21, passim; Lippmann, *Stakes of Diplomacy*, xxii. See also Ruhl F. Bartlett, *The League to Enforce Peace*, 37; *TMdoc*, 2:790–91, 1:215–16, 230; Charles Frederick Carter, *LEP*, 7. Holt resigned from the promediation American Neutral Conference Committee on 17 December 1917 in deference to the LEP's demand that he do so. See Warren F. Kuehl, *Hamilton Holt: Journalist, Internationalist, Educator*, 111. For *NR*, see Croly, "Structure of Peace," 289, 290, and 289–90, passim; "Appeal to the President," 304; "Note as Americanism," 229–30.

26. WW, "Unpublished Prolegomenon," 69–70. See too "Memorandum by Herbert Bruce Brougham," 458–59; *WHTP*, 102–3.

27. *TMdoc*, 1:96; WW, "Address to the Senate," 22 Jan. 1917, 536; WW to Lansing, 9 Dec. 1916, *PWW* 40:199; and WW, "An Appeal for a Statement of War Aims," 18 Dec. 1916, *PWW* 40:275. See also *TMdoc*, 1:257; "Peace without Victory," *Independent* 89 (5 Feb. 1917): 203; "America Speaks," 340–42.

28. WJB, "War in Europe," 14.

29. "For a Peace Conference of Neutral Nations," 598. See also WPP platform quoted in Degen, *History of the Woman's Peace Party*, 40–41; "Towards the Peace That Shall Last"; WJB, "Peace Day," 15; Eastman, "War and Peace," 363.

30. Cooley, "Enforcing Peace," *Public* 20 (2 Feb. 1917): 101; WJB and WHT, *World Peace*, 63; "The Week," *TN* 100 (11 Feb. 1915): 156; and "Critics of the League to Enforce Peace," *TN* 104 (4 Jan. 1917): 5; Devine, "Ourselves and Europe, II," 159, and WPP, quoted in ibid., 159, 41. Degen also notes this shift. See *History of the Woman's Peace Party*, 42, 154–59. See also Steinson, *American Women's Activism*, 142. For Kellogg, see "A Bill of Particulars," *TN* 103 (3 Aug. 1916): sec. 2, 1; for Jordan, see Louis P. Lochner, "Peace Challenging Preparedness," *Survey* 35 (30 Oct. 1915): 104; and "Colloquy with Members of the American Neutral Conference," 112. Jordan and Stephen Wise of the AUAM even agreed to be sponsors of the LEP program. See Bartlett, *League to Enforce Peace*, 215–16. RLF supported upholding peace machinery with public opinion and an economic boycott. See "Duty of Neutral Nations," 8.

31. WJB, "Labor's Interest in Peace," 9; Samuel Danziger, "A Disappointing Message," *Public* 18 (17 Dec. 1915): 1211; Stoughton Cooley, "Discounting the Future," *Public* 18 (26 Nov.

1915): 1138; "Colloquy with a Group of Antipreparedness Leaders," 645, 648; *AUAM Bulletin* no. 54 (24 July 1916): 1.

32. WJB, "Labor's Interest in Peace," 9; WJB, "Planning for World Peace," *Commoner* 16 (Mar. 1916): 1. See also WJB and WHT, *World Peace*, 36, 98–102, 113, 139.

33. WPP, quoted in Degen, *History of the Woman's Peace Party*, 41, and see 40–46, passim; Hague International Congress of Women, 1915, quoted in Degen, *History of the Woman's Peace Party*, 87; Howe, *Why War?* 340, and 339–43, passim, 348. See also "Platform of the American Union against Militarism," *Survey* 36 (22 Apr. 1916): 95; WJB, "Why Not a Referendum?" *Commoner* 16 (Feb. 1916): 6; RLF, "Consult the People!" *LFM* 8 (May 1916): 1; Ernest C. Bolt Jr., *Ballots before Bullets: The War Referendum Approach to Peace in America, 1914-1941*, 2–26, passim; Elizabeth McKillen, *Chicago Labor and the Quest for a Democratic Diplomacy, 1914-1924*, 36, 52–54; Knock, *To End All Wars*, 50–55. On the citizen commission idea and on the Mexican episode, see Crystal Eastman, "A Review," AUAM pamphlet, Oct. 1916, in Blanche Wiesen Cook, ed., *Crystal Eastman on Women and Revolution*, 250–51; Marchand, *American Peace Movement*, 243–44.

34. Paul Kellogg, "A Bill of Particulars," *TN* 103 (3 Aug. 1916): sec. 2, p. 1. Socialists and some labor radicals did call for the independence of colonies. See Knock, *To End All Wars*, 53, and McKillen, *Chicago Labor*, 30, 50–51. See also "Towards the Peace That Shall Last"; Pinchot, "Preparedness," 112–13; Howe, *Why War?* 339–50, passim.

35. WJB to WW, 1 Dec. 1914, *PWW* 31:379; Devine, "Ourselves and Europe, II," 158; "Colloquy with Members of the American Neutral Conference," 112. For pacifists applauding Wilson's 22 January 1917 address to the Senate, see, e.g., Wald and others to WW, 24 Jan. 1917, *PWW* 41:7–8.

36. Mead, "Compulsory Military Service," 1167; "Critics of the League to Enforce Peace," 6.

37. TR to Henry Sturgis Drinker, 9 Jan. 1917, *TRLET* 8:1142, 1143; TR in *NYT*, 22 January 1917, 5. Root made a similar objection to the LEP program. See Dubin, "Elihu Root," 449.

38. HCL, *War Addresses*, 271, 272, 260, and see 255–63, 266–71, 274–76, passim. See also Root, in Bacon and Scott, eds., *United States and the War*, 24–25; TR in *NYT*, 4 Jan. 1917, 3; Dubin, "Elihu Root," 447–48, 450–51.

39. TR, "Utopia or Hell," *Independent* 81 (4 Jan. 1915): 13, 16. William Clinton Olson speculates that TR left Austria-Hungary out of his plan because he did not expect it to survive the war. See Olson, "Theodore Roosevelt's Conception of an International League," 348.

40. TR, *NYT*, 29 Nov. 1914, 5:5; TR, *NYT*, 18 Oct. 1914, 5:1; TR, *NYT*, 1 Nov. 1914, 5:1.

41. Root, in Bacon and Scott, eds., *International Subjects*, 167, and see 166–67, 391, 406, and 405–9, passim, 399, 400–401, 415, 425. See also Herman, *Eleven against War*, 23–46; Jessup, *Elihu Root*, 2:373–75; Dubin, "Elihu Root," 439–42.

42. HCL to TR, 20 Jan. 1915, *HCL-TR*, 2:452–53; HCL, *War Addresses*, 31, and see 41–43; HCL, *LEP*, 165, 166.

43. HCL, *War Addresses*, 271, 259, 271. See also Root, in Bacon and Scott, eds., *International Subjects*, 157; "Roosevelt and Righteousness," 281; David Jayne Hill, *NSL*, 27.

44. TR, "World War," 177. See also TR, "Utopia or Hell," 16.

45. TR, *NYT*, 18 Oct. 1914, 5:1; HCL, quoted in Widenor, *Henry Cabot Lodge*, 188; TR to Arthur Hamilton Lee, 7 June 1916, *TRLET* 8:1053. See also Root, in Bacon and Scott, eds., *United States and the War*, 19–20, 25–26; Dubin, "Elihu Root," 447.

46. EMH to Grey, 11 May 1916, *PWW* 37:21; and WW to EMH, 12 May 1916, *PWW* 37:24; *TMdoc*, 1:96.

47. George Santayana, "A Communication," *NR* 6 (26 Feb. 1916): 100; "War as We See It," 103, and see 103–4, passim.

48. WW, "Address to the Senate," 22 Jan. 1917, 539.

49. See Widenor, *Henry Cabot Lodge,* 221–60, passim. Lodge also saw his support for a league as a way to keep the GOP united for the 1916 elections.

50. HCL, "The President's Plan for a World Peace," 1 Feb. 1917, *War Addresses,* 268.

4. Pursuing a Wilsonian Peace, 1914–15

1. WW, "An Appeal to the American People," 18 Aug. 1914, *PWW* 30:394, and 393–94, passim; WW, quoted in Link, *Wilson,* 3:87; Robert Lansing to WW, 22 Aug. 1914, *PWW* 30:436, and see 435–36, passim; WW to WJB, 22 Jan. 1915, *PWW* 32:104. See also Link, *Wilson,* 3:81–91, 137–58, 179–87. My understanding of the complexity of the issues discussed in this chapter draws from Link's *Wilson,* even though my interpretation of events is very different from his.

2. This summary of Britain's maritime system relies on John W. Coogan, *The End of Neutrality: The United States, Britain, and Maritime Rights, 1899–1915,* 155–64; and Link, *Wilson,* 3:106–7.

3. Coogan, *End of Neutrality,* 155–61, 173; Link, *Wilson,* 3:106–7.

4. This interpretation follows Coogan's. See his *End of Neutrality,* 160.

5. Wambaugh, quoted in Coogan, *End of Neutrality,* 173; Lansing to WW, 27 Sept. 1914, *PWW* 31:86; Lansing to Walter Hines Page, 26 Sept. 1914, *FRUS 1914 Supplement, The World War* (Washington, D.C.: 1928), 231; Lansing to WW, 27 Sept. 1914, *PWW* 31:86. This discussion relies on Coogan, *End of Neutrality,* 166–74.

6. HD, 30 Sept. 1914, *PWW* 31:109; and see Coogan, *End of Neutrality,* 179–80.

7. EMH to WW, 18 Sept. 1914, *PWW* 31:45; Cecil Arthur Spring Rice to WW, 19 Sept. 1914, *PWW* 31:58–59; James Viscount Bryce to WW, 24 Sept. 1914, *PWW* 31:82, and 81–82, passim; Page to WW, 6 Sept. 1914, *PWW* 31:8; EMH to WW, 6 Sept. 1914, *PWW* 31:5; Bryce to WW, 24 Sept. 1914, *PWW* 31:82.

8. HD, 28 Sept. 1914, *PWW* 31:95, and see 94–95, passim.

9. HD, 28 Sept. 1914, *PWW* 31:94–95; House, quoted in Link, *Wilson,* 3:205; HD, 28 Sept. 1914, *PWW* 31:94; EMH to WW, 8 Oct. 1914, *PWW* 31:137. See also WW to Bryce, 9 Oct. 1914, *PWW* 31:138; HD, 3 Dec. 1914, *PWW* 31:385.

10. WW to Spring Rice, 23 Oct. 1914, PWW 31:214. See also Coogan, *End of Neutrality,* 173–93; Link, *Wilson,* 3:112–31. My interpretation follows Coogan, based on the relevant documents in *PWW* 31:86–243.

11. WW, quoted in Joseph P. Tumulty, *Woodrow Wilson as I Know Him,* 231, and see 230–31, passim; WW to EMH, 29 Oct. 1914, *PWW* 31:246; Spring Rice to Grey, 9 Nov. 1914, *PWW* 31:292; Spring Rice to Grey, 13 Nov. 1914, *PWW* 31:315. On British mines, see Lansing to WJB, 18 Feb. 1915, *FRUS Lansing Papers, 1914–1920* (Washington, D.C.: 1939), 1:37–38; Coogan, *End of Neutrality,* 213–14; Link, *Wilson,* 3:132.

12. See Coogan, *End of Neutrality,* 198–99, 202–3, 208–16; Link, *Wilson,* 3:171; Viscount Grey, *Twenty Five Years,* 2:110–11.

13. WJB to WW, 17 Dec. 1914, *PWW* 31:477, 478, 480, and 477–80, passim. For anger at the British, see Coogan, *End of Neutrality,* 199–200, 203; Link, *Wilson,* 3:161.

244 NOTES TO PAGES 70–76

14. WW to Spring Rice, 23 Dec. 1914, *PWW* 31:514. See also HD, 18 Dec. 1914, *PWW* 31:489. On Lansing, see Coogan, *End of Neutrality,* 202. On Grey's defense, see Spring Rice to WW, 21 Dec. 1914, *PWW* 31:505–6.

15. WW to WJB, 26 Dec. 1914, *PWW* 31:528, 527, and see 526–27, 530, and 525–30, passim; EMH to WW, 31 Dec. 1914, *PWW* 31:553. Coogan drew my attention to the clause concerning "self-preservation." See his *End of Neutrality,* 207.

16. Diary of Chandler Parsons Anderson, 9 Jan. 1915, *PWW* 32:48–49n1.

17. Zimmermann, quoted in Link, *Wilson,* 3:210, and see 210–11, passim; HD, 16 Dec. 1914, *PWW* 31:468–69.

18. House, quoted in Link, *Wilson,* 3:211; diary of Chandler Parsons Anderson, 9 Jan. 1915, *PWW* 32:44; HD, 23 Dec. 1914, *PWW* 31:519, 518.

19. HD, 12 Jan. 1915, *PWW* 32:61; HD, 23 Dec. 1914, *PWW* 31:518, 519. See also WW to EMH, 16 Jan. 1915, *PWW* 32:81–82; WW to EMH, 17 Jan. 1915, *PWW* 32:83.

20. EMH to WW, 11 Feb. 1915, *PWW* 32:220.

21. EMH to WW, 15 Feb. 1915, *PWW* 32:237; EMH to WW, 18 Feb. 1915, *PWW* 32:255, and see 254; EMH to WW, 9 Mar. 1915, *PWW* 32:351. See also EMH to WW, 26 Mar. 1915, *PWW* 32:438.

22. EMH to WW, 23 Feb. 1915, *PWW* 32:277–78; EMH to WW, 29 Mar. 1915, *PWW* 32:455–56.

23. WW to EMH, 20 Feb. 1915, *PWW* 32:265; WW to EMH, 1 Apr. 1915, *PWW* 32:462. On the Berlin trip, see EMH to WW, 18 Feb. 1915, *PWW* 32:253; EMH to WW, 17 Feb. 1915, *PWW* 32:242; WW to EMH, 20 Feb. 1915, *PWW* 32:265; EMH to WW, 21 Feb. 1915, *PWW* 32:267–68; WW to EMH, 25 Feb. 1915, *PWW* 32:287.

24. WW to WJB, 27 Apr. 1915, *PWW* 33:81–82. See also WW to WJB, 28 Apr. 1915, *PWW* 32:85.

25. Spring Rice to Grey, 3 Sept. 1914, *PWW* 30:472. For Grey's description of the blockade, see Spring Rice to WW, 15 Oct. 1914, *PWW* 31:154–56.

26. Page to WW, 21 Oct. 1914, *PWW* 31:199–200; WW to Lansing, 15 Oct. 1914, *PWW* 31:154, and 154–56, passim.

27. Spring Rice to Grey, 19 Dec. 1914, *PWW* 31:499; EMH to WW, 22 Jan. 1915, *PWW* 32:108, 107. See also Spring Rice to Sir Valentine Chirol, 3 Nov. 1914, in Stephen Gwynn, ed., *The Letters and Friendships of Sir Cecil Arthur Spring Rice,* 2:241–42.

28. Coogan, *End of Neutrality,* 205; Asquith, quoted in ibid., 206.

29. EMH to WW, 26 Mar. 1915, *PWW* 32:438. For anger at home at the arms sales, see Link, *Wilson,* 3:161–70; Lansing to WW, 9 Dec. 1914, *PWW* 31:440–42; McKillen, *Chicago Labor,* 20–27; Hugo Münsterberg to WW, 7 and 19 Nov. 1914, *PWW* 31:276–78, 336–40. On the German admission that the arms sales were legal, see WJB to WW, 24 Dec. 1914, *PWW* 31:521–22.

30. Memorandum of the German government, 4 Feb. 1915, *FRUS 1915 Supplement, The World War* (Washington, D.C.: 1928), 96 and 96–97, passim.

31. WJB, quoted in Link, *Wilson,* 3:64, and see 132–36; "A Memorandum by Robert Lansing," 23 Oct. 1914, *PWW* 31:219, and see 219–20, passim.

32. Lansing to Stone, 20 Jan. 1915, *FRUS 1914 Supplement,* viii, and see vii–xiv, passim. See also Lansing to WW, 9 Dec. 1914, *PWW* 31:440–42, and see 433–46, passim; Link, *Wilson,* 3:167–70.

33. Lansing to Stone, 20 Jan. 1915, *FRUS 1914 Supplement,* ix, x. For the disingenuousness of the Civil War argument, see Lansing to Page, 21 Oct. 1915, *FRUS 1915 Supplement,* 579, 581, 585, 587, where the administration rejected any parallel between the British maritime system and American actions during the Civil War.

34. WW, "Remarks to the Belgian Commissioners," 16 Sept. 1914, *PWW* 31:34, and see 33–34, passim; WW to WJB, 12 Jan. 1915, *PWW* 32:60.

35. Lansing to WW, 7 Feb. 1915, *PWW* 32:195; WW to James Watson Gerard, 10 Feb. 1915, *PWW* 32:209, and see 208–10, passim.

36. WW to WJB, 26 Dec. 1914, *PWW* 31:529, 530, and see 525–31, passim. See also Coogan, *End of Neutrality,* 214–15, 221–23.

37. See WJB to Page, 10 Feb. 1915, *FRUS 1915 Supplement,* 100–101; Link, *Wilson,* 3:323–24.

38. WJB to WW, 15 Feb. 1915, *PWW* 32:235, and see 235–36, passim; WW to EMH, 20 Feb. 1915, *PWW* 32:265. See also WJB to WW, 15 Feb. 1915, n. 3, *PWW* 32:235–36; WJB to WW, 19 Feb. 1915, *PWW* 32:259–62.

39. Page to WW, 10 Mar. 1915, *PWW* 32:359, and see 358–59, passim. On Germany's position, see Link, *Wilson,* 3:333–34.

40. WW, "Appeal to the American People," 394; WW, "Remarks to the American Bar Association," 20 Oct. 1914, *PWW* 31:186; WW, "Annual Message to Congress," 8 Dec. 1914, *PWW* 31:422.

41. WW, "Annual Message to Congress," 8 Dec. 1914, 423.

5. Pursuing a Wilsonian Peace, 1915–17

1. See Coogan, *End of Neutrality,* 223–24; Link, *Wilson,* 3:337–40.

2. WW to WJB, 4 Mar. 1915, *PWW* 32:317; WW to Lansing, 28 Mar. 1915, *PWW* 32:449, and see 443–49, passim; WW to James Watson Gerard, 10 Feb. 1915, *PWW* 32:209. For the State Department's and the secretary of war's views, see Scott, quoted in Coogan, *End of Neutrality,* 228; WJB to WW, 22 Mar. 1915, *PWW* 32:413n2; Lindley Miller Garrison to WW, 20 Mar. 1915, *PWW* 32:407. My interpretation follows Coogan's. See his *End of Neutrality,* 235. For Link's view, see *Wilson,* 3:341–48.

3. WW to WJB, 24 Mar. 1915, *PWW* 32:424–25 (emphasis in original). See also Coogan, *End of Neutrality,* 230.

4. WW to WJB, 24 Mar. 1915, *PWW* 32:425; WJB to WW, 24 Mar. 1915, *PWW* 32:428; and WW to WJB, 25 Mar. 1915, *PWW* 32:432–33, 433.

5. WW to WJB, 24 Mar. 1915, *PWW* 32:425; WJB to WW, 24 Mar. 1915, *PWW* 32:428–29; WW to WJB, 25 Mar. 1915, *PWW* 32:432. On the drafts, see WW to WJB, 19 Mar. 1915, *PWW* 32:399–401; Lansing to WW, 28 Mar. 1915, *PWW* 32:443–49; Lansing to WW, 28 Mar. 1915, *PWW* 32:449.

6. EMH to WW, 9 May 1915, *PWW* 33:134; Page to WW, 8 May 1915, *PWW* 33:130.

7. WW to WJB, 10 May 1915, *PWW* 33:139; WW to WJB, 11 May 1915, *PWW* 33:154.

8. WW to WJB, 12 May 1915, *PWW* 33:176, 177, and see 174–78, passim; WJB to WW, 7 June 1915, *PWW* 33:358, and see 355–60, passim.

9. WJB to WW, 12 May 1915, *PWW* 33:166, and see 165–66, passim; WJB to WW, 5 June 1915, *PWW* 33:342, and see 342–43, passim; WJB to WW, 3 June 1915, *PWW* 33:324, and see

321–26, passim; WJB to WW, 7 June 1915, *PWW* 33:354–55, and see 351–55, passim; WJB to WW, 16 May 1915, *PWW* 33:207, and see 206–7, passim. For Lansing's hawkish views, see WJB to WW, 2 June 1915, *PWW* 33:312–13.

10. WW to WJB, 20 May 1915, *PWW* 33:224; "A Memorandum by Lindley Miller Garrison," 1 June 1915, *PWW* 33:296n4; WW to WJB, 14 May 1915, *PWW* 33:194; WW to WJB, 5 June 1915, *PWW* 33:343.

11. WW to Lansing, 21 July 1915, *PWW* 33:548, and see 547 and 545–48, passim.

12. WW, "Address in Cleveland on Preparedness," 47; Lansing to WW, 20 Aug. 1915, *PWW* 34:265; and see WW to Lansing, 21 Aug. 1915, *PWW* 34:271; WW to EBG, 19 Aug. 1915, *PWW* 34:257; WW to EBG, 22 Aug. 1915, *PWW* 34:290; WW to EBG, c. 23 Aug. 1915, *PWW* 34:298–99.

13. WW to Lansing, 27 Aug. 1915, *PWW* 34:341; WW to Lucy Marshall Smith, 15 Sept. 1915, *PWW* 34:474; WW to EMH, 20 Sept. 1915, *PWW* 34:493. For the threat to sever relations, see Link, *Wilson,* 3:569, 659–62, 674–76.

14. HD, 30 Mar. 1916, *PWW* 36:388–89; Page to WW, 30 Mar. 1916, *PWW* 36:385. See also WW, "Address to a Joint Session of Congress," 19 Apr. 1916, 506–10; HD, 28 Mar. 1916, *PWW* 36:375; Lansing to WW, 27 Mar. 1916, *PWW* 36:371–73; WW to Lansing, 30 Mar. 1916, *PWW* 36:381–82; Link, *Wilson,* 4:61–99.

15. WW to EBG, 18 Aug. 1915, *PWW* 34:242–43 (emphasis in original). For Britain's dependence on American war supplies at this time, see Link, *Wilson,* 3:604. On the negative reports concerning the Allied war effort, see, e.g., EMH to WW, 4 Aug. 1915, *PWW* 34:84–85.

16. McAdoo to WW, 23 Aug. 1915, *PWW* 34:294. See also McAdoo to WW, 21 Aug. 1915, *PWW* 34:275, 279, and see 275–80, passim; Link, 3:616–28; Lansing to WW, 25 Aug. 1915, *PWW* 34:316–17; WW to Lansing, 26 Aug. 1915, *PWW* 34:329; EMH to WW, 22 Jan. 1915, *PWW* 32:108.

17. Lansing, quoted in Link, *Wilson,* 3:597; WW to EMH, 18 May 1915, *PWW* 33:217; Lansing to Page, 21 Oct. 1915, *FRUS 1915 Supplement,* 589, and see 578–89, passim; WW to EMH, 18 Oct. 1915, *PWW* 35:81; Spring Rice to Grey, 7 Mar. 1916, *PWW* 36:269. See also Link, *Wilson,* 4:55–56, 146–47. For a very different interpretation of the October note, see Link, *Wilson,* 682–92.

18. HD, 8 Oct. 1915, *PWW* 35:43–44. For the delay on mediation, see WW to WJB, 27 Apr. 1915, *PWW* 33:81; Lansing to WW, 18 Aug. 1915, *PWW* 34:236–37; WW to Lansing, 19 Aug. 1915, *PWW* 34:248.

19. HD, 8 Oct. 1915, *PWW* 35:44; WW to EMH, 18 Oct. 1915, *PWW* 35:81, and see 80–82, passim; EMH to WW, 15 Feb. 1916, *PWW* 36:180n2; HD, 6 Mar. 1916, *PWW* 36:262. For the decision to send House to Europe, see HD, 15 Dec. 1915, *PWW* 35:356–59. See also WW to EMH, 24 Dec. 1915, *PWW* 35:387–88; Link, *Wilson,* 4:113. For the cable to Grey, see House to Grey, 7 Mar. 1916, *PWW* 36:266; HD, 7 Mar. 1916, *PWW* 36:266.

20. EMH to WW, 3 June 1914, *PWW* 30:140; HD, 30 Aug. 1914, *PWW* 30:462, and 16 Dec. 1914, *PWW* 31:469, and see 469–70. See also WW, "Draft of a Pan-American Treaty," 471–72. For House's prewar trip to Europe, see Link, *Wilson,* 2:316.

21. HD, 15 Oct. 1915, *PWW* 35:71n3, and see text on 71; EMH to WW, 10 Nov. 1915, *PWW* 35:186; WW to EMH, 11 Nov. 1915, *PWW* 35:187. For examples of late 1914–early 1915 British suggestions about America's upholding the peace, see HD, 23 Dec. 1914, *PWW* 31:518–20, and see n. 2 to this entry; EMH to WW, 9 Feb. 1915, *PWW* 36:205; EMH to WW, 16 June 1915, *PWW* 33:408.

22. Allan R. Millet and Peter Maslowski, *For the Common Defense: A Military History of the United States of America,* 339.

23. EMH to WW, 11 Jan. 1916, *PWW* 35:465; and see WW to EMH, 12 Feb. 1916, *PWW* 36:173; WW, "Address in Des Moines on Preparedness," 80; EMH to WW, 15 Feb. 1916, *PWW* 36:180n2; and see HD, 6 Mar. 1915, *PWW* 36:262.

24. EMH to Grey, 11 May 1916, *PWW* 37:21; and see WW to EMH, 12 May 1916, *PWW* 37:24; Lansing to WW, 3 May 1916, *PWW* 36:594; EMH to Grey, 11 May 1916, *PWW* 37:21; and see WW to EMH, 12 May 1916, *PWW* 37:24; EMH to WW, 9 May 1916, *PWW* 37:7; and see WW to EMH, 12 May 1916, *PWW* 37:24; EMH to WW, 17 May 1916, *PWW* 37:63; and see WW to EMH, 18 May 1916, *PWW* 37:68; EMH to Grey, 11 May 1916, *PWW* 37:21; and see WW to EMH, 12 May 1916, *PWW* 37:24.

25. EMH to WW, 14 May 1916, *PWW* 37:43; EMH to WW, 17 May 1916, *PWW* 37:63–64; and see WW to EMH, 18 May 1916, *PWW* 37:68; WW, "Address in Washington to the League to Enforce Peace," 116, and see 115–16, passim; "Colloquy with a Group of Anti-preparedness Leaders," 648, and see 645–46, passim; EMH to WW, 17 May 1916, *PWW* 37:64, and see 63–64, passim; WW to EMH, 18 May 1916, *PWW* 37:68. For WW and EMH backing down on pressing a peace bid in the summer of 1916, see also EMH to WW, 8 Apr. 1916, *PWW* 36:443–44. For Wilson's efforts on the naval bill, see Link, *Wilson,* 4:334–38.

26. WW to EMH, 7 Sept. 1915, *PWW* 34:426. See also Link, *Wilson,* 3:554–64, 645–51, 4:56–59.

27. WW, "Address in Cleveland on Preparedness," 47; WW, quoted in Ray Stannard Baker, *Woodrow Wilson: Life and Letters,* 5:77; WW, quoted in Tumulty, *Woodrow Wilson,* 234, and see 234–35, passim.

28. WW, "Address in Chicago on Preparedness," 65; WW to EBG, 20 Aug. 1915, *PWW* 34:261; WW to Grey, 6 Apr. 1916, *PWW* 36:421; HD, 30 Mar. 1916, *PWW* 36:388; WW to EBG, 20 Aug. 1915, *PWW* 34:261.

29. WJB to WW, 27 Apr. 1915, *PWW* 33:73, and see 72–73, passim; WW to WJB, 28 Apr. 1915, *PWW* 33:85; WJB to WW, 5 May 1915, *PWW* 33:106–8; and see Link, *Wilson,* 3:356–67.

30. WW, "An Address in Philadelphia to Newly Naturalized Citizens," 10 May 1915, *PWW* 33:149. On the *Lusitania,* see WW to EMH, 14 July 1915, *PWW* 33:505; Link, *Wilson,* 3:441–42, 4:90–100. On the *Ancona,* see Link, *Wilson,* 4:67–72.

31. WW, "Address to a Joint Session of Congress," 19 Apr. 1916, 510; HD, 11 Apr. 1916, *PWW* 36:460. See also Link, *Wilson,* 3:565–87, 653–81, 4:228–78.

32. For WW pressing the British, see, e.g., WW to EMH, 5 May 1915, *PWW* 33:105–6; WW to EMH, 19 July 1915, *PWW* 33:526. On the food-sub deal, see Link, *Wilson,* 3:392–95.

33. Lansing to WW, 7 Jan. 1916, *PWW* 35:448, and see 448–49, passim; Lansing to WW, 5 Feb. 1916, *PWW* 36:134, and see 133–34, passim; House, quoted in Link, *Wilson,* 4:162; 4:142–94.

34. See Chapter 3 in this volume.

35. WW to Lindley Miller Garrison, 19 Aug. 1915, *PWW* 34:248. See also Link, *Wilson,* 3:589–90, 592; Cooper, *Warrior and the Priest,* 252, 297–99.

36. See Link, *Wilson,* 3:591. WW apparently started to contemplate defense increases as early as February 1915. See Baker, *Life and Letters,* 6:8.

37. WW to EBG, 24 Aug. 1915, *PWW* 34:309. See also Chapter 2 in this volume.

38. "Memorandum by Chandler Parsons Anderson," 503–4, and see 501–4, passim;

WW, "Address in Pittsburgh on Preparedness," 29 Jan. 1916, *PWW* 36:27. See also Link, *Wilson*, 3:444; "A Press Release," 21 July 1915, *PWW* 34:3–4; EMH to WW, 14 July 1915, in Charles Seymour, ed., *Intimate Papers of Colonel House*, 1:19.

39. Count Johann Heinrich von Bernstorff to the German Foreign Office, 2 June 1915, *PWW* 33:318, and see 316–20, passim; Bernstorff to Theobald von Bethmann Hollweg, 29 May 1915, *PWW* 33:283, and see 279–84, passim; EMH to WW, 19 Nov. 1915, *PWW* 35:220, and see 220–21, passim. For House in Berlin, see Link, *Wilson*, 4:119–22.

40. WW, "Address in Pittsburgh on Preparedness," 34; WW, "Address in Cleveland on Preparedness," 43.

41. WW, "Address to a Joint Session of Congress," 19 Apr. 1916, 510; WW, "Address in St. Louis on Preparedness," 117; WW, "Address to a Joint Session of Congress," 510; WW, "Address in Chicago on Preparedness," 65.

42. WW to EMH, 24 Dec. 1915, *PWW* 35:388, 387. See also WW, "Address in Washington to the League to Enforce Peace," 113–16; WW to EMH, 29 May 1916, *PWW* 37:118. For an analysis of Wilson's stance on peace terms, see Chapter 3 in this volume.

43. WW, "Address in Pittsburgh on Preparedness," 33; WW, "Address in Chicago on Preparedness," 66, and see 66–67, passim; WW, "Address in St. Louis on Preparedness," 117; WW, "Address in Des Moines on Preparedness," 81; WW, "Address in Chicago on Preparedness," 65.

44. HD, 14 Nov. 1916, *PWW* 38:646. On the deterioration of relations with London in 1916, see Link, *Wilson*, 5:10–15, 18–24, 32–36, 65–71, 80. On liberal opinion in Britain, see, e.g., EMH to WW, 25 June 1916, *PWW* 37: 294–96; Laurence W. Martin, *Peace without Victory: Woodrow Wilson and the British Liberals*, 82–83. For Germany's conditional concession on the U-boat situation in 1916, see Lansing to WW, 6 May 1916, *PWW* 36:620–25. For Germany's October threat, see EMH to WW, 20 Oct. 1916, *PWW* 38:494–97.

45. On the retaliatory legislation and the treasury notes, see Link, *Wilson*, 5:70–71, 200–206. On WW's knowledge of Britain's financial situation, see "A News Report," 21 Nov. 1916, including *PWW* 40:19–20n1; Henry Pomeroy Davison, 25 Nov. 1916, *PWW* 40:75–76. On watering down the peace note, see Link, *Wilson*, 5:197–200, 209–19.

46. WW, "Address to the Senate," 22 Jan. 1917, 536, 534, 538, 535–36, and see 533–39, passim.

47. "Memoranda by Walter Hines Page," c. 23 Sept. 1916, *PWW* 38:246, 247, 252, 248, and see 257; Spring Rice to Grey, 4 Sept. 1916, *Letters and Friendships of Spring Rice*, 2:347, and see 346–47, passim; Spring Rice to Grey, 24 Nov. 1916, *Letters and Friendships of Spring Rice*, 2:356, and see 354–56, passim; Grey to EMH, 28 Aug. 1916, *PWW* 38:89; and see HD, 24 Sept. 1916, *PWW* 38:258; Trevelyan, quoted in Arthur S. Link, *President Wilson and His English Critics*, 15. British radicals outside of the government did cheer the speech. See Martin, *Peace without Victory*, 82–83.

48. The kaiser and Hindenburg, quoted in Link, *Wilson*, 5:234–35; Zimmermann, quoted in Fritz Fischer, *Germany's Aims in the First World War*, 299–300. See also Link, *Wilson*, 5:210–13, 233–35, 255; Fischer, *Germany's Aims*, 290–300, 303–4; Karl E. Birnbaum, *Peace Moves and U-boat Warfare: A Study of Imperial Germany's Policy towards the United States, April 18, 1916–January 9, 1917*, 102–5, 124, 130–34, 253–54, 268–69.

49. Holtzendorff and Hipper, quoted in Holger H. Herwig, *Politics of Frustration: The United States in German Naval Planning, 1889–1941*, 122, 124. See also Link, *Wilson*, 5:239–47; Fischer, *Germany's Aims*, 308, Birnbaum, *Peace Moves and U-boat Warfare*, 315–27, 337.

50. HD, 1 Feb. 1917, *PWW* 41:87; "A Memorandum by Louis Paul Lochner," 1 Feb. 1917, *PWW* 41:89; HD, 1 Feb. 1917, *PWW* 41:87.

51. Page to WW, 20 Jan. 1917, *PWW* 40:532.

52. Bernstorff to EMH, 27 July 1915, in Seymour, *Intimate Papers*, 1:27.

53. Mearsheimer, *Tragedy of Great Power Politics*, 158, and see 155–62, passim.

54. WW, "Address to the Senate," 534.

55. Lansing to WW, 6 May 1916, *PWW* 36:623. Historians after the war calculated that about 500,000 German civilians died as a result of the blockade. See Robert W. Tucker, *Woodrow Wilson and the Great War*, 225–26n7.

56. "Colloquy with Members of the American Neutral Conference," 114, and see 114–15, passim.

57. Coogan argues that Wilsonian mediation might have worked if WW had maintained America's neutral rights against both groups of belligerents. See Coogan, *End of Neutrality*, 256.

58. WW, "Address in Washington to the League to Enforce Peace," 114, 116.

6. Debating Wilsonianism

1. "Pacifism vs. Passivism," 7; *NR* on the arms embargo, quoted in Link, *Wilson*, 3:167; "Next Step," 323; editorial, *NR* 5 (29 Jan. 1916): 316. On a trade embargo, see "Our Relations with Great Britain," *NR* 5 (22 Jan. 1916): 290–91. On a cease-fire, see, e.g., "War at Any Price," 84–85. On submarines, see, e.g., "Submarines as Commerce Destroyers," *NR* 6 (4 Mar. 1916): 116–17. On Britain's maritime system, see "War as We See It," 102.

2. "The War Zone," *NR* 2 (13 Feb. 1915): 35; "The Crisis," *NR* 3 (15 May 1915): 25; "Next Step," 322, and see 322–23, passim.

3. "Next Step," 323; "Hostages to Peace," *NR* 3 (15 May 1915): 29; "If We Enter the War," 306, and 305–6, passim.

4. "Next Step," 323; "Our Relations with Great Britain," 292. See also "Aggressive Pacifism," 263–65.

5. "Appeal to the President," 304, and see 303–5, passim. See also Norman Angell, "A New Kind of War," *NR* 3 (31 July 1915): 327–29.

6. "Appeal to the President," 305; Croly, "Meaning of It," 11.

7. "Preparedness—A Trojan Horse," *NR* 5 (6 Nov. 1915): 6.

8. Editorial, *NR* 4 (28 Aug. 1915): 83; editorial, *NR* 6 (5 Feb. 1916): 1.

9. "Our Relations with Great Britain," 292.

10. "Mr. Wilson's Great Utterance," 102–3; "Note as Americanism," 230, and see 228–31, passim.

11. "Mr. Wilson's Great Utterance," 103–4; "Beneath the Outcry," *NR* 9 (30 Dec. 1916): 232, and see 231–32, passim.

12. See Chapters 2 and 3 in this volume.

13. *TMdoc*, 1:6, 180–81, 6.

14. WHT to WW, 10 May 1915, *PWW* 33:150, and see 150–51, passim; WHT, in *NYT*, 3 Sept. 1915, 3; WHT, quoted in Pringle, *Taft*, 2:881, and see 873–79, 927; WHT to WW, 10 May 1915, *PWW* 33:150. For LEP concern about forming too close a relationship with the Allies, see the exchange over a proposed WHT trip to London in late 1916 in *TMdoc*, 1:207–8, 215–17, 220–21, 224–26, 231.

15. TR, "Utopia or Hell," 14–15. See also TR, *NYT*, 8 Nov. 1914, 5:1. See also Root, in Bacon and Scott, eds., *International Subjects*, 441–47; Jessup, *Elihu Root*, 2:321–22; Robert

Bacon, *NSL*, 64; HCL to TR, 7 Dec. 1914, *HCL-TR*, 2:448; HCL to TR, 15 Jan. 1915, *HCL-TR*, 2:451; Garraty, *Henry Cabot Lodge*, 307; Widenor, *Henry Cabot Lodge*, 187, 205–6. Cooper inaccurately suggests that Lodge did not agree with TR's charges against Wilson on the Hague issue. See Cooper, *Warrior and the Priest*, 283.

16. TR, *NYT*, 8 Nov. 1914, 5:1; TR, "Utopia or Hell," 14–15; Root, in Bacon and Scott, eds., *International Subjects*, 444, and see 441–44, passim; TR, *NYT*, 29 Nov. 1914, 5:5; TR to Andrew Dickson White, 2 Nov. 1914, *TRLET* 8:828.

17. TR to James Bryce, 31 Mar. 1915, *TRLET* 8:914, and see 914–17, passim; TR to John St. Loe Strachey, 22 Feb. 1915, *TRLET* 8:898–99; TR to Cecil Arthur Spring Rice, 3 Oct. 1914, *TRLET* 8:822, and see 821–22, passim; TR to Miles Poindexter, 30 Jan. 1915, *TRLET* 8:886–87; TR to Spring Rice, 5 Feb. 1915, *TRLET* 8:889, and see 888–89, passim. On the ship purchase bill, see HCL, quoted in Garraty, *Henry Cabot Lodge*, 307; TR to James Bryce, 31 Mar. 1915, *TRLET* 8:914–15; HCL to TR, 15 Jan. 1915, *HCL-TR*, 2:451–52; Root, in Bacon and Scott, eds., *International Subjects*, 337–38. See also Widenor, *Henry Cabot Lodge*, 205–7; Leopold, *Elihu Root*, 104; Jessup, *Elihu Root*, 2:319–20, 322.

18. TR, *NYT*, 29 Nov. 1914, 5:5; HCL to TR, 15 Jan. 1915, *HCL-TR*, 2:451.

19. Root, in Bacon and Scott, eds., *International Subjects*, 438, and see 436–40, passim; TR, *Fear God*, 124, and see 123–35, passim; Root, in Bacon and Scott, eds., *International Subjects*, 440; TR in *NYT*, 11 May 1916, 5; Root, in Bacon and Scott, eds., *International Subjects*, 446.

20. TR, *Fear God*, 85; Root, in Bacon and Scott, eds., *International Subjects*, 447, and see 435–36; TR to Guy Emerson, 11 May 1916, *TRLET* 8:1041; TR, *Fear God*, 189, and see 179–80, 188–89; TR to HCL, 26 Jan. 1916, *TRLET* 8:1005, and 1005–6, passim.

21. TR in *NYT*, 29 Jan. 1917, 6; TR in *NYT*, 23 Jan. 1917, 3. See also HCL, *War Addresses*, 202, 205, 221–25, 229–30, 251–53, 279; Root, in Bacon and Scott, eds., *United States and the War*, 25–26.

22. TR, *Fear God*, iii, and see 83–85, and ibid., 355; Root, in Bacon and Scott, eds., *International Subjects*, 440, and see 437–40, passim; and Jessup, *Elihu Root*, 2:323. On Belgium, see the following discussion and see also TR to Spring Rice, 3 Oct. 1914, *TRLET* 8:821; TR, *NYT*, 8 Nov. 1914, 5:1. On the submarine crisis, see Widenor, *Henry Cabot Lodge*, 212–15; TR to Frederick Wallingford Whitridge, 6 Apr. 1915, *TRLET* 8:920; HCL to TR, 20 Dec. 1915, *HCL-TR*, 2:468–69.

23. HCL to TR, 5 July 1916, *HCL-TR*, 2:490. See also TR to Bernhard Dernburg, 4 Dec. 1914, *TRLET* 8:857.

24. See also Widenor, *Henry Cabot Lodge*, 195, for a similar interpretation.

25. TR to Presley Marion Rixey, 22 Feb. 1915, *TRLET* 8:903; TR to Arthur Hamilton Lee, 2 Sept. 1915, *TRLET* 8:968–70; TR to Lee, 17 June 1915, *TRLET* 8:937; TR, *NYT*, 4 Oct. 1914, 4:1. See also TR to Lee, 10 Nov. 1916, *TRLET* 8:1124; TR to Lee, 2 Sept. 1915, *TRLET* 8:966–67.

26. See Chapters 2 and 3 in this volume.

27. WJB, "Wasting Time," 5 (emphasis in original). See also Alice Hamilton, "The Attitude of Social Workers toward the War," *Survey* 36 (17 June 1916): 308.

28. WJB to WW, 10 Aug. 1914, *PWW* 30:372. See also Link, *Wilson*, 3:62–64.

29. WJB to William J. Stone, 20 Jan. 1915, *FRUS 1914 Supplement*, xii. See also Link, *Wilson*, 3:62. This interpretation is taken from Link, *Wilson*, 3:132–36.

30. See "Mr. Bryan on War Loans," *Commoner* 15 (Sept. 1915): 4.

31. WJB to WW, 29 Aug. 1914, *PWW* 30:459; Lansing to WJB, 9 Jan. 1915, *FRUS Lansing Papers,* 1:190, and see 189–90, passim; Lansing to WJB, 23 Jan. 1915, *FRUS Lansing Papers,* 1:194, and see 192–94, passim; WJB to WW, 29 Aug. 1914, *PWW* 30:459, and see 459–60, passim.

32. WJB to Stone, 20 Jan. 1915, *FRUS 1914 Supplement,* x; WJB to WW, 6 Jan. 1915, *PWW* 32:24 (emphasis in original). See also "Public Circular," *FRUS 1914 Supplement,* 573–74; Link, *Wilson,* 3:60–61; WJB to WW, 24 Dec. 1914, *PWW* 31:521–22. WJB also thought that arms embargos encouraged arms racing between states. See Lansing to WW, 6 Aug. 1915, *PWW* 34:114; Lansing to WW, 5 Aug. 1915, *PWW* 34:95–96.

33. "Force Only a Last Resort," *Commoner* 15 (July 1915): 2; WJB to WW, 24 Dec. 1914, *PWW* 31:521. See also Coogan, *End of Neutrality,* 173, 184–85, 204; Link, *Wilson,* 3:107.

34. WJB to Stone, 20 Jan. 1915, *FRUS 1914 Supplement,* viii; WJB to WW, 19 Jan. 1915, *PWW* 32:91.

35. WJB to WW, 15 Feb. 1915, *PWW* 32:236; WJB to WW, 29 Mar. 1915, *PWW* 32:454. On WJB's concern about the war getting more dangerous and his view of the blockade, see WJB to WW, 15 Feb. 1915, *PWW* 32:235.

36. WJB to WW, 12 May 1915, *PWW* 33:166; WJB to WW, 7 June 1915, *PWW* 33:354; WJB, quoted in Link, *Wilson,* 3:411; WJB to WW, 12 May 1915, *PWW* 33:166.

37. "Real Issue," 3.

38. See WJB to WW, 12 May 1915, *PWW* 33:166; WJB to WW, 12 May 1915, *PWW* 33:173; WJB to WW, 3 June 1915, *PWW* 33:321–25; WJB to WW, 5 June 1915, *PWW* 33:342; WJB to WW, 7 June 1915, *PWW* 33:353–55; "Two Points of Difference," *Commoner* 15 (June 1915): 2; Link, *Wilson,* 3:414.

39. "War in Europe and Its Lessons for Us," 14, and see 12–16, passim. See also WJB to WW, 9 June 1915, *PWW* 33:375–76; Link, *Wilson,* 3:410–25; "Reply to Roosevelt's Interview," *Commoner* 15 (Sept. 1915): 3.

40. WJB to WW, 12 May 1915, *PWW* 33:166; WJB to WW, 14 May 1915, *PWW* 33:192; WJB to WW, 3 June 1915, *PWW* 33:323 (emphasis in original).

41. WJB to WW, 1 May 1915, *PWW* 33:91; "National Honor," *Commoner* 15 (July 1915): 10; WJB to WW, 2 June 1915, *PWW* 33:310; WJB to WW, 3 June 1915, *PWW* 33:325, and see 321–25, passim. See also WJB to WW, 5 June 1915, *PWW* 33:342.

42. RLF, "Neutrality," *LFM* 7 (Sept. 1915): 1. See also RLF, "Duty of Neutral Nations," 8; Robert David Johnson, *The Peace Progressives and American Foreign Relations,* 56–68; Edward Devine, "America and Peace: 1915," *Survey* 33 (2 Jan. 1915): 387–88; McKillen, *Chicago Labor,* 26–32, and 20–54, passim; "Neutrality and War Supplies," *Public* 18 (30 July 1915): 733; Danziger, "Bryan's Adherence to Principle," *Public* 18 (18 June 1915): 585; Stoughton Cooley, "Peace, Not War," *Public* 18 (30 July 1915): 729; Danziger, "Two Wrongs Don't Make a Right," *Public* 19 (28 Apr. 1916): 385; Crystal Eastman Benedict, "A Platform of Real Preparedness," *Survey* 35 (13 Nov. 1915): 160–61; and John A. Thompson, *Reformers and War: American Progressive Publicists and the First World War,* 129–32.

43. "The Week," *TN* 100 (1 Apr. 1915): 344; "The Outlaw German Government," *TN* 100 (13 May 1915): 527; "Larger Effects," 553; "Not Two Governments, but Two Moralities," *TN* 100 (10 June 1915): 641. See also "Misrepresented Neutrality," *TN* 100 (4 Mar. 1915): 238–39; "The Question of a Loan to Europe," *TN* 101 (16 Sept. 1915): 349–50; "England's False Step," *TN* 100 (4 Mar. 1915): 238; "At Last a Blockade," *TN* 100 (25 Mar. 1915): 320; "The Week," *TN* 100 (8 Apr. 1915): 372; "Neutral Rights at Sea," *TN* 101 (23 Sept. 1915): 373. OGV and Paul

Kellogg also tended to support Wilson's diplomacy while urging him to take a tougher line against Britain in order to maintain neutrality. See OGV to WW, 14 May 1915, *PWW* 33:201; OGV, "A Tried Administration," *TN* 101 (12 Aug. 1915): 197–98; Michael Wreszin, *Oswald Garrison Villard: Pacifist at War,* 48, 50–51; Kellogg, "Bill of Particulars," sec. 2, 1.

44. "The President and Preparedness," *TN* 101 (21 Oct. 1915): 485; "The 'Preparedness' Flurry," *TN* 99 (3 Dec. 1914): 647; Crystal Eastman Benedict, "Correspondence," *NR* 3 (24 July 1915): 313. See also J. H. Dillard, "The Veil of Preparation," *Public* 18 (5 Nov. 1915): 1071; Addams and others to WW, 29 Oct. 1915, *PWW* 35:134–35.

45. Cooley, "An Impregnable Nation," *Public* 19 (10 Nov. 1916): 1063, and see 1062–63, passim; Milton Bronner, "Preparedness for Peace Means Preparedness for War," *LFM* 8 (Jan. 1916): 10; Pinchot, "Preparedness," 112, and see 110–12, passim.

46. WPP, quoted in Degen, *History of the Woman's Peace Party,* 46–47; Addams, "A Conference of Neutrals," *Survey* 35 (22 Jan. 1916): 495; WPP, quoted in Degen, *History of the Woman's Peace Party,* 46; "Colloquy with Members of the American Neutral Conference," 110; "Two Memoranda by Louis Paul Lochner," 12 Nov. 1915, *PWW* 35:197; "Colloquy with Members of the American Neutral Conference," 38:109; and see Degen, *History of the Woman's Peace Party,* 47. See also WJB to WW, 17 Dec. 1914, *PWW* 31:480–81; RLF, "Duty of Neutral Nations," 7. Kellogg wanted to time any mediation effort to Allied military gains. See Thompson, *Reformers and War,* 165.

47. See "Let the Jingoes Die First," *Commoner* 15 (Aug. 1915): 5; "Consult the People!" 1; Bolt, *Ballots before Bullets,* 5–27.

48. Link, *Wilson,* 2:149, 155, and see 153–55, passim.

49. WJB, "Courage, Physical or Moral," *Commoner* 15 (Dec. 1915): 6; "The Words of the Preacher," *TN* 102 (11 May 1916): 518–19.

50. "The Real Issue," *Commoner* 15 (June 1915): 3; Cooley, "President Wilson's Preparation Program," *Public* 18 (17 Dec. 1915): 1211; Wald, in *NYT,* 16 May 1916, 5; Eastman, quoted in Knock, *To End All Wars,* 66, and see 66–67, passim. Most pacifists supported Wilson in the 1916 election. See ibid., 93–95; Paolo E. Coletta, *William Jennings Bryan,* 3:38–42.

51. WW, "Address to the Senate," 22 Jan. 1917, 534; Lillian D. Wald and others to WW, 24 Jan. 1917, *PWW* 41:7–8; WJB to WW, 26 Jan. 1917, *PWW* 41:29.

7. Wilson at War

1. WW, "An Address to a Joint Session of Congress," 2 Apr. 1917, *PWW* 41:521; WW, "An Address to a Joint Session of Congress," 11 Nov. 1918, *PWW* 53:41.

2. WW comments, quoted in Arthur S. Link, "That Cobb Interview," 10–11.

3. WW, "An Address to a Joint Session of Congress," 26 Feb. 1917, *PWW* 41:285; WW, quoted in Link, "That Cobb Interview," 8. My interpretation here is based on my reading of the primary sources in *PWW* 41:71–527, passim; and on Link, *Wilson,* 5:290–531; Link, "That Cobb Interview," 8–10.

4. WW, "Address to a Joint Session of Congress," 2 Apr. 1917, 525; WW, quoted in Link, "That Cobb Interview," 8; WW, "Address to a Joint Session of Congress," 2 Apr. 1917, 525–26.

5. Page to WW, 9 Mar. 1917, *PWW* 41:373; "A News Report," c. 28 Feb. 1917, *PWW* 41:305n3. See also Lansing to WW, 13 Feb. 1917, *PWW* 41:213–14. On the Allies' gaining the upper hand

in the war, see Lippmann to WW, 31 Jan. 1917, *PWW* 41:83; WW to Lansing (Penfield), 28 Feb. 1917, *PWW* 41:300–301; Jusserand to Aristide Briand, 3 Mar. 1917, *PWW* 41:317; Lansing to WW (Harper), 16 Mar. 1917, *PWW* 41:416–17; Lansing to WW, 19 Mar. 1917, *PWW* 41:426; EMH to WW, 19 Mar. 1917, *PWW* 41:429. Daniel Smith asserts that by 1917 Wilson "feared that a German victory was probable." He provides no evidence for this assertion, however, and the documents cited here contradict it. See Smith, *Great Departure,* 82.

6. See EMH to WW, 8 Feb. 1917, *PWW* 41:165–67; WW, "Address to a Joint Session of Congress," 26 Feb. 1917, 283–87.

7. WW, "Address to a Joint Session of Congress," 2 Apr. 1917, 521. See also WW, "Address to a Joint Session of Congress," 26 Feb. 1917, 283–87; Lansing to WW, 9 Mar. 1917 (Daniels), *PWW* 41:371–72; Daniels diary, 12 Mar. 1917, *PWW* 41:395; "A Memorandum by Josephus Daniels," 13 Mar. 1917, *PWW* 41:395–98; Daniels diary, 20 Mar. 1917, *PWW* 41:444–45.

8. WW, "Address to a Joint Session of Congress," 2 Apr. 1917, 526; Polk to Jusserand, 3 Aug. 1917, *PWW* 43:360; Drummond to Balfour, 15 Nov. 1917, *PWW* 45:68; "Memorandum by Louis Paul Lochner," 90. See also WW to EMH, 22 Mar. 1918, *PWW* 47:105; "A Memorandum by WHT," c. 29 Mar. 1918, *PWW* 47:200–201; Geddes to Lloyd George, 13 Oct. 1918, *PWW* 51:327; HD, 15 Aug. 1918, *PWW* 49:266.

9. WW to EMH, 22 Mar. 1918, *PWW* 47:105; WW to EMH, 7 Sept. 1917, PWW 49:467–71, passim. See also HD, 15 Aug. 1917, *PWW* 49:265–66.

10. Polk to Jusserand, 3 Aug. 1917, *PWW* 43:360; WW to EMH, 7 Sept. 1917, *PWW* 49:469; "A Translation of a Memorandum by William Emmanuel Rappard," 1 Nov. 1917, *PWW* 44:488.

11. Wiseman to Reading, 16 Aug. 1918, *PWW* 49:274; WW, "An Address in the Metropolitan Opera House," 27 Sept. 1918, *PWW* 51:129; WW, "Second Inaugural Address," 5 Mar. 1917, *PWW* 41:334.

12. WW, "A Flag Day Address," 14 June 1917, *PWW* 42:502–4. See also WW, "An Address in Buffalo to the American Federation of Labor," 12 Nov. 1917, *PWW* 45:13; WW, "An Address," 6 Apr. 1918, *PWW* 47:269–70; WW, "A Message to a Farmers' Conference," 31 Jan. 1918, *PWW* 46:174–75.

13. WW, "To the Provisional Government of Russia," 22 May 1917, *PWW* 42:366; WW, "An Address to a Joint Session of Congress," 8 Jan. 1918, *PWW* 45:537–38. For WW's early expression of his new peace terms, see HD, 28 Apr. 1917, *PWW* 42:155–57; Balfour to Cecil, 23 May 1917, *PWW* 42:385; HD, 30 Apr. 1917, *PWW* 42:171–72.

14. HD, 13 Oct. 1917, *PWW* 44:379; WW, "Annual Message on the State of the Union," 4 Dec. 1917, *PWW* 45:200; Jusserand to the Foreign Ministry, 24 Apr. 1917, *PWW* 42:128–29; Baron Moncheur to Baron Charles de Broqueville, 14 Aug. 1917, *PWW* 43:468; "A Memorandum by Franklin Knight Lane," 1 Nov. 1918, *PWW* 51:548. On WW's pre–March 1918 policy, see Victor S. Mamatey, *The United States and East Central Europe, 1914–1918: A Study in Wilsonian Diplomacy and Propaganda,* 37–39, 45–68, 163, 175–81, 213–14, 219–32; "A Memorandum by Sidney Edward Mezes, David Hunter Miller, and Walter Lippmann," 4 Jan. 1918, *PWW* 45:463. On the policy after March 1918, see Wiseman to Drummond, 30 May 1918, *PWW* 48:205–6; WW to Lansing, 26 June 1918, *PWW* 48:435–37; Mamatey, *United States and East Central Europe,* 63–64, 141–43, 233–39, 252–72. On German-Austrian union, see Sir Geddes to George, 13 Oct. 1918, *PWW* 51:326; WW, "A Draft of a Note to the Austro-Hungarian Government," c. 19 Oct. 1918, *PWW* 51:383; EMH to WW, 29 Oct.

1918, *PWW* 51:502; WW to EMH, 30 Oct. 1918, PWW 51:511; Mamatey, *United States and East Central Europe,* 318–45. Mamatey, 351, errs in stating that WW never thought about a German-Austrian union.

15. Baron Moncheur to Baron Charles de Broqueville, 14 Aug. 1917, *PWW* 43:468, and see 468–69, passim. See also Lansing to WW, 13 Aug. 1917, *PWW* 43:445; WW to Lansing, 14 Aug. 1917, *PWW* 43:460; Kent to WW, 16 Aug. 1917, *PWW* 43:496; Daniels diary, 4 Dec. 1917, *PWW* 45:207; HD, 9 Jan. 1918, *PWW* 45:552–53; "A Memorandum by Sir William Wiseman," 23 Jan. 1918, *PWW* 46:87.

16. WW, "Address to a Joint Session of Congress," 8 Jan. 1918, 536, and see 537. See also HD, 9 Jan. 1918, *PWW* 45:552–53.

17. Balfour to WW, 18 May 1917, *PWW* 42:341, and see 341–42, passim. See also WW to Balfour, 19 May 1917, *PWW* 42:346; "Memorandum by Mezes, Miller, and Lippmann," 469, 473–74. On Prussia acting unjustly, see Jusserand to Pichon, 5 Dec. 1917, *PWW* 45:220. After January, Wilson did once waver on his view that Alsace-Lorraine should go back to France. See "Memorandum by WHT," 202.

18. WW, "Address to a Joint Session of Congress," 2 Apr. 1917, 521, and 521–22, passim; WW, "Flag Day Address," 499.

19. WW, "Address to a Joint Session of Congress," 2 Apr. 1917, 523; WW, "Annual Message on the State of the Union," 4 Dec. 1917, 198, and see 197–98, passim; WW, "Address in Buffalo to the American Federation of Labor," 13–14.

20. WW, "Flag Day Address," 502, and 502–3, passim; WW, "Annual Message on the State of the Union," 4 Dec. 1917, 196; Lansing to WW (Grew), 12 Nov. 1917, *PWW* 45:37, 36, and see 30–37, passim. On the peace resolution, see Klaus Epstein, *Matthias Erzberger and the Dilemma of German Democracy,* 182–213; David Stevenson, *The First World War and International Politics,* 149, 153–54. On Hertling's selection and his policies, see Epstein, *Matthias Erzberger,* 214–31; Martin Kitchen, *The Silent Dictatorship: The Politics of the German High Command under Hindenburg and Ludendorff, 1916–1918,* 149–50; Fischer, *Germany's Aims,* 477–88. For other alarming reports about the Reichstag majority, see WW to Lansing (Sosnowski), 21 Aug. 1917, *PWW* 44:3–4; Gompers to WW, 9 Feb. 1918, *PWW* 46:312; and see WW to Lansing, 13 Feb. 1918, *PWW* 46:334.

21. Brest-Litovsk, quoted in Stevenson, *First World War,* 201, and see 203–5, passim; Kitchen, *Silent Dictatorship,* 197, and see 196–99, passim.

22. Gompers to WW, 9 Feb. 1918, *PWW* 46:312; and see WW to Lansing, 13 Feb. 1918, *PWW* 46:334; Erzberger, quoted in Epstein, *Matthias Erzberger,* 234. See also ibid., 235; A. J. Ryder, *The German Revolution of 1918: A Study of German Socialism in War and Revolt,* 113–14, 116–18; Fischer, *Germany's Aims,* 506; Kitchen, *Silent Dictatorship,* 180–81, 199.

23. WW, "Remarks to Foreign Correspondents," 8 Apr. 1918, *PWW* 47:288; Wiseman to Drummond, 30 May 1918, *PWW* 48:206; Wiseman to Arthur Cecil Murray, 30 Aug. 1918, *PWW* 49:399. For the State Department memo, see Auchincloss to WW (Bullitt), 7 Mar. 1918, *PWW* 46: 567–69. Manfred Boemeke sees Brest-Litovsk as a turning point in WW's view of the German people, but he misses the doubts about Germany's character that WW had from April 1917 onward, and he ignores WW's broader reservations about the idea of peaceful democracies. See Boemeke, "Woodrow Wilson's Image of Germany, the War-Guilt Question, and the Treaty of Versailles," in Boemeke, Feldman, and Glaser, eds., *The Treaty of Versailles: A Reassessment after Seventy-Five Years,* 603–14.

24. WW, "Annual Message on the State of the Union," 4 Dec. 1917, 197; WW, "Flag Day

Address," 502. See also WW, "To the Provisional Government of Russia," 365–67; WW to Page, 27 Aug. 1917, *PWW* 44:57–59.

25. Baron Moncheur to Baron Charles de Broqueville, 14 Aug. 1917, *PWW* 43:467, and see 467–68, passim. On the "psychological basis" for peace, see Chapter 3 in this volume.

26. WW, "Address to a Joint Session of Congress," 2 Apr. 1917, 524; WW, "Address to a Joint Session of Congress," 8 Jan. 1918, 539; WW to Page, 27 Aug. 1917, *PWW* 44:58–59. See also WW, "Annual Message on the State of the Union," 4 Dec. 1917, 198.

27. WW, "Annual Message on the State of the Union," 4 Dec. 1917, 198.

28. Wiseman, "Notes on Interview with the President," 1 Apr. 1918, reprinted in W. B. Fowler, *British–American Relations, 1917–1918: The Role of Sir William Wiseman,* 270; WW, "Address," 269; WW, "Address in the Metropolitan Opera House," 129; WW, "Remarks to Foreign Correspondents," 287.

29. WW, "Address in the Metropolitan Opera House," 129; WW to St. Loe Strachey, 5 Apr. 1918, *PWW* 47:259; Wiseman to Reading, 16 Aug. 1918, *PWW* 49:274.

30. Wiseman to Murray, 14 Sept. 1918, *PWW* 51:8; WW, "Address in the Metropolitan Opera House," 130.

31. Wiseman to Murray, 30 Aug. 1918, *PWW* 49:399. Klaus Schwabe suggests this point as well, in a different context. See Schwabe, *Woodrow Wilson, Revolutionary Germany, and Peacemaking,* 113.

32. WW, "Address to a Joint Session of Congress," 8 Jan. 1918, 538; WW, "Remarks to Confederate Veterans in Washington," 5 June 1917, *PWW* 42:452; WW, "Address to a Joint Session of Congress," 2 Apr. 1917, 525; WW, "Second Inaugural Address," 334; WW, "Annual Message on the State of the Union," 4 Dec. 1917, 196.

33. Wiseman to Drummond, 30 May 1918, *PWW* 48:206; Sharp to Cambon, 7 Aug. 1917, *PWW* 43:388; Wiseman to Murray, 14 Sept. 1918, *PWW* 51:8; Jusserand to the Foreign Ministry, 7 Mar. 1917, *PWW* 41:356; WW to EMH, 21 July 1918, *PWW* 43:238 (emphasis in original).

34. WW to Page, 27 Aug. 1917, *PWW* 44:58; WW, "Annual Message on the State of the Union," 4 Dec. 1917, 198; Jusserand to the Foreign Ministry, 3 May 1917, *PWW* 42:212; Spring Rice to Balfour, 4 Jan. 1918, *PWW* 45:456; WW, "An Address at Mount Vernon," 4 July 1918, *PWW* 48:517; WW, "Address in the Metropolitan Opera House," 129, and see 127–32, passim.

35. See Lansing to WW, 17 May 1917, *PWW* 42:318; Lansing to WW, 25 Jan. 1918, *PWW* 46:96–97.

36. WW, "Address to a Joint Session of Congress," 8 Jan. 1918, 536. On the Allied treaties, see Spring Rice to Lloyd George, 26 Apr. 1917, *PWW* 42:140–41. On WW's inter-Allied conferences and the Supreme War Council, see David F. Trask, *The United States in the Supreme War Council: American War Aims and Inter-Allied Strategy, 1917–1918,* 20–37; Daniel R. Beaver, *Newton D. Baker and the American War Effort, 1917–1919,* 112–14. On the Allied peoples, see WW, "Address in the Metropolitan Opera House," 132. On avoiding the term "allies," see, e.g., WW to Herbert Clark Hoover, 10 Dec. 1917, *PWW* 45:256–57.

37. Baker to WW (Bliss), 27 May 1917, *PWW* 42:409–10 (emphasis in original); Baker to John Joseph Pershing, 26 May 1917, *PWW* 42:405. This paragraph relies on the relevant documents in *PWW* and on David R. Woodward, *Trial By Friendship: Anglo-American Relations, 1917–1918,* 37, 43, 50, 55, 58–59, 115–39, 151–69, 190–92, 198–99; Beaver, *Newton D. Baker,* 25–30, 40–47, 110–50, 156–59, 171–78.

38. WW to EMH, 21 July 1917, *PWW* 43:238; Daniels diary, 12 Oct. 1917, *PWW* 44:371.

39. Page to WW, 28 June 1917, *PWW* 43:34; "Memorandum by Sir William Wiseman," 174, and see 173–74, passim. See also Fowler, *British–American Relations,* 36–59; David F. Trask, *Anglo-American Naval Relations, 1917–1918: Captains and Cabinets,* 104–24; Woodward, *Trial By Friendship,* 62–64; Kennedy, *Over Here,* 326–31.

40. WW to Tumulty, c. 30 July 1917, *PWW* 43:318; WW, "Address to a Joint Session of Congress," 8 Jan. 1918, 535, and see 537–38; "Memorandum by Sir William Wiseman," 87.

41. WW to Lansing, 29 Jan. 1918, *PWW* 46:149; "Memorandum by John Howard Whitehouse," 14 Apr. 1917, *PWW* 42:66; WW to Page, 27 Aug. 1917, *PWW* 44:59; WW, "An Address to a Joint Session of Congress," 11 Feb. 1918, *PWW* 46:323.

42. My interpretation of Wilson's Russian policy during the war is based on documents in *PWW* 42–51 and George F. Kennan, *Soviet–American Relations, 1917–1920,* vol. 1, *Russia Leaves the War* and *Soviet–American Relations, 1917–1920,* vol. 2, *Decision to Intervene;* David S. Fogelsong, *America's Secret War against Bolshevism: U.S. Intervention in the Russian Civil War, 1917–1920;* Mamatey, *United States and East Central Europe;* Betty Miller Unterberger, "Woodrow Wilson and the Bolsheviks: The 'Acid Test' of Soviet–American Relations"; Eugene P. Trani, "Woodrow Wilson and the Decision to Intervene in Russia: A Reconsideration"; John W. Long, "American Intervention in Russia: The North Russian Expedition, 1918–1919." Overall, my views closely accord with Kennan's and Mamatey's in stressing WW's anti-German orientation in Russia. In contrast to these authors, and the others listed previously, Fogelsong focuses more on WW's ideological animus toward the Bolsheviks.

43. WW to Lamont, 31 Jan. 1918, *PWW* 46:179. See also Fogelsong, *America's Secret War,* 56–67, 76–114, 121–22, 188–202, 205–8; Kennan, *Russia Leaves the War,* 160–77; and *Decision to Intervene,* 31–57, 245–76. Unterberger especially stresses Wilson's commitment to the principle of noninterference in Russian political affairs. Trani stresses Wilson's desire to maintain good relations with the Allies, although he does not pay much attention to the fact that the brigading issue was straining U.S.–Allied ties at the time of Wilson's intervention decision. See Unterberger, "Woodrow Wilson and the Bolsheviks"; and Trani, "Woodrow Wilson and the Decision to Intervene in Russia."

44. Lansing to WW (Knight), 28 June 1918, *PWW* 48:459, and see 458–60, passim; Reading to WW, 3 July 1918, *PWW* 48:499, and see 496–501, passim; "A Memorandum by Robert Lansing," 6 July 1918, *PWW* 48:543, and see 542–43, passim; WW to Polk, 17 July 1918, *PWW* 48:641, and see 639–43, passim. See also Kennan, *Decision to Intervene,* passim; Fogelsong, *America's Secret War,* 143–87; Mamatey, *United States and East Central Europe,* 218–19, 275–92.

45. WW to Lansing, 18 Sept. 1918, *PWW* 51:50; Lansing to Barclay, 27 Sept. 1918, *PWW* 51:141, and 140–41, passim. See also Kennan, *Decision to Intervene,* 379; Fogelsong, *America's Secret War,* 168–73, 213–19.

46. Lansing to WW, 9 June 1917, *PWW* 42:470; and see Lansing to Smith, 12 June 1917, *PWW* 42:490–91; Lowry to WW, 12 June 1917, *PWW* 42:486; and see WW to Lowry, 13 June 1917, *PWW* 42:497; WW, "Annual Message on the State of the Union," 4 Dec. 1917, 196. On the assassination plot, see EMH to WW, 5 Feb. 1917, *PWW* 41:127–28.

47. Croly to WW, 19 Oct. 1917, *PWW* 44:410, and see 408–10, passim. See also House to WW (Lippmann), 17 Oct. 1917, *PWW* 44:393–94; WW to Tumulty, 18 Dec. 1917, *PWW* 45:320; Kent to WW, 28 Sept. 1918, *PWW* 51:147–48; and WW to Kent, 30 Sept. 1918, *PWW* 51:161.

48. Croly to WW, 19 Oct. 1917, *PWW* 44:409; Burleson to WW, 30 Oct. 1918, *PWW*

51:521. See also WW to Tumulty, 18 Dec. 1917, *PWW* 45:320; WW to Burleson, 29 Oct. 1918, *PWW* 51:483; George P. West, "A Talk with Mr. Burleson," *Public* 20 (12 Oct. 1917): 986. On the administration's actions against dissenters and aliens, see Kennedy, *Over Here*, 45–92.

49. WW, "Address to a Joint Session of Congress," 2 Apr. 1917, 522. See also Edward M. Coffman, *The War to End All Wars: The American Military Experience in World War I*, 24–29; Kennedy, *Over Here*, 93–154, 252–56; Robert H. Ferrell, *Woodrow Wilson and World War I, 1917–1921*, 99–102, 189.

50. "A Draft of a Proclamation," c. 1 May 1917, *PWW* 42:181, and see 180–82, passim; WW to Elizabeth Merrill Bass, 4 May 1917, *PWW* 42:214; WW to Gompers, 31 Aug. 1918, *PWW* 44:101.

51. WW, "A Statement on the Lever Bill," 19 May 1917, *PWW* 42:345. On this interpretation of the Sedition Act and on the APL, see O'Brian to Gregory, 18 Apr. 1918, *PWW* 47:363–65; WW to Lee Slater Overman, 20 Apr. 1918, *PWW* 47:381; Kennedy, *Over Here*, 80–81; Joan M. Jensen, *The Price of Vigilance*, 39–43. On voluntarism, see Kennedy, *Over Here*, 93–143, 252–56.

52. WW to Catt, 13 June 1918, *PWW* 48:303; WW, "An Address to the Senate," 30 Sept. 1918, *PWW* 51:159, 158.

53. WW, "Address at Arlington Cemetery on Memorial Day," 30 May 1917, *PWW* 42:423; WW, "Address to a Joint Session of Congress," 2 Apr. 1917, 525; WW, "Address at Arlington Cemetery," 423.

54. Friedrich Oederlin to WW, 6 Oct. 1918, *PWW* 51:253.

55. Lansing to WW (Herron), 5 Oct. 1918, *PWW* 51:243; Bullitt, quoted in Schwabe, *Woodrow Wilson*, 41; HD, 9 Oct. 1918, *PWW* 51:278; Tumulty to WW, 8 Oct. 1918, *PWW* 51:268n2, and see 268–69, passim.

56. Lansing to Oederlin, 8 Oct. 1918, *PWW* 51:269; Tumulty, *Woodrow Wilson*, 312.

57. Diary of Henry Fountain Ashurst, 14 Oct. 1918, *PWW* 51:339, and see 338–40, passim; Lawrence to WW, 13 Oct. 1918, *PWW* 51:320; Bliss to Baker and March, 7 Oct. 1918, *PWW* 51:262. On Allied military and political leaders, see Bliss to Lansing and others, 8 Oct. 1918, *PWW* 51:272–75; Cecil to the British embassy, Washington, 9 Oct. 1918, *PWW* 51:288–89. For the timing of the receipt of Bliss's message of 7 October, see March to Bliss, 8 Oct. 1918, *PWW* 51:272; Wiseman to Reading and Drummond, 9 Oct. 1918, *PWW* 51:291. On the submarine attack, see Geddes to Lloyd George, 13 Oct. 1918, *PWW* 51:326n2, and 325–26, passim. For Germany's reply, see HD, 13 Oct. 1918, *PWW* 51:317n6. My interpretation of the German note follows Bullitt Lowry, *Armistice 1918*, 34.

58. WW, "Draft of a Note to the German Government," 14 Oct. 1918, *PWW* 51:333–34.

59. Jusserand to Barclay, 11 Oct. 1918, *PWW* 51:308; WW, "Draft of a Note to the German Government," 333; Geddes to Lloyd George, 13 Oct. 1918, *PWW* 51:325. Wilson by this point also worried that talk of an armistice could sap the will to fight in America and among the Entente. This fear reinforced the president's desire to make sure that any armistice crippled Germany's ability to resume the war. See Jusserand to Barclay, 11 Oct. 1918, *PWW* 51:307; HD, 13 Oct. 1918, *PWW* 51:315.

60. "Memorandum by Sir William Wiseman," 352, and see 347–48. See also David Stevenson, *French War Aims against Germany, 1914–1919*, 121. Significantly, Wilson by mid-October had already decided on a key peace term, namely that Alsace-Lorraine should go back to France. See diary of Henry Fountain Ashurst, 14 Oct. 1918, *PWW* 51:339; "Memorandum by Sir William Wiseman," 351.

61. "Memorandum by Sir William Wiseman," 348; "Memorandum by Franklin Knight Lane," 415. For the cable, see Lansing to WW, 15 Oct. 1918, *PWW* 51:345–46. On German constitutional changes, see Schwabe, *Woodrow Wilson,* 61–63; Arno J. Mayer, *Politics and Diplomacy of Peacemaking: Containment and Counterrevolution at Versailles, 1918–1919,* 64. On Wilson and the revised Allied military terms, see WW to Baker, 18 Oct. 1918, *PWW* 51:373; "An Admonitory Message," 22 Oct. 1918, *PWW* 51:411–12. By accepting the idea that the Allied military advisors would set terms, Wilson also put pressure on the Allies to accept an armistice and forego a full-scale invasion of Germany. See "Memorandum by Franklin Knight Lane," 415; Schwabe, *Woodrow Wilson,* 66–69.

62. WW to Lansing, 23 Oct. 1918, *PWW* 51:418–19.

63. Baker to WW, 28 Oct. 1918, *PWW* 51:472; WW to EMH, 28 Oct. 1918, *PWW* 51:473.

64. Baker to WW (Bliss), 24 Oct. 1918, *PWW* 51:430, 434–35, and see 425–36, passim; Baker to WW (March to Pershing), 28 Oct. 1918, *PWW* 51:472; WW to EMH, 28 Oct. 1918, *PWW* 51:473; Baker to WW (Pershing), 26 Oct. 1918, *PWW* 51:455, and see 454–55, passim. Bliss in his letter of 24 October was specifically discussing the terms he conveyed to the administration on 8 October. See Bliss to Lansing and others, 8 Oct. 1918, *PWW* 51:272–75. Wilson received another report on France's preferred armistice terms on 26 October and a full report on Foch's proposed terms on 27 October. See Baker to WW (Pershing), 26 Oct. 1918, *PWW* 51:454–55; EMH to WW, 27 Oct. 1918, *PWW* 51:462–64. For careful studies of the armistice presenting a very different interpretation of the crucial issue of Foch's terms, see Lowry, *Armistice,* 39–40, 95–96; Schwabe, *Woodrow Wilson,* 87–92; Inga Floto, *Colonel House in Paris: A Study of American Policy at the Paris Peace Conference, 1919,* 42–47; Knock, *To End All Wars,* 182–83.

65. Baker to WW (Bliss), 3 Nov. 1918, *PWW* 51:571; Lowry, *Armistice,* 80; Baker to WW (Bliss), 24 Oct. 1918, *PWW* 51:435; WW to Lansing, 23 Oct. 1918, *PWW* 51:418. On the final terms, see EMH to WW, 4 Nov. 1918, *PWW* 51:581–82. On the naval terms, see Trask, *Captains and Cabinets,* 328–36, 342–48. On Lloyd George and Foch's terms, see EMH to WW, 30 Oct. 1918, *PWW* 51:516; EMH to WW, 30 Oct. 1918, *PWW* 51:511. See also EMH to WW, 1 Nov. 1918, *PWW* 51:542. For a second negative Bliss comment about Foch's terms, see Baker to WW (Bliss), 4 Nov. 1918, *PWW* 51:585. For Bliss's proposal to disarm Germany, see Baker to WW (Bliss), 24 Oct. 1918, *PWW* 51:434–35, and see 430–36, passim.

66. EMH to WW, 30 Oct. 1918, *PWW* 51:515; EMH to WW, 4 Nov. 1918, *PWW* 51:581.

67. EMH to WW, 30 Oct. 1918, *PWW* 51:511–13, 514; and see WW to EMH, 31 Oct. 1918, *PWW* 51:533; WW to EMH, 4 Nov. 1918, *PWW* 51:575.

68. WW to EMH, 30 Oct. 1918, *PWW* 51:513. On economic sanctions, see WW to EMH, 7 Sept. 1918, *PWW* 49:469; "A Memorandum by Sir Eric Geddes," 7 Nov. 1918, *PWW* 51:633–34. Wilson also alluded to the league's blockade powers in his Fourteen Points Address. See WW, "Address to a Joint Session of Congress," 8 Jan. 1918, 536–37.

69. EMH to WW, 30 Oct. 1918, *PWW* 51:515; WW to EMH, 31 Oct. 1918, *PWW* 51:533; EMH to WW, 3 Nov. 1918, *PWW* 51:569; EMH to WW, 5 Nov. 1918, *PWW* 51:594. See also Lowry, *Armistice,* 91; Schwabe, *Woodrow Wilson,* 91–92.

70. See Schwabe, *Woodrow Wilson,* 73, 79; Lansing to WW, 30 Oct. 1918, *PWW* 51:518–20.

71. Lansing to WW, 31 Oct. 1918, *PWW* 51:527–28; Schwabe, *Woodrow Wilson,* 74.

72. "A Memorandum by Homer Stille Cummings," c. 8 Nov. 1918, *PWW* 51:647; WW, "Address to a Joint Session of Congress," 11 Nov. 1918, 42; and see WW to EMH, 10 Nov.

1918, *PWW* 51:25; WW, "Address to a Joint Session of Congress," 11 Nov. 1918, 43, and see 42–43, passim. See also Baker to WW, 6 Nov. 1918, *PWW* 51:607; Lansing to WW (Bullitt), 7 Nov. 1918, *PWW* 51:622–23; Schwabe, *Woodrow Wilson*, 79–80.

73. See Mearsheimer, *Tragedy of Great Power Politics*, 368.

74. EMH to WW, 3 Nov. 1918, *PWW* 51:569; Lansing to Oederlin, 8 Oct. 1918, *PWW* 51:269.

75. WW, "A Statement to the American People," 26 July 1918, *PWW* 49:97; Daniels diary, 16 Oct. 1918, *PWW* 51:347; Cummings to WW, 7 Nov. 1918, *PWW* 51:629, and see 629–31, passim.

76. WW, "Address to a Joint Session of Congress," 8 Jan. 1918, 536.

77. WW, "A Message to Teachers," 28 June 1918, *PWW* 51:455; WW, "Address in the Metropolitan Opera House," 132.

78. Wiseman to Reading, 5 Sept. 1918, *PWW* 49:454, and see 453–54, passim. Casualty statistics are from Woodward, *Trial by Friendship*, 157. On Allied irritation with Wilson, see, e.g., Lloyd George to Geddes, 12 Oct. 1918, *PWW* 51:313.

79. Philip Kerr, Lloyd George's secretary, quoted in George W. Egerton, *Great Britain and the Creation of the League of Nations: Strategy, Politics, and International Organization, 1914–1919*, 82. See also G. R. Conyne, *Woodrow Wilson: British Perspectives, 1912–21*, 144–45; Woodward, *Trial by Friendship*, 218–19; Stevenson, *French War Aims*, 101; Egerton, *Great Britain and the Creation of the League of Nations*, 34–35, 53–59, 65–68, 74, 82; Link, *English Critics*, 17.

80. Maj. Gen. Sir Charles Sackville-West, quoted in Woodward, *Trial by Friendship*, 159. British and American efforts to buck-pass to each other is a major theme in Woodward, although he tends to make the point most explicitly with regard to the British. See Woodward, *Trial by Friendship*, passim. On the British, see also Brock Millman, *Pessimism and British War Policy, 1916–1918*. On buck-passing in general, see Mearsheimer, *Tragedy of Great Power Politics*, 157–62.

81. "Memorandum by Sir Eric Geddes," 634, and see 633–34, passim.

82. On Erzberger, see Epstein, *Matthias Erzberger*, 250–56. On the Reichstag and the Fourteen Points, and on the German government's views of Wilson's program and a liberal peace, see Schwabe, *Woodrow Wilson*, 22–24, 28, 34–37, 48, 55, 95–96, 98, 109.

83. WW, "Address to a Joint Session of Congress," 11 Nov. 1918, 41.

8. National Security Debates, 1917–18

1. *WHTP*, 128; "Justification," *NR* 10 (10 Feb. 1917): 37, and see 36–38, passim; "Where the Threads Converge," *NR* 10, suppl. (10 Mar. 1917): 29, and see 26–29, passim.

2. Lippmann to WW, 15 June 1917, *PWW* 42:525. See also "The Tasks of America," *NR* 11 (26 May 1917): 95; "Breaking Up Mid-Europe," *NR* 11 (2 June 1917): 121–22; "What Democracy Demands of the Allies," *NR* 11 (9 June 1917): 146–48; "Our President," *Independent* 90 (23 June 1917): 530; editorial, *NR* 13 (8 Dec. 1917): 133; editorial, *NR* 13 (12 Jan. 1918): 292; "Memorandum by Mezes, Miller, and Lippmann," 459–73; "The United States Comes of Age," *Independent* 93 (19 Jan. 1918): 89.

3. "Time and Victory," *NR* 12 (27 Oct. 1917): 341. See also WW, "Annual Message on the State of the Union," 4 Dec. 1917, 194–202; and editorial, *NR* 13 (8 Dec. 1917): 133; "For a Holy War," *Independent* 92 (15 Dec. 1917): 497.

4. "The Issue and Our Critics," *NR* 16 (19 Oct. 1918): 341–42; "The Germans and Their Government," *NR* 13 (29 Dec. 1917): 232; "The Foes of American Unity," *NR* 17 (9 Nov. 1918): 29; "The Necessary Step," *NR* 12 (1 Sept. 1917): 118; "Germans and Their Government," 233.

5. "Germans and Their Government," 233, 232, and see 231–33, passim. See also "The German Government and the German People," *Independent* 91 (15 Sept. 1917): 410–11; "The New German Attitude," *NR* 11 (28 July 1917): 345–46; editorial, *NR* 11 (2 June 1917): 118–19; Hamilton Holt et al., "To the Socialists of Russia," *Independent* 90 (19 May 1917): 328.

6. "The Great German Offensive," *NR* 14 (9 Mar. 1918): 159; "A Victory of Justice vs. a Victory of Power," *NR* 16 (5 Oct. 1918): 272, and see 271–73, passim. See also "The Only Way," *Independent* 93 (30 Mar. 1918): 509; "The President Voices the World's Desire," *Independent* 96 (12 Oct. 1918): 39.

7. Editorial, *NR* 17 (16 Nov. 1918): 54; editorial, *NR* 17 (9 Nov. 1918): 24. See also "Peace on Our Own Terms," *Independent* 96 (26 Oct. 1918): 111.

8. "Issue and Our Critics," 341; editorial, *NR* 16 (19 Oct. 1918): 325; editorial, *NR* 17 (16 Nov. 1918): 54; editorial, *NR* 16 (26 Oct. 1918): 357; "Foes of American Unity," 28, and 27–30, passim. The *Independent* was more wary of letting a democratic Germany into the league immediately. See "Put Germany on Probation," *Independent* 96 (9 Nov. 1918): 145.

9. Walling, *LEP 1918*, 153, and 152–53, passim; Dabney, *LEP 1918*, 48; Shaw, *LEP 1918*, 64–65, and 63–65, passim. See also *WHTE*, 34. Marburg, in contrast, sharply distinguished between the German people and the German autocracy and still wanted a democratic Germany admitted to the league of nations. See *TMdoc*, 1:288, 399, 2:539; Marburg, *NYT*, 24 Nov. 1918, 4:11.

10. Walling, *LEP 1918*, 152; WHT, *LEP 1918*, 17, and 17–18, passim; Walling, *LEP 1918*, 159.

11. Creel to WW (Angell), 15 July 1918, *PWW* 48:617. On concern about Allied war aims and the need to get the Allies to commit to international reform, see "The Next Step toward Peace," *NR* 12 (8 Sept. 1917): 146–47; Holt, "A League of Nations Now?" *Survey* 40 (31 Aug. 1918): 607–8; *TMdoc*, 1:312–15, 440–41, and see nn. 71, 72 to this letter, 479–80. On Angell's close relationship with NR, see Arno J. Mayer, *Political Origins of the New Diplomacy, 1917–1918*, 337–38; David W. Levy, *Herbert Croly of the New Republic: The Life and Thought of an American Progressive*, 223.

12. *TMdoc*, 1:477. See also *TMdoc*, 1:440–41, 479–80, 452–53, 2:483–84, 499; *WHTP*, 97.

13. *WHTE*, 93, and see 92–94. For *NR*, see, e.g., editorial, *NR* 13 (1 Dec. 1917): 105; editorial, *NR* 13 (8 Dec. 1917): 134–35; "Japan Is Menacing," *NR* 14 (9 Mar. 1918): 160–61; "For and Against the Bolsheviki," *NR* 14 (6 Apr. 1918): 280–82; "Alternative Policies in Russia," *NR* 15 (20 July 1918): 329; editorial, *NR* 16 (31 Aug. 1918): 120–21. On the LEP, see *TMdoc*, 1:300–301, 428–29; Talcott Williams, *LEP 1918*, 141–42. See also Christopher Lasch, *The American Liberals and the Russian Revolution*, 38–39, and passim.

14. Croly to WW, 19 Oct. 1917, *PWW* 44:409; "The Morality of Conscription," *NR* 11 (5 May 1917); 8; "Morale," *NR* 10 (21 Apr. 1917): 338; George Soule, "Selecting for Service," *NR* 12 (13 Oct. 1917): 296; "The Fighting Hope," *NR* 11 (23 June 1917): 199. See also *WHTE*, 2, 20, 39–40; John Spargo, *LEP 1918*, 70–74; "The Railroads Nationalized," *Independent* 93 (5 Jan. 1918): 8; "Seeing the War Through," *NR* 14 (30 Mar. 1918): 248–50; Edward A. Filene, *LEP 1918*, 25–29; "A Better World Already," *Independent* 94 (29 June 1918): 491.

15. "War Propaganda," *NR* 12 (6 Oct. 1917): 256, and see 255–57, passim; EMH to WW (Lippmann), 17 Oct. 1917, *PWW* 44:393, and see 393–94, passim; "Economic Dictatorship in War," *NR* 11 (12 May 1917): 37, and see 37–38, passim; "After the War—Reaction or Reconstruction," *NR* 13 (19 Jan. 1918): 333, and see 331–33, passim.

16. *WHTE,* 110, and see 109–10, passim, 36–37, 31, and see 29–31, passim.

17. EMH to WW (Lippmann-Cobb Memo), 29 Oct. 1918, *PWW* 51:504; "Issue and Our Critics," 341; "Nationalism and Internationalism," *NR* 17 (2 Nov. 1918): 5; League of Free Nations Association, "Statement of Principles," *TN* 107 (30 Nov. 1918): 651, and 650–51, passim. For background on the LFNA, see Wolfgang J. Helbich, "American Liberals in the League of Nations Controversy," 568–77.

18. LEP, "Victory Program," 23 Nov. 1918, reprinted in Bartlett, *League to Enforce Peace,* 221–22. On Marburg and Holt, compare the draft convention for the league written by a committee chaired by Marburg with the Victory Program. See "The United Nations," *Independent* 93 (26 Jan. 1918): 141–42; and the Victory Program in Bartlett, *League to Enforce Peace,* 221–22. Holt, Edward Filene, and Thomas R. White of the LEP all signed on to the LFNA as well. On the LEP and the LFNA, see also Helbich, "American Liberals in the League of Nations Controversy," 573–75.

19. Victory Program in Bartlett, *League to Enforce Peace,* 221; *TMdoc,* 2:564, and 563–64, passim; "United Nations," 141–42; *TMdoc,* 2:794, and see 791–94, passim. See also *TMdoc,* 2:721–51; Warren F. Kuehl, *Seeking World Order: The United States and International Organization to 1920,* 240–44.

20. Amos Pinchot et al., "Referendum," *Public* 20 (17 Feb. 1917): back cover; WJB, "An Appeal for Peace," *Commoner* 17 (Feb. 1917): 2; AUAM, "The Argument against War," *NR* 10 (31 Mar. 1917): 275; Pinchot et al., "Do the People Want War?" *NR* 10 (3 Mar. 1917): 145. See also RLF, "The Armed Ship Bill Meant War," *LFM* 9 (Mar. 1917): 1–4; Kellogg, "The Fighting Issues," *Survey* 37 (17 Feb. 1917): 572–77; "A League of Armed Neutrals," *TN* 104 (15 Feb. 1917): 178–79; Degen, *History of the Woman's Peace Party,* 180–91; Steinson, *American Women's Activism,* 220–48.

21. Editorial, *Public* 20 (22 June 1917): 593; editorial, *Public* 20 (15 June 1917): 567; "The American Tradition and the War," *TN* 104 (26 Apr. 1917): 726, and see 725–26, passim; "A Message to the Russians," *Public* 20 (22 June 1917): 596. See also Crystal Eastman to Emily G. Balch, 14 June 1917, in Cook, ed., *Crystal Eastman,* 254–57; WJB, "We Must Win," *Commoner* 17 (July 1917): 1; Stephen Wise, "What We Are Fighting For," *Public* 20 (23 Nov. 1917): 1126–29; "A Protest" (Kellogg comment), *Survey* 37 (10 Mar. 1917): 675; Kellogg, "Swords and Ploughshares," *Survey* 38 (4 Aug. 1917): 406; James L. Abrahamson, "David Starr Jordan and American Antimilitarism," 81–84; Steinson, *American Women's Activism,* 249–95; Erika A. Kuhlman, *Petticoats and White Feathers: Gender Conformity, Race, the Progressive Peace Movement, and the Debate over War, 1895–1919,* 73–75, 80–83; Lawrence Levine, *Defender of the Faith: William Jennings Bryan, the Last Decade, 1915–1925,* 136–37; James Weinstein, *The Decline of Socialism in America, 1912–1925,* 119–31.

22. "Questions for American Conservatives," *NR* 16 (21 Sept. 1918): 214; "Moving for Disarmament," *TN* 105 (11 Oct. 1917): 385; "Moves toward Peace," *Public* 20 (27 July 1917): 715–16; Louis F. Post, "Peace after the War," *Public* 20 (28 Dec. 1917): 1272, and see 1272–74, passim. On arms limitation, see LFNA, "Statement of Principles," *TN* 107 (30 Nov. 1918): 650; *TMdoc,* 1:393; "The Question of Disarmament," *Independent* 91 (1 Sept. 1917): 306–7; *WHTP,* 150. Kellogg and other ex-AUAM leaders were the driving forces behind the LFNA. See Helbich, "American Liberals in the League of Nations Controversy," 568–70. See also Thompson, *Reformers and War,* 150–227.

23. On the socialists, see Weinstein, *Decline of Socialism,* 120–23, 126–27, 141, 162–69; Majority Report of the St. Louis Convention, 14 Apr. 1917, in Chambers, ed., *Eagle and the Dove,* 114–16. On the People's Council, see Steinson, *American Women's Activism,* 265–83;

Resolutions of the People's Council, 31 May 1917, in Chambers, ed., *Eagle and the Dove,* 117–19. On La Follette, see Nancy C. Unger, *Fighting Bob La Follette, the Righteous Reformer,* 243–61; RLF, "A Just and Durable Peace," *LFM* 9 (May 1917): 1–2.

24. Randolph S. Bourne, in Carl Resek, ed., *War and the Intellectuals: Essays by Randolph S. Bourne, 1915–1919,* 24, 32, 34, and see 22–35, passim.

25. Bourne, in ibid., 75, 38, 35, 34, 33, 18, and see 22–35 and 65–88, passim.

26. TR, *Foes of Our Own Household,* 34, and see 34–35, passim; TR to John Callan O'Laughlin, 13 Apr. 1917, *TRLET* 8:1173. See also Root, in Bacon and Scott, eds., *United States and the War,* 27–31; Widenor, *Henry Cabot Lodge,* 264.

27. TR, *KAS,* 153; Root, in Bacon and Scott, eds., *United States and the War,* 41, and see 40–41, passim.

28. HCL, *CR,* 65th Cong., 1st sess., 28 Apr. 1917, 1440; TR to George Eugenievich, 20 July 1917, *TRLET* 8:1212; TR, *The Great Adventure: Present Day Studies in American Nationalism,* 90. See also Root, in Bacon and Scott, eds., *United States and the War,* 39–41.

29. TR, *Great Adventure,* 87, 77; TR, *KAS,* 155; HCL, "The Necessary Guarantees of Peace," *Scribner's Magazine* 64 (Nov. 1918): 623, and see 622–24, passim. See also Root, in Robert Bacon and James Brown Scott, eds., *Men and Policies: Addresses by Elihu Root,* 198; Jessup, *Elihu Root,* 2:324–25; HCL, "America's War Aims," *Current History* 9 (Oct. 1918): 141–42.

30. HCL, "Necessary Guarantees of Peace," 622, and see 622–24, passim; TR, *Great Adventure,* 195.

31. TR, *KAS,* 247; TR, *Great Adventure,* 68, and see 67–68, passim; TR, *KAS,* 193; HCL, quoted in Garraty, *Henry Cabot Lodge,* 340. See also HCL, *Senate and the League of Nations,* 92–94.

32. TR, *KAS,* 245; TR, *Great Adventure,* 67, 195–96; TR, *KAS,* 248. Lodge avoided discussing the league of nations during the war. See Widenor, *Henry Cabot Lodge,* 290–91. Root's contradictory position on a league mirrored TR's. See Root, in Bacon and Scott, eds., *Miscellaneous Addresses,* 288, 293; Root, in Bacon and Scott, eds., *United States and the War,* 83; Root to EMH, 16 Aug. 1918, *PWW* 49:269–72.

33. Root, in Bacon and Scott, eds., *Men and Policies,* 193; TR to Miles Poindexter, 22 May 1918, *TRLET* 8:1335, and see 1320–35, passim; TR, *KAS,* 131, and see 129–32, passim; HCL, "America's War Aims," 142; Root, in Bacon and Scott, eds., *Men and Policies,* 200, and see 196, 199–201.

34. For the Taft-TR reconciliation, see TR to Taft, 15 Aug. 1918, *TRLET* 8:1362; Pringle, *Taft,* 910–12; Widenor, *Henry Cabot Lodge,* 291–92; *NYT,* 1 Nov. 1918, 14.

35. See Widenor, *Henry Cabot Lodge,* 274, 277–78; TR to Albert Jeremiah Beveridge, 31 Oct. 1918, *TRLET* 8:1385.

36. On TR's son, see TR to George V, 22 July 1918, *TRLET* 8:1353. On Lodge's son-in-law, see Garraty, *Henry Cabot Lodge,* 339–40.

37. TR, *KAS,* 76–77; HCL, "Necessary Guarantees of Peace," 624; Catt to WW, 29 Sept. 1918, *PWW* 51:156; *Public,* quoted in Widenor, *Henry Cabot Lodge,* 286.

38. WHT, *LEP 1918,* 17. Marc Trachtenberg discusses this point in connection with liberal thought about the war. See his "Versailles after Sixty Years," 490–97.

39. "Foes of American Unity," 29. See also "Why the President Did It," *NR* 17 (2 Nov. 1918): 4.

40. "Memorandum by Mezes, Miller, and Lippmann," 465; "President Voices the

World's Desire," 39; "Issue and Our Critics," 342; George Creel to WW (Angell), 15 July 1918, *PWW* 48:620, and 619–20, passim. See also LFNA, "Statement of Principles," 651.

41. Lowell, *LEP 1918,* 41.

9. Wilson and the Versailles Treaty

1. Meeting of the Council of Four, 12 June 1919, *PWW* 60:446.

2. WW to Tumulty, 10 Jan. 1919, *PWW* 53:709; "Memorandum by David Lloyd George," 262. See also Meeting of the Supreme War Council, 13 Jan. 1919, *PWW* 54:40; Meeting of the Council of Four, 26 Mar. 1919, *PWW* 56:289–90; Meeting of the Supreme War Council, 24 Jan. 1919, *PWW* 54:242.

3. Meeting of the Council of Four, 27 Mar. 1919, *PWW* 56:316; Meeting of the Council of Ten and of the Supreme War Council, 12 Feb. 1919, *PWW* 55:104, and see 105; Meeting of the Supreme War Council, 17 Mar. 1919, *PWW* 56:26; Meeting of the Council of Ten, 28 Jan. 1919, *PWW* 54:324–25. See also WW, "Remarks to Members of the Democratic National Committee," 28 Feb. 1919, *PWW* 55:317–18; Meeting of the Council of Four, 15 Apr. 1919, *PWW* 57:359–62; Meeting of the Council of Four, 2 May 1919, *PWW* 58:342–43; Meeting of the Council of Four, 19 May 1919, *Mantoux,* 2:116–17; Meeting of the Council of Four, 12 June 1919, 438–39, 446. This view agrees with Schwabe's. See his *Woodrow Wilson,* 191–253, 395–400.

4. Grayson diary, 8 Dec. 1918, *PWW* 53:336–37; Wiseman to the Foreign Office, 15 Dec. 1918, *PWW* 53:395; Geddes, quoted in Mayer, *Politics and Diplomacy of Peacemaking,* 157; see also 133–66, 177–86; Schwabe, *Woodrow Wilson,* 284, 293, 295. Schwabe also makes the point about Wilson's concern to keep the current Allied leadership in power.

5. WW to Daniels, 16 Nov. 1918, *PWW* 53:98. For Progressive views, see, e.g., LFNA, "Statement of Principles," 650.

6. Meeting of the Commission on the League of Nations, 11 Feb. 1919, *PWW* 55:77–78; "A Memorandum by Sidney Edward Mezes," 31 Mar. 1919, *PWW* 56:472, and 471–73, passim; Grayson diary, 8 Dec. 1918, *PWW* 53:339. On the disarmament terms, see, e.g., Meeting of the Supreme War Council, 12 Feb. 1919, *PWW* 55:95–109; Meeting of the Supreme War Council, 17 Mar. 1919, 14–49; on the Rhineland, see Meeting of the Supreme War Council, 17 Mar. 1919, 26; on Poland, see Meeting of the Council of Ten, 19 Mar. 1919, *PWW* 56:94; Meeting of the Council of Four, 11 June 1919, *PWW* 60:404–6; Piotr S. Wandycz, "The Polish Question," in Boemeke, Feldman, and Glaser, eds., *Treaty of Versailles,* 325–28; Schwabe, *Woodrow Wilson,* 239; on the Tyrol and Czechoslovakia, see EMH to WW (Lippmann-Cobb Memorandum), 29 Oct. 1918, *PWW* 51:501; WW, "Remarks to Members of the Democratic National Committee," 317–18; Coolidge to the American Commissioners, 7 Apr. 1919, *PWW* 57:96–97; WW to Lansing, 2 July 1919, *PWW* 61:371; Clemenceau to WW, 31 Mar. 1919, *PWW* 56:478; Arthur Walworth, *Wilson and His Peacemakers: American Diplomacy at the Paris Peace Conference, 1919,* 54–55, 98, 263.

7. "A Declaration," 8 Feb. 1919, *PWW* 55:33, and 29–34, passim; Meeting of the Council of Four, 28 Mar. 1919, *PWW* 56:364–65. See also Alan Sharp, *The Versailles Settlement: Peacemaking in Paris, 1919,* 77–95, 113–16.

8. Meeting of the Council of Four, 2 Apr. 1919, *Mantoux,* 1:120–21; Meeting of the Council of Four, 9 Apr. 1919, *Mantoux,* 1:197; Meeting of the Council of Four, 8 Apr. 1919,

Mantoux, 1:190; Lansing to WW, 8 Apr. 1919, *PWW* 57:131. My interpretation here follows Schwabe, *Woodrow Wilson*, 248–49. On the general point of Wilson's punitive orientation at the peace conference, see ibid., 393–402; Levin, *Woodrow Wilson and World Politics*, 123–82; Boemeke, "Woodrow Wilson's Image of Germany," 603–14; Trachtenberg, "Versailles after Sixty Years," 487–506.

9. Grayson diary, 8 Dec. 1918, *PWW* 53:338; Bullitt diary, 10 Dec. 1918, *PWW* 53:352; WW, "An Address to the Third Plenary Session of the Peace Conference," 14 Feb. 1919, *PWW* 55:166.

10. Meeting of the Council of Ten, 27 Jan. 1919, *PWW* 54:294, 293; WW, "Address to the Third Plenary Session of the Peace Conference," 172. See also Elisabeth Glaser, "The Making of the Economic Peace," in Boemeke, Feldman, and Glaser, eds., *Treaty of Versailles*, 379; Articles 264–70 of the Versailles treaty.

11. Lansing to the Swiss Minister, 5 Nov. 1918, *FRUS 1918 Supplement, The World War* (Washington, D.C.: 1933), 1:469; Lansing and others to WW, 19 Feb. 1919, *PWW* 55:210, and see 210–11, passim. My understanding of the reparations issue is indebted to Sharp, *Versailles Settlement*, 77–101; Sally Marks, "Smoke and Mirrors: In Smoke-Filled Rooms and the Galerie des Glaces," in Boemeke, Feldman, and Glaser, eds., *Treaty of Versailles*, 337–70; David Stevenson, *Cataclysm: The First World War as Political Tragedy*, 420–21; and Schwabe, *Woodrow Wilson*, 243–48, 285–88, 362–74.

12. See Articles 231–36 of the Versailles treaty.

13. Article 231 of the Versailles treaty; McCormick diary, 9 June 1919, *PWW* 60:306; Meeting of the Council of Four, 9 June 1919, *PWW* 60:317–18, and see 319. On Allied leaders falling from power, see Schwabe, *Woodrow Wilson*, 293.

14. "A Memorandum," 28 Mar. 1919, *PWW* 56:371; Article 430 of the Versailles treaty. See also Keith L. Nelson, *Victors Divided: America and the Allies in Germany, 1918–1923*, 66–123; and Sharp, *Versailles Settlement*, 106–13.

15. See Ferdinand Foch to WW, 14 Mar. 1919, *PWW* 55:502–10; Meeting of the Council of Four, 27 Mar. 1919, 318–20; Raymond Poincaré to Clemenceau, 28 Apr. 1919, *PWW* 58:211–14; HD, 14 Apr. 1919, *PWW* 57:335; Ray Baker diary, 2 Apr. 1919, *PWW* 56:542; Meeting of the Council of Four, 22 Apr. 1919, *Mantoux*, 1:319. See also Stephen A. Schuker, "The Rhineland Question," in Boemeke, Feldman, and Glaser, eds., *Versailles Treaty*, 306–9; Walter A. McDougall, *France's Rhineland Diplomacy*, 67–72.

16. Meeting of the Council of Four, 6 May 1919, *PWW* 58:488; "A Report of a Press Conference," 10 July 1919, *PWW* 61:421; Meeting of the Council of Ten, 27 Jan. 1919, 293. See also WW to Tumulty, 9 May 1919, *PWW* 58:602; Meeting of the Council of Ten, 27 Jan. 1919, 295; Meeting of the Council of Ten, 28 Jan. 1919, 325. On the Saarland, see Stevenson, *French War Aims*, 177–79. On disarmament, see Meeting of the Supreme War Council, 17 Mar. 1919, 19; Articles 11 and 213 of the Versailles treaty. On Germany and the League, see Meeting of the Council of Four, 12 June 1919, 459–60; Article 1 of the Versailles treaty. For WW believing that other nations saw America as "unselfish," see Grayson diary, 22 Feb. 1919, *PWW* 55:224.

17. "A Memorandum by Isaiah Bowman," 10 Dec. 1918, *PWW* 53:354, and see 354–55, passim; Bullitt diary, 10 Dec. 1918, *PWW* 53:350–51.

18. David Hunter Miller, *The Drafting of the Covenant*, 1:169, and see 168–69, passim; 181, and see 180–81, passim; Meeting of the League of Nations Commission, 11 Feb. 1919, *PWW* 55:74, 79, and see 74–80, passim.

19. Meeting of the League of Nations Commission, 11 Feb. 1919, 76, and see 75–76, passim.

20. Meeting of the League of Nations Commission, 10 Apr. 1919, *PWW* 57:226, and 226–32, passim; Meeting of the League of Nations Commission, 24 Mar. 1919, *PWW* 56:231.

21. Meeting of the League of Nations Commission, 26 Mar. 1919, *PWW* 56:301–2; Meeting of the League of Nations Commission, 10 Apr. 1919, 230, 228, and see 227–32, passim.

22. WW, "An Address in Reno," 22 Sept. 1919, *PWW* 63:436; WW to McCall, 28 Feb. 1919, *PWW* 55:329; Meeting of the League of Nations Commission, 10 Apr. 1919, 227, 230 (emphasis in original); WW, "A Luncheon Address in San Francisco," 17 Sept. 1919, *PWW* 63:319; Hitchcock to EBG, 13 Nov. 1919, *PWW* 64:30; Meeting of the League of Nations Commission, 11 Apr. 1919, *PWW* 57:255, and see 255–56, passim. See also John Milton Cooper Jr., *Breaking the Heart of the World: Woodrow Wilson and the Fight for the League of Nations,* 259–60, 266–67; Herbert F. Margulies, *The Mild Reservationists and the League of Nations Controversy in the Senate,* 64–65.

23. WW, "Draft Letter to Henry Cabot Lodge," 14 Aug. 1919, *PWW* 62:279; Hitchcock to EBG, 13 Nov. 1919, *PWW* 64:30; WW, "An Address in the St. Paul Auditorium," 9 Sept. 1919, *PWW* 63:142 (emphasis added); "The Covenant of the League of Nations," 28 Apr. 1919, *PWW* 58:191.

24. "A Conversation with Members of the Senate Foreign Relations Committee," 19 Aug. 1919, *PWW* 62:354, 361; WW, "Draft Letter to Henry Cabot Lodge," 279.

25. WW, "An Address in the Indianapolis Coliseum," 4 Sept. 1919, *PWW* 63:23; WW, "An Address in the Seattle Arena," 13 Sept. 1919, *PWW* 63:257; WW, "Address in the Indianapolis Coliseum," 23; WW, "A Luncheon Address to the St. Louis Chamber of Commerce," 5 Sept. 1919, *PWW* 63:38.

26. "Covenant of the League of Nations," 191; "Conversation with Members of the Senate Foreign Relations Committee," 343; WW, "An Address in the Princess Theater in Cheyenne," 24 Sept. 1919, *PWW* 63:479; "Conversation with Members of the Senate Foreign Relations Committee," 353–54, 343, 392, and see 361.

27. "Notes of a Press Conference by Walter Edward Weyl," 27 June 1919, *PWW* 61:241; WW, "Address in the Princess Theater in Cheyenne," 479.

28. WW, "An Address in the Tabernacle in Salt Lake City," 23 Sept. 1919, *PWW* 63:452–53; "Covenant of the League of Nations," 191.

29. WW, "Address in the Indianapolis Coliseum," 215, and see 214–15, passim; WW, "An Address at the Metropolitan Opera House," 4 Mar. 1919, *PWW* 55:419, and see 414; WW, "Address in the St. Paul Auditorium," 141–42.

30. WW, "Luncheon Address to the St. Louis Chamber of Commerce," 35; WW, "Address in the Indianapolis Coliseum," 27; "Conversation with Members of the Senate Foreign Relations Committee," 354.

31. WW, "An After-Dinner Speech in Los Angeles," 20 Sept. 1919, *PWW* 63:407; "Conversation with Members of the Senate Foreign Relations Committee," 392; WW, "An Address in the Marlow Theater in Helena," 11 Sept. 1919, *PWW* 63:184; WW, "An Address at Bismarck," 10 Sept. 1919, *PWW* 63:157, and see 161; WW, "An Address to His Fellow Passengers," 4 July 1919, *PWW* 61:380, and see 380–81, passim; WW, "Address in the St. Paul Auditorium," 141, and see 139–42, passim; WW, "Address in the Marlow Theater in Helena," 183; WW, "An Address in the San Francisco Civic Auditorium," 17 Sept. 1919, *PWW* 63:333; "Conversation with Members of the Senate Foreign Relations Committee," 389.

32. WW, "An Address in the Coliseum in Sioux Falls," 8 Sept. 1919, *PWW* 63:113; WW, "An Address in the Des Moines Coliseum," 6 Sept. 1919, *PWW* 63:77; WW, "Address in the St. Paul Auditorium," 145; WW, "An Address at Coeur d'Alene," 12 Sept. 1919, *PWW* 63:214; WW, "An Address in Boston," 24 Feb. 1919, *PWW* 55:242; WW, "An Address to the Columbus Chamber of Commerce," 4 Sept. 1919, *PWW* 63:11.

33. WW, "A Luncheon Address in San Francisco," 343; WW, "After-Dinner Speech in Los Angeles," 402. On America's relative self-sufficiency, see Davis to WW, 9 May 1919, *PWW* 58:596; WW, "An Address in the Minneapolis Armory," 9 Sept. 1919, *PWW* 63:136; WW, "Address in Bismarck," 155; WW, "Address in the Seattle Arena," 257.

34. WW, "Address in the St. Louis Coliseum," 46; WW, "An Address in Convention Hall in Kansas City," 6 Sept. 1919, *PWW* 63:69; WW, "A Luncheon Address in Portland," 15 Sept. 1919, *PWW* 63:279; WW, "Address in the Coliseum in Sioux Falls," 112; WW, "Address in Convention Hall in Kansas City," 69; WW, "Address in the Des Moines Coliseum," 78.

35. For German views, see Schwabe, "Germany's Peace Aims," in Boemeke, Feldman, and Glaser, eds., *Treaty of Versailles,* 44–47; Schwabe, *Woodrow Wilson,* 186–87; Tasker Howard Bliss to WW, 1 Apr. 1919, *PWW* 56:492–93; A. J. Nicholls, *Weimar and the Rise of Hitler,* 55–56. For recent assessments of the peace treaty that tend to see its terms as not unreasonable or unworkable, see Margaret MacMillan, *Paris 1919: Six Months That Changed the World,* esp. 481–94; Sharp, *Versailles Settlement;* David Stevenson, "French War Aims" in Boemeke, Feldman, and Glaser, eds., *Treaty of Versailles,* 108–89; Marks, "Smoke and Mirrors," 337–70; Stevenson, *Cataclysm,* 409–30.

36. Quoted in Epstein, *Matthias Erzberger,* 304; quoted in Schwabe, *Woodrow Wilson,* 335, 334–35, and see also 332–36.

37. Quoted in Schwabe, *Woodrow Wilson,* 335; quoted in Epstein, *Matthias Erzberger,* 304; Count Ulrich Karl Christian von Brockdorff-Rantzau to Clemenceau, 29 May 1919, *PWW* 59:579; Grayson diary, 23 June 1919, *PWW* 61:79n2.

38. Schwabe, "Germany's Peace Aims," 64; Epstein, *Matthias Erzberger,* 325. See also Nicholls, *Weimar and the Rise of Hitler,* 61–62, 72–73.

39. WW, "Address in Convention Hall in Kansas City," 73; WW, "Address in the Des Moines Coliseum," 83. See also WW, "Address at Coeur d'Alene," 214; WW, "Luncheon Address in San Francisco," 342; WW, "An Address in Shrine Auditorium in Los Angeles," 20 Sept. 1919, *PWW* 63:410.

40. Hoover to WW, 11 Apr. 1919, *PWW* 57:272. See also Ray Baker diary, 3 May 1919, *PWW* 58:419; Smuts to WW, 14 May 1919, *PWW* 59:149–50; Bullitt to WW, 17 May 1919, *PWW* 59:232–33; Smuts to Lloyd George, 22 May 1919, *PWW* 59:413–19; Smuts to WW, 30 May 1919, *PWW* 59:616–18; "A Memo by Herbert Clark Hoover," 5 June 1919, *PWW* 60:194–96; Trachtenberg, "Versailles after Sixty Years," 495–98; Martin, *Peace without Victory,* 204–7.

41. "A Memorandum by Robert Lansing," 20 Aug. 1919, *PWW* 62:429, and see 428–29, passim; Lansing to Wallace, 10 Feb. 1920, *PWW* 64:402; WW to Hitchcock, 8 Mar. 1920, *PWW* 65:69. See also Daniel M. Smith, *Aftermath of War: Bainbridge Colby and Wilsonian Diplomacy, 1920–1921,* 32–74. On Shantung and Fiume, see Seth P. Tillman, *Anglo-American Relations at the Paris Peace Conference of 1919,* 315–43.

42. WW, "Luncheon Address in San Francisco," 317; WW, "Address in Reno," 436. See also WW, "Address in the Seattle Arena," 260.

43. Meeting of the Council of Ten, 28 Jan. 1919, 325–26; Grayson diary, 4 Dec. 1919, *PWW* 53:314, and see 314–15, passim; EMH to WW, 9 Apr. 1919, *PWW* 57:179. See also Tillman, *Anglo-American Relations,* 287–95.

44. For an early postwar example of Wilson's saying America would abandon the Allies if they pursued a peace based on the balance of power, see WW, "An Address in Free Trade Hall," 30 Dec. 1918, *PWW* 53:550.

45. WW, "Address in the Coliseum in Sioux Falls," 113; WW to David Lloyd George, 5 May 1919, *PWW* 58:448, and see 446–48, passim; Plenary Session of a Meeting of the Inter-Allied Conference on the Preliminaries of Peace, 31 May 1919, *PWW* 59:628–29. On war debts, see Ellen Schrecker, *The Hired Money: The French Debt to the United States, 1917–1929*, 41–59, 70–71. For Allied bitterness at Wilson's apparent indifference to the price they paid in lives and money to fight the war, see, e.g., "A Memorandum," 30 Dec. 1918, *PWW* 53:565–67; Meeting of the Council of Four, 28 Mar. 1919, 366.

46. Diary of Josephus Daniels, 1 Apr. 1919, *PWW* 56:519; diary of Lord Robert Cecil, 8 Apr. 1919, *PWW* 57:142; Ray Baker diary, 3 May 1919, *PWW* 58:420n1; HD, 31 May 1919, *PWW* 59:644.

10. National Security Debates, 1918–20

1. "The Open Menace of Secrecy," *TN* 107 (28 Dec. 1918): 792; "The Madness at Versailles," *TN* 108 (17 May 1919): 778; OGV, "The Truth about the Peace Conference," *TN* 108 (26 Apr. 1919): 646; RLF, "The Versailles Treaty," 13 Nov. 1919, in Robert S. Maxwell, ed., *La Follette*, 71, and see 56–71, passim; "Madness at Versailles," 778. See also "The Allied Intervention in Russia and Hungary," *Liberator* (June 1919), in Cook, ed., *Crystal Eastman*, 298–99; Johnson, *Peace Progressives*, 99–103.

2. Lincoln Colcord, "Why Wilson Was Defeated at Paris," *TN* 108 (17 May 1919): 782; OGV, "Truth about the Peace Conference," 647.

3. RLF, quoted in Belle Case La Follette and Fola La Follette, *Robert La Follette*, 2:970, 969; "The Net Result," *TN* 108 (22 Feb. 1919): 268; RLF, "Versailles Treaty," 59, 71, 57, and see 57–61, 70–71, passim. See also Johnson, *Peace Progressives*, 82–85, 97–99; Ralph Stone, *Irreconcilables*, 39–40; Ambrosius, *American Diplomatic Tradition*, 93, 136.

4. See "Net Result," 268; "The Testing of France," *TN* 108 (22 Feb. 1919): 269; OGV, "Truth about the Peace Conference," 646; "Madness at Versailles," 778–79; A. A. Berle Jr., "The Betrayal at Paris," *TN* 109 (9 Aug. 1919): 170–71; editorial, *TN* 109 (4 Oct. 1919): 449; RLF, "Versailles Treaty," 60–64; John Kenneth Turner, "A Pledge to the World," *TN* 109 (5 July 1919): 14–16; George W. Norris, *CR*, 66th Cong., 1st sess., 15 July 1919, 2592–93.

5. "Isolation and World Recovery," *TN* 110 (6 Mar. 1920): 286.

6. "A More Excellent Way," *TN* 108 (8 Mar. 1919): 342; "Mr. Wilson Rants," *TN* 109 (4 Oct. 1919): 453. See also Johnson, *Peace Progressives*, 99–102.

7. William E. Borah, *CR*, 65th Cong., 1st sess., 4 Apr. 1917, 253. See also Borah, *CR*, 65th Cong., 1st sess., 26 July 1917, 5496–97; Robert James Maddox, *William E. Borah and American Foreign Policy*, 16–17, 21–26; Johnson, *Peace Progressives*, 56–68, 80; Marian C. McKenna, *Borah*, 165–66.

8. William E. Borah, *CR*, 65th Cong., 3d sess., 6 Dec. 1918, 196–97, and see 190–91. See also Johnson, *Peace Progressives*, 80–102; Maddox, *William E. Borah*, 59–67; McKenna, *Borah*, 150–53.

9. William E. Borah, *CR*, 65th Cong., 3d sess., 14 Jan. 1919, 1387.

10. William E. Borah, *CR*, 65th Cong., 3d sess., 6 Dec. 1918, 190; Borah, *CR*, 65th Cong., 3d sess., 14 Jan. 1919, 1385, and see 1384–86, passim; Borah, "The League of Nations," 19 Nov.

1919, in Horace Green, ed., *American Problems: A Selection of Speeches and Prophecies by William Borah,* 120, and see 119–23, passim; Borah, *CR,* 65th Cong., 3d sess., 14 Jan. 1919, 1387. See also Johnson, *Peace Progressives,* 71–77.

11. Walter Lippmann, "Bolshevism," *NR* 18, suppl. (22 Mar. 1919): 13; "La Victoire Desintegrale," *NR* 18 (15 Mar. 1919): 203.

12. "Peace at Any Price," *NR* 19 (24 May 1919): 100; "Europe Proposes," *NR* 19 (17 May 1919): 71, and 67–71, passim; "Mr. Wilson and His Promises," *NR* 19 (24 May 1919): 105, 106, and see 104–6, passim; "A Punic Peace," *NR* 19 (17 May 1919): 73, and 71–73, passim; "Joy among the Philistines," *NR* 19 (7 June 1919): 169.

13. "Agitation for a League of Nations without Criticism," *NR* 18 (15 Mar. 1919): 201; Walter Lippmann, "Amendments," *NR* 18, suppl. (22 Mar. 1919): 10; "Peace at Any Price," 102; "'Must'?" *NR* 19 (31 May 1919): 135. See also "The A. B. C. of Alliances," *NR* 19 (24 May 1919): 110.

14. "'Must'?" 135, and see 134–35, passim; "Will the Republicans Save the League?" *NR* 20 (24 Sept. 1919): 216, and see 216–17, passim.

15. LFNA, "Statement of Principles," 650.

16. "Should American Questions Be Excepted from Compulsory Conference?" *NR* 18 (12 Apr. 1919): 325, and see 325–26, passim. See also "Will the Republicans Save the League?" 215–19.

17. For *NR*'s posture on postwar defense plans, see editorial, *NR* 20 (1 Oct. 1920): 244; "The Essentials of an Anglo-American Understanding," *NR* 21 (17 Dec. 1919): 66–69.

18. My understanding of the mild reservationists relies heavily on Margulies, *Mild Reservationists.*

19. Paul Kellogg, "To the Unfinished Work," *Survey* 42 (5 July 1919): 514; "A Protest and Some Comments," *NR* 19 (9 July 1919): 325, and see 325–27, passim. For antireservationists who had no real problem with the peace terms imposed on Germany, see "The Empire That Was," *Independent* 98 (17 May 1919): 235; Holt, "What Is This Treaty of Peace?" *Independent* 99 (12 July 1919): 49–50; WJB, "Welcome, World Peace," *Commoner* 19 (May 1919), 1; *TMdoc,* 2:654, 656–58. On the LFNA, see LFNA cablegram to Wilson, 28 May 1919, printed on the back cover of *NR* 19 (25 June 1919); "A Cablegram to the President," *Survey* 42 (21 June 1919): 451; Helbich, "American Liberals in the League of Nations Controversy," 579–90. On the WPP, see Degen, *History of the Woman's Peace Party,* 228–46; Steinson, *American Women's Activism,* 360–70; Knock, *To End All Wars,* 254.

20. Kellogg, "To the Unfinished Work," 514; *TMdoc,* 2:664, 755, 759–60, and see 755–62, passim. See also Holt, "Article X: The Soul of the Covenant," *Independent* 99 (5 July 1919): 15–16; Holt, "No Reservations," *Independent* 99 (9 Aug. 1919): 183–84.

21. Holt, "Article X," 15; *TMdoc,* 2:624; see also 2:854; Holt, "Compromize," *Independent* 101 (10 Jan. 1920): 59, 74; Helbich, "American Liberals in the League of Nations Controversy," 592–93; WJB, "Exaggeration on Both Sides," *Commoner* 19 (Dec. 1919): 1–2.

22. *WHTP,* 183, and see 182–83, passim; *WHTE,* 210, and see 210–12, passim, 216, and see 215–16, passim. See also Cooper, *Breaking the Heart of the World,* 99–100; Margulies, *Mild Reservationists,* 32–33, 82, 97, 131, 158; Irvine L. Lenroot, *CR,* 66th Cong., 1st sess., 24 July 1919, 3092–93.

23. *WHTP,* 193, 237, 284; Colt, *CR,* 66th Cong., 1st sess., 17 July 1919, 2721; Porter J. McCumber, *CR,* 66th Cong., 1st sess., 18 June 1919, 1268. On the League as a bulwark against Bolshevism, see Margulies, *Mild Reservationists,* xi; *WHTP,* 175–77. On faith in collective security theory, see, e.g., Le Baron Colt, *CR,* 66th Cong., 1st sess., 17 July 1919, 2721.

24. *WHTE*, 193, 266; Frank Kellogg, *CR*, 66th Cong., 1st sess., 7 Aug. 1919, 3687.

25. Lowell, in William H. Taft et al., *The Covenanter: An American Exposition of the Covenant of the League of Nations*, 127–28; *WHTE*, 159, and see 158–59, passim.

26. Lodge reservations, reprinted in Thomas A. Bailey, *Woodrow Wilson and the Great Betrayal*, 388–89. On the negotiations over the reservations, see Cooper, *Breaking the Heart of the World*, 177–78, 223–26; Margulies, *Mild Reservationists*, 103–5, 127–48; Widenor, *Henry Cabot Lodge*, 330.

27. *TMdoc*, 2:755; Lenroot, *CR*, 66th Cong., 1st sess., 24 July 1919, 3094.

28. *CR*, 66th Cong., 1st sess., 17 Nov. 1919, 8634; McCumber, *CR*, 66th Cong., 1st sess., 17 Nov. 1919, 8638; Walter Edge, *CR*, 66th Cong., 1st sess., 17 Nov. 1919, 8639.

29. HCL, *CR*, 65th Cong., 3d sess., 21 Dec. 1918, 727; HCL to TR, 26 Nov. 1918, *TR-HCL* 2:547; HCL, *CR*, 65th Cong., 3d sess., 21 Dec. 1918, 727–28. See also TR's praise for HCL's speech in TR, *KAS*, 287–88; Widenor, *Henry Cabot Lodge*, 295.

30. Root, in Bacon and Scott, eds., *Men and Policies*, 262, 264, and see 262–65, passim; HCL, *Senate and the League of Nations*, 257, 258; Root, in Bacon and Scott, eds., *Men and Policies*, 220. See also Stone, *Irreconcilables*, 78–79; TR to Richard Derby, 30 Dec. 1918, *TRLET* 8:1420.

31. "A Conversation with Members of the Senate Foreign Relations Committee" (Brandegee), 19 Aug. 1919, *PWW* 62:393, and see also 691; Root, quoted in Widenor, *Henry Cabot Lodge*, 338; HCL, *Senate and the League of Nations*, 228–29, and see 255. See also Jessup, *Elihu Root*, 2:394–95; Stone, *Irreconcilables*, 55–56.

32. Frank Brandegee, *CR*, 66th Cong., 1st sess., 19 Nov. 1919, 8776; Knox, *CR*, 65th Cong., 3d sess., 18 Dec. 1918, 605, 603. See also William R. Keylor, "'Lafayette, We Have Quit!': Wilsonian Policy and French Security after Versailles," 51–53, nn. 6, 64; Widenor, *Henry Cabot Lodge*, 304, 324–25; Root, in Bacon and Scott, eds., *Men and Policies*, 269, 274; Leopold, *Elihu Root*, 133; TR, *KAS*, 277; TR to George Haven Putnam, 15 Nov. 1918, *TRLET* 8:1395, and see 1394–95, passim; Knox, *CR*, 66th Cong., 1st sess., 10 June 1919, 894; Jessup, *Elihu Root*, 2:382; Ambrosius, *Wilsonianism*, 91–99; Stone, *Irreconcilables*, 26–27, 41, 48, 110–11, 180; Keylor, "The Rise and Demise of the Franco-American Guarantee Pact, 1919–1921," 367–77.

33. TR, *KAS*, 263–65; Root, in Bacon and Scott, eds., *Men and Policies*, 272, and see 251–66, 269–76; see also 251–66; *NYT*, 20 Mar. 1919, 4 (HCL-Lowell debate); Cooper, *Breaking the Heart of the World*, 77–79, 105–8; Widenor, *Henry Cabot Lodge*, 318–19, 328–30. For Root's endorsement of the Lodge reservations, see Root, in Bacon and Scott, eds., *Men and Policies*, 218–19.

34. HCL, *Senate and the League of Nations*, 401–2; Root, in Bacon and Scott, eds., *Men and Policies*, 292, 273, 293; HCL, quoted in Widenor, *Henry Cabot Lodge*, 318; Root, in Bacon and Scott, eds., *Men and Policies*, 216. On Atlanticist dismay with Wilson's domestic policies, see also HCL to TR, 15 Nov. 1918, *TR-HCL* 2:544; Kennedy, *Over Here*, 244–45.

35. HCL, *Senate and the League of Nations*, 231, and see 230–34, 256–58, 405, 407, and see 405–10, passim. See also Root, in Bacon and Scott, eds., *Men and Policies*, 262–64; Stone, *Irreconcilables*, 78–79; Widenor, *Henry Cabot Lodge*, 319–20, 347–48.

36. TR, *KAS*, 262–63. See also Ambrosius, *Wilsonianism*, 91–97; Ambrosius, *American Diplomatic Tradition*, 47, 101–4, 144–51, 211–15; Bailey, *Great Betrayal*, 225–26, 272–73; Cooper, *Breaking the Heart of the World*, 58, 77–81, 101–8, 302–3, 328–29, 424–26; Margulies, *Mild Reservationists*, 23, 33–44, 243–45; Stone, *Irreconcilables*, 31, 46, 90–93, 112–13, 115–17;

Widenor, *Henry Cabot Lodge,* 301–4, 308–10, 316–19, 320–21, 328–29, 332, 352. On the Allies, see also HCL, *CR,* 65th Cong., 3d sess., 21 Dec. 1918, 728; TR, *KAS,* 276–77; Root, in Bacon and Scott, eds., *Men and Policies,* 263, 266.

37. Johnson, quoted in Stone, *Irreconcilables,* 146. The 80 percent figure is from Cooper, *Breaking the Heart of the World,* 425.

38. Bailey, *Great Betrayal,* 277. See also Cooper, *Breaking the Heart of the World,* 333–34, 336–47, 359–62; Margulies, *Mild Reservationists,* 172–73, 182, 242–43. Cooper and Bailey agree that the treaty would have passed had Wilson not intervened concerning Article 10. See Bailey, *Great Betrayal,* 276–77; Cooper, *Breaking the Heart of the World,* 413–14.

39. WW, "Address in the Princess Theater in Cheyenne," 479, and see 479–80, passim; WW to Hitchcock, 8 Mar. 1920, *PWW* 65:68, and see 67–71. Holt and Marburg agreed with this assessment. See Holt, "Defeat the Reservations," *Independent* 100 (8 Nov. 1919): 61; *TMdoc,* 2:758–59.

40. See EMH to WW (Miller), 25 June 1919, *PWW* 61:181–82; Miller to Gordon Auchincloss, 26 June 1919, *PWW* 61:235; Holt, "No Reservations,"; WW, "Draft of a Letter to Henry Cabot Lodge," 14 Aug. 1919, *PWW* 62:280; *TMdoc,* 2:662–63; Margulies, *Mild Reservationists,* 71–72; Cooper, *Breaking the Heart of the World,* 149.

41. Wiseman to Balfour, 18 July 1919, *PWW* 61: 542; Link et al., eds., "Introduction," *PWW* 61:ix; Diary of Robert Lansing, 25 Aug. 1919, *PWW* 62:507. See also "A News Report," 19 July 1919, *PWW* 61:544–47; Bert E. Park, "Wilson's Neurologic Illness during the Summer of 1919," *PWW* 62:628–38; WW, "A Memorandum," 3 Sept. 1919, *PWW* 62:621; Ambrosius, *American Diplomatic Tradition,* 183–84; Cooper, *Breaking the Heart of the World,* 152–57. My interpretation concerning the political necessity for Wilson to negotiate with the mild reservationists follows Margulies. See *Mild Reservationists,* 41–72, 88–95. Cooper heavily stresses the impact of Wilson's health on the course of the treaty fight. See Cooper, *Breaking the Heart of the World,* passim.

42. Bert E. Park, "Woodrow Wilson's Stroke of Oct. 2, 1919," *PWW* 63:642, and see 639–46, passim. See also Irwin Hood Hoover, "The Facts about President Wilson's Illness," undated, in *PWW* 63:632–38; Margulies, *Mild Reservationists,* 107–10, 181–82; Cooper, *Breaking the Heart of the World,* 247–49, 257–63, 288–89, 297–329, 339–40, 345–47. On the treaty provisions other than Article 10 being vital to the League's structure for peace, see, e.g., WW, "Address in the Indianapolis Coliseum," 19–21, 27; *WHTE,* 297–306.

Conclusion

1. Platform, quoted in Margulies, *Mild Reservationists,* 269. See also Smith, *Aftermath of War,* 32–74; Ambrosius, *American Diplomatic Tradition,* 259–65; Margulies, *Mild Reservationists,* 261–70; Edward M. Coffmann, *The Hilt of the Sword: The Career of Peyton C. March,* 174–81, 189–210; Bernard L. Boylan, "Army Reorganization, 1920: The Legislative Story," 115–28.

2. Cooper, *Breaking the Heart of the World,* 429, 433, 415. See also Knock, *To End All Wars,* passim; Bailey, *Great Betrayal,* v–vi, 356–69; Link, *Revolution, War, and Peace,* 127–28, and passim; Arthur S. Link, *The Higher Realism of Woodrow Wilson,* passim.

3. Holt, "Article X," 15. See also Roland Stromberg, *Collective Security and American Foreign Policy: From the League of Nations to NATO,* 14–43.

4. Walter Lippmann, "A World Pool," *NR* 8, suppl. (22 Mar. 1918): 8; Miller, *Drafting of the Covenant,* 1:165.

5. See Cooper, *Breaking the Heart of the World,* 416–33; Smith, *America's Mission,* 105–6.

6. WW, "Address to a Joint Session of Congress," 8 Jan. 1918, 538.

7. FDR, "Address to the Governing Board of the Pan-American Union," 14 Apr. 1937, *PPAFDR* 5:158; FDR, "Fireside Chat," 3 Sept. 1939, *PPAFDR* 8:461–62; FDR, "Annual Message," 6 Jan. 1941, *PPAFDR* 9:672; FDR, "Atlantic Charter," 14 Aug. 1941, *PPAFDR* 10:315.

8. Melvyn P. Leffler, *A Preponderance of Power: National Security, the Truman Administration, and the Cold War,* 1–24.

9. Kennan, quoted in John Lewis Gaddis, *Strategies of Containment: A Critical Appraisal of Postwar American National Security Policy,* 50; Truman, quoted in Leffler, *Preponderance of Power,* 495. See also Leffler, *Preponderance of Power,* 356, 495–96.

10. For an interesting analysis of how fears of militarism played into debates over Truman's military and foreign policies, see Michael J. Hogan, *A Cross of Iron: Harry S. Truman and the Origins of the National Security State, 1945–1954,* passim. Hogan traces the framework of this debate to World War II, missing its origin in World War I.

11. George H. W. Bush, "Address to the United Nations," 1 Oct. 1990, http://www.miller center.Virginia.edu/Scripps/diglibrary/prezspeeches/ghbush (accessed 31 Jan. 2007).

12. Defense Guidance Statement, quoted in Christopher Layne, "The Unipolar Illusion: Why New Great Powers Will Rise," 6, and see passim. On the writing and revision of the statement, see James Mann, *Rise of the Vulcans: The History of Bush's War Cabinet,* 208–15.

Select Bibliography

Primary Sources

COLLECTIONS

Bacon, Robert, and James Brown Scott, eds. *Addresses on International Subjects by Elihu Root.* Cambridge, Mass.: Harvard Univ. Press, 1916.

——. *Men and Policies: Addresses by Elihu Root.* Cambridge, Mass.: Harvard Univ. Press, 1926.

——. *Miscellaneous Addresses by Elihu Root.* Cambridge, Mass.: Harvard Univ. Press, 1917.

——. *The United States and the War, the Mission to Russia, Political Addresses by Elihu Root.* Cambridge, Mass.: Harvard Univ. Press, 1918.

Baker, Ray Stannard. *Woodrow Wilson: Life and Letters.* 8 vols. New York: Doubleday, Doran and Co., 1939.

Bryan, William Jennings. *Speeches of William Jennings Bryan.* New York: Funk and Wagnalls, 1909, 1913.

Chambers, John Whiteclay, II, ed. *The Eagle and the Dove: The American Peace Movement and United States Foreign Policy, 1900–1922.* New York: Garland, 1976, and 2d ed., 1991.

Cook, Blanche Wiesen, ed. *Crystal Eastman on Women and Revolution.* New York: Oxford Univ. Press, 1978.

Davidson, John Wells, ed. *A Crossroads of Freedom: The 1912 Campaign Speeches of Woodrow Wilson.* New Haven, Conn.: Yale Univ. Press, 1956.

Green, Horace, ed. *American Problems: A Selection of Speeches and Prophecies by William Borah.* New York: Duffield and Company, 1924.

Gwynn, Stephen, ed. *The Letters and Friendships of Sir Cecil Spring Rice.* Vol. 2. Boston: Houghton Mifflin, 1929.

Hendrick, Burton S., ed. *The Life and Letters of Walter H. Page.* 3 vols. Garden City, N.J.: Doubleday Page, 1925.

Hughes, Charles Evans. *Addresses of Charles Evans Hughes, 1906–1916.* New York: G. P. Putnam's Sons, 1916.

Israel, Fred, ed. *The State of the Union Messages of the Presidents, 1790–1966.* 3 vols. New York: Chelsea House, 1967.

Lane, Anne Wintermute, and Louise Herrick Wall, eds. *The Letters of Franklin K. Lane.* Boston: Houghton Mifflin, 1922.

Lansing, Robert. *War Memoirs of Robert Lansing, Secretary of State*. New York: Bobbs-Merrill, 1935.

Latane, John H., ed. *Development of the League of Nations Idea: Documents and Correspondence of Theodore Marburg*. 2 vols. New York: Macmillan, 1932.

League to Enforce Peace. *Enforced Peace: Proceedings of the First Annual National Assemblage of the League to Enforce Peace, Washington, May 26–27, 1916*. New York: League to Enforce Peace, 1916.

———. *Win the War for Permanent Peace: Addresses Made at the National Convention of the League to Enforce Peace in Philadelphia, May 16–17, 1918*. New York: League to Enforce Peace, 1918.

Link, Arthur S., ed. *The Papers of Woodrow Wilson*. 69 vols. Princeton, N.J.: Princeton Univ. Press, 1966–94.

Link, Arthur S., and Manfred F. Boemeke, trans. and eds. *The Deliberations of the Council of Four (March 24–June 28, 1919): Notes of the Official Interpreter, Paul Mantoux*. 2 vols. Princeton, N.J.: Princeton Univ. Press, 1992.

Lodge, Henry Cabot. *Speeches and Addresses, 1884–1909*. New York: Houghton Mifflin, 1909.

———. *War Addresses, 1915–1917*. Boston: Houghton Mifflin, 1917.

Lodge, Henry Cabot, and Charles F. Redmond, eds. *Selections from the Correspondence of Theodore Roosevelt and Henry Cabot Lodge, 1884–1918*. 2 vols. New York: Charles Scribner's and Sons, 1925. Reprint, New York: Da Capo Press, 1971.

Marburg, Theodore, and Horace Flack, eds. *Taft Papers on the League of Nations*. New York: Macmillan, 1971.

Maxwell, Robert S., ed. *La Follette*. Englewood Cliffs, N.J.: Prentice Hall, 1969.

Morison, Ellting E., ed. *The Letters of Theodore Roosevelt*. 8 vols. Cambridge, Mass.: Harvard Univ. Press, 1951–54.

National Security League. *Proceedings of the National Security Congress, January 20–22, 1916*. New York: National Security League, 1916.

Navy League of the United States. *Pamphlets*. Vol. 1. New York: Navy League, 1916.

Resek, Carl, ed. *War and the Intellectuals: Essays by Randolph S. Bourne, 1915–1919*. New York: Harper and Row, 1964.

Richardson, James P., ed. *A Compilation of the Messages and Papers of the Presidents*. 20 vols. New York: Bureau of National Literature, 1897–1916.

Roosevelt, Theodore. *Addresses and Papers of Theodore Roosevelt*. 1909.

———. *Addresses and Presidential Messages, 1902–1904*. New York: G. P. Putnam's Sons, 1904.

Rosenman, Samuel, ed. *Public Papers and Addresses of Franklin D. Roosevelt*. 13 vols. New York: Russell and Russell, 1950–69.

Scott, James Brown, ed. *Official Statements of War Aims and Peace Proposals, December 1916 to November 1918*. Washington, D.C.: Carnegie Endowment for International Peace, 1921.

Seymour, Charles, ed. *The Intimate Papers of Colonel House*. 4 vols. Boston: Houghton Mifflin, 1926–28.

Stout, Ralph, ed. *Roosevelt in the Kansas City Star: War-time Editorials*. Boston: Houghton Mifflin, 1921.

Survey Associates Records/Paul U. Kellogg. Social Welfare History Archives. University of Minnesota.

Vivian, James F., ed. *William Howard Taft: Collected Editorials, 1917–1921*. New York: Praeger, 1990.

World Peace Foundation. *Pamphlet Series.* Vols. 5–6. Boston: World Peace Foundation, 1915–16.

BOOKS

Addams, Jane. *Peace and Bread in Time of War.* New York: Kings Crown Press, 1945.

Axson, Stockton. *Brother Woodrow: A Memoir of Woodrow Wilson.* Ed. Arthur S. Link. Princeton, N.J.: Princeton Univ. Press, 1993.

Bryan, William Jennings, and William Howard Taft. *World Peace: A Written Debate between William Howard Taft and William Jennings Bryan.* New York: George H. Doran and Company, 1917.

Croly, Herbert. *The Promise of American Life.* New York: Bobbs-Merrill, 1965.

Gompers, Samuel. *Seventy Years of Life and Labor: An Autobiography.* Ithaca, N.Y.: Cornell Univ. Press, 1984.

Grey, Viscount, of Fallodon. *Twenty-five Years, 1892–1916.* Vol. 2. London: Hodder & Stoughton, 1925.

Howe, Frederic C. *Why War?* New York: Charles Scribner's Sons, 1916.

Hughes, Charles Evans. *The Pathway of Peace.* New York: Harper and Brothers, 1925.

Hull, William. *The New Peace Movement.* Boston: World Peace Foundation, 1912.

Jay, John, Alexander Hamilton, and James Madison. *The Federalist Papers.* New York: New American Library, 1961.

Jordan, David Starr. *War and Waste.* New York: Doubleday, 1913.

La Follette, Belle Case, and Fola La Follette. *Robert La Follette.* Vol. 2. New York: Macmillan, 1953.

Lane, Winthrop. *Military Training in Schools and Colleges of the United States: The Facts and an Interpretation.* New York: Committee on Military Training, 1925.

Lippmann, Walter. *Drift and Mastery.* Madison: Univ. of Wisconsin Press, 1985.

———. *The Stakes of Diplomacy.* New York: Henry Holt, 1915, 1917.

Lodge, Henry Cabot. *The Senate and the League of Nations.* New York: Charles Scribner's Sons, 1925.

Mahan, Alfred Thayer. *Armaments and Arbitration.* New York: Harper and Brothers, 1912.

———. *The Interest of America in International Conditions.* Boston: Little, Brown and Company, 1910.

Miller, David Hunter. *The Drafting of the Covenant.* 2 vols. New York: G. P. Putnam's Sons, 1928.

Reinsch, Paul S. *World Politics at the End of the Nineteenth Century as Influenced by the Oriental Situation.* New York: Macmillan, 1904.

Roosevelt, Theodore. *An Autobiography.* New York: Da Capo Press, 1985.

———. *Fear God and Take Your Own Part.* New York: George H. Doran, 1916.

———. *The Foes of Our Own Household.* New York: George H. Doran, 1917.

———. *The Great Adventure: Present Day Studies in American Nationalism.* New York: Charles Scribner's Sons, 1918.

———. *The New Nationalism.* Englewood Cliffs, N.J.: Prentice Hall, 1961.

———. *The Strenuous Life.* New York: Century Company, 1905.

Root, Elihu. *America's Message to the Russian People.* Boston: Marshall Jones, 1918.

Taft, William H., George W. Wickersham, A. Lawrence Lowell, and Henry W. Taft. *The Covenanter: An American Exposition of the Covenant of the League of Nations.* New York: Doubleday, Page, 1919.

Tumulty, Joseph P. *Woodrow Wilson as I Know Him.* New York: Garden City, 1925.

Upton, Emery. *The Military Policy of the United States.* Washington, D.C.: Government Printing Office, 1912.

Villard, Oswald Garrison. *Fighting Years: Memoirs of a Liberal Editor.* New York: Harcourt Brace and Co., 1939.

———. *Preparedness.* New York: New York Evening Post, 1915.

Wald, Lillian D. *Windows on Henry Street.* Boston: Little, Brown and Co., 1934.

Weyl, Walter. *American World Policies.* Seattle: University of Washington, 1973.

———. *The End of the War.* New York: Macmillan, 1918.

PERIODICALS

American Legion Monthly
Annals of the American Academy of Political and Social Science
The Arena
Atlantic Monthly
Century
The Commoner
Congressional Annals
Current History
Harper's Weekly
Independent
International Conciliation
La Follette's Magazine
Literary Digest
Nation
New Republic
New York Times
North American Review
Outlook
Popular Science Monthly
Public
Saturday Evening Post
Survey
Scribner's Magazine
Wall Street Journal

Public Documents

Department of State. *Papers Relating to the Foreign Relations of the United States, The Lansing Papers, 1914–1920.* Vol. 1. Washington, D.C., 1939.

———. *Papers Relating to the Foreign Relations of the United States, 1914, suppl., The World War.* Washington, D.C., 1928.

———. *Papers Relating to the Foreign Relations of the United States, 1915, suppl., The World War.* Washington, D.C., 1928.

———. *Papers Relating to the Foreign Relations of the United States, 1916, suppl., The World War.* Washington, D.C., 1929.

———. *Papers Relating to the Foreign Relations of the United States, 1918, suppl., The World War.* Washington, D.C., 1933.

———. *Papers Relating to the Foreign Relations of the United States, The Paris Peace Conference, 1919.* Vol. 5. Washington, D.C., 1946.

House Military Affairs Committee. *Army Reorganization Hearings.* 66th Cong., 1st sess., 1919. 2 vols. Washington, D.C.: Government Printing Office, 1919.

Senate Committee on Military Affairs Hearings. *Preparedness for National Defense: Hearings.* 64th Cong., 1st sess., 1916.

United States Congress. *Congressional Record,* 63d Cong., 2d sess., through 65th Cong., 3d sess. Washington, D.C., 1914–19.

United States Department of Commerce. *Historical Statistics of the United States.* Vol. 2. Washington, D.C.: Government Printing Office, 1975.

Secondary Sources

Abrahamson, James L. "David Starr Jordan and American Antimilitarism." *Pacific Northwest Quarterly* 67 (Apr. 1976): 76–87.

Alonso, Harriet Hyman. *Peace as a Women's Issue: A History of the U.S. Movement for World Peace and Women's Rights.* Syracuse, N.Y.: Syracuse Univ. Press, 1993.

Ambrosius, Lloyd E. *Wilsonianism: Woodrow Wilson and His Legacy in American Foreign Relations.* New York: Palgrave Macmillan, 2002.

———. *Wilsonian Statecraft: Theory and Practice of Liberal Internationalism during World War I.* Wilmington, Del.: Scholarly Resources, 1991.

———. "Woodrow Wilson and George W. Bush: Historical Comparisons of Ends and Means in Their Foreign Policies." *Diplomatic History* 30 (June 2006): 509–43.

———. *Woodrow Wilson and the American Diplomatic Tradition: The Treaty Fight in Perspective.* New York: Cambridge Univ. Press, 1987.

Bailey, Thomas A. *Woodrow Wilson and the Great Betrayal.* Chicago: Quadrangle Books, 1963.

Bailyn, Bernard. *The Ideological Origins of the American Revolution.* Cambridge, Mass.: Belknap Press, 1967.

Bartlett, Ruhl F. *The League to Enforce Peace.* Chapel Hill: Univ. of North Carolina Press, 1944.

Beale, Howard K. *Theodore Roosevelt and the Rise of America to a World Power.* Baltimore: Johns Hopkins Univ. Press, 1956.

Beaver, Daniel R. *Newton D. Baker and the American War Effort, 1917–1919.* Lincoln: Univ. of Nebraska Press, 1966.

Beisner, Robert L. *Twelve Against Empire.* New York: McGraw-Hill, 1968.

Bird, Kai, and Martin J. Sherwin. *American Prometheus: The Triumph and Tragedy of J. Robert Oppenheimer.* New York: Alfred A. Knopf, 2005.

Birnbaum, Karl E. *Peace Moves and U-Boat Warfare: A Study of Imperial Germany's Policy towards the United States, April 18, 1916–January 9, 1917.* New York: Archon Books, 1970.

Boemeke, Manfred G., Gerald D. Feldman, and Elizabeth Glaser, eds. *The Treaty of Versailles: A Reassessment after Seventy-five Years.* Washington, D.C.: German Historical Institute, 1998.

Bolt, Ernest C., Jr. *Ballots Before Bullets: The War Referendum Approach to Peace in America, 1914–1941.* Charlottesville: Univ. Press of Virginia, 1977.

Boylan, Bernard L. "Army Reorganization, 1920: The Legislative Story." *Mid-America* 49 (Apr. 1967): 115–28.

Buehrig, Edward H. *Woodrow Wilson and the Balance of Power.* Bloomington: Indiana Univ. Press, 1955.

Burk, Kathleen. *Britain, America and the Sinews of War, 1914–1918.* Boston: George Allen and Unwin, 1985.

Calhoun, Frederick S. *Power and Principle: Armed Intervention in Wilsonian Foreign Policy.* Kent, Ohio: Kent State Univ. Press, 1986.

Campbell, John P. "Taft, Roosevelt, and the Arbitration Treaties of 1911." *Journal of American History* (Sept. 1966): 289–91.

Chambers, Clarke A. *Paul Kellogg and the Survey: Voices for Social Welfare and Social Justice.* Minneapolis: University of Minnesota, 1971.

Chambers, John Whiteclay, II. *To Raise an Army: The Draft Comes to Modern America.* New York: Free Press, 1987.

———. *The Tyranny of Change: America in the Progressive Era, 1890–1920.* 2d ed. New York: St. Martin's Press, 1992.

Chickering, Roger. *Imperial Germany and the Great War, 1914–1918.* Cambridge, Mass.: Harvard Univ. Press, 1998.

Clements, Kendrik A. *William Jennings Bryan: Missionary Isolationist.* Knoxville: Univ. of Tennessee Press, 1982.

Clifford, John Garry. *The Citizen Soldiers: The Plattsburg Training Camp Movement, 1913–1920.* Lexington: Univ. Press of Kentucky, 1972.

Coffman, Edward M. *The Hilt of the Sword: The Career of Peyton C. March.* Madison: Univ. of Wisconsin Press, 1966.

———. *The War to End All Wars: The American Military Experience in World War I.* Madison: Univ. of Wisconsin Press, 1986.

Coletta, Paolo E. "Norman Graebner and the Realist View of American Diplomatic History." *Diplomatic History* 11 (Summer 1987): 252–64.

———. *William Jennings Bryan.* 3 vols. Lincoln: Univ. of Nebraska Press, 1969.

Collin, Richard H. *Theodore Roosevelt, Culture, Diplomacy, and Expansion.* Baton Rouge: Louisiana State Univ. Press, 1985.

Conyne, G. R. *Woodrow Wilson: British Perspectives, 1912–21.* London: Macmillan, 1992.

Coogan, John W. *The End of Neutrality: The United States, Britain, and Maritime Rights, 1899–1915.* Ithaca, N.Y.: Cornell Univ. Press, 1981.

Cooper, John Milton, Jr. *Breaking the Heart of the World: Woodrow Wilson and the Fight for the League of Nations.* New York: Cambridge Univ. Press, 2001.

———. *The Vanity of Power: American Isolationism and the First World War, 1914–1917.* Westport, Conn.: Greenwood, 1969.

———. *The Warrior and the Priest: Woodrow Wilson and Theodore Roosevelt.* Cambridge, Mass.: Belknap Press, 1983.

———. "World War I in American Historical Writing." In *Causes and Consequences of World War I,* ed. John Milton Cooper Jr., 3–31. New York: Quadrangle Books, 1972.

Costigliola, Frank. *Awkward Dominion: American Political, Economic, and Cultural Relations with Europe.* Ithaca, N.Y.: Cornell Univ. Press, 1984.

Crackel, Marcus. *Mr. Jefferson's Army: Political and Social Reform of the Military Establishment, 1801–1809.* New York: New York Univ. Press, 1987.

Cress, Lawrence D. *Citizens in Arms: The Army and Militia in American Society to the War of 1812.* Chapel Hill: Univ. of North Carolina Press, 1982.

Dallek, Robert. *The American Style of Foreign Policy.* New York: Alfred A. Knopf, 1983.

Dalton, Kathleen. *Theodore Roosevelt: A Strenuous Life.* New York: Alfred A. Knopf, 2002.

De Beneditti, Charles. *Origins of the Modern American Peace Movement, 1915–1929.* Millwood, N.Y.: Kto Press, 1978.

DeConde, Alexander, ed. *Isolation and Security.* Durham, N.C.: Duke Univ. Press, 1957.

Degen, Mary Louise. *The History of the Woman's Peace Party.* New York: Burt Franklin Reprints, 1974.

Dubin, Martin David. "Elihu Root and the Advocacy of a League of Nations, 1914–1917." *Western Political Quarterly* 19 (Sept. 1966): 439–55.

Duffus, R. L. *Lillian Wald: Neighbor and Crusader.* New York: Macmillan, 1939.

Early, Frances H. *A World without War: How U.S. Feminists and Pacifists Resisted World War I.* Syracuse, N.Y.: Syracuse Univ. Press, 1997.

Edwards, John Carver. *Patriots in Pinstripe: Men of the National Security League.* Washington, D.C.: Univ. Press of America, 1982.

Egerton, George W. *Great Britain and the Creation of the League of Nations: Strategy, Politics, and International Organization, 1914–1919.* Chapel Hill: Univ. of North Carolina Press, 1978.

Epstein, Klaus. *Matthias Erzberger and the Dilemma of German Democracy.* Princeton, N.J.: Princeton Univ. Press, 1959.

Esposito, David M. *The Legacy of Woodrow Wilson: American War Aims in World War I.* Westport, Conn.: Praeger, 1996.

Farrell, John C. *Beloved Lady: A History of Jane Addams' Ideas on Reform and Peace.* Baltimore: Johns Hopkins Univ. Press, 1967.

Fass, Paula S. *The Damned and the Beautiful: American Youth in the 1920s.* New York: Oxford Univ. Press, 1977.

Ferguson, Niall. *The Pity of War: Explaining World War I.* New York: Basic Books, 1999.

Ferrell, Robert H. *Woodrow Wilson and World War I, 1917–1921.* New York: Harper and Row, 1985.

Finnegan, John Patrick. *Against the Specter of a Dragon: The Campaign for American Preparedness, 1914–1917.* Westport, Conn.: Greenwood Press, 1974.

Fischer, Fritz. *Germany's Aims in the First World War.* New York: W. W. Norton, 1967.

Floto, Inga. *Colonel House in Paris: A Study of American Policy at the Paris Peace Conference, 1919.* Princeton, N.J.: Princeton Univ. Press, 1980.

Fogelsong, David S. *America's Secret War against Bolshevism: U.S. Intervention in the Russian Civil War, 1917–1920.* Chapel Hill: Univ. of North Carolina Press, 1995.

Forcey, Charles. *The Crossroads of Liberalism: Croly, Weyl, Lippmann, and the Progressive Era, 1900–1925.* New York: Oxford Univ. Press, 1961.

Fowler, W. B. *British–American Relations, 1917–1918: The Role of Sir William Wiseman.* Princeton, N.J.: Princeton Univ. Press, 1969.

Gaddis, John Lewis. "The Corporatist Synthesis: A Skeptical View." *Diplomatic History* 10 (Fall 1986): 357–62.

———. *Strategies of Containment: A Critical Appraisal of Postwar American National Security Policy.* New York: Oxford Univ. Press, 1982.

Gardner, Lloyd C. *Safe for Democracy: The Anglo-American Response to Revolution, 1913–1923.* New York: Oxford Univ. Press, 1984.

Garraty, John A. *Henry Cabot Lodge: A Biography.* New York: Alfred A. Knopf, 1953.

Gelfand, Lawrence E. *The Inquiry: American Preparations for Peace, 1917–1919.* New Haven, Conn.: Yale Univ. Press, 1963.

Gilbert, Martin. *The First World War: A Complete History.* New York: Henry Holt, 1994.

Gilderhus, Mark T. *Pan-American Visions: Woodrow Wilson in the Western Hemisphere, 1913–1921.* Tucson: Univ. of Arizona Press, 1986.

Ginger, Ray. *Eugene V. Debs: The Making of an American Radical.* New York: Collier Books, 1977.

Graebner, Norman A. *America as a World Power: A Realist Appraisal from Wilson to Reagan.* Wilmington, Del.: Scholarly Resources, 1984.

Gregory, Ross. *The Origins of American Intervention in the First World War.* New York: W. W. Norton, 1971.

———. *Walter Hines Page: Ambassador to the Court of St. James.* Lexington: Univ. Press of Kentucky, 1970.

Grenville, John A. S., and Berkeley George Young. *Politics, Strategy and American Diplomacy: Studies in Foreign Policy, 1873–1917.* New Haven, Conn.: Yale Univ. Press, 1966.

Guinn, Paul. *British Strategy and Politics, 1914–1918.* London: Oxford Univ. Press, 1965.

Harbaugh, William Henry. *Power and Responsibility: The Life and Times of Theodore Roosevelt.* New York: Farrar, Straus, and Cuday, 1961.

Hawley, Ellis. "The Discovery and Study of a 'Corporate Liberalism.'" *Business History Review* 52 (Autumn 1978): 309–20.

———. *The Great War and the Search for a Modern Order.* New York: St. Martin's Press, 1979.

Healy, David. *U.S. Expansionism.* Madison: Univ. of Wisconsin Press, 1970.

Helbich, Wolfgang J. "American Liberals in the League of Nations Controversy." *Public Opinion Quarterly* 31 (Winter 1967–78): 568–96.

Herman, Sondra R. *Eleven against War: Studies in American Internationalist Thought, 1898–1921.* Stanford, Calif.: Hoover Institution Press, 1969.

Herring, George C. "James Hay and the Preparedness Controversy, 1915–1916." *Journal of Southern History* 30 (Nov. 1964): 383–404.

Herwig, Holger H. *Politics of Frustration: The United States in German Naval Planning, 1889–1941.* Boston: Little, Brown, 1976.

Higginbotham, Don. "The Debate over National Military Institutions." In *The American Revolution: Changing Perspectives,* ed. William M. Fowler Jr. and Wallace Coyle, 149–68. Boston: Northeastern Univ. Press, 1979.

Hirschfeld, Charles. "Nationalist Progressivism and World War I." *Mid-America* 45 (July 1963): 139–56.

Hofstadter, Richard. *The Age of Reform.* New York: Vintage Books, 1955.

Hogan, Michael J. "Corporatism: A Positive Appraisal." *Diplomatic History* 10 (Fall 1986): 363–71.

———. *A Cross of Iron: Harry S. Truman and the Origins of the National Security State, 1945–1954.* New York: Cambridge Univ. Press, 2000.

Hogan, Michael J., and Thomas G. Paterson, eds. *Explaining the History of American Foreign Relations.* Cambridge: Cambridge Univ. Press, 1991.

Hunt, Michael H. *Ideology and U.S. Foreign Policy.* New Haven, Conn.: Yale Univ. Press, 1987.

Jaffe, Lorna S. *The Decision to Disarm Germany: British Policy towards Postwar German Disarmament, 1914–1919.* Boston: Allen and Unwin, 1985.

Jensen, Joan M. *The Price of Vigilance.* New York: Rand McNally, 1968.

Jessup, Philip. *Elihu Root.* 2 vols. New York: Dodd and Mead, 1938.

Johnson, Robert David. *The Peace Progressives and American Foreign Relations.* Cambridge, Mass.: Harvard Univ. Press, 1995.

Karsten, Peter. *The Military in America.* New York: Free Press, 1980.

Keller, Morton. *In Defense of Yesterday: James M. Beck and the Politics of Conservatism, 1861–1936.* New York: Coward-McCann, 1958.

Kennan, George F. *American Diplomacy.* Chicago: Univ. of Chicago Press, 1984.

——. *Soviet–American Relations, 1917–1920.* Vol. 1, *Russia Leaves the War.* Princeton, N.J.: Princeton Univ. Press, 1956.

——. *Soviet–American Relations, 1917–1920.* Vol. 2, *The Decision to Intervene.* Princeton, N.J.: Princeton Univ. Press, 1958.

Kennedy, David M. *Over Here: The First World War and American Society.* New York: Oxford Univ. Press, 1980.

Kennedy, Paul. *The Rise and Fall of Great Powers: Economic Change and Military Conflict from 1500 to 2000.* New York: Random House, 1987.

——. *Strategy and Diplomacy, 1870–1945.* London: Fontana, 1984.

Kennedy, Ross A. "Uncertain Security: American Political Ideology and the Problem of Militarism, 1890–1941." Ph.D. diss., University of California, Berkeley, 1994.

——. "Woodrow Wilson, World War I, and an American Conception of National Security." *Diplomatic History* 25 (Winter 2001): 1–31.

Keylor, William R. "'Lafayette, We Have Quit!': Wilsonian Policy and French Security after Versailles." In *Two Hundred Years of Franco-American Relations: Papers of the Bicentennial Colloquium of the Society for French Historical Studies,* ed. Charles K. Warner and Nancy L. Roelker, 45–58. Newport, R.I.: Society for French Historical Studies, 1978.

——. "The Rise and Demise of the Franco-American Guarantee Pact, 1919–1921." *Proceedings of the Annual Meeting of the Western Society for French History,* vol. 15, ed. William Roosen, 367–77. Flagstaff: Northern Arizona University, 1988.

Kitchen, Martin. *The Silent Dictatorship: The Politics of the German High Command under Hindenburg and Ludendorff, 1916–1918.* New York: Holme and Meier, 1976.

Kloppenberg, James T. *Uncertain Victory: Social Democracy and Progressivism in European and American Thought, 1870–1920.* New York: Oxford Univ. Press, 1986.

Knock, Thomas J. *To End All Wars: Woodrow Wilson and the Quest for a New World Order.* New York: Oxford Univ. Press, 1992.

Kohn, Richard H. *The Eagle and Sword: The Federalists and the Creation of the Military Establishment in America, 1783–1802.* New York: Free Press, 1975.

Kuehl, Warren F. *Hamilton Holt: Journalist, Internationalist, Educator.* Gainesville: Univ. of Florida Press, 1960.

——. *Seeking World Order: The United States and International Organization to 1920.* Nashville, Tenn.: Vanderbilt Univ. Press, 1969.

Kuhlman, Erika A. *Petticoats and White Feathers: Gender Conformity, Race, the Progressive Peace Movement, and the Debate Over War, 1895–1919.* Westport, Conn.: Greenwood Press, 1997.

LaFeber, Walter. *The New Empire.* Ithaca, N.Y.: Cornell Univ. Press, 1963.

Lane, Jack C. *Armed Progressive: General Leonard Wood.* San Rafael, Calif.: Presidio Press, 1978.

Larson, Simeon. *Labor and Foreign Policy: Gompers, the AFL, and the First World War, 1914–1918*. Rutherford, N.J.: Fairleigh Dickinson Univ. Press, 1975.

Lasch, Christopher. *The American Liberals and the Russian Revolution*. New York: McGraw-Hill, 1972.

———. *The New Radicalism in America, 1889–1963: The Intellectual as a Social Type*. New York: W. W. Norton, 1965.

Layne, Christopher. "Kant or Cant: The Myth of the Democratic Peace." *International Security* 19 (Fall 1994): 5–49.

———. "The Unipolar Illusions: Why New Great Powers Will Rise." *International Security* 17 (Spring 1993): 5–51.

Leffler, Melvyn P. *The Elusive Quest: America's Pursuit of European Stability and French Security, 1919–1933*. Chapel Hill: Univ. of North Carolina Press, 1979.

———. *A Preponderance of Power: National Security, the Truman Administration, and the Cold War*. Stanford, Calif.: Stanford Univ. Press, 1992.

Leopold, Richard W. *Elihu Root and the Conservative Tradition*. Boston: Little, Brown and Company, 1954.

Levin, N. Gordon, Jr. *Woodrow Wilson and World Politics: America's Response to War and Revolution*. New York: Oxford Univ. Press, 1968.

Levine, Lawrence. *Defender of the Faith: William Jennings Bryan, The Last Decade, 1915–1925*. 1967. Reprint, Cambridge, Mass.: Harvard Univ. Press, 1987.

Levy, David W. *Herbert Croly of the New Republic: The Life and Thought of an American Progressive*. Princeton, N.J.: Princeton Univ. Press, 1985.

Link, Arthur S. *The Higher Realism of Woodrow Wilson*. Nashville: Vanderbilt Univ. Press, 1971.

———. *President Wilson and His English Critics*. London: Oxford Univ. Press, 1959.

———. "That Cobb Interview." *Journal of American History* 72 (June 1985): 7–17.

———. *Woodrow Wilson*. 5 vols. Princeton, N.J.: Princeton Univ. Press, 1947–65.

———. *Woodrow Wilson: Revolution, War, and Peace*. Arlington Heights, Ill.: Harlan Davidson, 1979.

Livermore, Seward W. *Woodrow Wilson and the War Congress, 1916–1918*. Seattle: Univ. of Washington Press, 1968.

Long, John W. "American Intervention in Russia: The North Russian Expedition, 1918–1919." *Diplomatic History* 6 (Winter 1982): 45–67.

Lowry, Bullitt. *Armistice 1918*. Kent, Ohio: Kent State Univ. Press, 1996.

MacMillan, Margaret. *Paris 1919: Six Months That Changed the World*. New York: Random House, 2003.

Maddox, Robert James. *William E. Borah and American Foreign Policy*. Baton Rouge: Louisiana State Univ. Press, 1969.

Mahon, John K. *History of the Militia and the National Guard*. New York: Macmillan, 1983.

Mamatey, Victor S. *The United States and East Central Europe, 1914–1918: A Study in Wilsonian Diplomacy and Propaganda*. Princeton, N.J.: Princeton Univ. Press, 1957.

Mann, James. *Rise of the Vulcans: The History of Bush's War Cabinet*. New York: Penguin, 2004.

Marchand, C. Roland. *The American Peace Movement and Social Reform, 1898–1918*. Princeton, N.J.: Princeton Univ. Press, 1972.

Margulies, Herbert F. *The Mild Reservationists and the League of Nations Controversy in the Senate.* Columbia: Univ. of Missouri Press, 1989.

Marks, Frederick W., III. "Morality as a Drive Wheel in the Diplomacy of Theodore Roosevelt." *Diplomatic History* 2 (Winter 1978): 43–62.

Marks, Sally. "The Myths of Reparations." *Central European History* 11 (Sept. 1978): 231–55.

Martin, Laurence W. *Peace without Victory: Woodrow Wilson and the British Liberals.* New Haven, Conn.: Yale Univ. Press, 1958.

May, Ernest. *The World War and American Isolation, 1914–1917.* Chicago: Quadrangle Books, 1959.

Mayer, Arno J. *Political Origins of the New Diplomacy, 1917–1918.* New Haven, Conn.: Yale Univ. Press, 1959.

———. *Politics and Diplomacy of Peacemaking: Containment and Counterrevolution at Versailles, 1918–1919.* New York: Alfred A. Knopf, 1967.

McCormick, Thomas J. "Drift or Mastery? A Corporatist Synthesis for American Diplomatic History." *Reviews in American History* 10 (Dec. 1982): 318–30.

McDougall, Walter A. *France's Rhineland Diplomacy, 1914–1924: The Last Bid for a Balance of Power in Europe.* Princeton, N.J.: Princeton Univ. Press, 1978.

McKenna, Marian C. *Borah.* Ann Arbor: Univ. of Michigan Press, 1961.

McKillen, Elizabeth. *Chicago Labor and the Quest for a Democratic Diplomacy, 1914–1924.* Ithaca, N.Y.: Cornell Univ. Press.

Mearsheimer, John. "The False Promise of International Institutions." *International Security* 19 (Winter 1994): 5–49.

———. *The Tragedy of Great Power Politics.* New York: W. W. Norton, 2001.

Millet, Allan R., and Peter Maslowski. *For the Common Defense: A Military History of the United States of America.* New York: Free Press, 1984.

Millman, Brock. *Pessimism and British War Policy, 1916–1918.* London: Frank Cass, 2001.

Mulder, John M. *Woodrow Wilson: The Years of Preparation.* Princeton, N.J.: Princeton Univ. Press, 1978.

Murphy, Paul L. *World War I and the Origin of Civil Liberties in the United States.* New York: W. W. Norton, 1979.

Nelson, Keith L. *Victors Divided: America and the Allies in Germany, 1918–1923.* Berkeley: Univ. of California Press, 1975.

Nicholls, A. J. *Weimar and the Rise of Hitler.* New York: St. Martin's Press, 2000.

Ninkovich, Frank. "Theodore Roosevelt: Civilization as Ideology." *Diplomatic History* 10 (Summer 1986): 221–45.

———. *The Wilsonian Century: U.S. Foreign Policy since 1900.* Chicago: Univ. of Chicago Press, 1999.

Noble, David W. "The *New Republic* and the Idea of Progress, 1914–1920." *Mississippi Valley Historical Review* 38 (Dec. 1951): 388–400.

Nordlinger, Eric A. *Isolationism Reconfigured: American Foreign Policy for a New Century.* Princeton, N.J.: Princeton Univ. Press, 1995.

Olson, William C. "Theodore Roosevelt's Conception of an International League." *World Affairs Quarterly* 29 (Jan. 1959): 329–53.

Oren, Ido. "The Subjectivity of the 'Democratic' Peace: Changing U.S. Perceptions of Imperial Germany." *International Security* 20 (Autumn 1995): 147–84.

Osgood, Robert E. *Ideals and Self-Interest in America's Foreign Relations: The Great Twentieth-Century Transformation.* Chicago: Univ. of Chicago Press, 1953.

Palmer, Frederick. *Bliss, Peacemaker: The Life and Letters of General Tasker Howard Bliss.* New York: Dodd and Mead, 1934.

Parrini, Carl. *Heir to Empire: United States Economic Diplomacy, 1916–1923.* Pittsburgh, Penn.: Univ. of Pittsburgh Press, 1969.

Parsons, Edward B. *Wilsonian Diplomacy: Allied–American Rivalries in War and Peace.* St. Louis, Mo.: Forum Press, 1978.

Patterson, David S. *Toward a Warless World: The Travail of the American Peace Movement, 1887–1914.* Bloomington: Indiana Univ. Press, 1976.

Pearlman, Michael. *To Make Democracy Safe for America: Patricians and Preparedness in the Progressive Era.* Chicago: Univ. of Illinois Press, 1984.

Perkins, Bradford. "The Tragedy of American Diplomacy: Twenty-Five Years After." *Reviews in American History* 12 (Mar. 1984): 1–18.

Peterson, H. C., and Gilbert C. Fite. *Opponents of War, 1917–1918.* Seattle: Univ. of Washington Press, 1968.

Powaski, Ronald E. *Toward an Entangling Alliance: American Isolationism, Internationalism, and Europe, 1901–1950.* New York: Greenwood Press, 1991.

Pringle, Henry F. *The Life and Times of William Howard Taft.* 2 vols. New York: Farrar and Rinehart, 1939.

Roberts, Priscilla. "The Anglo-American Theme: American Visions of an Atlantic Alliance, 1914–1933." *Diplomatic History* 21 (Summer 1997): 333–64.

Ryder, A. J. *The German Revolution of 1918: A Study of German Socialism in War and Revolt.* New York: Cambridge Univ. Press, 1967.

Safford, Jeffrey J. *Wilsonian Maritime Diplomacy, 1913–1921.* New Brunswick, N.J.: Rutgers Univ. Press, 1978.

Schafter, Ronald. *America in the Great War: The Rise of the War Welfare State.* New York: Oxford Univ. Press, 1991.

Schelling, Thomas C. *The Strategy of Conflict.* Cambridge, Mass.: Harvard Univ. Press, 1980.

Schrecker, Ellen. *The Hired Money: The French Debt to the United States, 1917–1929.* New York: Arno Press, 1978.

Schwabe, Klaus. *Woodrow Wilson, Revolutionary Germany, and Peacemaking, 1918–1919: Missionary Diplomacy and the Realities of Power.* Chapel Hill: Univ. of North Carolina Press, 1985.

Schwoerer, Lois. *"No Standing Armies!": The Antimilitary Ideology in Seventeenth Century England.* Baltimore: Johns Hopkins Univ. Press, 1974.

Scott, James Brown. *Robert Bacon: Life and Letters.* New York: Arno Press, 1975.

Sharp, Alan. *The Versailles Settlement: Peacemaking in Paris, 1919.* New York: St. Martin's Press, 1991.

Sherwin, Martin J. *A World Destroyed: The Atomic Bombs and the Grand Alliance.* New York: Vintage Books, 1977.

Skowronek, Stephen. *Building a New American State.* New York: Cambridge Univ. Press, 1982.

Smith, Daniel M. *Aftermath of War: Bainbridge Colby and Wilsonian Diplomacy, 1920–1921.* Philadelphia: American Philosophical Society, 1970.

———. *The Great Departure: The United States and World War I, 1914–1920.* New York: John Wiley and Sons, 1965.

———. *Robert Lansing and American Neutrality, 1914–1917.* New York: Da Capo Press, 1972.

Smith, Tony. *America's Mission: The United States and the Worldwide Struggle for Democracy in the Twentieth Century.* Princeton, N.J.: Princeton Univ. Press, 1994.

Snell, John L. "Wilson's Peace Program and German Socialism, January–March 1918." *Mississippi Valley Historical Review* 38 (Sept. 1951): 187–214.

Sprout, Harold, and Margaret Sprout. *Toward a New Order of Sea Power: American Naval Policy and the World Scene, 1918–1922.* Princeton, N.J.: Princeton Univ. Press, 1940.

Sprout, Margaret. *The Rise of American Naval Power, 1776–1918.* Princeton, N.J.: Princeton Univ. Press, 1939.

Steel, Ronald. *Walter Lippmann and the American Century.* New York: Vintage Books, 1980.

Steinson, Barbara J. *American Women's Activism in World War I.* New York: Garland, 1982.

Stevenson, David. *Cataclysm: The First World War as Political Tragedy.* New York: Basic Books, 2004.

———. *The First World War and International Politics.* New York: Oxford Univ. Press, 1988.

———. *French War Aims against Germany, 1914–1919.* New York: Oxford Univ. Press, 1982.

Stone, Ralph. *The Irreconcilables: The Fight against the League of Nations.* New York: W. W. Norton and Company, 1970.

Stromberg, Roland. *Collective Security and American Foreign Policy: From the League of Nations to NATO.* New York: Praeger Press, 1963.

Stuart, Reginald C. *War and American Thought: From the Revolution to the Monroe Doctrine.* Kent, Ohio: Kent State Univ. Press, 1982.

Symonds, Craig L. *Navalists and Antinavalists.* Cranbury, N.J.: Associated Univ. Presses, 1980.

Thelan, David P. *Robert M. La Follette and the Insurgent Spirit.* Boston: Little, Brown and Company, 1976.

Thompson, John A. *Reformers and War: American Progressive Publicists and the First World War.* New York: Cambridge Univ. Press, 1987.

Thorburn, Neil. "A Progressive and the First World War: Frederic C. Howe." *Mid-America* 51 (Apr. 1969): 108–18.

Tilchin, William N. *Theodore Roosevelt and the British Empire.* New York: St. Martin's Press, 1997.

Tillman, Seth P. *Anglo-American Relations at the Paris Peace Conference of 1919.* Princeton, N.J.: Princeton Univ. Press, 1961.

Tompkins, E. Berkeley. *Anti-Imperialism in the United States: The Great Debate, 1890–1920.* Philadelphia: Univ. of Pennsylvania Press, 1970.

Trachtenberg, Marc. *History and Strategy.* Princeton, N.J.: Princeton Univ. Press, 1991.

———. *Reparation in World Politics: France and European Economic Diplomacy, 1916–1923.* New York: Columbia Univ. Press, 1980.

———. "Versailles after Sixty Years." *Journal of Contemporary History* 17 (July 1982): 487–506.

Trani, Eugene P. "Woodrow Wilson and the Decision to Intervene in Russia: A Reconsideration." *Journal of Modern History* 48 (Sept. 1976): 440–61.

Trask, David F. *Anglo-American Naval Relations, 1917–1918: Captains and Cabinets.* Columbia: Univ. of Missouri Press, 1972.

———. *The United States in the Supreme War Council: American War Aims and Inter-Allied Strategy, 1917–1918.* Middleton, Conn.: Wesleyan Univ. Press, 1961.

Tucker, Robert W. *Woodrow Wilson and the Great War: Reconsidering America's Neutrality, 1914–1917.* Charlottesville: Univ. of Virginia Press, 2007.

Unger, Nancy C. *Fighting Bob La Follette the Righteous Reformer.* Chapel Hill: Univ. of North Carolina Press, 2000.

Unterberger, Betty Miller. "Woodrow Wilson and the Bolsheviks: The 'Acid Test' of Soviet-American Relations." *Diplomatic History* 11 (Spring 1987): 71–90.

Waltz, Kenneth. *Theory of International Politics.* Reading, Mass.: Addison-Wesley, 1979.

Walworth, Arthur. *America's Moment: 1918—American Diplomacy at the End of World War I.* New York: W. W. Norton, 1977.

———. *Wilson and His Peacemakers: American Diplomacy at the Paris Peace Conference, 1919.* New York: W. W. Norton, 1986.

Ward, Robert D. "The Origins and Activities of the National Security League, 1914–1919." *Mississippi Valley Historical Review* 47 (June 1960): 59–64.

Weigley, Russell F. *The American Way of War: A History of United States Military Strategy and Policy.* New York: Macmillan, 1973.

———. *History of the United States Army.* New York: Macmillan, 1967.

Weinberg, Gerhard L. *Germany, Hitler, and World War II.* New York: Cambridge Univ. Press, 2004.

Weinstein, James. *The Decline of Socialism in America, 1912–1925.* New York: Monthly Review Press, 1967.

Widenor, William C. *Henry Cabot Lodge and the Search for an American Foreign Policy.* Berkeley: Univ. of California Press, 1980.

Wiebe, Robert H. *The Search for Order, 1877–1920.* New York: Hill and Wang, 1967.

Williams, William Appleman. *The Tragedy of American Diplomacy.* New York: Dell, 1972.

Woodward, David R. *Trial by Friendship: Anglo-American Relations, 1917–1918.* Lexington: Univ. Press of Kentucky, 1993.

Wreszin, Michael. *Oswald Garrison Villard: Pacifist at War.* Bloomington: Indiana Univ. Press, 1965.

Wright, Gordon. *The Ordeal of Total War, 1939–1945.* New York: Harper and Row, 1968.

Index

Adamson Act, 22

Addams, Jane, xii, 2, 121, 130, 210. *See also* pacifists

Advisory Commission of the Council of National Defense, 147

agrarian progressives, xii

Allied Supreme War Council, 141, 145, 152, 198

All-Russian Congress of Soviets, 135

Alsace-Lorraine, 32, 50–51, 132–33, 140, 149, 151–52, 161, 166–67, 175, 185, 196, 204

Ambrosius, Lloyd, 49, 229n3

American Commission to Negotiate Peace (ACNP), 198

American Federation of Labor (AFL), xii, 147

American Neutral Conference Committee, 241n25

American Protective League, 147

American Union against Militarism (AUAM), xii, 2, 10–11, 26, 33, 55–56, 89, 120, 126–27, 172, 241n30

Ancona, 91

Anderson, Chandler P., 28, 31, 71, 94

Angell, Norman, 168, 180

Arabic, 84–86, 91

Archangel, 144–45

armistice negotiations, 148–55

Asquith, Herbert, 30, 74

Atlanticists, xiii, 6–7, 64–65, 93, 99, 206, 229n3; on American belligerency, 174; on balance of power, 22–23; on collective security, 43, 57–58, 60, 63, 176, 203, 215–16, 222; on economics, 35; on Germany, 179; on an international peace league, 163, 176–77, 179, 203, 216, 218; on militarism, 20–22, 163, 217; on national security, 21, 24–25, 36–37, 63, 125, 217, 224; on power politics, 15–20, 23, 217; on preparedness, 21, 36, 112, 124–25, 178; on

the ship-purchase controversy, 110–11; on the Versailles treaty, 203, 217; on Wilson's diplomacy, 104, 109–14, 123, 128, 146. *See also* universal military training

Austria-Hungary, 17, 91, 129, 133, 174–75

Axson, Stockton, 15

Bailey, Thomas, 219

Balfour, Arthur James, 134

Balkans, 51, 132

Beale, Howard K., 36

Belarus, 135

Belgium, 13, 19–20, 71–73, 76, 79, 95, 98, 106, 109–10, 112, 114–16, 122, 132, 175, 184, 196, 204

Bernstorff, Count Johann Heinrich von, 68, 71, 85, 90, 94, 98–100

Bliss, Gen. Tasker Howard, 142, 149, 152–53

Bohemia, 185

Bolshevik Revolution, 143–44, 155, 183

Bolsheviks, 135, 144–45, 157, 168–69, 194, 204, 207

Borah, William E., 206–7, 221

Bourgeois, Leon, 190

Bourne, Randolph, 171, 173–74, 177–79, 181

Brandegee, Frank, 216

Brest-Litovsk peace talks, 135–36, 138–39, 143, 149, 157, 208, 254n23

Bryan, William Jennings, xii, 57, 81–82, 120, 239n4; on American neutrality, 54; on collective security, 55–56; on German-American relations, 77, 83, 91, 118–19; on national security, 27, 172; on power politics, 8, 10, 55, 125; protest of British maritime policies, 70, 117–19; on Roosevelt, 125; as secretary of state, 73, 75, 121; on the Versailles treaty, 210; on Wilson's diplomacy, 114–19, 122, 127

Bryce, James, 68, 98

286